AWS Tools for PowerShell

Administrate, maintain, and automate your infrastructure with ease

Ramesh Waghmare

BIRMINGHAM - MUMBAI

AWS Tools for PowerShell 6

First published: August 2017

Production reference: 1020817

Published by Packt Publishing Ltd.
Livery Place
35 Livery Street
Birmingham
B3 2PB, UK.

ISBN 978-1-78588-407-8

www.packtpub.com

Credits

Author
Ramesh Waghmare

Reviewer
Mark Andrews

Commissioning Editor
Vijin Boricha

Acquisition Editor
Shrilekha Inani

Content Development Editor
Abhishek Jadhav

Technical Editor
Aditya Khadye

Copy Editors
Yesha Gangani
Juliana Nair

Project Coordinator
Judie Jose

Proofreader
Safis Editing

Indexer
Aishwarya Gangawane

Graphics
Kirk D'Penha

Production Coordinator
Aparna Bhagat

About the Author

Ramesh Waghmare is a technology evangelist who has been in the IT industry for over 20 years and has extensively worked in ICT operations, software development, deployment, and critical systems production support. Throughout his IT career, he has had the opportunity to work in roles such as senior developer, senior database administrator, manager, and architect, which have helped him to build expertise in various IT solutions and implementations from the business perspective and its simplicity to use.

He is a strategic thinker, focusing always on quality delivery to the client ensuring satisfaction at both ends. He has experience of leading and managing a team of technical and non-technical team members. He is a natural leader who inspires, is curious, and is very self-aware. He has a strategic mindset with practical orientation that enables team growth and continuous improvement with a positive outlook. He has strong organizational, analytical, and problem-solving skills, with incredible attention to detail. He has successfully implemented solutions involving cross-functional/cross-geography teams.

He is a sound expert in database technologies such as Oracle, MYSQL, and SQL Server, and in operating systems such as Linux, UNIX, and Windows. In addition, he has a great understanding of open source databases. He is also a certified AWS solution architect and has helped a number of clients to move from their isolated data centers to the public/private cloud.

He has also published a Kindle version of the book called *AWS for Oracle DBA and Architect*.

Academically, he has completed his MBA in information system, backed by an engineering degree in computer science. He is also a certified AWS solution architect and DevOps engineer at a professional level, holding other several key industry standard certifications.

I would like to thank my wife, Swati, who constantly inspired and kept me motivated during the writing of this book. My kids, Pranet, Neil, and Shara, also sacrificed their playtime because of my dedication to this book. Love to all the kids.

About the Reviewer

Mark Andrews' career in technology has been a varied one. Over the last 20 years, he has held several different positions, ranging from customer service to quality assurance. Throughout all of these positions, the responsibility of configuration and build management has always fallen either to Mark personally or to one of the groups that he managed. His "keeping a hand in" management style has kept him closely involved in the scripting and automation framework for this area. Creating scripted frameworks that intercommunicate across machine/operating system/domain boundaries is a passion for him.

He has also worked on the following books:

- *PowerShell 3.0 Advanced Administration Handbook*
- *Windows PowerShell 4.0 for .NET Developers*
- *PowerShell for SQL Server Essentials*
- *Microsoft Exchange Server PowerShell Essentials*
- *Microsoft Exchange Server PowerShell Cookbook (Third Edition)*

www.PacktPub.com

For support files and downloads related to your book, please visit www.PacktPub.com.

Did you know that Packt offers eBook versions of every book published, with PDF and ePub files available? You can upgrade to the eBook version at www.PacktPub.com and as a print book customer, you are entitled to a discount on the eBook copy. Get in touch with us at service@packtpub.com for more details.

At www.PacktPub.com, you can also read a collection of free technical articles, sign up for a range of free newsletters and receive exclusive discounts and offers on Packt books and eBooks.

https://www.packtpub.com/mapt

Get the most in-demand software skills with Mapt. Mapt gives you full access to all Packt books and video courses, as well as industry-leading tools to help you plan your personal development and advance your career.

Why subscribe?

- Fully searchable across every book published by Packt
- Copy and paste, print, and bookmark content
- On demand and accessible via a web browser

Customer Feedback

Thanks for purchasing this Packt book. At Packt, quality is at the heart of our editorial process. To help us improve, please leave us an honest review on this book's Amazon page at `https://www.amazon.com/dp/1785884077`.

If you'd like to join our team of regular reviewers, you can e-mail us at `customerreviews@packtpub.com`. We award our regular reviewers with free eBooks and videos in exchange for their valuable feedback. Help us be relentless in improving our products!

Table of Contents

Preface

PowerShell, originally developed by Microsoft, is a popular scripting language. With the cloud infrastructure addition and the heterogonous environment, there is a high degree of complexity in the IT environment. Without automating your routine task, it is practically impossible to keep the required governance, compliance, and control in your IT shop. Though there are many scripting tools available on the market that you can make use of to automate your workload, PowerShell stands out from others. With increasing complexity in the IT environment, you need a tool that can provide you a single pane to work with multiple cloud and hybrid environments. PowerShell provides you with that unified experience. It is a command-line and scripting language. Most of the industry-leading product creators have a module for PowerShell that can work with their product, whereas this is not the case with other tools. PowerShell is object-based, and this gives the incredible flexibility to filter, sort, measure, group, compare, or take other actions on objects as they pass through the PowerShell pipeline. Last year, Microsoft announced that PowerShell 6 is open source and will support Linux, macOS, and other platforms in addition to Windows. That makes PowerShell an even stronger candidate for providing universal shell to work in multicloud, hybrid, and heterogeneous environments.

In this book, we will explore how you can interact and work with many AWS services via PowerShell. We will learn how we can build highly available and fault-tolerant applications using Elastic Load Balancer and Auto Scaling. In addition, we will learn how Elastic Beanstalk and CloudFormation will help you to deploy the AWS infrastructure and application. We will also touch upon the popular MySQL Relational Database Service and learn how to spin up and work with DB Instances. Finally, we will learn about built-in monitoring and auditing capabilities that you should always consider in your AWS infrastructure.

What this book covers

Chapter 1, *PowerShell Essentials*, introduces the PowerShell and its cmdlet structure, provides ways to get help on specific cmdlets, and helps you build parameterized scripts with your own built-in help. We will also cover risk mitigation parameters in PowerShell that are required to know when you work in a highly complex environment.

Chapter 2, *The AWS Overview*, introduces you with AWS Cloud and helps you to understand the several benefits that AWS Cloud brings to the table. It also walks you through the different services provided by AWS and the signing up process with AWS.

Chapter 3, *Installing PowerShell Core and AWS Tools*, walks you through the installation process of PowerShell 6 and AWS Tools for PowerShell 6. It also discusses the security aspects in PowerShell and updating the new versions of AWS Tools as and when available.

Chapter 4, *AWS Identity and Access Management*, focuses on creating the PowerShell profile for storing the AWS credential. In addition, you will learn how to create IAM users, groups, and roles.

Chapter 5, *AWS Virtual Private Cloud*, dives more into the foundational network that you can consider before deploying your AWS infrastructure. It discusses more about the various components around building your AWS private network.

Chapter 6, *AWS Elastic Compute Cloud*, explains the EC2 service and also discusses how you can spin up and work with virtual machines in the cloud. It also focuses on the storage that can be used while working with EC2.

Chapter 7, *AWS Simple Storage Service*, introduces you the object store provided by AWS and discusses the various storage classes used by S3. You will learn about creating buckets and managing bucket permissions.

Chapter 8, *Elastic Load Balancer*, discusses two types of load balancer that are available with AWS and provides insight on how both of them work.

Chapter 9, *Auto Scaling*, focuses on the core components of horizontal scaling on AWS. It will cover fleet management and dynamic scaling of your application infrastructure.

Chapter 10, *Laying Foundation for RDS Databases*, introduces you to various aspects of Relational Database Service and helps you build the foundation for your RDS database deployment.

Chapter 11, *DB Instance Administration and Management*, introduces you to RDS storage types, licensing on RDS, maintenance windows, and working with DB instances. You will also learn multi-AZ deployment and running backups on RDS.

Chapter 12, *Working with RDS Read Replicas*, discusses MySQL read replica and how we can balance the traffic between multiple read replicas.

Chapter 13, *AWS Elastic Beanstalk,* focuses on deploying the application using Elastic Beanstalk. You will learn various deployment strategies that you can use while deploying your application on Elastic Beanstalk.

Chapter 14, *AWS CloudFormation,* discusses how you can build a CloudFormation template to deploy your AWS infrastructure. You will learn about the CloudFormation template YAML format and the structuring around it. We will also discuss submitting the template and tracking events generated by the stack creation process.

Chapter 15, *AWS CloudWatch,* introduces you to the in-built monitoring service and explains how we can create metrics and alarms using CloudWatch. It also focuses on CloudWatch Logs, which can be used for monitoring your application and server log files.

Chapter 16, *AWS Resource Auditing,* discusses the two most important management services, CloudTrail and Config. We will learn how you can enable CloudTrail and Config in your AWS account.

What you need for this book

You need an AWS account and basic knowledge of cloud computing. If you have some scripting experience using PowerShell, it would be a big plus. In addition, if you have any other cloud experience, that will help you to understand the concepts very easily.

In this book, you will need the following software:

- PowerShell 6
- AWS Tools for the PowerShell.NetCore module

Internet connectivity is required to install both the modules mentioned.

Who this book is for

This book is for all the cloud professionals who want to know the working of PowerShell with the AWS Cloud. If you are new to AWS, you can always refer to https://aws.amazon .com/ and read about various services provided by AWS. Mostly, DevOps cloud engineers will benefit the most from this book as it demonstrates command-line capability of doing many things via PowerShell.

Conventions

In this book, you will find a number of text styles that distinguish between different kinds of information. Here are some examples of these styles and an explanation of their meaning. Code words in text, database table names, folder names, filenames, file extensions, pathnames, dummy URLs, user input, and Twitter handles are shown as follows: "Once you start PowerShell, you can mostly use `get-host` or `$PSVersionTable` to check the version of PowerShell."

A block of code is set as follows:

```
{
  "Id": "key-consolepolicy-3",
  "Version": "2012-10-17",
  "Statement": [
    {
      "Sid": "Enable IAM User Permissions",
      "Effect": "Allow",
      "Principal": {
        "AWS": [
          "arn:aws:iam::072316406132:root"
        ]
      },
```

Any command-line input or output is written as follows:

```
PS C:\>Get-Service
```

New terms and **important words** are shown in bold. Words that you see on the screen, for example, in menus or dialog boxes, appear in the text like this: "You can start an ISE environment by clicking on **Windows PowerShell ISE.**"

 Warnings or important notes appear like this.

 Tips and tricks appear like this.

Reader feedback

Feedback from our readers is always welcome. Let us know what you think about this book-what you liked or disliked. Reader feedback is important for us as it helps us develop titles that you will really get the most out of. To send us general feedback, simply e-mail feedback@packtpub.com, and mention the book's title in the subject of your message. If there is a topic that you have expertise in and you are interested in either writing or contributing to a book, see our author guide at www.packtpub.com/authors.

Customer support

Now that you are the proud owner of a Packt book, we have a number of things to help you to get the most from your purchase.

Downloading the color images of this book

We also provide you with a PDF file that has color images of the screenshots/diagrams used in this book. The color images will help you better understand the changes in the output. You can download this file from https://www.packtpub.com/sites/default/files/down loads/AWSToolsforPowerShell6_ColorImages.pdf.

Errata

Although we have taken every care to ensure the accuracy of our content, mistakes do happen. If you find a mistake in one of our books-maybe a mistake in the text or the code-we would be grateful if you could report this to us. By doing so, you can save other readers from frustration and help us improve subsequent versions of this book. If you find any errata, please report them by visiting http://www.packtpub.com/submit-errata, selecting your book, clicking on the **Errata Submission Form** link, and entering the details of your errata. Once your errata are verified, your submission will be accepted and the errata will be uploaded to our website or added to any list of existing errata under the Errata section of that title. To view the previously submitted errata, go to https://www.packtpub.com/book s/content/support, and enter the name of the book in the search field. The required information will appear under the **Errata** section.

Piracy

Piracy of copyrighted material on the Internet is an ongoing problem across all media. At Packt, we take the protection of our copyright and licenses very seriously. If you come across any illegal copies of our works in any form on the Internet, please provide us with the location address or website name immediately so that we can pursue a remedy. Please contact us at `copyright@packtpub.com` with a link to the suspected pirated material. We appreciate your help in protecting our authors and our ability to bring you valuable content.

Questions

If you have a problem with any aspect of this book, you can contact us at `questions@packtpub.com`, and we will do our best to address the problem.

1
PowerShell Essentials

PowerShell is marching toward one of the greatest scripting and automation tools of all time. It is increasingly important to learn PowerShell if you are working with Microsoft products and surrounding ecosystems. Considering various limitations on the command-line management exposed using MS-DOS, Microsoft started to develop a new approach to the command-line management way back in 2002 and introduced a shell called **Monad**. It was September 2006 when Microsoft renamed Monad to PowerShell Version 1. Since then, there have been several versions released, and the current stable version is PowerShell 5. Last year, in 2016, Microsoft announced PowerShell Core 6 on GitHub, being not only open source but also cross-platform. This is what will make PowerShell more popular because of its capability to automate things on Linux as well as macOS.

So, where is PowerShell heading from here on? What is the future of PowerShell? Microsoft is aware of the fact that every business will have a cloud-first strategy and a complex infrastructure to manage. Microsoft's initial intention was to ease the Windows-based server administration and maintenance, but now they are strategically moving ahead to make PowerShell as a standard scripting platform for customers so that it can be used on Windows, Linux, and macOS. The open source nature of PowerShell will fuel the PowerShell growth and will help to build the trusted artifact gallery quickly. Businesses will adopt the multi-cloud strategy and there is no single answer of how to best manage multi-cloud. Management is absolutely the secret ingredient for multi-cloud, and there is no common API that is available to manage multi-cloud effectively. Over a period of time, PowerShell will become a mature scripting language to manage the multi-cloud and hybrid environment. And this is one of the biggest intentions of Microsoft, making it cross-platform in the PowerShell Core.

In this chapter, we will learn about the PowerShell cmdlet and how to get help on each cmdlet. We will also touch base on how PowerShell cmdlets are structured. In addition, we will learn about risk mitigation parameters and building your own help for the scripts that you create.

Why PowerShell?

If you are an IT admin or a developer, you will want to learn PowerShell. Learning PowerShell will enhance your ability to manage your entire IT infrastructure. It is a very rich scripting environment, but I do not want you to limit your thinking that it is just a scripting language. First, it can perform the same task on thousands of servers without logging in and help IT admins or developers to keep all the work consistent on all the servers. This is amazing, isn't it? Second, it is also used for **task automation**. When we think about the server configuration or deployment, we can use PowerShell to do all kinds of things that we want in our environment. Third, it is also **object oriented**. What I mean here is that everything we do inside of PowerShell is treated like an object, even if the object is a service, process, or just a server. Because of its object-oriented capability, many developers started using PowerShell even though it traditionally looks like an IT admin tool.

Microsoft is putting its full weight behind PowerShell. PowerShell is not going away; it is rather creating a big footprint in the task automation area, as Microsoft announced its intention to make PowerShell open sourced. They know that customers are really having heterogeneous environment in their IT shops, and this is why they thought to make PowerShell available to the community so that it becomes standard for IT automation in data centers. Microsoft also made it mandatory to have a PowerShell support for each product they released. Other vendors such as NetApp, IBM, VMWare, Dell, AWS, and several others have strong support for PowerShell. So, PowerShell is going to stay, and your reward for learning PowerShell is the improved ability to control and automate many technologies that it integrates and works with.

Running PowerShell

Different versions of Windows come with different version of PowerShell. For example, Windows 8 and Windows Server 2013 have PowerShell 3.0, whereas Windows 8.1 comes with PowerShell 4.0 by default. On Windows 10 and later, you see PowerShell 5 installed by default. For now, we will just focus on running PowerShell on your Windows desktop. I am running Windows 10 at the time of writing this book; thus I will use Windows 10 to demonstrate the concept to know more about PowerShell. At the same time, this chapter is not intended to make you an expert in PowerShell scripting; it is rather to help you know the very basics of the PowerShell environment so that you are all set for the journey that you are planning in this book to learn AWS Tools for PowerShell Core. This would help if you are new to PowerShell. You do not need to be an expert, but understanding the basic commands in PowerShell will help you. If you are keen to learn more about PowerShell, my suggestion is to consider buying other PowerShell-related books or take some online training to gain more insight into this beautiful scripting language.

You only need to type the first few letters of the word PowerShell on the start screen. As we discussed earlier, Microsoft announced PowerShell Core 6, which is still in beta at the time of writing this book. So, I have downloaded the PowerShell Core 6 beta version from the GitHub repository. I will be using PowerShell Core 6 on Windows 10 as we move forward. You may want to pin PowerShell into your taskbar rather than starting this way, by typing in the start screen window every time you run PowerShell:

There are four options that you will see in most of the Windows PowerShell environment. If you see (**x86**) in the options, such as **Windows PowerShell (x86)** or **Windows PowerShell ISE (x86)**, it means that it is 32-bit binaries for PowerShell, and without (x86) they are 64-bit binaries available for PowerShell. Windows PowerShell ISE is a nice GUI and an **Integrated Scripting Environment** (**ISE**). You can start an ISE environment by clicking on **Windows PowerShell ISE** ;or by just running the `ise` command inside PowerShell. The best thing about ISE is that it has a lot of advantages to it. Not only can you see the scripting pane at the top, which allows you to write rich and robust scripts, but you can also have error checks and debugging built into it, so you can step through the script one at a time if you want to do so.

Once you start PowerShell, you can mostly use `get-host` or `$PSVersionTable` to check the version of PowerShell. `get-host` works in all versions of PowerShell, whereas `$PSVersionTable` works in PowerShell version 2 and later.

```
PS C:\> get-host

Name              : ConsoleHost
Version           : 6.0.0
InstanceId        : 97e3ac95-bce3-40a3-8763-ebd1fb6f8334
UI                : System.Management.Automation.Internal.Host.InternalHostUserInterface
CurrentCulture    : en-AU
CurrentUICulture  : en-US
PrivateData       : Microsoft.PowerShell.ConsoleHost+ConsoleColorProxy
DebuggerEnabled   : True
IsRunspacePushed  : False
Runspace          : System.Management.Automation.Runspaces.LocalRunspace


PS C:\> $PSVersionTable

Name                       Value
----                       -----
PSVersion                  6.0.0-beta
PSEdition                  Core
BuildVersion               3.0.0.0
CLRVersion
GitCommitId                v6.0.0-beta.1
OS                         Microsoft Windows 10.0.14393
Platform                   Win32NT
PSCompatibleVersions       {1.0, 2.0, 3.0, 4.0...}
PSRemotingProtocolVersion  2.3
SerializationVersion       1.1.0.1
WSManStackVersion          3.0
```

Reading the PowerShell language

PowerShell is a natural language that you can learn quickly. There are four types of commands that PowerShell can run. Those are windows native, aliases, scripts, and cmdlet. Many people think that the only thing that PowerShell can do is run cmdlet, but that's not all true. Certainly, cmdlets are more popular, but in addition, you can run Windows native commands, aliases, and scripts. Cmdlets have a unique structure. There are thousands of cmdlet provided by AWS for managing the AWS infrastructure. Almost all the cmdlets work in a similar way, and this simplifies the scripting. All cmdlets have two parts. The first part is a verb and the second part is a noun. Usually, the verb indicates an action for the command, and the noun indicates a specific service or program. Set, get, add, and remove are some of the most popular verbs that you will see in PowerShell.

General syntax for cmdlet is:

Cmdlet structure: <verb> - <noun>

Dash (-) in between the verb and noun completes the Windows PowerShell command. It is also a PowerShell convention to use singular nouns. While it is not universally applied, if you are not sure whether a noun is singular or plural, go with singular. Let's say, if you want to see list of services running on Windows, then Get-Service is the cmdlet that you can use and not Get-Services:

```
PS C:\>Get-Service
```

Note that PowerShell cmdlets are not case sensitive, so if you type Get-Service or get-service in the PowerShell command prompt, both of them are going to yield the same result. You can get the list of common verbs used by PowerShell by running the following:

```
PS C:\>Get-Verb
```

This will give you an idea of how many verbs that PowerShell uses.

Getting and exploring help options

Microsoft has designed PowerShell in such a way that it is easy to use for complex scripting and automation tasks, and it is also easy to use for an interactive command. The standard naming convention used for a PowerShell cmdlet will assist you in figuring out how to accomplish certain tasks. Understanding the help system capability in PowerShell will help you to write the complex scripting cases in a large infrastructure setup, and the help system in PowerShell will become your most important resource. On some Windows systems, in case you do not find the help system installed, you can update it using the update-Help cmdlet:

```
PS C:\>Update-Help -Force
```

Force with Update-Help indicates that the Update-Help cmdlet does not follow the once-per-day limitation; it skips version checking and downloads files that exceed the 1 GB limit. Also, you need to ensure that you started PowerShell as an administrator before attempting to run this command.

The Get-Help cmdlet displays information about the necessary help for any other cmdlet that you need the information for. You can seek help on any cmdlet using Get-Help. For example, if you want to seek information on the Get-Process cmdlet, then you can use the following command:

```
PS C:\>Get-Help Get-Process
```

```
PS C:\> Get-Help Get-Process
NAME
    Get-Process

SYNOPSIS
    Gets the processes that are running on the local computer or a remote computer.

SYNTAX
    Get-Process [[-Name] <String[]>] [-ComputerName <String[]>] [-FileVersionInfo] [-Module] [<CommonParameters>]

    Get-Process [-ComputerName <String[]>] [-FileVersionInfo] -Id <Int32[]> [-Module] [<CommonParameters>]

    Get-Process [-ComputerName <String[]>] [-FileVersionInfo] -InputObject <Process[]> [-Module] [<CommonParameters>]

    Get-Process -Id <Int32[]> -IncludeUserName [<CommonParameters>]

    Get-Process [[-Name] <String[]>] -IncludeUserName [<CommonParameters>]

    Get-Process -IncludeUserName -InputObject <Process[]> [<CommonParameters>]

DESCRIPTION
    The Get-Process cmdlet gets the processes on a local or remote computer.

    Without parameters, this cmdlet gets all of the processes on the local computer. You can also specify a particular process by process name or process ID (PID) or pass a
    process object through the pipeline to this cmdlet.

    By default, this cmdlet returns a process object that has detailed information about the process and supports methods that let you start and stop the process. You can also
    use the parameters of the Get-Process cmdlet to get file version information for the program that runs in the process and to get the modules that the process loaded.

RELATED LINKS
    Online Version: http://go.microsoft.com/fwlink/?linkid=821590
    Debug-Process
    Get-Process
    Start-Process
    Stop-Process
    Wait-Process

REMARKS
    To see the examples, type: "get-help Get-Process -examples".
    For more information, type: "get-help Get-Process -detailed".
    For technical information, type: "get-help Get-Process -full".
    For online help, type: "get-help Get-Process -online"
```

The output shows the help for Get-Process. I would encourage you to check the following commonly used variant of the Get-Help cmdlet, which would feed you more detailed information on the specific cmdlet. This is what will help you to understand the command usage in detail when you start scripting:

```
PS C:\>Get-Help Get-Process -ShowWindow
PS C:\>Get-Help Get-Process -Detailed
PS C:\>Get-Help Get-Process -Full
PS C:\>Get-Help Get-Process -Online
```

Discovering cmdlets and aliases

If you are new to PowerShell, you must be excited to know about all the cmdlets and aliases available. It is an easy language to read and learn. You might want to know how many cmdlets and aliases are out there that you can use in your scripting language. Wait, that's very simple. You can unleash the list of all cmdlets and aliases just using a couple of commands. Get-Command is the cmdlet that will list you all the available cmdlets:

```
PS C:\>Get-Command
```

You can further narrow down the discovery using some keyword, and this is major plus point, which lets you quickly search and use the appropriate cmdlet in your script. You do not need to remember any cmdlet; just think of a specific action or service that you want to do, and pass it on to the Get-Command cmdlet to further refine the search. If you want to list all the process-related cmdlets, then you can use this:

```
PS C:\>Get-Command *process*
```

Once you see the available list, you can pick up the most appropriate one and get help using the Get-Help cmdlet. This is the best way to learn about various cmdlets. There is nothing like a fixed set of cmdlets available. This list is growing everyday. As and when you add a module, a new set of cmdlets associated with the service or product will be added in the list. Moving further, when we install AWS Tools for PowerShell, a new set of cmdlets will be added, and we will be making use of this new set of cmdlets to work with AWS Cloud.

Another way you can work with commands inside PowerShell is via aliases. Aliases are how you can bridge your knowledge about cmdlets, where you are coming from to where you want to go inside of PowerShell. For example, Get-ChildItem is the cmdlet used for listing all the items in the present working directory, or you can specify the location. If you are a Windows guy, using dir for quite a long time, you may prefer to continue to use this instead of using Get-ChildItem. If you are a Linux guy, then you may prefer to use ls. So, if you type dir, ls, or gci at the command prompt, then all of them will lead to the same result as thrown by Get-ChildItem. Are dir, ls, and gci different commands? The answer is NO. dir, ls, and gci are the aliases for Get-ChildItem. So, if you type Get-Alias in the command prompt, it will list you all the aliases defined in the PowerShell. You can also create your own aliases using Set-Alias. To get the list of existing alias, you can run the following command:

```
PS C:\>Get-Alias
```

You can specify the name of the alias with `Get-Alias` to know the parent cmdlet; for example:

```
PS C:\>Get-Alias dir
PS C:\>Get-Alias ls
PS C:\>Get-Alias gci
```

```
PS C:\> Get-Alias dir

CommandType     Name                                Version    Source
-----------     ----                                -------    ------
Alias           dir -> Get-ChildItem

PS C:\> Get-Alias ls

CommandType     Name                                Version    Source
-----------     ----                                -------    ------
Alias           ls -> Get-ChildItem

PS C:\> Get-Alias gci

CommandType     Name                                Version    Source
-----------     ----                                -------    ------
Alias           gci -> Get-ChildItem
```

Learning cmdlets

There are thousands of cmdlets available. Don't worry. It's not very scary. Don't think that you need to remember all those cmdlets to be a good IT admin or a developer. I do not know anybody who claims that he knows all the cmdlets. As I said earlier, the number of cmdlets are increasing day by day; what is important to know is how to get help on those cmdlets, discover the cmdlets, and learn the properties associated with specific cmdlets. Let's dive a little deeper into one cmdlet called `Get-Service`. Now, if you run this cmdlet in the PowerShell command prompt, you find that it returned just three columns.

```
PS C:\> Get-Service

Status     Name               DisplayName
------     ----               -----------
Running    AdobeARMservice    Adobe Acrobat Update Service
Stopped    AJRouter           AllJoyn Router Service
Stopped    ALG                Application Layer Gateway Service
Running    ApHidMonitorSer... Alps HID Monitor Service
Stopped    AppIDSvc           Application Identity
Running    Appinfo            Application Information
```

Does that mean that it has just got three columns? The answer is NO. There are methods and properties associated with each cmdlet. You can learn more about those methods and properties using the `Get-Member` cmdlet with `Get-Service`.

```
PS C:\> Get-Service | Get-Member


   TypeName: System.ServiceProcess.ServiceController

Name                     MemberType    Definition
----                     ----------    ----------
Name                     AliasProperty Name = ServiceName
RequiredServices         AliasProperty RequiredServices = ServicesDependedOn
Continue                 Method        void Continue()
Dispose                  Method        void Dispose(), void IDisposable.Dispose()
Equals                   Method        bool Equals(System.Object obj)
GetHashCode              Method        int GetHashCode()
GetType                  Method        type GetType()
Pause                    Method        void Pause()
Refresh                  Method        void Refresh()
Start                    Method        void Start(), void Start(string[] args)
Stop                     Method        void Stop()
WaitForStatus            Method        void WaitForStatus(System.ServiceProcess.ServiceControllerStatus desiredStatus), void Wait
CanPauseAndContinue      Property      bool CanPauseAndContinue {get;}
CanShutdown              Property      bool CanShutdown {get;}
CanStop                  Property      bool CanStop {get;}
DependentServices        Property      System.ServiceProcess.ServiceController[] DependentServices {get;}
DisplayName              Property      string DisplayName {get;}
MachineName              Property      string MachineName {get;}
ServiceHandle            Property      System.Runtime.InteropServices.SafeHandle ServiceHandle {get;}
ServiceName              Property      string ServiceName {get;}
ServicesDependedOn       Property      System.ServiceProcess.ServiceController[] ServicesDependedOn {get;}
ServiceType              Property      System.ServiceProcess.ServiceType ServiceType {get;}
StartType                Property      System.ServiceProcess.ServiceStartMode StartType {get;}
Status                   Property      System.ServiceProcess.ServiceControllerStatus Status {get;}
ToString                 ScriptMethod  System.Object ToString();
```

This way you can learn about the cmdlet that you plan to use in your scripting. You can now see that there are several properties and methods that you can make use of instead of the default output. Usually, if you are a developer, you will love to know more about the methods so that you can interact with the service using code.

Let's assume that you are interested in `Name`, `Status`, and `StartType`. You can tweak the output now using `Format-List` or `Format-Table` cmdlet as follows:

```
PS C:\>Get-Service | Format-List Name, Status, StartType
PS C:\>Get-Service | Format-Table Name, Status, StartType
```

Risk mitigation parameters

PowerShell has two risk mitigation parameters called `WhatIf` and `Confirm`. They are very useful for testing complicated scripts without risking the code running amok. By appending `WhatIf` and `Confirm`, you get a preview of what could have happened without risking the damage. Let's take a real-life example of a file deletion using a wildcard. Consider that there are some files, and you plan to delete them. But you want to ensure that you are deleting the right set of files that you intend to delete. Because you are using a wildcard, the consequences could be very serious. Hence, it is always prudent to ensure that you are not risking the run of the command. Lets assume that you want to remove `file*.txt` files from some directory; you can use `WhatIf` something like following:

```
PS C:\>Get-Childitem C:\somedata\file*.txt -Recurse | Remove-Item -WhatIf
```

```
PS C:\> Get-Childitem C:\somedata\file*.txt -Recurse | Remove-Item -WhatIf
What if: Performing the operation "Remove File" on target "C:\somedata\file1.txt".
What if: Performing the operation "Remove File" on target "C:\somedata\file2.txt".
What if: Performing the operation "Remove File" on target "C:\somedata\file3.txt".
What if: Performing the operation "Remove File" on target "C:\somedata\file4.txt".
What if: Performing the operation "Remove File" on target "C:\somedata\file5.txt".
```

In the example, we used `file*.txt` (with a wildcard), and the command did not make any permanent change when you appended the command with `WhatIf`. The command run is just letting us know that if you run it without `WhatIf`, it is going to delete all those five files. Likewise, you can use `Confirm` by appending at the end of the command to get a confirmation if the specific file can be deleted or not:

```
PS C:\>Get-Childitem C:\somedata\file*.txt -Recurse | Remove-Item -Confirm
```

```
PS C:\> Get-Childitem C:\somedata\file*.txt -Recurse | Remove-Item -Confirm

Confirm
Are you sure you want to perform this action?
Performing the operation "Remove File" on target "C:\somedata\file1.txt".
[Y] Yes  [A] Yes to All  [N] No  [L] No to All  [S] Suspend  [?] Help (default is "Y"): N

Confirm
Are you sure you want to perform this action?
Performing the operation "Remove File" on target "C:\somedata\file2.txt".
[Y] Yes  [A] Yes to All  [N] No  [L] No to All  [S] Suspend  [?] Help (default is "Y"): N

Confirm
Are you sure you want to perform this action?
Performing the operation "Remove File" on target "C:\somedata\file3.txt".
[Y] Yes  [A] Yes to All  [N] No  [L] No to All  [S] Suspend  [?] Help (default is "Y"): N
```

These two risk mitigation parameters are really powerful when you start rolling out the script to hundreds of servers, and it will help to ease your anxiety a little bit.

Working with output

As you work with PowerShell, sending out output and controlling the formatting of the output is very easy. Redirecting output is also a common use of the **Pipe** (|) operator that you find in PowerShell. There are different ways to deal with the output of the commands. As highlighted earlier, you can use the `Format-List` and `Format-Table` cmdlet to get the required properties in the output. In case you want to save the output to the file, you can use the `out-file` or `export-csv` parameter with the cmdlet. For example, let's say you want to save the services output to the file, then you simply use this:

```
PS C:\>Get-Service | out-file C:\services.txt
```

Or you use this:

```
PS C:\>Get-Service | export-csv C:\services.txt
```

One of the best things that you can find in PowerShell is called a **grid view**. It allows you to output the data to the GUI where you can work with it a little bit easier, especially when you are looking to manipulate data and get a quick peek on what's going on in a particular server or what's happening with a particular cmdlet. `Out-GridView` offers a great alternative instead of trying to figure out how to output to a file or a different table:

```
PS C:\>Get-Service | Out-GridView
```

This will just display the default properties into the grid view and not all the properties. But wait, you cannot combine `Out-GridView` with the `Format-List` and `Format-Table` commands. If you want to control what parameters go into the grid view, then the `Select-Object` cmdlet is what comes to the rescue:

```
PS C:\>Get-Service | Select-Object DisplayName,Status | Out-GridView
```

If you want all the parameters to send to the grid view, then you can use this:

```
PS C:\>Get-Service | Select-Object * | Out-GridView
```

If you are looking to get the quick details, then the grid view is the way to go.

Running PowerShell remotely

One of the advantages of PowerShell is accessing the remote servers. Running commands on remote servers is called PowerShell remoting, and this is not something new. Many IT admins run PowerShell on their client-side desktops and access servers located in different data centers to ease the administrative effort. In the cmdlets, there is a `ComputerName` parameter that you can use to run the command on the remote server. You just need to ensure that the `ComputerName` parameter specified is seen on the network and has a remoting option enabled. Let's say you want to run the `Get-Service` cmdlet on the server called `apps1`, then you can run this:

```
PS C:\>Get-Service -ComputerName apps1
```

So, all the cmdlets that you run locally can be run on the remote server just by specifying the `ComputerName` parameter with it.

PowerShell is locked down by default. In order to enable remoting, you have to run the `Enable-PsRemoting` cmdlet:

```
PS C:\> Enable-PsRemoting -Force
```

This command starts the **Windows Remote Management** (**WinRM**) service, sets it to start automatically with your system, and creates a firewall rule that allows incoming connections. The `Force` part of the command tells PowerShell to perform these actions without prompting you for each step. You should restart the WinRM service so that new settings can take effect:

```
PS C:\Restart-Service WinRM
```

For testing the connection, you can use this:

```
PS C:\Test-WsMan <RemoteComputer>
PS C:\Enter-PsSession -ComputerName <RemoteComputer>
```

Or you can run any other cmdlet with `ComputerName` parameter.

 Please note that when you deal with servers in multiple `domains` or the servers in `WorkGroup`, there could be some challenges establishing the connectivity with remote servers, as they are sometimes tricky to work with. It is always good to work with your system administrator in case you end up with issues regarding PowerShell remoting.

Building parameterized script

When you start building script for automation that can be used by yourself and others repeatedly for doing some task, building parameterized script is the key. In PowerShell, it is very easy to build the parameterized script using just a simple `param` keyword in the script file. You may have solved the problem using individual cmdlets, and you now want that one to be used repeatedly for building an automation. Let's review the following script for a better understanding of using parameters:

```
PS D:\scripts> Get-Content .\DiskInfo.ps1
param(
        [Parameter(Mandatory=$true)]
        [string[]] $Drive,
        $NotForUse
)

Get-CimInstance -ComputerName APPS1 -ClassName Win32_LogicalDisk -filter "DeviceID='$Drive'" |
Select-Object -Property @{n="ComputerName";e={$_.PSComputerName}},@{n="FreeGB";e={$_.FreeSpace / 1gb -as [int]}}
PS D:\scripts>
```

I created a file called `DiskInfo.ps1` in the `D:\scripts` directory. This script provides you with free GB available on the drive that you pass to this script. I am using `Get-CimInstance` to get me the computer name and free GB. The `param` keyword at the top of the script can be seen. You might just need to get a feeling of writing that syntax and nothing more. To make the drive letter mandatory, I used a keyword called `Mandatory=$true`. Once you saved the file, the script can be run as follows:

```
PS :\D>.\DiskInfo.ps1 –Drive C:
```

The beauty of the script is that when you start hitting the tab after the script name on the command prompt, it starts displaying you the parameters that can be passed to the script, which is amazing. This is the way you start building a new set of cmdlets for you. There is nothing else that needs to be done to build your own cmdlets.

Comment-based help

Another very important thing in PowerShell that you must know is that you can build the script with in-built help. There are no separate files that you need to maintain for your script. This is an amazing capability. There are two ways that you can write help lines in your PowerShell Script. You can either use a **hash** (#) in the line to indicate it's a help, or you can make use of the <#..#> block level comment. Let's use the following script to continue the discussion:

```
PS D:\scripts> Get-Content .\PS_Comment.ps1
<#
.Synopsis
This is an example of building parameterized script
.Description
This script checks free space on the given drive
.Parameter ComputerName
This is name of the Computer for which script needs to be run
.Parameter Drive
This indicates drive letter for which free space need to be checked
.Parameter NotForUse
This is sample added parameter
.Example
Connecting to Local Computer
DiskInfo -Computername localhost
.Example
Connecting to Remote Computer
DiskInfo -ComputerName remote_machine
#>

param(
        [Parameter(Mandatory=$true)]
        [string[]] $Computername,
        $Drive,
        $NotForUse
)

# Main Code Below

Get-CimInstance -ComputerName $Computername -ClassName Win32_LogicalDisk -filter "DeviceID='$Drive'" |
Select-Object -Property @{n="ComputerName";e={$_.PSComputerName}},@{n="FreeGB";e={$_.FreeSpace / 1gb -as [int]}}
PS D:\scripts>
```

I specified a block level comment in <#..#> with some other interesting things. Once the parsing engine sees the block of lines inside <#..#>, it starts ignoring the text and knows that it is help comment. But pay special attention to the lines inside that block, which are started with a **dot** (.). It has a special meaning in PowerShell. PowerShell starts building your help file once it sees this dot. This is extremely helpful in PowerShell when you build a complex script that can be used by others. There is no need to maintain a separate help file. It is just like the help you seek for any other cmdlet available in PowerShell. You can simply now type the following and see the magic:

```
PS C:\>Get-Help .\PS_Comment.ps1 -detailed
```

```
PS D:\scripts> get-help .\PS_Comment.ps1 -detailed

NAME
    D:\scripts\PS_Comment.ps1

SYNOPSIS
    This is an example of building parameterized script


SYNTAX
    D:\scripts\PS_Comment.ps1 [-Computername] <String[]> [[-Drive] <Object>] [[-NotForUse] <Object>] [<CommonParameters>]


DESCRIPTION
    This script checks free space on the given drive


PARAMETERS
    -Computername <String[]>
        This is name of the Computer for which script needs to be run

    -Drive <Object>
        This indicates drive letter for which free space need to be checked

    -NotForUse <Object>
        This is sample added parameter

    <CommonParameters>
        This cmdlet supports the common parameters: Verbose, Debug,
        ErrorAction, ErrorVariable, WarningAction, WarningVariable,
        OutBuffer, PipelineVariable, and OutVariable. For more information, see
        about_CommonParameters (https://go.microsoft.com/fwlink/?LinkID=113216).

    -------------------------- EXAMPLE 1 --------------------------

    PS C:\>Connecting to Local Computer

    DiskInfo -Computername localhost



    -------------------------- EXAMPLE 2 --------------------------

    PS C:\>Connecting to Remote Computer
```

So, you just built a help file that looks like the cmdlet help.

Summary

PowerShell is not new. It has been here since 2006, but mostly used in the Windows environment. There have been different versions released until now, the most recent being PowerShell 5 on Windows. PowerShell Core 6 is now an open source project that is being delivered not just on Windows but also on Linux and macOS. PowerShell Core 6 is what Microsoft are planning to support on a multi-platform environment; and at the time of writing this book, it has just been moved from alpha to beta. Looking into future, managing multi-cloud and hybrid heterogeneous environments, Microsoft sees a strong demand for a universal shell to manage the complex IT shops and drive automation. Because PowerShell provides a unified experience and single pane to interact with multiple vendor products, it will be helpful to manage multi-cloud, hybrid, and heterogeneous environments. So, stay tuned and keep learning PowerShell Core 6. In the next chapter, we will review some of the AWS services that we will touch base in rest of the book.

2
The AWS Overview

Cloud computing is the most discussed area these days and has created a huge footprint in IT. It is popularly known as cloud, and it is simply an on-demand provisioning of the IT resources on a pay-as-you-go basis. Most of us use cloud computing all day long without realizing it. When we sit at the PC and type a query into our favorite web search engine, the computer that we are using isn't playing much part in finding the answers for the query we submitted. Our computer is just no more than a messenger. The words of the query are swiftly shuttled over the internet, and through search engine providers, hundreds of thousands of clustered computers dig out the results and send them promptly back to us. The real work done by the search engine provider could be in any part of the world; most likely, we do not care. What we care about is the result we wanted for the query that we submitted. In the cloud environment, computing resources such as servers, storage, network, applications, and processes are managed by the cloud provider and seems to be centralized in nature for the user. The user uses these resources when needed. The user can also Scale-Out depending on the workload.

Organizations often adopt new technologies to enable the most efficient practices for the businesses to increase high availability, data reliability, and availability. As companies use more data types from many sources, complexity and risks are escalating. Organizations continue to introduce a new way to manage their data, as it is becoming critical for them to be competitive and be ahead in the game. With increasing datasets, structured and unstructured, companies are finding it difficult to provision the computing power to process the data and finding a way to enable an extreme provisioning of computing resources when needed, while minimizing the cost and maintaining security. Cloud computing is what organizations are finding as a solution to the on-demand provisioning of the resources, which enables then to stay in the game and be competitive.

In this chapter, we will discuss various benefits offered by cloud computing, common challenges that industries face in migrating to cloud, the AWS global infrastructure, security and compliance, and various AWS services. In addition, we will touch upon the signing up process and how you can get supported on AWS.

Disruptive innovations - AWS Cloud

Amazon Web Service (**AWS**) started it's journey as an online bookseller way back in 1996. Amazons online business model was a completely new concept. Its business model gave birth to a new type of industry itself. As an online bookseller, they achieved tremendous success. It was its own business that outstripped the capability of all the existing software and could not scale any more. Considering its growth, they wanted a kind of IT infrastructure that could scale based on the requirements, while maintaining its system and application performance.

It is surprising to see how Amazon became one of the leading cloud provider of the time. Around 2000 to 2002, they felt that everything that could be done in the software to optimize its applications and business logic had reached its peak and their complex pieces of software could not evolve anymore. They went through serious introspection and concluded that a service-oriented architecture would give them a level of isolation to build software components rapidly and independently. Service-oriented architectures is what they used internally for all its purposes, and they thought to commercialize that self-service platform for the benefit of the world, as they knew that there are many out there facing the same challenges as they had. So, in 2006, they launched **Simple Storage Service** (**S3**) and **Elastic Compute Cloud** (**EC2**). Behind Amazon's successful evolution from a retailer to a technology platform is its **service-oriented architecture** (**SOA**), which broke new technological grounds and proved that SOAs can deliver on their promises.

When you look at the size of the cloud market, it is astonishing that AWS is the undisputed leader and will probably be so for the foreseeable future. You may wonder how AWS built such a dominance in the market. Well, this is a classic case of disruption dynamics. In the early days, when AWS thought that service-oriented architecture was the solution largely needed in the industry, they did not have any support from other big players sitting across the lake, so the big IT giants stayed away from the idea that Amazon wanted to pursue. This gave AWS almost 6 to 7 years' head start to be ahead in the game. Now, other cloud players have a lot more work to do to catch up with the amount of pure functionality that AWS offers to its customers and which they are adding to on a regular basis.

The benefits of AWS cloud computing

AWS Cloud provides various services in regard to compute, storage, networking, applications, and many more supportive services. These sets of services offer numerous benefits. At a high level, these benefits are highlighted in the following list. These benefits are very attractive to most organizations from a cost and scalability perspective:

- **No capital expenditure**: There is no need to invest heavily in setting up your own data centers. All of your organization's upfront capital investment is not needed anymore. You simply spin up the servers and make use of the various AWS services on a pay-as-you-go model. You have only your operational cost when you work with AWS. You stop incurring cost when you stop using AWS resources.

- **No maintenance of data centers**: AWS Cloud has sophisticated data centers connected to multiple grids, which are well designed for failure and security. Your organization immediately starts saving money by moving to the cloud, as they do not need to maintain their own data centers.

- **Lower variable cost**: By using AWS Cloud, you can get huge benefits from massive economies of scale. As more organizations start using the cloud, the cost of services goes down. You can also commit on the usage of the service for a certain number of years, which helps you to save around 40% to 60% rather than using on-demand resources.

- **No capacity planning needed**: In the traditional IT world, when you operate in your own data center, there is always a need to have some capacity planned for the next 1 to 3 years in order to allow your application to handle spiky loads. This requires a lot more planning and time investment to get that in shape. With AWS, you can simply scale and Scale-Down in a few minutes. There is no need as such to guess the capacity anymore. You get it when you need it.

- **Increase agility**: This is something very exciting that is achieved using AWS Cloud. You get a server in a minute and can start working on your application development, or make use of the blue/green model without heavily investing in the infrastructure. Agility is the key factor to choose from cloud services.

Common challenges of shifting to the cloud

As the race begins, every enterprise wants to be in the race getting to the cloud. There are several cloud providers with various on-demand services, but organizations do not know where to get started. Integrating the cloud with your on-premise data center requires various considerations, and it's not simply lift and shift. When you consider the cloud, a detailed assessment will be needed to see if existing application is a better fit for the cloud movement or whether it should be re-designed depending on the cloud capability and services. Based on my experience, most applications need some kind of rewriting to make them suitable for the cloud environment.

Here are some of the known challenges that have been noticed:

- **Incompatibility:** Can I lift my application and database and put them in the cloud to work? It is the first question that organizations want to know. There is often disconnect between what they have in-house and how they would be consuming in the cloud service. In most cases, lift and shift may not work and a detailed assessment would be needed by the experts.

- **Security:** Security is a concern whether you are on-premise or in the cloud. How security is perceived and what level of data protection would be required decides whether a public or private cloud would be suitable. The security of your cloud environment is a shared responsibility between you and AWS. AWS owns the underlying platform security, whereas you would be responsible for the application and database side of the security. I would say that the cloud is more secure than your on-premise data center, as AWS has heavily invested in the security and compliance, as they know that if they want to be successful as a provider, they have to ensure that security is not compromised at any stage. As a consumer, it is of the utmost importance to review the security elements, which would be more appropriate to your applications and enterprise.

- **Reliability:** For a reliable environment, when designing your application and databases, you should consider the failure aspects of your cloud environment. Most of the cloud providers have a built-in fault tolerance and the disclosed SLA of 99.95% to 99.99% availability of various services. What is most important is to consider the designing aspects of your application reliability and fault tolerance. Whether cloud applications should be self-healing or the cloud infrastructure should provide resiliency services to applications that have not been designed *for fail* is something to be discussed and reviewed.

- **Network:** With the proliferation of the internet and availability of the cloud provider's data center in each part of the world, network bandwidth would not be an issue if you are planning to house your production application in the cloud. But there are several aspects you should consider about accessing your environment from your on-premise user base for maintenance or deployment.

Overall, there is a high possibility that you maybe still in a position to adopt the cloud for each application that you run on-premise and still ensure that all the aforementioned roadblocks are addressed. The cloud is becoming more popular and fancier nowadays and I am sure that every cloud provider could take it to the next level, ensuring every application can be run on the cloud.

The AWS global infrastructure

AWS serves over a million active customers in more than 190 countries. They are steadily expanding the global infrastructure to help customers achieve lower latency and higher throughput, and to ensure that customers data resides only in the region they specifies. AWS data centers are available in multiple locations worldwide.

AWS infrastructure is built around regions and availability zones. In a region, there are multiple availability zones. Each region is strategically selected by AWS around the world. AWS plans at least three availability zones in each region. You can have more than that in some of the regions. These availability zones across the regions are connected with very low latency networks so that you can build fault tolerant and highly available applications. At the time of writing this book, there were 16 regions and 42 availability zones. They keep adding regions and availability zone. I would encourage you to check for the latest AWS **Global Infrastructure** footprint on the AWS website.

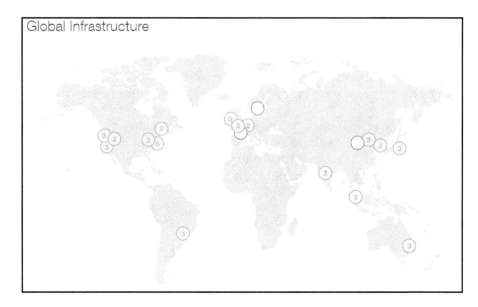

Image source: https://aws.amazon.com/

Because of the multiple regions, you can retain complete control and ownership over the region in which your data is physically located, making it easy to meet regional compliance and data residency requirements.

Security and compliance

Security is the shared responsibility between AWS and the customer. One portion of the cloud is secured by AWS and another portion of the cloud is your responsibility:

- **Security:** Cloud security at AWS is the highest priority. As an AWS customer, you will benefit from a data center and network architecture built to meet the requirements of the most security-sensitive organizations. This means that you can have the security you need but without the capital outlay and with much lower operational overhead than in an on-premise environment. You get access to hundreds of tools and features to help you to meet your security objectives. AWS provides security specific tools and features across network security, configuration management, access control, and data encryption. And finally, AWS environments are continuously audited with certifications from accreditation bodies across geographies and verticals. In the AWS environment, you can take advantage of automated tools for asset inventory and privileged access reporting.

- **Compliance:** AWS Cloud has a strong control in place to maintain the security and data protection in the cloud. Like security, compliance is also a shared responsibility between AWS and the customer. The AWS IT infrastructure is designed and managed in alignment with best security and a variety of IT security standards. AWS recently introduced AWS Artifact, which allows you to download the compliance report on-demand for its infrastructure for various bodies. The following is a list of many certifications and standards that AWS complies to:

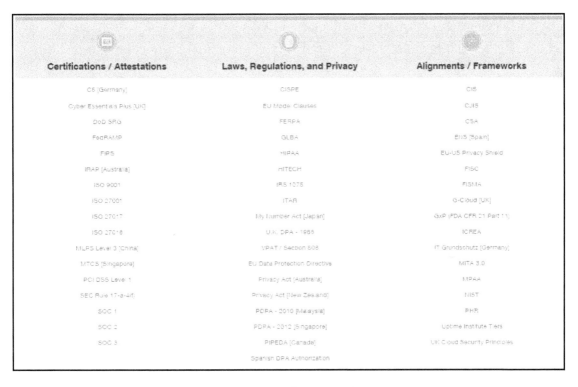

Image source: https://aws.amazon.com/

AWS services

AWS consists of broadly 18 categories of services at the time of writing this book, and you can use the combinations tailored to your business or organizational needs. All the services can be managed using AWS Console, AWS CLI, or PowerShell. You will be learning some of the PowerShell cmdlets for AWS Tools provided by AWS in other chapters:

- Compute
- Storage
- Database
- Networking and content delivery
- Migration
- Developer tools
- Management tools
- Security, identity, and compliance
- Artificial intelligence
- Analytics
- Internet of Things
- Contact center
- Game development
- Mobile services
- Application services
- Messaging
- Business productivity
- Desktop and apps streaming

Putting focus on all those services is out of the scope in this book, but I highly recommend that you review each and every service documentation on the AWS site so that you know what you can do with AWS Cloud and how these services can be used. The major intention of this chapter is to introduce you to AWS, and the intention of this book is to learn the AWS Tools for PowerShell. I just picked up few services out of those categories, which you will learn as we move forward in this book. In addition to this, I would like to highlight that AWS keeps adding services on a regular basis; thus, by the time this book is released, you may find some more.

Virtual Private Cloud

Amazon **Virtual Private Cloud** (**VPC**) lets you logically isolate the portion of the AWS Cloud in a region. AWS provides one default VPC in each region so that you can be ready to spin up resources as soon as you sign up. You can create your own VPC and spin up resources within your VPC. The default VPC that you get has all the public subnets. You can use your own IP address range for creating a new VPC and can plan to extend your on-premise data center. The VPC network resembles a traditional network that you build on-premise. You can also control the traffic coming in and going out of your VPC. You can also generate a detailed flow log on the VPC, which will help you to do analysis on the traffic flowing in and out for a better security control.

Elastic Compute Cloud

AWS EC2 can be thought of as *Virtual Machine in the cloud* or *Servers in the Cloud*. EC2 is a part of the compute category, and you get the processing power based on your needs. The beauty of this service is that there are several types of server configuration available to choose from. And you can switch from one type of server to another with minimal effort if needed. In AWS terminology, you will find that it is called EC2 Instances. So if somebody is talking about the EC2 Instance, it is a server in the cloud. The elastic nature of this compute service makes the choice between big versus small and few versus many an easy one, because this can quickly be changed when using AWS. Amazon **Elastic Block Store** (**EBS**) is part of this service, which provides you with persistent data storage for your application and database needs. Whether your application needs more IOPS or Throughput, both the solutions are now provided as part of the EBS. EBS Volumes are automatically replicated in the Availability Zone where it is created. So, high availability and durability is part of the service.

Simple Storage Service

Amazon **Simple Storage Service** (**S3**) is the most popular object store. You can keep plain text files, backup copies, archives, various log files, images, videos, and audio in S3. S3 is a highly available and durable data store. This service provides with you various storage classes to store your objects so that you can reduce the cost further. Files are stored as flat organizations inside buckets. You only pay for the space that you use. There is no commitment as such. You can also use S3 for hosting static websites. This service is tightly integrated with other services; thus you can use it to store all kinds of data, and access it when needed with other services. S3 also provides you with the ability to define policies and Access Control Lists to control the access to your buckets.

Glacier

AWS Glacier is another available object storage option. Glacier storage is like an extension of S3, but it is intended for infrequently accessed datasets. You can think of it as primarily suitable for data archiving and where a retrieval time of several hours is acceptable. Glacier storage offers the same high durability as S3 but with a very low cost. Objects in Glacier are managed through S3. Objects are not associated or managed with Glacier directly upon upload. Rather than this, the existing Amazon S3 objects are transitioned to Glacier when the data is ready for archiving. AWS also added additional retrieval options from Glacier that you can choose from to get the data quickly out of Glacier.

CloudWatch

AWS provides services to assist in monitoring. One such service is CloudWatch. CloudWatch is a resource and application monitoring service that can help customers to get alerted when thresholds are breached. It allows for the monitoring of resources immediately and automatically without the need to install or configure any software. It allows for visibility into resource utilization performance and traffic load patterns. It provides tools to gather and graph resources metrics, such as CPU utilization, disk I/O, and network traffic. Alarms can be set when metrics breach certain thresholds. These alarms then can trigger actions such as sending notifications or starting processes automatically to handle the issue. Most of the services available on AWS support CloudWatch as a monitoring tool. The use of CloudWatch is free, but if you intend to go for detailed monitoring, then there is some fees to pay.

Simple Notification Service

AWS **Simple Notification Service (SNS)** is a fully managed service, which provides a simple way to notify applications or people or various other endpoints by creating topics and using a publish-subscribe protocol. SNS allows messages to be published from within an application or directly from the console and have those messages delivered to subscribers via several protocols. Messages are first published to the centralized topics, then the subscriber to the topic receives the messages. It is used in cases where the same single messages are to be sent to many subscribers. SNS supports different protocols such as emails, HTTP, SMS, and so on.

The cost of the service is very low, and you pay only for what you use. For example, the IT production support team needs to be notified when there are issues with a production server; then CloudWatch can monitor the health, and an alarm can be raised when a specific event occurs. These alarms can be configured such that when raised, they publish a message to the SNS topic, then the subscriber to the topic will receive the message.

Relational Database Service

AWS **Relational Database Service (RDS)** provides a way to set up, operate, and scale relational databases in the cloud. Currently, RDS supports MySQL, Postgres, Aurora, MariaDB, Oracle, and the SQL Server database engine. RDS helps to speed up the development process by allowing quick access to the full featured database engine without the need to install or configure the software. As part of the RDS service, AWS takes care of backups and storing the backups for a configurable retention period and enables point in time recovery. By utilizing the multi-AZ setup, you can achieve a highly available and fault tolerant database. RDS also allows you create the read replicas for some of the database engine, which helps to ease the burden on the read intensive database. AWS also takes care of the patch and security management of the RDS instance, which eases the burden of ongoing database administration.

CloudFormation

AWS **CloudFormation** allows customer to write infrastructure as a code. It provides an easy way to developers and system administrator to create and manage the collection of AWS resources as a single stack. It allows for the definition of an entire application stack to exist as either a single or set of text-based template files. A version controlled system can then be used to manage different versions of the application infrastructure. CloudFormation template helps customers to quickly and consistently build the stack for different environments. The CloudFormation also offers real-time audit logs of events that can occur during the deployment process of the stack. By defining the stack policies, you can prevent unauthorized access to the CloudFormation stack resources. It is tightly integrated in the AWS platform and almost all the services can be created using CloudFormation.

Identify and Access Management

AWS **Identity and Access Management** (**IAM**) lets you create users and control access for those users on AWS services using policies. IAM allows you to do the following things:

- **Manage IAM users and their access:** You can create users in IAM, assign them individual security credentials (access keys, passwords, and multi-factor authentication devices), or request temporary security credentials to provide users access to AWS services and resources. You can manage permissions in order to control which operations a user can perform.
- **Manage IAM roles and their permissions:** You can create roles in IAM, and manage permissions to control which operations can be performed by the entity or AWS service that assumes the role. You can also define which entity is allowed to assume the role.
- **Manage federated users and their permissions:** You can enable identity federation to allow existing identities (for example, users) in your enterprise to access the AWS Management Console, to call AWS APIs, and to access resources without the need to create an IAM user for each identity.

CloudTrail

AWS **CloudTrail** allows customers to record the API calls made to the AWS account. This is very useful for auditing purpose, so you know what users are doing. The audit log provided by CloudTrail is much more useful to troubleshoot operational and security incidents, which, in turn, helps the organization to demonstrate its compliance with policies and regulatory standards. The CloudTrail log is saved in the S3 bucket, and you can send CloudTrail logs to CloudWatch for monitoring specific events. CloudTrail events can be processed by one trail for free. There is a charge for processing events by additional trails.

AWS Config

AWS **Config** is a really important and awesome service. It is fully managed by AWS and provides you with an inventory of your AWS resources. It also lets you audit the resource configuration history and notifies you of resource configuration changes. Over a period of time, as a cloud admin, you will fall in love with this service. To better understand it, let's say that there is a need for you to modify the instance type from **m3.large** to **c4.large**.

Once you modify the instance type, all the data related to the previous state of the instance is lost. And in case you need those configurational details of the instance before the modification event, you have no way to get that information. This is where AWS Config plays a vital role. You can record the configurational changes of the instance and other resources that are available on AWS. So, this service helps you to track down the changes made to your resources on AWS.

AWS Elastic Beanstalk

AWS provides a number of services to help with implementing elasticity, deployment, and configuration management of the applications. There are tradeoffs between those services depending on the amount of control versus the convenience desired. AWS **Elastic Beanstalk** is at the convenience end of the spectrum, whereas AWS Ops Works and CloudFormation are more on the *control* side of the spectrum. It is a fully managed AWS service, which allows you to simply upload the application to AWS and AWS takes care of the rest. This service handles provisioning of all the required resources to run the application in the cloud. It takes care of capacity provisioning, load balancing, Auto Scaling, and application health monitoring. AWS is continuously adding to the list of platforms supported by Elastic beanstalk. Currently, it supports programming languages such as Java, PHP, Python, Node.js, Ruby, .NET, Java SE, Docker container, and Go. There is no additional charge for the AWS Beanstalk services. You only pay for the resources that Elastic Beanstalk launches for you.

Laying out foundations

Laying foundations for your AWS journey is very crucial. If you are architecting your organization application framework on AWS, then just spinning up EC2 or RDS for moving your on-premise applications and databases are not enough. You should understand the frameworks and tools provided by AWS to lay the foundations. Overall there are four areas that you can focus on:

- **Accounts**: Some organizations might want to create a single AWS root account and host different types of environments in different VPCs or some might think that having different accounts for different environments is a right thing to do. You should think about the account structure that will make sense in your organization. Nothing wrong or right, but it would help you to segregate environments appropriately. Hence, understanding where development, testing, and production should be hosted would help you in the longer run.

- **Billing**: It may not be your core activity, but understanding how the billing structure is organized or required in your organization will help you to structure your practices. When organizations have multiple accounts on AWS, then consolidated billing will give a total cost picture.
- **Access keys**: It is very important to decide upon a key management strategy. You may not want to end up managing keys for each server that you will access. Some cloud module demands access key and secret access key, which is not considered to be best practice, but that is how it is designed by many vendors. In such cases, understand deeply how to integrate vendor applications/modules with your AWS account. Also secure the AWS root account access key and secret key.
- **Groups and roles**: Use IAM groups to manage console users and API access. If you want RDS, SNS, S3, and Glacier services to interact with your EC2 instance, then think about having a role created for EC2 and assign it to each EC2 instance at the launch stage itself.

The AWS sign up

If you are new to AWS and want to make use of the free tier that AWS provides, then simply visit `https://aws.amazon.com/` and **Create a Free Account**. This is the best way to get started with AWS. The sign-up process is not complicated; it just involves entering your details and credit card. Though you select the free tier, the process would prompt you to enter your credit card details. I feel AWS is just keeping the details for an individual identity purpose and nothing else. AWS won't charge your credit card for the free tier if you are using free tier services only. If you provide an expired credit card or cancelled credit card, the AWS account will not be activated. Otherwise, you have the AWS dashboard ready for you straight away to get started.

At the time of writing this book, I noticed the following screen, and this is always changing, but the web address is same all the time. So, just remember the preceding web address.

Image source: https://aws.amazon.com/

During the process, you will also receive an automated phone call from AWS, which will prompt you to enter the four-digit PIN displayed on the screen. As soon as you enter it, your account will be activated and you will see the AWS dashboard in front of you. I also noticed that AWS keeps changing the look and feel of the dashboard. You can set your dashboard by AWS Services or Categories.

Click on **Show Categories** and see what you get.

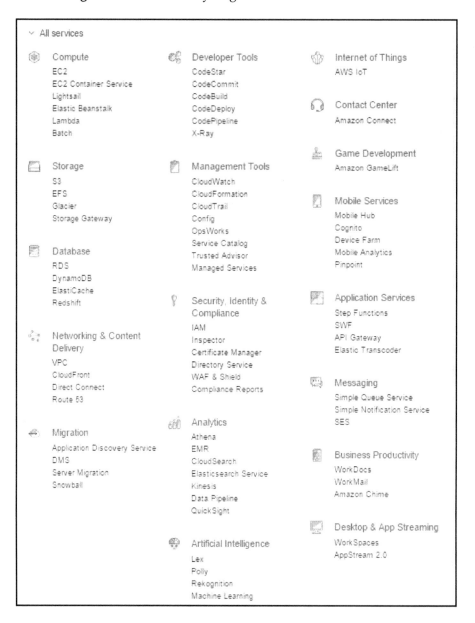

Image source: https://aws.amazon.com/

As I hinted at earlier, you must review the free tier details before you spin up EC2 servers for your testing. Only **t2.micro** instances are covered under the free tier categories and not others. This may not be suitable all the time for your test installation and testing, as you would be restricted by instance memory. A **t2.micro** instance provides just 1 GB of RAM and some application installations need more than that.

 I would encourage you to review the updated details at `https://aws.ama zon.com/free/`.

The organization provided AWS account

If you are working in an organization, and they provided you with AWS account, then get account-specific links from an internal department who is in charge of the root account. The root account is the account used for signing up with AWS. For example, in the previous section you created the free tier account using your own details, which can be considered as a root account. In organizations, usually there would be someone who is responsible for managing the root account as it is a very powerful account. If you try to log in using `https ://aws.amazon.com/console/`, then you may end up with a user not found error as this link validates against all global AWS customers. It is very important to understand these differences when you manage the root account and other AWS users in the organization.

Get supported

Whether your organization is new to AWS, or continuing to increase the adoption of AWS services as they develop applications and build business solutions, AWS support can provide a unique combination of tools and expertise to help you do amazing things with AWS. There are four support tiers available for your organization to consider. You can see the support details at `https://aws.amazon.com/premiumsupport/`.

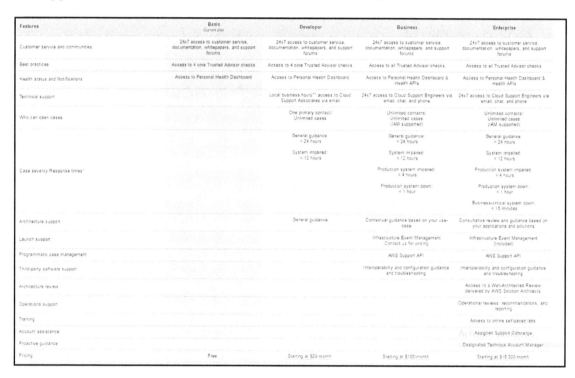

Features	Basic (Current plan)	Developer	Business	Enterprise
Customer service and communities	24x7 access to customer service, documentation, whitepapers, and support forums	24x7 access to customer service, documentation, whitepapers, and support forums	24x7 access to customer service, documentation, whitepapers, and support forums	24x7 access to customer service, documentation, whitepapers, and support forums
Best practices	Access to 4 core Trusted Advisor checks	Access to 4 core Trusted Advisor checks	Access to all Trusted Advisor checks	Access to all Trusted Advisor checks
Health status and Notifications	Access to Personal Health Dashboard	Access to Personal Health Dashboard	Access to Personal Health Dashboard & Health APIs	Access to Personal Health Dashboard & Health APIs
Technical support		Local business hours access to Cloud Support Associates via email	24x7 access to Cloud Support Engineers via email, chat, and phone	24x7 access to Cloud Support Engineers via email, chat, and phone
Who can open cases		One primary contact/ Unlimited cases	Unlimited contacts/ Unlimited cases (IAM supported)	Unlimited contacts/ Unlimited cases (IAM supported)
Case severity/ Response times		General guidance: < 24 hours; System impaired: < 12 hours	General guidance: < 24 hours; System impaired: < 12 hours; Production system impaired: < 4 hours; Production system down: < 1 hour	General guidance: < 24 hours; System impaired: < 12 hours; Production system impaired: < 4 hours; Production system down: < 1 hour; Business-critical system down: < 15 minutes
Architecture support		General guidance	Contextual guidance based on your use-case	Consultative review and guidance based on your applications and solutions
Launch support			Infrastructure Event Management Contact us for pricing	Infrastructure Event Management (Included)
Programmatic case management			AWS Support API	AWS Support API
Third-party software support			Interoperability and configuration guidance and troubleshooting	Interoperability and configuration guidance and troubleshooting
Architecture review				Access to a Well-Architected Review delivered by AWS Solution Architects
Operations support				Operational reviews, recommendations, and reporting
Training				Access to online self-paced labs
Account assistance				Assigned Support Concierge
Proactive guidance				Designated Technical Account Manager
Pricing	Free	Starting at $29/month	Starting at $100/month	Starting at $15,000/month

In addition to the AWS support, in case you want to engage with a managed cloud provider, there are many out there to choose from. Usually, it is good practice to be with any one of them if you are new to AWS and do not know the various techniques that you can use for billing and cost optimization. The managed cloud provider can play a role to optimize your cost and also provide a level of support that you need to manage your AWS cloud regularly.

Summary

AWS is a digital ocean and is becoming more and more relevant today. Sailing through it requires the use of proper navigational instruments, otherwise you will be lost or it will cost you more. Up to now, you could say that you do not know AWS, but that is something that cannot be said anymore.

For IT staff in any organization, knowing AWS is a need and not a choice. These days, if you do not know cloud computing technologies such as AWS or Azure, you will become obsolete. AWS is more popular for its IaaS platform, not PaaS or SaaS. There could be situations where you cannot do one-to-one mapping for your on-premise applications with the AWS infrastructure. The success of the AWS integration in your business depends upon whether you have utilized the strength of the AWS cloud or not. There are a lot of materials posted on the AWS website to get started with. Reviewing some of the webinars or short *getting started videos* would help you. Knowing the AWS cloud's strength and building upon it is crucial to maximize your cloud investment. Consider the architecture that suites your organization. Utilize the best practice for your deployment and maximize ROI. There are tons of organizations using it, and a number of use cases are available widely on the internet. Research what you need and what you are trying to achieve from your cloud investment. All in all, cloud is going to stay and soon will become the de facto standard in IT by creating huge footprint. In next chapter, we will learn how to install PowerShell 6 and AWS Tools for PowerShell 6.

3
Installing PowerShell Core and AWS Tools

Let's understand PowerShell and PowerShell Core. PowerShell has been around for use on Windows systems since 2006. It is known as a task automation and a configuration management framework, particularly known for Windows systems until now. PowerShell is built on .NET Framework. .NET Framework is a software framework that runs primarily on Windows. PowerShell Core is built on top of .NET Core. .NET Core is a cross-platform and open source managed software framework similar to .NET Framework. Going forward, PowerShell for Windows and PowerShell Core would be PowerShell. Presently, I feel these two terminologies are used because the community wants to identify the open source related effort for PowerShell as PowerShell Core. With the release of PowerShell 6.0, Microsoft has officially made PowerShell open source, providing the capability to access to Linux, macOS systems, and many more. Going forward, there would be slight change in the way that PowerShell has been defined so far. Now, PowerShell is a task automation and is distributed as a heterogeneous scalable configuration management framework.

The goalpost is very clear--PowerShell for every system. Microsoft understands the necessity of the customer to manage complex heterogeneous IT environments, and they want to have a universal shell that can support multiple systems, which will benefit their huge customer base and simplify the administration and management for complex IT systems. The cloud is redefining many things and adding more complexities in managing the infrastructure. By having one unified shell, we can bridge the gap to manage multiple cloud systems in addition to on-premise data centers. The open source will allow for a cross-pollination of administrators to manage multiple types of server operating systems from any system. This level of flexibility is unprecedented and will be useful for standardizing the management of different platforms. PowerShell is the answer here.

In this chapter, we will learn about installing PowerShell 6 on Windows and Linux operating systems. In addition, we will also learn about installing AWS modules on PowerShell 6.

AWS Tools for PowerShell

The AWS Tools for Windows PowerShell and AWS Tools for PowerShell Core are PowerShell modules that are built on the functionality exposed by the AWS SDK for .NET. With AWS PowerShell tools, you can script, maintain, and automate various AWS operations on AWS resources from the PowerShell command line. You may be thinking why is PowerShell used for AWS instead of AWS CLI provided by AWS, which is supported on many different platforms as well? The question is obvious. I personally started using AWS CLI when I started working on AWS for maintaining and automating some workloads. But over time, when you start managing Windows, Linux, and other platforms, the complexity increases. And that's where I thought that PowerShell provides the single pane which is needed to schedule the same kind of script without any modifications on other platforms. Another important aspect is that the output generated by AWS CLI commands are just textual, and you would require many other utilities to format the output in order to pass on to the other subprograms. This is the beauty of PowerShell. The output can act as an object, and you pick up the properties that you want to manipulate, which makes scripting very easy.

AWS Tools for Windows PowerShell is particularly for Windows-based systems and can be downloaded from `https://aws.amazon.com/powershell/`. You will find the MSI installer on the top right on the previous link and upon successful installation, you will get the `AWSPowerShell` module installed in your PowerShell.

AWS Tools for PowerShell Core are meant for all the platforms, and at the time of writing this book, it was still in beta. This new module is known as the AWS Tools for PowerShell Core Edition or `AWSPowerShell.NetCore`. Just like PowerShell itself, this new module can be used on Windows, Linux, and the OS X platform. The `AWSPowerShell.NetCore` module is built on top of the .NET Core version of the AWS SDK for .NET.

 Note that updates to the new module for new service features may lag a little behind the sister AWS Tools for Windows PowerShell (`AWSPowerShell`) module, while the .NET Core version of the AWS SDK for .NET is in beta. I feel that once `AWSPowerShell.NetCore` is live, then the `AWSPowerShell` module will be deprecated.

Currently, there is a high compatibility between AWS Tools for Windows PowerShell and AWS Tools for PowerShell Core. There will be some exceptions though. I see that some of the cmdlets, which were available for some of the AWS services, are not seen in the `AWSPowerShell.NetCore` module. If they are not seen, it does not mean the functionality is removed; it means it could have been renamed to some other cmdlet. You will get that idea as you scan through the AWS PowerShell cmdlet. You may find those subtle differences in the documentation.

Installing PowerShell 6 On Windows

The best place to download PowerShell 6 is from the PowerShell GitHub community. The link for the community is `https://github.com/PowerShell/PowerShell`. There are several platforms you can see on this link for which you can download the PowerShell installer. The list of platforms as of now are shown here:

Platform	Downloads	How to Install
Windows 10 / Server 2016 (x64)	.msi	Instructions
Windows 8.1 / Server 2012 R2 (x64)	.msi	Instructions
Windows 7 / Server 2008 R2 (x64)	.msi	Instructions
Windows 7 (x86)	.msi	Instructions
Ubuntu 16.04	.deb	Instructions
Ubuntu 14.04	.deb	Instructions
Debian 8	.deb	Instructions
CentOS 7	.rpm	Instructions
Red Hat Enterprise Linux 7	.rpm	Instructions
OpenSUSE 42.1	.rpm	Instructions
Arch Linux		Instructions
Many Linux distributions	.AppImage	Instructions
macOS 10.12	.pkg	Instructions
Docker		Instructions

Before installing, review the **How to Install** instructions set for the specific platform. For Windows, the installation is very straightforward. Download the MSI installer and run the installer. By default, it will be installed in `C:\Program Files\PowerShell\`. Now to run, just open the file explorer and navigate to the `C:\Program Files\PowerShell\6.0.0-beta.2` directory. You may have a different directory structure, so follow what you see there after the install. Right-click on `powershell.exe`, and run it as an administrator or simply double-click on it. That's it. PowerShell 6 is running on your machine. You can pin `powershell.exe` to the taskbar for a quick run. You can make use of the `Get-Host` cmdlet to check the installed version.

Installing PowerShell 6 on Linux

For Linux installation, there are several ways. As indicated previously, you can download the `rpm` package, or you can do it using the `yum` install. Here, I am demonstrating on Red Hat 7 using `yum`, which is quiet easy. Just make sure your Linux server is connected to the internet; if not, download the `rpm` package and install it. As highlighted earlier, do not forget to review the instruction set for your platform. Sometimes, there are little deviations from version to version, and some known issues are highlighted. So, instead of scratching your head, a quick scan through the instruction set is a real good help.

PowerShell Core for Linux is published on official Microsoft repositories for easy installation. Perform the following instructions as a root user or your user needs to have `sudo` rights:

```
# Register the Microsoft RedHat repository
curl https://packages.microsoft.com/config/rhel/7/prod.repo | sudo tee
/etc/yum.repos.d/microsoft.repo
# Install PowerShell
yum install -y powershell
# Start PowerShell
powershell
```

```
[root@ip-172-31-61-33 ~]# which powershell
/usr/bin/which: no powershell in (/usr/local/sbin:/usr/local/bin:/sbin:/bin:/usr/sbin:/usr/bin:/root/bin)
[root@ip-172-31-61-33 ~]# cat /etc/redhat-release
Red Hat Enterprise Linux Server release 7.3 (Maipo)
[root@ip-172-31-61-33 ~]# curl https://packages.microsoft.com/config/rhel/7/prod.repo | sudo tee /etc/yum.repos.d/microsoft.repo
  % Total    % Received % Xferd  Average Speed   Time    Time     Time  Current
                                 Dload  Upload   Total   Spent    Left  Speed
100   193  100   193    0     0    516      0 --:--:-- --:--:-- --:--:--   517
[packages-microsoft-com-prod]
name=packages-microsoft-com-prod
baseurl=https://packages.microsoft.com/rhel/7/prod/
enabled=1
gpgcheck=1
gpgkey=https://packages.microsoft.com/keys/microsoft.asc
[root@ip-172-31-61-33 ~]# sudo yum install -y powershell
```

After installing, you can use the Linux `which` command to check the path of the `powershell` executable.

```
[root@ip-172-31-61-33 ~]# which powershell
/bin/powershell
[root@ip-172-31-61-33 ~]# powershell
PowerShell
Copyright (C) Microsoft Corporation. All rights reserved.

PS /root> Get-Host


Name            : ConsoleHost
Version         : 6.0.0
InstanceId      : 4a369fd3-c67c-4e76-9f07-2df44ce749c1
UI              : System.Management.Automation.Internal.Host.InternalHostUserInterface
CurrentCulture  : en-US
CurrentUICulture : en-US
PrivateData     : Microsoft.PowerShell.ConsoleHost+ConsoleColorProxy
DebuggerEnabled : True
IsRunspacePushed : False
Runspace        : System.Management.Automation.Runspaces.LocalRunspace
```

Prerequisites for AWS Tools

In order to use AWS Tools for PowerShell, you need to have the minimum configuration running:

- Microsoft Windows XP or higher versions
- Windows PowerShell 2.0 or higher versions (PowerShell 5.1 or later for Tools for PowerShell Core)

On Linux servers, if you install PowerShell using `yum`, the dependency modules will be installed automatically. With the `rpm` type install, you may need to install a couple of individual modules before you attempt to install PowerShell on Linux. Likewise, there are some dependencies for each platform, which can be seen as part of the documentation. I encourage you to refer to a platform-specific documentation. In this book, I will touch base on Linux and Windows related prerequisites only. On Red Hat, the PowerShell install using the `yum` installer will install the modules `libunwind` and `uuid`.

Downloading and installing AWS Tools

The installation of the `AWSPowerShell.NetCore` module is pretty simple. The only thing I would like to highlight is for you to make use of the `$PSHOME/Modules` directory as a target for installation of the module. The module can be installed using the `Install-Module` cmdlet. Note that you need to start PowerShell using the administrator or root privilege.

Note that currently, you can only see the MSI installer on `https://aws.amazon.com/power shell/`. This installer is only for **PowerShell on Windows**. This module is called `AWSPowerShell`. At the time of writing this book, a new module for AWS Tools for PowerShell was called `AWSPowerShell.NetCore`, which was published on the PowerShell Gallery only and can be installed as follows:

```
PS C:\> Install-Package -Name AWSPowerShell.NetCore -Source
https://www.powershellgallery.com/api/v2/ -ProviderName NuGet -
ExcludeVersion -Destination $PSHOME/Modules
```

- On Windows:

- On Linux:

If you install the `AWSPowerShell.NetCore` module in the `$PSHOME/Modules` directory, you do not need to adjust the `$env:PSModulePath` environment variable. Every time you start PowerShell, `AWSPowerShell.NetCore` will be loaded. My recommendation would be using the `$PSHOME/Modules` path if you are new to PowerShell. If you install it in a different directory, then you can plan to update the default PowerShell profile so that the module gets loaded every time you start PowerShell.

You can check whether `AWSPowerShell.NetCore` is installed or not using the following:

- On Linux:

  PS /root>Get-Module -ListAvailable

```
PS /root> Get-Module -ListAvailable


    Directory: /opt/microsoft/powershell/6.0.0-beta.2/Modules


ModuleType Version     Name                                ExportedCommands
---------- -------     ----                                ----------------
Binary     3.3.98.0    AWSPowerShell.NetCore               {Add-AASScalableTarget, Add-ACMCertificateTag, Add-ADSConfigurationItemsToApplication, Add-ASAA...
Manifest   1.1.0.0     Microsoft.PowerShell.Archive        {Compress-Archive, Expand-Archive}
Manifest   3.0.0.0     Microsoft.PowerShell.Host           {Start-Transcript, Stop-Transcript}
Manifest   3.1.0.0     Microsoft.PowerShell.Management      {Add-Content, Clear-Content, Clear-ItemProperty, Join-Path...}
Manifest   3.0.0.0     Microsoft.PowerShell.Security       {Get-Credential, Get-ExecutionPolicy, Set-ExecutionPolicy, ConvertFrom-SecureString...}
Manifest   3.1.0.0     Microsoft.PowerShell.Utility        {Format-List, Format-Custom, Format-Table, Format-Wide...}
Script     1.1.4.0     PackageManagement                   {Find-Package, Get-Package, Get-PackageProvider, Get-PackageSource...}
Script     3.3.9       Pester                              {Describe, Context, It, Should...}
Script     1.1.3.1     PowerShellGet                       {Install-Module, Find-Module, Save-Module, Update-Module...}
Script     0.0         PSDesiredStateConfiguration         {ThrowError, Get-PSMetaConfigDocumentInstVersionInfo, New-DscChecksum, ValidateNodeResourceSour...
Script     1.2         PSReadLine                          {Get-PSReadlineKeyHandler, Set-PSReadlineKeyHandler, Remove-PSReadlineKeyHandler, Get-PSReadlin...
```

- On Windows:

  PS C:\>Get-Module -ListAvailable

```
PS C:\> Get-Module -ListAvailable


    Directory: C:\program files\powershell\6.0.0-beta.2\Modules


ModuleType Version     Name                                ExportedCommands
---------- -------     ----                                ----------------
Binary     3.3.98.0    AWSPowerShell.NetCore               {Add-AASScalableTarget, Add-ACMCertificateTag, Add-ADSConfigurationItemsToApplication, Add-ASAA...
Manifest   1.0.0.0     CimCmdlets                          {Get-CimAssociatedInstance, Get-CimClass, Get-CimInstance, Get-CimSession...}
Manifest   1.1.0.0     Microsoft.PowerShell.Archive        {Compress-Archive, Expand-Archive}
Manifest   3.0.0.0     Microsoft.PowerShell.Diagnostics    {Get-WinEvent, New-WinEvent, Get-Counter, Import-Counter...}
Manifest   3.0.0.0     Microsoft.PowerShell.Host           {Start-Transcript, Stop-Transcript}
Manifest   1.0.0.0     Microsoft.PowerShell.LocalAccounts  {Add-LocalGroupMember, Disable-LocalUser, Enable-LocalUser, Get-LocalGroup...}
Manifest   3.1.0.0     Microsoft.PowerShell.Management      {Add-Content, Clear-Content, Clear-ItemProperty, Join-Path...}
Manifest   3.0.0.0     Microsoft.PowerShell.Security       {Get-Acl, Set-Acl, Get-PfxCertificate, Get-Credential...}
Manifest   3.1.0.0     Microsoft.PowerShell.Utility        {Format-List, Format-Custom, Format-Table, Format-Wide...}
Manifest   3.0.0.0     Microsoft.WSMan.Management           {Disable-WSManCredSSP, Enable-WSManCredSSP, Get-WSManCredSSP, Set-WSManQuickConfig...}
Script     4.2.3       NTFSSecurity                        {Add-NTFSAccess, Clear-NTFSAccess, Disable-NTFSAccessInheritance, Enable-NTFSAccessInheritance...}
Script     1.1.4.0     PackageManagement                   {Find-Package, Get-Package, Get-PackageProvider, Get-PackageSource...}
Script     3.3.9       Pester                              {Describe, Context, It, Should...}
Script     1.1.3.1     PowerShellGet                       {Install-Module, Find-Module, Save-Module, Update-Module...}
Script     0.0         PSDesiredStateConfiguration         {ThrowError, Get-PSMetaConfigDocumentInstVersionInfo, New-DscChecksum, ValidateNodeResourceSour...
Script     1.0.0.0     PSDiagnostics                       {Disable-PSTrace, Disable-PSWSManCombinedTrace, Disable-WSManTrace, Enable-PSTrace...}
Script     1.2         PSReadLine                          {Get-PSReadlineKeyHandler, Set-PSReadlineKeyHandler, Remove-PSReadlineKeyHandler, Get-PSReadlin...
Manifest   1.3.0.0     SecurityPolicyDsc
Manifest   1.2.0.0     xSystemSecurity
```

You might get the long list depending on the different modules that are installed on your Windows machine.

Enabling script execution

The PowerShell execution policy is the setting that determines the type of PowerShell scripts that can be run on the system. I noticed that by default, PowerShell is configured to prevent the execution of the scripts on Windows, whereas this is *unrestricted* on Linux. The execution policy is never meant to be a security control for IT admin and developers; however, it is just a precautionary measure for them not to shoot themselves in their feet. That is why there are several ways to bypass the policy in PowerShell.

Windows PowerShell execution policies are as follows. I feel Linux will be always set as *Unrestricted*. All these policies are meant for the Windows PowerShell environment. Likewise, for other platforms, I am not sure how these policies are treated. There is no clear documentation on the usage of these policies on other platforms. But overall, for the sake of information, I have outlined the purposes of each known execution policy on the Windows platform:

- **Restricted**: This is the default execution policy on most of the Windows systems. This policy setting allows you to run individual cmdlets but not scripts.
- **RemoteSigned**: This policy requires the digital signature from a trusted publisher on scripts and configuration files that are downloaded from the internet. If you have written the script locally, it can run on the local machine. Running locally does not require any digital signature with this policy. This is the one recommended for AWS Tools for PowerShell.
- **Unrestricted**: As the name implies, there is no restriction as such. You can run local or any scripts downloaded from the internet. Setting the execution policy to *Unrestricted* will risk running malicious code. Hence, never plan to set this in your production environment.
- **AllSigned**: In many IT shops, setting the execution policy to *AllSigned* is the ultimate goal. This policy requires a digital signature from the trusted publisher on scripts and configuration files that are downloaded from the internet as well as any scripts that you run locally.
- **Bypass:** This policy means nothing is blocked and there are no warnings generated. This execution policy is designed for configurations in which a Windows PowerShell script is built into a larger application, or for configurations in which Windows PowerShell is the foundation for a program that has its own security model.
- **Undefined:** Setting this means that there is no execution policy in the current scope. If the execution policy in all the scopes is *Undefined*, the effective execution policy is *Restricted*, which is the default execution policy.

The execution policy can be set at the different levels. It is also important to understand the scope of the execution policy as well. The execution policy can be set at `Process`, `CurrentUser`, and `LocalMachine` or at the group level in Windows. `LocalMachine` is the default when setting an execution policy in PowerShell.

You can view the current execution policy setting with scope as follows:

```
PS C:\>Get-ExecutionPolicy -List | Format-Table -AutoSize
```

```
PS C:\> Get-ExecutionPolicy -List | Format-Table -AutoSize

        Scope ExecutionPolicy
        ----- ---------------
MachinePolicy       Undefined
   UserPolicy       Undefined
      Process       Undefined
  CurrentUser       Undefined
 LocalMachine      Restricted

PS C:\>
```

In order to change the execution policy to `RemoteSigned`, you can use this:

```
PS C:\>Set-ExecutionPolicy RemoteSigned
PS C:\>Set-ExecutionPolicy -ExecutionPolicy RemoteSigned
```

```
PS C:\> Set-ExecutionPolicy RemoteSigned
PS C:\> Get-ExecutionPolicy -List | Format-Table -AutoSize

        Scope ExecutionPolicy
        ----- ---------------
MachinePolicy       Undefined
   UserPolicy       Undefined
      Process       Undefined
  CurrentUser       Undefined
 LocalMachine    RemoteSigned

PS C:\>
```

Note that you need to start PowerShell using the administrator credential in Windows PowerShell in order to change the policy. If you are running PowerShell 6.0, the `AWSPowerShell.NetCore` module is loaded automatically whenever you run one of the AWS cmdlets. This lets you use the AWS cmdlets interactively, even if the execution policy on your system is set to disallow the script execution.

Finding the AWS Tool version

Amazon Web Services periodically release the new version of AWS Tools for Windows PowerShell and AWS Tools for PowerShell Core to support new AWS services and features. You can use `Get-AWSPowerShellVersion` to see what version of AWS Tools you have installed on your system:

```
PS C:\> Get-AWSPowerShellVersion
```

```
PS C:\> Get-AWSPowerShellVersion

AWS Tools for PowerShell Core
Version 3.3.98.0
Copyright 2012-2017 Amazon.com, Inc. or its affiliates. All Rights Reserved.

Amazon Web Services SDK for .NET
Core Runtime Version 3.3.14.0
Copyright 2009-2015 Amazon.com, Inc. or its affiliates. All Rights Reserved.

Release notes: https://aws.amazon.com/releasenotes/PowerShell

This software includes third party software subject to the following copyrights:
- Logging from log4net, Apache License
[http://logging.apache.org/log4net/license.html]

PS C:\>
```

`Get-AWSPowerShellVersion` has a parameter called `ListServices`, which you can use to see a list of AWS services that are supported in the current version of AWS Tools. I noticed that this keeps changing a lot. Almost all the services supported through APIs can be seen in this list. Always review the list of services supported by AWS Tools. I feel most of the core services that you might use on a day-to-day basis are already in the list:

```
PS C:\> Get-AWSPowerShellVersion -ListServices
```

```
PS C:\> Get-AWSPowerShellVersion -ListServices

AWS Tools for PowerShell Core
Version 3.3.98.0
Copyright 2012-2017 Amazon.com, Inc. or its affiliates. All Rights Reserved.

Amazon Web Services SDK for .NET
Core Runtime Version 3.3.14.0
Copyright 2009-2015 Amazon.com, Inc. or its affiliates. All Rights Reserved.

Release notes: https://aws.amazon.com/releasenotes/PowerShell

This software includes third party software subject to the following copyrights:
- Logging from log4net, Apache License
[http://logging.apache.org/log4net/license.html]


Service                   Noun Prefix API Version
-------                   ----------- -----------
AWS AppStream             APS         2016-12-01
AWS Batch                 BAT         2016-08-10
AWS Budgets               BGT         2016-10-20
AWS Certificate Manager   ACM         2015-12-08
AWS Cloud Directory       CDIR        2016-05-10
AWS Cloud HSM             HSM         2014-05-30
AWS CloudFormation        CFN         2010-05-15
```

The list displayed in the command output is not complete. I have only taken a screenshot of a few services to display. Run the `Get-AWSPowerShellVersion` cmdlet with the `ListServices` parameter for the complete list.

Updating AWS Tools for PowerShell

AWS keeps releasing a new version of the AWS Tools module both on Windows and PowerShell Core. As discussed earlier, you can determine the current version of AWS Tool by running the `Get-AWSPowerShellVersion` cmdlet. Currently, you can install Windows-based AWS Tools from `https://aws.amazon.com/powershell/`. For PowerShell Core, check the available version in the PowerShell Gallery. I think AWS Tool releases are too frequent, and they are targeting new releases every other 2 weeks. So, there is a need for you to understand the update process so that you know how to do or automate by writing your own script.

In case you have AWS Tools for PowerShell Core installed, plan to uninstall it before you attempt re-installation of the module. To uninstall, you can use this:

```
PS C:\> Uninstall-Package -Name AWSPowerShell.NetCore -AllVersions
```

When uninstallation is finished, install the updated package by running the following command. By default, this command installs the latest version of the AWS Tools for PowerShell Core. This package is available from the PowerShell Gallery, but the easiest method of installation is to run `Install-Package`:

```
PS C:\> Install-Package -Name AWSPowerShell.NetCore -Source
https://www.powershellgallery.com/api/v2/ -ProviderName NuGet -
ExcludeVersion -Destination $PSHOME/Modules
```

Summary

Microsoft's intention of making PowerShell open source is very loud. Now, PowerShell supports different platforms, and it will soon become the de facto scripting and automation tool because of its several in-built capabilities. Despite of AWS's own CLI, AWS supports on PowerShell is an indication that they see PowerShell is a universal shell. The installation of AWS Tools is simple. This chapter was particularly focused on getting PowerShell 6 and installing AWS Tools on PowerShell 6. In the next chapter, you will learn about AWS Identity and Access Management, which will provide you with an idea about managing AWS access and permissions.

4

AWS Identity and Access Management

AWS **Identity and Access Management** (**IAM**) allows you to manage AWS users, groups, roles, and access to various application services. IAM provides access and access permissions to AWS resources, such as EC2, RDS, DynamoDB, S3, and so on. It is a global service to all the AWS regions. It means that creating a user in IAM, will apply to all the AWS regions. Here are some common uses of IAM:

- Users to access accounts or specific services
- IAM roles to allow other resources to assume some permissions
- Groups to tie users
- Policies for more fine grained access
- Creating API keys for programmable access to AWS resources
- Defining a password policy
- Managing MFA requirements per user basis

When you create a user in IAM, it has no permission on any AWS resource or service. This is called a non-explicit deny rule set for all new users. In order to allow them to access certain resources, you have to assign them permissions or add them as part of the IAM group. When you sign up on the AWS website for the first time using your email ID and credit card, you get an account. That account is a root account. Remember this: a root account is a very powerful account and does not need any permissions. You can do all the things with your AWS resources using a root account. For all other users, you have to assign permissions in order to grant them access on some specific AWS services or resources.

As a best practice, you should not be using the root account to perform day-to-day operations. Root accounts should be locked down, and you should use other IAM users to perform day-to-day work. This way, if an IAM user is compromised, you can delete the IAM user and the associated access keys. But, if your root account is compromised, nothing can be done. If your root account is compromised, the only option is to go on a long vacation. So be careful. It is also a best practice to follow the **Principal of Least Privilege** when you administer AWS accounts, users, groups, and roles. When an AWS root account is created, it is a best practice to complete the following tasks as mentioned:

- Delete your root access keys
- Activate MFA on your root account
- Create individual IAM users
- Create user groups to assign permissions
- Apply an IAM password policy

As soon you log in using your root credentials on `https://aws.amazon.com/`, navigate to the IAM service by clicking on **All Services** | **Security, Identity & Compliance** | **IAM**, and perform the tasks mentioned in the list.

In this chapter, we will learn about the AWS shared responsibility model, setting up AWS Tools in PowerShell to access the AWS Cloud, managing AWS credentials, credential search order, creating IAM users, creating IAM groups, creating roles, accessing the AWS console, and defining IAM policies. In addition, we will touch upon one use case relating to access key rotation.

The AWS-shared responsibility model

In AWS, security is of paramount importance. Under the shared responsibility model, AWS provides a secure infrastructure, compute, storage, networking, database services, and some other high-level services. AWS customers are responsible for protecting the confidentiality, integrity, and availability of their data in the cloud for meeting specific business requirements for information protection. So in short, AWS manages the security *of* the cloud, and security *in* the cloud is the customer's responsibility. Here is the graphical information with regards to the shared responsibility model. This is taken from the AWS whitepaper:

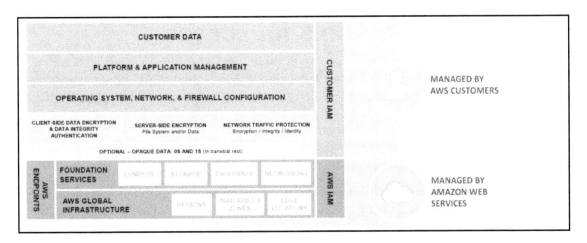

Image source: https://aws.amazon.com/

In regards to the EC2 service, under the shared responsibility model, AWS is responsible for the host operating system virtualization layer down to the physical security of the facilities, and you would be responsible for the following:

- Operating systems
- Application software
- Data-in-transit
- Data-at-rest
- Data stores
- Access keys
- Policies and configurations
- Amazon Machine Images
- Security Groups
- Network ACL

Setting up AWS Tools for access

Once you have installed **AWS Tools for PowerShell**, the next thing you need is the AWS access key. Without the access key, you cannot run the `AWSPowerShell.NetCore` cmdlet. All of them will result in an error. So first, let's get the access key. As we discussed earlier, it is not a best practice to create an access key for a root user. Root user accounts must be locked down and should not be used in any API action. For access keys, you need to create a user. So, open the IAM console by navigating to **All Services** | **Security, Identity & Compliance** | **IAM**.

From the navigation menu, click on **Users**. Click on **Add User**. Fill in the username of your choice. You may have some specific naming convention to name the user though. Tick the checkbox as **Programmatic Access**. On the next screen, select **Attach existing policies directly** and the first one on the top, **AdministratorAccess**. Click on **Review** and then **Create user**. As soon as you hit **Create user**, you will see that the **Access Key** and **Secret Access Key** are displayed on the screen. Copy the credentials and secure them. There will be an option as well to download the `Download.csv` file; this file will contain the same information displayed on the screen.

You are all set. If you followed the preceding instructions, you added an IAM user, and assigned the administrator policy, you will be allowed to do almost all the things that you can do with a root account, except billing-related aspects. You can now use this access and a secret access key to set up AWS Tools to access AWS from PowerShell. There are several ways to specify credentials. The preferred approach is to use a profile rather than incorporating literal credentials into your command line:

```
PS C:\> Set-AWSCredentials -AccessKey {xx} -SecretKey {xx} -StoreAs
{MyProfileName}
```

```
PS C:\> Set-AWSCredentials -AccessKey AKIAIVQ7QQR7ISZUBY2A -SecretKey +PTZ9DPU0+0NnFfqgQE0UhxxBdhv0QBt9Ej0nh16 -StoreAs PowerShellProfile
PS C:\> Get-AWSCredentials -ListProfileDetail

ProfileName        StoreTypeName        ProfileLocation
-----------        -------------        ---------------
PowerShellProfile NetSDKCredentialsFile

PS C:\>
```

`GET-AWSCredentials` tells you that `PowerShellProfile` is created. You can use the `Initialize-AWSDefaults` cmdlet to specify the default profile for every PowerShell session:

```
PS C:\> Initialize-AWSDefaults -ProfileName {MyProfileName} -Region {us-
west-2}
```

You can see that I created a profile called `PowerShellProfile`, and I will make that profile as the default one for us.

```
PS C:\> Initialize-AWSDefaults -ProfileName PowerShellProfile -Region us-west-2
PS C:\> Get-AWSCredentials -ListProfileDetail

ProfileName        StoreTypeName        ProfileLocation
-----------        -------------        ---------------
PowerShellProfile  NetSDKCredentialsFile
default            NetSDKCredentialsFile

PS C:\>
```

After running the `Initialize-AWSDefaults` cmdlet, you can now see that there is a default profile added. For the list of regions supported by `AWSPowerShell.NetCore`, you can use the `Get-AWSRegion` cmdlet:

PS C:\> Get-AWSRegion

```
PS C:\> Get-AWSRegion

Region         Name                        IsShellDefault
------         ----                        --------------
ap-northeast-1 Asia Pacific (Tokyo)        False
ap-northeast-2 Asia Pacific (Seoul)        False
ap-south-1     Asia Pacific (Mumbai)       False
ap-southeast-1 Asia Pacific (Singapore)    False
ap-southeast-2 Asia Pacific (Sydney)       False
ca-central-1   Canada (Central)            False
eu-central-1   EU Central (Frankfurt)      False
eu-west-1      EU West (Ireland)           False
eu-west-2      EU West (London)            False
sa-east-1      South America (Sao Paulo)   False
us-east-1      US East (Virginia)          False
us-east-2      US East (Ohio)              False
us-west-1      US West (N. California)     False
us-west-2      US West (Oregon)            True

PS C:\>
```

You can see that in the output, `us-west-2` is set as the default region. You can now validate the access to your AWS account by simply running the `Get-S3Bucket` cmdlet:

PS C:\>Get-S3Bucket

If you have any S3 bucket created, this will list all the available buckets in your S3. That's it, your PowerShell AWS Tools module for `AWSPowerShell.NetCore` is all set to rock, and you will be able to perform almost all the things that you can do on the AWS console.

Managing AWS credentials

There are several ways to supply the AWS credentials. You can specify credential per-command, per-session, or for all the sessions. You should avoid exposing credentials in the command line in the form of literals, or supplying them each time you run the AWS cmdlet. For any cmdlet, there are some common parameters that you can supply each time you run the AWS-specific cmdlet. Those are mostly `Access Key`, `Secret Access Key`, `Region`, `ProfileName`, `ProfileLocation`, and so on. Exposing your AWS credentials in the cmdlet is not considered as a best practice. Instead, create a profile for each set of credentials that you want to use, and store the profile in the credential store. Specify the correct profile by name in your command, and let PowerShell retrieve the associated credentials from the store. You can create the different profiles using `Set-AWSCredentials`:

```
PS C:\> Set-AWSCredentials -AccessKey {xx} -SecretKey {xx} -StoreAs
{MyProfileName}
```

If you are interested to know the other options, then refer to the online documentation. I would restrict credential management using profiles to avoid confusion in this book. If you created the profile using the `Set-AWSCredentials` cmdlet and want to make it a default profile for the session, then you can simply use the `ProfileName` parameter with the `Set-AWSCredentials` cmdlet:

```
PS C:\> Set-AWSCredentials -ProfileName {MyProfileName}
```

You can also specify `ProfileName` with the other cmdlet. For example, if you do not have any default profile set, then you can supply a profile to the AWS-related cmdlet:

```
PS C:\> Get-S3Bucket -ProfileName {MyProfileName}
```

The AWS credential search order

AWS Tools stores the credential in the `C:\Users\username>\AppData\Local\AWSToolkit\RegisteredAccounts.json` file. This files stores your access and secret access keys in an encrypted format. Even if you copy this file to a different computer, you cannot use it. This is the first file that AWS Tools for PowerShell searches on the Windows platform for the AWS credentials. You can also write the credentials to a different file as follows:

```
PS C:\> Set-AWSCredentials -AccessKey {xx} -SecretKey {xx} -StoreAs
{ProfileName} -ProfilesLocation c:\AWSTools\MyCredential
```

By default, on a Windows platform, AWS Tools for Windows PowerShell modules read profiles from the file `C:\Users<userid>\.aws\credentials`. Don't get confused here. I specifically mentioned AWS Tools for Windows PowerShell and not AWS Tools for PowerShell Core. AWS Tools for PowerShell Core still store credentials in the location, `C:\Users\username>\AppData\Local\AWSToolkit\RegisteredAccounts.json`. On Linux, the file is at `~/.aws/credentials`. Here are the high-level steps for the credential search:

- Literal credentials in the cmdlet
- Profile names or profile locations
- Credentials specified by the credential parameter
- PowerShell session profiles
- Default profiles set in PowerShell for the AWS access
- The EC2 instance credential if EC2 instance is configured for an IAM role

Creating IAM users

When you sign up with AWS, you get a root account. A root account is a very powerful account and its use should be avoided for your day-to-day operations. For security reasons, you can create individual IAM users to manage identity and permissions for AWS resources. You can create users using the PowerShell cmdlet provided, you have rights to do so. Identify and Access Management is a global service and is identified as the IAM service. An IAM user is an entity that you create in AWS to represent the person, or the service that uses it to interact with AWS. A user in the AWS consists of a name and credentials. If you want to know all the cmdlets that are provided for an IAM service, you can use this:

```
PS C:\> Get-Command -Module AWSPowerShell.NetCore -Name "*-IAM*"
```

All the cmdlets in regard to this service will be listed. You can make use of the New-IAMUser cmdlet to add a user in your AWS account:

```
PS C:\> New-IAMUser -UserName Ramesh
```

This will create a user in your AWS account. All IAM users start with a non-explicit deny rule. Hence, a user that we created does not have permission.

```
PS C:\> New-IAMUser -UserName Ramesh


Arn             : arn:aws:iam::072316406132:user/Ramesh
CreateDate      : 6/5/2017 1:38:02 PM
PasswordLastUsed : 1/1/0001 12:00:00 AM
Path            : /
UserId          : AIDAIIROGQFGVBDKMAUXY
UserName        : Ramesh
```

Let's now move to the next section to understand IAM groups.

Creating IAM groups

An IAM group is a collection of IAM users. Groups let you specify permissions for multiple users, which can make it easier to manage the permissions for users. For example, you could have a group called developer and give that group the types of permissions that they typically need. If the developer group only needs full access to S3 and dynamo DB, then you can create a group called `developer` and assign policies to it which are only meant for access to S3 and dynamo DB. Similarly, if you have an admin group for managing AWS resources, then you can create an admin group and assign administrator-related policies to that group. If a user changes jobs in your organization, instead of editing that user's permissions, you can remove him or her from the old group, and add them to the appropriate new groups. You can use `Get-IAMGroupList` for viewing the existing group and `New-IAMGroup` to create the new group:

```
PS C:\> Get-IAMGroupList
PS C:\> New-IAMGroup -GroupName developer
```

```
PS C:\> Get-IAMGroupList
PS C:\> New-IAMGroup -GroupName developer


Arn         : arn:aws:iam::072316406132:group/developer
CreateDate  : 6/5/2017 1:52:35 PM
GroupId     : AGPAJ7QFAJES6UK5NLGAK
GroupName   : developer
Path        : /


PS C:\> Get-IAMGroupList


Arn         : arn:aws:iam::072316406132:group/developer
CreateDate  : 6/5/2017 1:52:35 PM
GroupId     : AGPAJ7QFAJES6UK5NLGAK
GroupName   : developer
Path        : /
```

The `developer` group is created, but still there are no policies assigned to it and no user added to it. Let's plan to see what are the AWS policies available for `S3` and `DynamoDB`. You can use the `Get-IAMPolicies` cmdlet to retrieve the full list of IAM policies available for you to choose from. You have to have a practice of reading that data, and choosing the one which is most appropriate for the group. I mostly filter it as follows:

```
PS C:\> Get-IAMPolicies | where-object {$_.PolicyName -like "*S3*"}
|format-table -Property PolicyName,Arn
PS C:\> Get-IAMPolicies | where-object {$_.PolicyName -like "*dynamo*"}
|format-table -Property PolicyName,Arn
```

```
PS C:\> Get-IAMPolicies | where-object {$_.PolicyName -like "*S3*"} |format-table -Property PolicyName,Arn

PolicyName                 Arn
----------                 ---
AmazonDMSRedshiftS3Role    arn:aws:iam::aws:policy/service-role/AmazonDMSRedshiftS3Role
AmazonS3FullAccess         arn:aws:iam::aws:policy/AmazonS3FullAccess
AmazonS3ReadOnlyAccess     arn:aws:iam::aws:policy/AmazonS3ReadOnlyAccess


PS C:\> Get-IAMPolicies | where-object {$_.PolicyName -like "*dynamo*"} |format-table -Property PolicyName,Arn

PolicyName                     Arn
----------                     ---
AmazonDynamoDBFullAccess       arn:aws:iam::aws:policy/AmazonDynamoDBFullAccess
AWSLambdaDynamoDBExecutionRole arn:aws:iam::aws:policy/service-role/AWSLambdaDynamoDBExecutionRole
AmazonDynamoDBReadOnlyAccess   arn:aws:iam::aws:policy/AmazonDynamoDBReadOnlyAccess
AmazonDynamoDBFullAccesswit... arn:aws:iam::aws:policy/AmazonDynamoDBFullAccesswithDataPipeline
AWSLambdaInvocation-DynamoDB   arn:aws:iam::aws:policy/AWSLambdaInvocation-DynamoDB
```

You can see that `Get-IAMPolicies` returned a number of policies that you can choose from for `S3` and `DynamoDB`. We will plan to grant `AmazonS3FullAccess` and `AmazonDynamoDBFullAccess` to the `developer` group that we created earlier. In order to attach a policy to the developer, you need to know the ARN for the policy. You can see in the output that there are two columns that we selected. You can use the `Register-IAMGroupPolicy` cmdlet to attach policies to a particular group:

```
PS C:\> Register-IAMGroupPolicy -GroupName developer -PolicyArn
arn:aws:iam::aws:policy/AmazonS3FullAccess
PS C:\> Register-IAMGroupPolicy -GroupName developer -PolicyArn
arn:aws:iam::aws:policy/AmazonDynamoDBFullAccess
```

This cmdlet will not return any output if it runs successfully. Both the policies will be added after the `Register-IAMGroupPolicy` is run. Now, you can add the user `Ramesh` to the developer group using `Add-IAMUserToGroup`:

```
PS C:\>Add-IAMUserToGroup -UserName "Ramesh" -GroupName "developer"
```

The IAM user `Ramesh` is now part of the IAM group called `developer`. But hold on, how can you access AWS using that user? The next section will help you to understand that.

You can directly assign the policies to the IAM user as well instead of granting it via a group. You can use the `Register-IAMUserPolicy` cmdlet. Granting policies via a group is considered as a best practice to ease administration on the AWS Cloud. Let's attach the `PowerUserAccess` policy to the user `Ramesh`:

```
PS C:\> Register-IAMUserPolicy -UserName Ramesh -PolicyArn
arn:aws:iam::aws:policy/PowerUserAccess
```

Accessing the AWS console

In order to allow access to the AWS console, you need to create the IAM profile for the user `Ramesh`. You can use the `New-IAMLoginProfile` cmdlet for this purpose:

```
PS C:\> New-IAMLoginProfile -UserName Ramesh -Password Test123 -
PasswordResetRequired $false
```

If you want to enforce the password change at first log in, then you can use the `PasswordResetRequired $true` parameter with the cmdlet.

```
PS C:\> New-IAMLoginProfile -UserName Ramesh -Password Test123 -PasswordResetRequired $false
New-IAMLoginProfile : One or more errors occurred. (Password does not conform to the account password policy.)
At line:1 char:1
+ New-IAMLoginProfile -UserName Ramesh -Password Test123 -PasswordReset ...
+ CategoryInfo          : InvalidOperation: (Amazon.PowerShe...inProfileCmdlet:NewIAMLoginProfileCmdlet) [New-IAMLoginProfile], InvalidOperationExcepti
   on
+ FullyQualifiedErrorId : System.AggregateException,Amazon.PowerShell.Cmdlets.IAM.NewIAMLoginProfileCmdlet

PS C:\> New-IAMLoginProfile -UserName Ramesh -Password Test1234 -PasswordResetRequired $false

CreateDate          PasswordResetRequired UserName
----------          --------------------- --------
6/5/2017 2:22:11 PM False                 Ramesh
```

If you are fail to set the password and do not know the password rules, then make use of the `Get-IAMAccountPasswordPolicy` cmdlet. This will list the rules enforced at the AWS account level:

```
PS C:\> IAMAccountPasswordPolicy
```

```
PS C:\> Get-IAMAccountPasswordPolicy

AllowUsersToChangePassword : False
ExpirePasswords            : False
HardExpiry                 : False
MaxPasswordAge             : 0
MinimumPasswordLength      : 8
PasswordReusePrevention    : 0
RequireLowercaseCharacters : True
RequireNumbers             : True
RequireSymbols             : False
RequireUppercaseCharacters : True
```

Now, get the AWS account alias using this:

```
PS C:\> Get-IAMAccountAlias
```

And make use of the alias returned by the `Get-IAMAccountAlias` cmdlet to sign in to the AWS console using the following:

```
https://<account-alias>.signin.aws.amazon. com/console.
```

Accessing AWS via CLI

There are two types of ways to access the AWS services and resources. One is through the AWS console, and we have discussed the process on how to sign on; and the second way is through the CLI/API calls. For accessing via CLI, you need an access key and a secret access key for programmatic access. You can check the access key associated with a specific IAM user using `Get-IAMAccessKey`; and you can create a new access key using `New-IAMAccessKey`:

```
PS C:\> Get-IAMAccessKey –UserName Ramesh
PS C:\> New-IAMAccessKey –UserName Ramesh
```

```
PS C:\> Get-IAMAccessKey -UserName Ramesh
PS C:\> New-IAMAccessKey -UserName Ramesh


AccessKeyId      : AKIAIDT3Y5MSGWJL4PFA
CreateDate       : 6/5/2017 2:42:21 PM
SecretAccessKey  : 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
Status           : Active
UserName         : Ramesh


PS C:\> Get-IAMAccessKey -UserName Ramesh

AccessKeyId          CreateDate          Status UserName
-----------          ----------          ------ --------
AKIAIDT3Y5MSGWJL4PFA 6/5/2017 2:42:21 PM Active Ramesh
```

Note that this is the only time you can see the `SecretAccessKey` displayed on the screen. You cannot retrieve it later. Save it securely. If you miss it, then you need to create a new one and deactivate the old one. Recycling and maintaining the access key falls under customer responsibilities. Now, you can use the access key and the secret access key for any programmatic access. It will assume the same policies that you assigned earlier to the developer group. You can think of the access key as the user ID and the secret access key as the password to your AWS account.

If you want to change the status of the specified access key from **active** to **inactive** or vice versa, then use the `Update-IAMAccessKey` cmdlet:

```
PS C:\> Update-IAMAccessKey -UserName Ramesh -AccessKeyId
AKIAIDT3Y5MSGWJL4PFA -Status Inactive
```

```
PS C:\> Get-IAMAccessKey -UserName Ramesh

AccessKeyId            CreateDate         Status  UserName
-----------            ----------         ------  --------
AKIAIDT3Y5MSGWJL4PFA 6/5/2017 2:42:21 PM Active  Ramesh


PS C:\>
PS C:\> Update-IAMAccessKey -UserName Ramesh -AccessKeyId AKIAIDT3Y5MSGWJL4PFA -Status Inactive
PS C:\> Get-IAMAccessKey -UserName Ramesh

AccessKeyId            CreateDate          Status   UserName
-----------            ----------          ------   --------
AKIAIDT3Y5MSGWJL4PFA 6/5/2017 2:42:21 PM Inactive Ramesh
```

Removing a policy from the group

If you want to remove a policy from the group, then use the `Unregister-IAMGroupPolicy` cmdlet. This one will remove the policy from the group. The following command will not return any output if it runs successfully:

```
PS C:\>Unregister-IAMGroupPolicy -GroupName developer -PolicyArn
arn:aws:iam::aws:policy/AmazonDynamoDBFullAccess
```

Revoking a policy from the user

If you have assigned the policy directly to the IAM user, then the `Unregister-IAMUserPolicy` cmdlet can be used:

```
PS C:\>Unregister-IAMUserPolicy -UserName Ramesh -PolicyArn
arn:aws:iam::aws:policy/PowerUserAccess
```

If you want to detach all the policies directly assigned to the user, then use `Get-IAMAttachedUserPolicies`, and pipe it to `Unregister-IAMUserPolicy` for that specific user:

```
PS C:\>Get-IAMAttachedUserPolicies -UserName Ramesh | Unregister-IAMUserPolicy -Username Ramesh
```

What are IAM roles?

IAM roles allow you to make AWS resources and service calls without supplying any long-term credentials. They are not associated with any specific user or group; rather, trusted entities assume a role and perform actions, providing the role has permissions. Using IAM roles is a best practice wherever you can, as it helps you to maintain security. You do not need to have a process to recycle the credentials. Roles take care of the recycling of credentials automatically.

Before you can create an IAM role using a PowerShell cmdlet, you must create a trust policy. A trust policy permits AWS services such as EC2 to assume an IAM role on behalf of your application. To create the trust policy, copy the following policy and paste it in a text file and save it with the name, `EC2_Trust_Policy_4_Apps.json`. `New-IAMRole` is the cmdlet that can be used to create a role.

To check the trust policy in PowerShell, use `Get-Content`:

```
PS C:\> Get-Content -Raw D:\EC2_Trust_Policy_4_Apps.json
```

Once your policy document is right, create a role using `New-IAMRole`:

```
PS C:\> New-IAMRole -AssumeRolePolicyDocument (Get-Content -raw
D:\EC2_Trust_Policy_4_Apps.json) -RoleName WorldPressAppRole
```

```
PS C:\> Get-Content -raw D:\EC2_Trust_Policy_4_Apps.json
{
  "Version": "2012-10-17",
  "Statement": [
    {
      "Effect": "Allow",
      "Principal": {
        "Service": "ec2.amazonaws.com"
      },
      "Action": "sts:AssumeRole"
    }
  ]
}
PS C:\> New-IAMRole -AssumeRolePolicyDocument (Get-Content -raw D:\EC2_Trust_Policy_4_Apps.json) -RoleName WorldPressAppRole


Arn                     : arn:aws:iam::072316406132:role/WorldPressAppRole
AssumeRolePolicyDocument : %7B%0A%20%20%22Version%22%3A%20%222012-10-17%22%2C%0A%20%20%22Statement%22%3A%20%5B%0A%20%20%20%20%7B%0A%20%20%20%20%20%20%22Effe
                          ct%22%3A%20%22Allow%22%2C%0A%20%20%20%20%20%20%22Principal%22%3A%20%7B%0A%20%20%20%20%20%20%20%20%22Service%22%3A%20%22ec2.amazon
                          aws.com%22%0A%20%20%20%20%20%7D%2C%0A%20%20%20%20%20%20%22Action%22%3A%20%22sts%3AAssumeRole%22%0A%20%20%20%20%7D%0A%20%20%5D%
                          0A%7D
CreateDate              : 6/5/2017 5:49:56 PM
Description             :
Path                    : /
RoleId                  : AROAJOFJELFO6XSCZ4HB4
RoleName                : WorldPressAppRole
```

You will learn how to assign roles in Chapter 6, *AWS Elastic Compute Cloud*. A trust policy document is needed to create the role. For writing a trust policy document, you should check some of the IAM documentations online. If your role requirements change, and you need to modify the permissions you granted your EC2 instance via the IAM role, you can replace the policy attached to the IAM role. However, this will also modify the permissions for other EC2 instances that use this IAM role:

```
PS C:\> Update-IAMAssumeRolePolicy -WorldPressAppRole ClientRole -
PolicyDocument (Get-Content -Raw D:\New_Trust_Policy_4_Apps.json)
```

IAM policies

A policy is a document that formally states one or more permissions. You apply permissions to IAM users, groups, and roles by creating policies. There are two types of IAM policies.

- **Managed policies**: These are standalone policies that you can attach to multiple users, groups, and roles in the AWS account. Managed policies can be **AWS Managed** and **Customer Managed**. If you are new to the AWS, then start using AWS Managed policies.
- **Inline policies**: These are policies that you create and manage; they are embedded directly into a single user, group, or role. Resource-based policies are another form of inline policy.

You can use the Get-IAMPolicies cmdlet for the AWS Managed and Customer Managed IAM policies:

```
PS C:\> Get-IAMPolicies | where-object {$_.PolicyName -like "*EC2*"}
|format-table -Property PolicyName
```

AWS Managed and Customer Managed policies can be clearly seen on the IAM console. However, I have not seen any parameter or method with the Get-IAMPolicies cmdlet that can tell you whether the policy is AWS Managed or Customer Managed. Maybe this is something that will be added in a future version.

You can create a custom policy using `New-IAMPolicy`. In this case, you need to create the policy document. I have created a policy document in JSON format, and then created a custom policy.

```
PS C:\> Get-Content -Raw D:\MyCustomPolicy.json
{
  "Version": "2012-10-17",
  "Statement": [
    {
      "Action": [
        "s3:GetBucketLocation",
        "s3:GetBucketNotification",
        "s3:GetBucketTagging",
        "s3:List*",
        "ses:Get*",
        "ses:List*",
        "sns:GetTopicAttributes",
        "sns:List*",
        "sqs:GetQueueAttributes",
        "sqs:ListQueues",
        "tag:Get*"
      ],
      "Effect": "Allow",
      "Resource": "*"
    }
  ]
}
PS C:\> New-IAMPolicy -PolicyName MyAppCustomPolicy -PolicyDocument (Get-Content -Raw D:\MyCustomPolicy.json)


Arn             : arn:aws:iam::072316406132:policy/MyAppCustomPolicy
AttachmentCount : 0
CreateDate      : 6/5/2017 7:11:43 PM
DefaultVersionId : v1
Description     :
IsAttachable    : True
Path            : /
PolicyId        : ANPAIONWILCYMEJP6H5Q4
PolicyName      : MyAppCustomPolicy
UpdateDate      : 6/5/2017 7:11:43 PM
```

Dropping groups, roles, and users

At times, if you want to delete the group that you created, you can use the `Remove-IAMGroup` cmdlet. In order to drop the group, you need to ensure that there are no attached policies or users assigned to the group:

```
PS C:\> Remove-IAMUserFromGroup -GroupName developer -UserName Ramesh
PS C:\> Remove-IAMGroup -GroupName developer
```

For the AWS role deletion, you can use the `Remove-IAMRole` cmdlet. The role must not have any policies attached. The following example deletes the role named `WorldPressAppRole` from the current IAM account. Before you can delete the role, you must first use the `Unregister-IAMRolePolicy` command to detach any managed policies. Inline policies are also deleted with the role.

```
PS C:\> Remove-IAMRole -RoleName WorldPressAppRole
```

To delete the specific IAM user from your AWS account, you can use the `Remove-IAMUser` cmdlet. The user you are deleting must not belong to any groups or have any access keys, signing certificates, or attached policies.

```
PS C:\>Remove-IAMUser -UserName Ramesh
```

Dropping PowerShell AWS profiles

You can have multiple AWS credential profiles created. There is a frequent need to drop the profile that is not needed anymore. In such cases, you can use the `Remove-AWSCredentialProfile` cmdlet to remove the unwanted AWS credential profile. First, check what profiles are available in your PowerShell:

```
PS C:\> Get-AWSCredential -ListProfileDetail
```

Once you identify the profile, you can remove them:

```
PS C:\> Remove-AWSCredentialProfile -ProfileName TestProfile
```

```
PS C:\> Get-AWSCredential -ListProfileDetail

ProfileName        StoreTypeName        ProfileLocation
-----------        -------------        ---------------
PowerShellProfile  NetSDKCredentialsFile
default            NetSDKCredentialsFile
TestProfile        NetSDKCredentialsFile


PS C:\> Remove-AWSCredentialProfile -ProfileName TestProfile

Confirm
Are you sure you want to perform this action?
Performing the operation "Remove-AWSCredentialProfile" on target "TestProfile".
[Y] Yes  [A] Yes to All  [N] No  [L] No to All  [S] Suspend  [?] Help (default is "Y"): Y
PS C:\> Get-AWSCredential -ListProfileDetail

ProfileName        StoreTypeName        ProfileLocation
-----------        -------------        ---------------
PowerShellProfile  NetSDKCredentialsFile
default            NetSDKCredentialsFile
```

The use case - access key rotation

For CLI access, you have to have an access key. This poses a security risk. Recycling access keys and secret access keys on a regular basis is considered as a well-known security best practice. This way you can reduce the impact on the business if the keys are comprised. Having an established process ensuring operational success, without impacting application functionality, is a key to ensuring that recycling the key is not a challenging task and is error free.

In order to rotate access keys and secret access keys, you should follow these steps:

- **Create a second access key**: While the first access key is still active, you can create the second access key using the `New-IAMAccessKey` cmdlet. The new access key created will be active by default.

  ```
  PS C:\>New-IAMAccessKey -UserName Ramesh
  ```

  Access keys and secret access keys will be displayed on the screen. As mentioned earlier, this is the only time that you will see the secret key on the screen. Save and secure it.

- **Update all your applications and tools to use the new access key**: Follow your own process to update the keys. If you have anything built to propagate the key to your code, then use that or manually update the keys wherever you need to do so.

- **Determine if the first access key is still in use**: `Get-IAMAccessKeyLastUsed` is the cmdlet that you can use to check the status of the access key. You can wait for several days and check once again. This way you will have an idea of whether the old access keys are being used or not.

- **Change the status of the first access key to inactive**: If there is no use of the first key, then you can plan to make the first key inactive rather than directly deleting it. This way you are setting up yourself for the second check if the access key is needed or not. Wait for a week and review the application or tool health for any mishap.

  ```
  PS C:\>Update-IAMAccessKey -UserName Ramesh -AccessKeyId
  AIDAIIROGQFGVBDKMAUXY -Status Inactive
  ```

- **Validate that your applications and tools are working**: After changing the key, if your application is working and if no part of the application is broken, then you can assume that application has an updated key. If a part of the application or the entire application stops working, then you can reactivate the key that was disabled or replaced with the new key.

- **Delete inactive access key**: After you wait for some period of time to ensure that all applications and tools have been updated, you can delete the first access key. `Remove-IAMAccessKey` is a cmdlet that you can use to delete the access key pair associated with the specified IAM user.

 If you do not specify a username, IAM determines the username implicitly based on the AWS access key ID signing the request. Because this action works for access keys under the AWS account, you can use this action to manage root credentials even if the AWS account has no associated users.

```
PS C:\>Remove-IAMAccessKey -AccessKeyId AIDAIIROGQFGVBDKMAUXY -
UserName Ramesh -Force
```

Summary

AWS IAM is a feature of your AWS account offered at no additional charge. You will be charged only for the use of other AWS products by your IAM users. AWS Identity Access and Management gives you an ability to provide shared access to your AWS account. You can also use IAM to define granular level permissions to tighten the access to practice the *Principle of Least Privilege*. The IAM-specific PowerShell cmdlets allow you to perform all the IAM-related tasks that you can perform using the console. The command-line tools such as PowerShell are useful if you want to build scripts that perform AWS tasks and automation. Using a command-line tool can be faster and more convenient than using the AWS console. We have seen some of the cmdlets that you can make use of on a regular basis to perform your day-to-day functions, but by no means is this information sufficient to make you an expert in IAM. This chapter specifically helps you to understand how PowerShell can help you automate as much as you can to perform your tasks. In the next chapter, you will learn more about the networking foundation needed on AWS for running applications.

5
AWS Virtual Private Cloud

Laying foundations for your AWS journey is crucial. Do not assume that just creating a root account and some IAM users is the thing you need to do in order to get started on AWS. Spinning up servers for your application and database workload requires planning, and it starts with defining the networking component on AWS. This brings in a lot more complexity when you have the hybrid environment. Most importantly, you should understand the framework and tools provided by AWS to lay down this foundation. Usually, it is a best practice to start thinking about the account management practices that you want to use for your AWS journey. Some organizations consider creating a single AWS root account and hosting different types of environment in different VPCs, or some might think that having different accounts for different environments is the right thing to do. You should think about the account structure that will make sense in your organization. Nothing wrong or right, but it would help you to segregate environments appropriately. Hence understanding where development, testing, and production should be hosted would help you in the long run.

In this chapter, we will learn about the virtual private cloud and associated components that you must know in order to deploy a successful foundation for your AWS infrastructure.

Laying the foundation

To better understand the networking components on AWS, let's consider the example architecture here. This will help you to understand various networking components considered at various layers of the architecture. This is just a sample architecture that we are considering and could be suitable for most of the deployment. In the example architecture, there is a VPC, which spans across two availability zones. In each availability zone, there are two subnets created. On the left-hand side of the **Availability Zone**, we have **Subnet 1** as the **public** subnet and **Subnet 3** as the **private** subnet. On the right-hand side of the **Availability Zone**, we have **Subnet 2** as the **public** Subnet and **Subnet 4** as the **private** one. There are a couple of Route Tables and one **Internet Gateway** for routing the traffic. You will also see a NAT Gateway that accepts traffic from **private** subnets and interacts with the open internet for the software updates. The **Network Access Control List** and **Security Group** act as a firewall. The end user is connected to the EC2 instance via a web browser, which comes through the IGW and hits the public network defined in the **VPC**. **Bastion Host** is a kind of jump server that sits in the **public** subnet and acts as the critical access point in the following architecture. We will make use of the AWS tools for the PowerShell cmdlet to define the following networking components and use this architecture in the rest of the chapters for discussing AWS services:

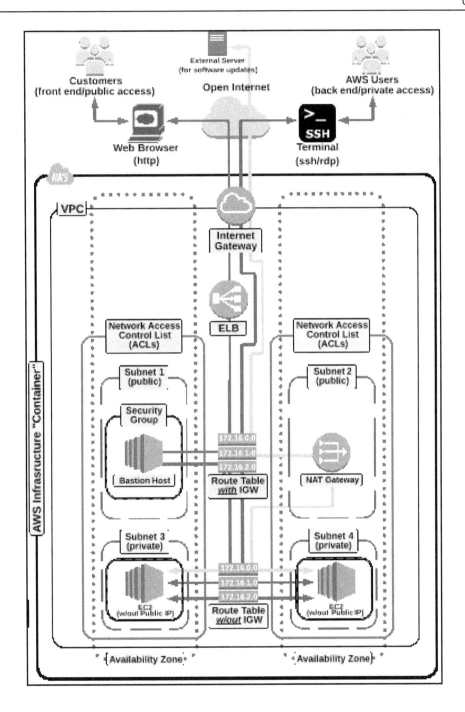

Virtual Private Cloud

Amazon **Virtual Private Cloud** (**VPC**) enables you to isolate and launch AWS Resources into the virtual network. VPC closely resembles a traditional network that you define in your on-premise with the benefits of using an elastic and scalable architecture. You can define public and private subnets in your virtual cloud, and it provides an ability to extend your existing corporate network to the cloud. VPC always houses within an AWS region and cannot span the region. However, VPC can span across multiple availability zones in the given region. Spanning VPC across multiple availability zones allow you to provision redundant resources in separate availability zone while having them accessible on the same network. This forms the foundation for a high availability and fault tolerant architecture.

AWS provides a DNS server for your VPC, so each instance that you spin up has a hostname. However, you can run your own DNS servers by changing the DHCP option set configuration within the VPC. There are several other benefits of using VPC, such as defining a custom IP address range (CIDR block) for each VPC and the subnet within the VPC. Also, it provides an ability to launch instances in the specific subnet for better control. VPC allows you to extend your on-premise network into the cloud with VPN or a direct connect.

When you create an AWS account, you get one default VPC in each region. This default VPC has a preconfigured setup and is meant to allow the user easy access to the VPC without having to configure it from scratch. You can assume that all the underlying dirty work for the default VPC, including Route Table, Internet Gateway, and subnets, are taken care of by AWS. The default VPC is not suitable for your production application deployment, but this is something that will help to test your prototype to start with. Each instance that you start in the default VPC will have a private and public IP address assigned. In the default VPC, all the subnets have route to the internet. In short, the default VPC is public. You are allowed to create only five more VPCs in each region. If you want to create more than five VPCs, you need to contact AWS to get the limit increased.

If you notice, when you log onto the AWS Console, the VPC service is seen under the **Networking & Content Delivery** category, as shown in the following diagram. If you perform an operation via the console for this service, I do not feel that there will be much confusion around it. But, if you try to perform a VPC-related operation via the PowerShell cmdlet, you would feel that all the VPC-related cmdlets are specified under the **Amazon Elastic Computer Cloud** service.

However, on the AWS console, you will see that the AWS **Elastic Compute Cloud (EC2)** service comes under the **Compute** category and not under **Networking & Content Delivery**. Because of this, you can get a little lost. This is somewhat confusing to the new guys when they start working with the AWS console, though I am not sure why it is like that. Even if you discover all the VPC-related cmdlets in PowerShell, you will notice that most of them have an EC2 keyword in them.

To list all the available cmdlets in PowerShell in regards to VPC, you run this:

```
PS C:\>Get-Command -Name *Vpc*
```

To list all the available VPCs in your account for the given region, you can use this:

```
PS C:\>Get-EC2Vpc | Format-Table -AutoSize
```

```
PS C:\> Get-EC2Vpc | Format-Table -AutoSize

CidrBlock     DhcpOptionsId InstanceTenancy Ipv6CidrBlockAssociationSet IsDefault State     Tags     VpcId         VpcState  Tag
---------     ------------- --------------- --------------------------- --------- -----     ----     -----         --------  ---
10.11.0.0/16  dopt-d928d0bc default         {}                          False     available {Name}   vpc-849c2ae3  available {Name}
172.31.0.0/16 dopt-d928d0bc default         {}                          True      available {Name}   vpc-0ac0136e  available {Name}

PS C:\>
```

The output shows the `CidrBlock` range for a couple of VPCs that are created in the account. For each `CidrBlock`, you will see `VpcId` assigned by AWS. In almost all the operations, you would be referencing `VpcId` for the network allocation, including a subnet and not the CIDR block itself. We will discuss subnets later. The `IsDefault` attribute indicates that the given VPC is a default VPC in the region, and if you do not specify the VPC for spinning up your resources, by default, that will be used by AWS. `DhcpOptionsId` is what you can change when you have a custom DNS. I will not be covering changing the DHCP option set in detail in this book, because it will require a lot of other understanding and demonstration. We will go with the default DNS server that AWS assigned to the VPC.

If you want to see what tags are given to the VPC, then you have a little more work to do to pull out that information, as you will notice that tags are just named **{Name}**:

```
PS C:\>$resultVPC=Get-EC2Vpc -VPCId vpc-849c2ae3
PS C:\>$resultVPC.tags
```

```
PS C:\> $resultVPC=Get-EC2Vpc -VPCId vpc-849c2ae3
PS C:\> $resultVPC.tags

Key   Value
---   -----
Name  ramesh_vpc


PS C:\>
```

For creating a new VPC in your AWS account, you must choose the CIDR block range that is suitable for your AWS deployment. You should choose the CIDR block range that is not overlapping anywhere else in your organization if you are planning to extend your on-premise data center to AWS Cloud. Having an overlap of the CIDR block range can create issues for VPN connections, and there is nothing you can do about it. You have to redeploy your AWS resources once again in a different VPC in case that happens. You cannot rename or easily move the resources out of the VPC.

`New-EC2Vpc` creates a VPC with the specified IPv4 CIDR block. The smallest VPC you can create uses a /28 netmask (16 IPv4 addresses) and the largest uses a /16 netmask (65,536 IPv4 addresses). You can optionally request an Amazon-provided IPv6 CIDR block for the VPC. In our example, we will only use the IPv4 CIDR block range. If you are new to this CIDR block notation, I would recommend that you review some of the materials available online to increase your learning reward.

To create a new VPC, you can use this:

```
PS C:\> New-EC2Vpc -CidrBlock 10.0.0.0/16 -InstanceTenancy default
```

```
PS C:\> New-EC2Vpc -CidrBlock 10.0.0.0/16 -InstanceTenancy default

CidrBlock                   : 10.0.0.0/16
DhcpOptionsId               : dopt-d928d0bc
InstanceTenancy             : default
Ipv6CidrBlockAssociationSet : {}
IsDefault                   : False
State                       : pending
Tags                        : {}
VpcId                       : vpc-a6bb60df


PS C:\> Get-EC2VPC |Format-Table -AutoSize

CidrBlock      DhcpOptionsId InstanceTenancy Ipv6CidrBlockAssociationSet IsDefault State     Tags     VpcId        VpcState  Tag
---------      ------------- --------------- --------------------------- --------- -----     ----     -----        --------  ---
10.11.0.0/16   dopt-d928d0bc default         {}                          False     available {Name}   vpc-849c2ae3 available {Name}
172.31.0.0/16  dopt-d928d0bc default         {}                          True      available {Name}   vpc-0ac0136e available {Name}
10.0.0.0/16    dopt-d928d0bc default         {}                          False     available {}       vpc-a6bb60df available {}


PS C:\>
```

Now, a new VPC with `VpcID vpc-a6bb60df` and `CidrBlock 10.0.0.0/16` is created and made available, but it is not fully ready to use, unless we create Route Tables, Internet Gateway, NAT Gateway, and subnets. Go back and review the foundation architecture that we discussed earlier in this chapter and see where the VPC fits in. We have just created that outer framework, and other network components are still pending.

Before proceeding, let's ensure that the two most important attributes on the VPCs are set. They are **Enable DNS HostNames** and **Enable DNS Support**. Attribute `enableDnsHostnames`, if enabled, will allocate DNS hostnames to instances in VPC; and attribute `enableDnsSupport`, if enabled, supports DNS resolution. You cannot modify both of them simultaneously. You have to issue an individual cmdlet to enable them. You can enable the DNS hostname only if you have enabled DNS support.

To check if VPC attributes are set or not, you can use this:

```
PS C:\> Get-EC2VpcAttribute -VpcId vpc-a6bb60df -Attribute
enableDnsHostnames
PS C:\> Get-EC2VpcAttribute -VpcId vpc-a6bb60df -Attribute enableDnsSupport
```

To enable VPC attributes, you run this:

```
PS C:\> Edit-EC2VpcAttribute -VpcId vpc-a6bb60df -EnableDnsHostnames $true
PS C:\> Edit-EC2VpcAttribute -VpcId vpc-a6bb60df -EnableDnsSupport $true
```

```
PS C:\> Get-EC2VpcAttribute -VpcId vpc-a6bb60df -Attribute enableDnsSupport

EnableDnsHostnames EnableDnsSupport VpcId
------------------ ---------------- -----
False              True             vpc-a6bb60df


PS C:\> Get-EC2VpcAttribute -VpcId vpc-a6bb60df -Attribute enableDnsHostnames

EnableDnsHostnames EnableDnsSupport VpcId
------------------ ---------------- -----
False              False            vpc-a6bb60df


PS C:\> Edit-EC2VpcAttribute -VpcId vpc-a6bb60df -EnableDnsHostnames $true
PS C:\> Edit-EC2VpcAttribute -VpcId vpc-a6bb60df -EnableDnsSupport $true
PS C:\>
```

Internet Gateways

Internet Gateway (IGW) is a VPC component that allows communication between instances in your VPC and the open internet. IGW is horizontally scaled, redundant, and highly available. It imposes no availability risks or bandwidth constraints on your network traffic. Only one IGW can be attached to the VPC at a time. An IGW cannot be detached from the VPC if there are active resources running inside your VPC, such as the EC2 and RDS instances. You must attach IGW to the VPC if the resources inside the VPC need to connect to the open internet. The default VPC that you get in each region has an IGW attached to it by default. Let's create and assign the new IGW to the VPC we created earlier.

To check all the relevant IGW cmdlets, you can use this:

```
PS C:\> Get-Command *InternetGateway*
```

To list the number of IGW and its association with VPC, you run this:

```
PS C:\> Get-EC2InternetGateway
```

To create a new IGW, you can issue this:

```
PS C:\> New-EC2InternetGateway
```

```
PS C:\> Get-EC2InternetGateway

Attachments      InternetGatewayId Tags
-----------      ----------------- ----
{vpc-0ac0136e}   igw-b5c0fed0      {Name}
{vpc-849c2ae3}   igw-f6abfb92      {}

PS C:\> Get-EC2VPC |Format-Table -AutoSize

CidrBlock        DhcpOptionsId InstanceTenancy Ipv6CidrBlockAssociationSet IsDefault State     Tags   VpcId        VpcState  Tag
---------        ------------- --------------- --------------------------- --------- -----     ----   -----        --------  ---
10.11.0.0/16     dopt-d928d0bc default         {}                          False     available {Name} vpc-849c2ae3 available {Name}
172.31.0.0/16    dopt-d928d0bc default         {}                          True      available {Name} vpc-0ac0136e available {Name}
10.0.0.0/16      dopt-d928d0bc default         {}                          False     available {}     vpc-a6bb60df available {}

PS C:\> New-EC2InternetGateway

Attachments InternetGatewayId Tags
----------- ----------------- ----
{}          igw-4b55c22d      {}
```

`New-EC2InternetGateway` creates an IGW that can be used to attach to your VPC. It returns `InternetGatewayId`, which you can use to associate with the VPC. You can attach the IGW using the `Add-EC2InternetGateway` cmdlet:

```
PS C:\> Add-EC2InternetGateway –InternetGatewayId igw–4b55c22d –VpcId vpc–
a6bb60df
```

```
PS C:\> Get-EC2InternetGateway

Attachments      InternetGatewayId Tags
-----------      ----------------- ----
{vpc-0ac0136e}   igw-b5c0fed0      {Name}
{vpc-849c2ae3}   igw-f6abfb92      {}
{}               igw-4b55c22d      {}

PS C:\> Add-EC2InternetGateway -InternetGatewayId igw-4b55c22d -VpcId vpc-a6bb60df
PS C:\> Get-EC2InternetGateway

Attachments      InternetGatewayId Tags
-----------      ----------------- ----
{vpc-0ac0136e}   igw-b5c0fed0      {Name}
{vpc-849c2ae3}   igw-f6abfb92      {}
{vpc-a6bb60df}   igw-4b55c22d      {}
```

By default, when you create an IGW, it is not attached to any VPC and as mentioned earlier; you can only attach one IGW to the VPC.

Route Tables

A **Route Table** is what basically directs the traffic in the VPC. AWS defines a Route Table as a set of rules called routes that are used to determine where network traffic is directed. Each Route Table has two main components called target and destination. The target indicates where the data is being routed to, and the destination indicates the CIDR block range of the target where the data is routed to. With the default VPC, you get one Route Table, which is assigned to the default VPC. It is considered a best practice to leave the default Route Table as it is and create new Route Tables for your own custom VPC. There are two main characteristics that you must know about the Route Table. First, by default, all the subnet traffic is allowed to the other available subnet within your VPC, and is called as a local route. Second, you can modify the local route. The best thing is you can have multiple active routes in the VPC. If you want to delete the specific route, you cannot delete it if it has a subnet associated.

To get the list of cmdlets associated with the Route Table operation, you can use this:

```
PS C:\> Get-Command *RouteTable*
```

In the architecture diagram that we used earlier, we wanted to create two Route Tables, one for the public subnet and the other for the private subnet. To get the list of available Route Tables, you can use this:

```
PS C:\> Get-EC2RouteTable |Format-Table –AutoSize
```

To create a new Route Table, you run this:

```
PS C:\> New-EC2RouteTable –VpcId vpc-a6bb60df
```

`New-EC2RouteTable` allows you to create a Route Table for the specified VPC. After you create a Route Table, you can add routes and associate the Route Table with a subnet. In this example, we have created two Route Tables: `rtb-50472228` and `rtb-c24421ba`. For further discussion, let's ensure that we set only one of them as a public Route Table. In our example, we will set the Route Table, `rtb-50472228`, as public and `rtb-c24421ba` as private. We have just created a Route Table, there is no IGW attached to the public Route Table. Let's first attach the IGW to the public Route Table. You can use the `New-EC2Route` cmdlet for doing this:

```
PS C:\> New-EC2Route –RouteTableId rtb-50472228 –DestinationCidrBlock
0.0.0.0/0 –GatewayId igw-4b55c22d
```

Now, the Route Table called `rtb-50472228` has a route to internet, and subnets associated with this Route Table will be called public subnets.

```
PS C:\> New-EC2Route -RouteTableId rtb-50472228 -DestinationCidrBlock 0.0.0.0/0 -GatewayId igw-4b55c22d
True
```

Subnets

Subnets are a part of the VPC. By creating different subnets in the given VPC, you are creating different subnetworks for your infrastructure. The scope of the VPC is the region. VPC cannot span across regions, but it can span across all the availability in that region. The scope of the subnet is the availability zone, and it cannot span across different availability zones in that region. This is very important to understand when you work with subnets, and design the fault tolerant application that spreads across multiple availability zone. Each subnet that you create must be associated with the Route Table. One Route Table can have multiple subnets associated to it.

There are two types of subnets. First, the **public subnet**; this has a route to the internet. This is the subnet, which is associated with the Route Table that has IGW attached to it. Second, the **private subnet**; this does not have route to the internet, and is associated with the Route Table to which there is no IGW attached to it. As there is no IGW attached to the Route Table associated with the private subnet, instances launched in the private subnet cannot communicate with the internet and, hence, cannot download software patches. This is where NAT Gateway comes in to the picture and helps to solve this problem.

In the default VPC, there are subnets created which have routes to the internet. For your own deployment, there is a need to create the different subnets so that public facing applications are deployed in the public subnets, and others are deployed in the private subnet for better control. Running instances in private subnets tightens the security, and it is very useful when you want to secure your application from the open internet.

To get the list of cmdlets for a subnet, you can use the following command:

```
PS C:\> Get-Command *subnet*
```

To get the list of subnets created, you can run the following command:

```
PS C:\> Get-EC2Subnet |Select-Object
VpcID,SubnetID,State,CidrBlock,AvailabilityZone |Format-Table -AutoSize
```

To create a new subnet in the given VPC, you use the following command:

```
PS C:\>New-EC2Subnet -VpcId vpc-a6bb60df -CidrBlock 10.0.1.0/24 -
AvailabilityZone us-east-1a
```

```
PS C:\> New-EC2Subnet -VpcId vpc-a6bb60df -CidrBlock 10.0.1.0/24 -AvailabilityZone us-east-1a


AssignIpv6AddressOnCreation : False
AvailabilityZone            : us-east-1a
AvailableIpAddressCount     : 251
CidrBlock                   : 10.0.1.0/24
DefaultForAz                : False
Ipv6CidrBlockAssociationSet : {}
MapPublicIpOnLaunch         : False
State                       : pending
SubnetId                    : subnet-b262c19e
Tags                        : {}
VpcId                       : vpc-a6bb60df
```

I have created and run three additional subnets as follows:

```
PS C:\>New-EC2Subnet -VpcId vpc-a6bb60df -CidrBlock 10.0.2.0/24 -
AvailabilityZone us-east-1b
PS C:\>New-EC2Subnet -VpcId vpc-a6bb60df -CidrBlock 10.0.3.0/24 -
AvailabilityZone us-east-1a
PS C:\>New-EC2Subnet -VpcId vpc-a6bb60df -CidrBlock 10.0.4.0/24 -
AvailabilityZone us-east-1b
```

Now, we have four subnets. Unless we assign them a proper route, we cannot say that these subnets are public or private. There is no association as such to the Route Table. You can list all the subnets created in the VPC as follows:

```
PS C:\> Get-EC2Subnet |Select-Object
VpcID,SubnetID,State,CidrBlock,AvailabilityZone |Where-Object VpcID -eq
'vpc-a6bb60df' |Format-Table -AutoSize
```

```
PS C:\> Get-EC2Subnet |Select-Object VpcID,SubnetID,State,CidrBlock,AvailabilityZone |Where-Object VpcID -eq 'vpc-a6bb60df' |Format-Table -AutoSize

VpcId        SubnetId       State     CidrBlock   AvailabilityZone
-----        --------       -----     ---------   ----------------
vpc-a6bb60df subnet-c843dd80 available 10.0.2.0/24 us-east-1b
vpc-a6bb60df subnet-b29d3e9e available 10.0.3.0/24 us-east-1a
vpc-a6bb60df subnet-b262c19e available 10.0.1.0/24 us-east-1a
vpc-a6bb60df subnet-f042dcb8 available 10.0.4.0/24 us-east-1b
```

Let's associate the subnets `subnet-c843dd80` and `subnet-b29d3e9e` to the Route Tables `rtb-50472228` and `subnet-b262c19e`, and `subnet-f042dcb8` to the Route Table `rtb-c24421ba`. `Register-EC2RouteTable` associates a subnet with the Route Table:

```
PS C:\> Register-EC2RouteTable -RouteTableId rtb-50472228 -SubnetId subnet-c843dd80
```

For the rest of the three subnet associations, see this:

```
PS C:\> Register-EC2RouteTable -RouteTableId rtb-50472228 -SubnetId subnet-c843dd80
rtbassoc-feb0f685
PS C:\> Register-EC2RouteTable -RouteTableId rtb-50472228 -SubnetId subnet-b29d3e9e
rtbassoc-1dbef866
PS C:\> Register-EC2RouteTable -RouteTableId rtb-c24421ba -SubnetId subnet-b262c19e
rtbassoc-11b8fe6a
PS C:\> Register-EC2RouteTable -RouteTableId rtb-c24421ba -SubnetId subnet-f042dcb8
rtbassoc-7cbef807
PS C:\>
```

NAT Gateway

IGW is used to direct the traffic to the open internet and is associated with the Route Table intended for public subnets. This means the connection to a particular instance can be initiated from the open internet and from the instance itself. For a private subnet, you cannot initiate the connection from the open internet. But for software patches downloads, or to interact with other AWS services, you need to have a route to the internet so that the connection initiated from the instance should be able to download the patches or work with other AWS services; but no one should be able to initiate the connection from the open internet. This is where we need the NAT Gateway.

The NAT Gateway enables instances in a private subnet to connect to the open internet or to other AWS services, but it prevents the open internet from initiating the connection to those private instances. The NAT Gateway is highly available and fully managed by AWS. It has the capability to burst up to 10 Gbps. The software used on the NAT Gateway is highly optimized for NAT traffic.

To find out all the cmdlets related to the NAT Gateway, you can use this:

```
PS C:\> Get-Command *NatGateway*
```

To check the list of NAT Gateways created in the region, you run this:

```
PS C:\> Get-EC2Natgateway
```

Before you create a NAT Gateway, you must first create an Elastic IP address for a VPC, using this:

```
PS C:\> New-EC2Address -Domain Vpc
```

An important thing to note here is that you should associate the NAT Gateway with a public subnet while creating it. There must be a route to the internet for the subnet in which you run your NAT Gateway. subnet-c843dd80 and subnet-b29d3e9e are the public subnets that we created earlier. You can just associate the NAT Gateway to one of the public subnets. To associate the NAT Gateway with a public subnet, you run this:

```
PS C:\> New-EC2NatGateway -SubnetId subnet-c843dd80  -AllocationId
eipalloc-929853a2
```

```
PS C:\> New-EC2Address -Domain Vpc

AllocationId      Domain PublicIp
------------      ------ --------
eipalloc-929853a2 vpc    34.201.232.104

PS C:\> New-EC2NatGateway -SubnetId subnet-c843dd80  -AllocationId eipalloc-929853a2

ClientToken NatGateway
----------- ----------
            Amazon.EC2.Model.NatGateway
```

You get `AllocationId` associated with the EIP when you create it. So at the time of the NAT Gateway creation, you associate AllocationId instead of the EIP itself. You can now get the list of available NAT Gateways using this:

```
PS C:\> Get-EC2Natgateway |Select-Object NatGatewayId,State,VpcId |Where-
Object State -eq 'available'
```

```
PS C:\> Get-EC2Natgateway |Select-Object NatGatewayId,State,VpcId |Where-Object State -eq 'available'

NatGatewayId            State      VpcId
------------            -----      -----
nat-0c08f0ce9062ab192 available vpc-a6bb60df
```

You must add this NAT Gateway on the private Route Table in order to allow private instances to receive updates from the internet. This can be done using this:

```
PS C:\> New-EC2Route -RouteTableId rtb-c24421ba -DestinationCidrBlock
0.0.0.0/0 -GatewayId nat-0c08f0ce9062ab192
```

```
PS C:\> New-EC2Route -RouteTableId rtb-c24421ba -DestinationCidrBlock 0.0.0.0/0 -GatewayId nat-0c08f0ce9062ab192
True
```

Overall, you create a NAT Gateway on the public subnet, but add it to the Route Table designated for the private subnet. Keep this thing in mind as there is a lot of confusion seen when people work with NAT Gateways. If you allocate a private subnet to the NAT Gateway, it may not error out; but after allocating it on the private Route Table, you will not be able to download patches or interact with other AWS services.

Network Access List

The **Network Access Control List** (**NACL**) sits outside the subnet and acts as a firewall. It functions at the subnet level and is an optional layer of security. NACL supports the `ALLOW` and `DENY` rules for the traffic travelling into or out of the subnet. Every time you create a new VPC, AWS creates a default NACL for you and associates it with the VPC. By default, all the inbound and outbound traffic is allowed on the subnet. The default inbound rule looks something like this:

Rule #	View: All rules ▼ Type	Protocol	Port Range	Source	Allow / Deny
100	ALL Traffic	ALL	ALL	0.0.0.0/0	ALLOW
*	ALL Traffic	ALL	ALL	0.0.0.0/0	DENY

And outbound rules are also similar to inbound rules, which allow all the traffic to flow from and to the subnet.

Rule #	Type	Protocol	Port Range	Destination	Allow / Deny
View: All rules ▾					
100	ALL Traffic	ALL	ALL	0.0.0.0/0	ALLOW
*	ALL Traffic	ALL	ALL	0.0.0.0/0	DENY

NACL is stateless. This means that the return traffic must be allowed through the outbound rule. It processes rules in the order of the number when deciding whether to allow the traffic. `Rule#` mentioned as * is called the **catch all** deny rule. This means that unless the protocol/port is explicitly allowed, the traffic will be denied. To understand the rule processing better, let's review the following inbound rule:

Rule #	Type	Protocol	Port Range	Source	Allow / Deny
View: All rules ▾					
60	SSH (22)	TCP (6)	22	0.0.0.0/0	ALLOW
70	HTTPS (443)	TCP (6)	443	0.0.0.0/0	ALLOW
80	HTTPS (443)	TCP (6)	443	0.0.0.0/0	DENY
100	ALL Traffic	ALL	ALL	0.0.0.0/0	ALLOW
*	ALL Traffic	ALL	ALL	0.0.0.0/0	DENY

You see that I have added `Rule#` in an increment of 10, which is considered as a best practice when you create your own custom NACL. Having it in an increment of 10 will allow you to plug in a new rule when needed. That's the theme behind it and nothing else. As long as `Rule#` is in increment, you are fine. `Rule# 60` will be processed first, which allows traffic from all the sources. `Rule# 70` will be processed next, which allows HTTPS traffic from all the sources. Now, `Rule# 80` will be simply discarded, because NACL has already processed the rule for the same protocol and port earlier.

To get the list of network ACL related cmdlets, you can run the following command:

```
PS C:\> Get-Command *NetworkAcl*
```

To list all the network ACL in your region, you can use the following command:

```
PS C:\> Get-EC2NetworkAcl | Select-Object VpcId,NetworkAclId,IsDefault
```

To create a new network ACL, you need to know the VpcId for which you would be creating NACL. You can use the following command:

```
PS C:\> New-EC2NetworkAcl -VpcId vpc-a6bb60df
```

```
PS C:\> New-EC2NetworkAcl -VpcId vpc-a6bb60df


Associations : {}
Entries      : {Amazon.EC2.Model.NetworkAclEntry, Amazon.EC2.Model.NetworkAclEntry}
IsDefault    : False
NetworkAclId : acl-882c6df1
Tags         : {}
VpcId        : vpc-a6bb60df
```

You can add the rule using New-EC2NetworkAclEntry. This cmdlet creates a rule in a network ACL with the specified rule number. Each network ACL has a set of numbered ingress rules and a separate set of numbered egress rules:

```
PS C:\> New-EC2NetworkAclEntry -NetworkAclId acl-882c6df1 -Egress $false -
RuleNumber 50 -Protocol 17 -PortRange_From 53 -PortRange_To 53 -CidrBlock
0.0.0.0/0 -RuleAction allow
```

In order to assign the newly created NACL, you have to first get the NACL association ID of the subnet for which you are planning to assign the newly created NACL. I have not seen NACL association ID visible on the AWS console. This is needed when you plan to assign a new NACL to the subnet via PowerShell. Let's pick up the one subnet that we created earlier in the private subnet and assign the NACL that we created to it.

To get the current NACL association ID for the subnet, you can run this:

```
PS C:\> (Get-EC2NetworkAcl -NetworkAclId acl-27c7825e).Associations
```

```
PS C:\> (Get-EC2NetworkAcl -NetworkAclId acl-27c7825e).Associations

NetworkAclAssociationId NetworkAclId SubnetId
----------------------- ------------ --------
aclassoc-5d2ceb2e       acl-27c7825e subnet-b29d3e9e
aclassoc-6f2fe81c       acl-27c7825e subnet-f042dcb8
aclassoc-9d2becee       acl-27c7825e subnet-c843dd80
aclassoc-ff23e48c       acl-27c7825e subnet-b262c19e
```

Let's plan to assign the NACL to the subnet, `subnet-f042dcb8`. The `Set-EC2NetworkAclAssociation` cmdlet changes the network ACL to which a subnet is associated with:

```
PS C:\> Set-EC2NetworkAclAssociation -AssociationId aclassoc-6f2fe81c -
NetworkAclId acl-882c6df1
```

```
PS C:\> Set-EC2NetworkAclAssociation -AssociationId aclassoc-6f2fe81c -NetworkAclId acl-882c6df1
aclassoc-5a71b329
PS C:\> (Get-EC2NetworkAcl -NetworkAclId acl-27c7825e).Associations

NetworkAclAssociationId NetworkAclId SubnetId
----------------------- ------------ --------
aclassoc-5d2ceb2e       acl-27c7825e subnet-b29d3e9e
aclassoc-9d2becee       acl-27c7825e subnet-c843dd80
aclassoc-ff23e48c       acl-27c7825e subnet-b262c19e


PS C:\> (Get-EC2NetworkAcl -NetworkAclId acl-882c6df1).Associations

NetworkAclAssociationId NetworkAclId SubnetId
----------------------- ------------ --------
aclassoc-5a71b329       acl-882c6df1 subnet-f042dcb8
```

In the preceding screenshot, you can see that for NACL `acl-27c7825e`, there are only three subnets associated, which is the default NACL. And for the custom NACL `acl-882c6df1`, there is one subnet association now. You can check the inbound and outbound rules set on the specific NACL using this:

```
PS C:\> (Get-EC2NetworkAcl -NetworkAclId acl-882c6df1).Entries |format-
table -AutoSize
```

```
PS C:\> (Get-EC2NetworkAcl -NetworkAclId acl-882c6df1).Entries |format-table -AutoSize

CidrBlock Egress IcmpTypeCode Ipv6CidrBlock PortRange Protocol RuleAction RuleNumber
--------- ------ ------------ ------------- --------- -------- ---------- ----------
0.0.0.0/0 True                                        -1       allow      100
0.0.0.0/0 True                                        -1       deny       32767
0.0.0.0/0 False                                       -1       allow      100
0.0.0.0/0 False                                       -1       deny       32767
```

The `Egress` column in the preceding output indicates whether the rule is inbound or outbound. The Egress value, True, suggests that it is for the outbound traffic; and false indicates that it is for the inbound rule. -1 indicates it is for all the traffic.

Security Groups

Security Groups are another layer of protection for the instances. They are pretty much similar to NACL. They also allow and deny the traffic. Unlike NACL, they are stateful. This means that the return traffic is allowed regardless of the inbound rule. As mentioned, NACL sits outside the subnet and evaluates the traffic before sending it in and out of the subnet, whereas Security Groups protect the traffic to flow into the instances. A Security Group sits inside the subnet, but it is not specifically assigned to one subnet. This is also a second level of firewall. Security Groups support only the allow rule, and all the rules are evaluated before allowing the traffic to flow. You get one Security Group in each region by default when you set up your AWS account, and it is associated with the default VPC. Afterwards, every time you create a new VPC, a new Security Group is created. There are a number of situations where you would prefer to create your own Security Group instead of using the default one. You can implement some best practices such as creating a Security Group for your web access, allowing only the HTTP traffic, and considering the functionality of the application only for backend access, such as SSH. Security Groups are associated with a specific VPC and can be used for all the resources wherever applicable.

Type	Protocol	Port Range	Source
ALL Traffic	ALL	ALL	sg-5be1fd25

The default Security Group allows all the traffic to come from all the other sources wherever the default Security Group is assigned. The source column indicates that all the traffic from the Security Group called `sg-5be1fd25` is allowed. The source could be a range of IPs, one single server, or a Security Group.

To get the list of cmdlets in regard to the Security Group, you can use the following command:

```
PS C:\> Get-Command *SecurityGroup*
```

To list the Security Groups for the region, you can use the following command:

```
PS C:\> Get-EC2SecurityGroup |Select-Object VpcId,GroupId, GroupName,
Description
```

To create a new Security Group for the VPC, you can use the following command:

```
PS C:\> New-EC2SecurityGroup -GroupName My-test-Group -Description "My
First Security Group" -VpcId vpc-a6bb60df
```

You can grant the traffic to flow using `Grant-EC2SecurityGroupIngress`:

```
PS C:\> $ip1 = @{ IpProtocol="tcp"; FromPort="22"; ToPort="22";
IpRanges="0.0.0.0/0" }
PS C:\> $ip2 = @{ IpProtocol="tcp"; FromPort="3389"; ToPort="3389";
IpRanges="0.0.0.0/0" }
PS C:\> Grant-EC2SecurityGroupIngress -GroupId sg-6fd1361e -IpPermission @(
$ip1, $ip2 )
```

```
PS C:\> (Get-EC2SecurityGroup -GroupId sg-6fd1361e).IpPermissionsEgress |Format-Table -AutoSize

FromPort IpProtocol IpRanges   Ipv6Ranges PrefixListIds ToPort UserIdGroupPairs UserIdGroupPair IpRange
-------- ---------- --------   ---------- ------------- ------ --------------- --------------- -------
       0 -1         {0.0.0.0/0} {}              {}           0 {}              {}              {0.0.0.0/0}


PS C:\> (Get-EC2SecurityGroup -GroupId sg-6fd1361e).IpPermissions |Format-Table -AutoSize
PS C:\> $ip1 = @{ IpProtocol="tcp"; FromPort="22"; ToPort="22"; IpRanges="0.0.0.0/0" }
PS C:\> $ip2 = @{ IpProtocol="tcp"; FromPort="3389"; ToPort="3389"; IpRanges="0.0.0.0/0" }
PS C:\> Grant-EC2SecurityGroupIngress -GroupId sg-6fd1361e -IpPermission @( $ip1, $ip2 )
PS C:\> (Get-EC2SecurityGroup -GroupId sg-6fd1361e).IpPermissions |Format-Table -AutoSize

FromPort IpProtocol IpRanges   Ipv6Ranges PrefixListIds ToPort UserIdGroupPairs UserIdGroupPair IpRange
-------- ---------- --------   ---------- ------------- ------ --------------- --------------- -------
      22 tcp        {0.0.0.0/0} {}              {}          22 {}              {}              {0.0.0.0/0}
    3389 tcp        {0.0.0.0/0} {}              {}        3389 {}              {}              {0.0.0.0/0}
```

I suggest that you always make use of `GroupID` instead of `GroupName`. If you use `GroupName`, it will try to search the group in the default VPC. If you use `GroupID`, it will go through and automatically associate it with the VPC for which you created the Security Group. If you are not familiar about the CIDR block notation, then `0.0.0.0/0` indicates that that source is from anywhere in the world. As long as there is access to an instance, you will be allowed when `IpRange` is `0.0.0.0/0`. It is not necessary that you need to always set that. You can also specify your own IP address to allow the traffic just from your workstation. Practice *The Principle of Least Privilege* in this case as well.

Summary

Building network components carefully on AWS is a key for your cloud success. This helps you design your portion of the cloud securely. Remember that security in the cloud is a shared responsibility. Designing and securing your own network falls under the customer area of responsibility. AWS Virtual Private Cloud can help you to define, isolate, and secure your network in the cloud. In addition, it provides you with an ability to extend your on-premise network to the cloud. We have discussed several VPC components in the chapter, which form the basis for your AWS network. Understanding how to build your wall brick by brick helps you in designing your network. We have seen several key components such as Route Tables, IGW, NAT Gateway, Subnets, NACL, and Security Groups. In the next chapter, you will learn how to spin up resources in the VPC that you built.

6

AWS Elastic Compute Cloud

AWS **Elastic Compute Cloud** (**EC2**) is the first service that AWS launched back in 2006. AWS EC2 is nothing but servers in the cloud known as **EC2 instances**. When AWS first launched this service, it only offered one type of EC2 instance to the customer, which was **m1.small** with 1vCPU, 1.7 GiB RAM, and 160 GB of storage. It was supported only on the Linux platform and was offered with on-demand pricing. This is called a first generation type of instances and number 1 in **m1.small** indicates the generation number. Though it was only one type of instance offered by AWS, it was a very attractive offering for the customer because of the **on-demand** pricing nature of the computing. This really formed the basis for further innovation in cloud computing for AWS. Considering the humongous success of the EC2 on-demand offering and understanding customer expectations, AWS released various types of instance categories every year. Today, there are a number of instance categories to choose from. Note that the **instance category** and the **instance family** are used interchangeably. Here are all the types of instance families available currently on AWS:

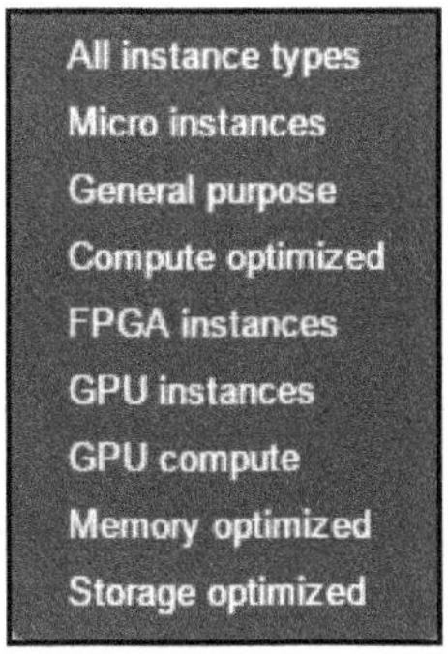

All instance types

Micro instances

General purpose

Compute optimized

FPGA instances

GPU instances

GPU compute

Memory optimized

Storage optimized

Under each instance family, you find that there are different models available. These models are named **m4.large**, **c4.large**, **c4.xlarge**, and so on. These models represent the vCPU, RAM, storage, and bandwidth for the EC2 instance. There are many models available under each family to choose from. In the following example, you will see that for the compute family, there are several other models available. You can choose the one that best fits your needs.

Model	vCPU	Mem (GiB)	Storage	Dedicated EBS Bandwidth (Mbps)
c4.large	2	3.75	EBS-Only	500
c4.xlarge	4	7.5	EBS-Only	750
c4.2xlarge	8	15	EBS-Only	1,000
c4.4xlarge	16	30	EBS-Only	2,000
c4.8xlarge	36	60	EBS-Only	4,000

Several models are created by which you can achieve vertical and horizontal Scaling-In the cloud when needed. If you look at the models, they are almost double in size than the previous one. The keyword after the dot in the model numbers is analogous to the t-shirt sizes that we buy, such as large, x-large, 2x-large, and so on. These sizes represent the instance size available under each model. These models provide flexibility to the customer to start with minimal capacity and scale to the larger instance size only when needed.

Currently, here are some of the abbreviations used by AWS for the instance family:

- **General purpose or multi-purpose**: m
- **Compute optimized**: c

- **Memory optimized or RAM optimized**: r or x
- **GPU optimized**: g, p, or f
- **Storage optimized**: d
- **IO optimized**: i
- **Low cost, burstable performance**: t

EC2 is a really big topic to discuss and is a basis for every other service that AWS offers. You can find the details of each instance family and its related models at `https://aws.amazon.com/ec2/instance-types/`. It's better to refer to this web page frequently to check what type of instance family is introduced, updated, and added by AWS. This page is frequently updated and I see that every other month, something new is added.

In this chapter, we will discuss the characteristics offered by EC2, various purchasing options, understanding various IP addresses on EC2, and storage options on EC2. In addition, we will learn how to spin up and work around EC2 instances for your day-to-day tasks.

The characteristics of AWS EC2

AWS EC2 is a truly virtual computing environment, which provides you with re-sizable compute capacity in the cloud with the intention of making cloud computing easier. You get a variety of operating systems to choose from, and you can run as many as you want or as few servers as you desire. The basic characteristics of the AWS EC2 service are:

- **Elasticity**: It allows you to increase and decrease the capacity based on your needs.
- **Fully controlled**: You get a root/administrator access to each EC2 instance. You can control start, stop, and restart using the AWS console, through CLI, or API.
- **Flexible**: You get multiple instance types that you can choose from with different operating systems.
- **Scalable**: You can achieve vertical and horizontal scaling when needed.
- **Reliable**: Instances can be rapidly and predictably provisioned.
- **Secure**: It works in conjunction with AWS VPC, which provides you with an isolated network in the cloud.
- **Inexpensive**: You get instances with an on-demand pricing option, which you pay for hourly, with no commitment.
- **Easy to spin**: Using existing images, you just spin up EC2 instances in a minute.

The EC2 instance purchasing options

AWS offers several purchasing options to the customer and allow customers to choose the best option that fits their workload. Almost every customer goes for a mix of purchasing options, which allows you to save a lot and satisfy the workload requirements.

On-demand

This is the first default option that usually customers start with on AWS. Under this purchasing option, you pay for the compute capacity by the hour with no long-term commitments. You spin up the EC2 instance when you need it and destroy it when you are done. You only get charged for the time that you use the compute capacity. This option is very attractive to support spiky workloads or when you do not have any clarity on the capacity that you need to start with.

Reserved

Under this purchasing option, you commit to AWS that you need a compute capacity for a certain number of years. You can either make a low one-time payment or a lump-sum payment to receive a significant discount on the hourly charge. This is the most suitable option for running RDBMS database servers. If you know the demand of your application workload, this is the option that you can think of so that you never run out of capacity in the given availability zone.

Spot

This is a very interesting option that AWS offers to the customer. Spot instances are spare EC2 instances on AWS cloud. When you have time insensitive or transient workloads, this purchasing option is something you can think of. Under this option, you bid for unused capacity on the AWS cloud. The price that you get depends on the real-time supply and demand. When your bid price exceeds the spot price and if the spot capacity is available, your spot instance is launched and will keep running until the spot market price exceeds your bid. You only get 2 minutes of warning before the spot instance is terminated. Hence, you have to make use of spot instances in such a way that you are not losing any data.

Dedicated

AWS has a dedicated hardware option as well. Under this purchasing option, your EC2 instances will be hosted only on the hardware dedicated to your account. This option is more suitable for the **Bring Your Own License** (**BYOL**) and for highly sensitive/regulated workloads. Because you get a dedicated host under this option, it is a highly costly option offered by AWS as compared to the other purchasing options.

Understanding IP addresses on EC2

This is a very common topic of confusion when you start working on EC2. So, let's discuss some of the aspects with regards to IP addressing on EC2. There are two types of IP addresses that EC2 instances can have. One is the public IP address and the other one is a private IP address. As you know, public IP addresses can be reached over the internet, whereas a private IP address cannot. It's very important for you to understand the IP addressing on the EC2 instance in order to design your fault tolerant and highly available environment. Once you launch an EC2 instance, it is assigned a private IP address at boot time, and the IP address is picked up from the subnet range in which you can launch the EC2 instance. So, every time you launch an EC2 instance, it will have a private IP address assigned. However, you can have public IP addresses assigned to the EC2 instance if you want it at boot time or later. This means your single EC2 instance can have both IP addresses--**public** and **private**. An EC2 instance private IP address will never change during the lifespan of that EC2 instance, but the public IP address can change in some situations.

When the EC2 instance is rebooted, AWS reboots the same virtual machine. The original virtual machine assigned to your EC2 instance is not returned back to AWS. In this case, the public IP address assigned to the EC2 instance will not change. When you stop an EC2 instance, the associated virtual machine is returned to AWS, and when you restart an EC2 instance, a new virtual machine is provisioned for you, so the EC2 instance will have a new public IP address.

Storage options on EC2

There are couple of storage options available to you when you make use of EC2. The first one is an instance storage and the other one is the Elastic Block Storage.

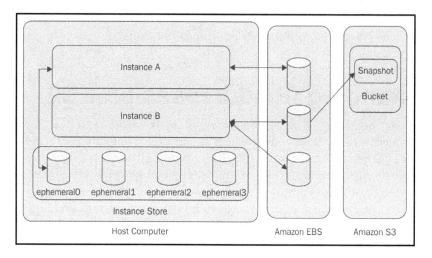

Instance storage

Instance storage comes with the host computer and is physically attached to the host computer. Instance storage comes with SSD and HDD offerings. The data on instance store is ephemeral in nature. This is also called a non-persistent data store. The amount of storage and the type that you get is totally dependent on the instance type. The data on the instance store is dependent upon the instance lifecycle. The instance store data persists only when the operating system in the EC2 instance is rebooted or the instance is restarted. The data on instance store is lost when an underlying drive fails, and the instance is terminated, or the EBS-backed instance has stopped. There are some situations where you could still use instance stores, as they are physically attached to the host computer and offer excellent performance. They also offer performance without IO restrictions. Other things that you should know about the instance store is that the data on the instance store is not replicated, and there is no out-of-the-box support for backups and snapshots. In case you want to replicate the data on the instance store, then you have to manually implement replication at the OS level.

Elastic Block Storage

Elastic Block Storage (**EBS**) is a block storage as a service. Because it is a service, it is massively distributed on the physical hardware. You can create and attach EBS volumes using the console, CLI, or API. EBS volumes are network attached devices and automatically replicate within the availability zone in which they are created. They are tightly integrated with S3 for snapshotting. We will see more about S3 in the next chapter. Because they are a network attached storage, you can use EBS-optimized instances to deliver dedicated Throughput between EC2 and EBS. You can use EBS for a persistent block-level storage. The data on EBS volumes is independent of the instance lifecycle. You can attach multiple volumes to one EC2 instance but cannot assign the same volume to multiple EC2 instances at a time. When you attach an EBS volume to the running instance, it will be automatically detached when the instance is terminated with the data intact on the volume, whereas EBS volumes that are created and attached to an EC2 instance at launch time, are deleted when the instance is terminated. However, you can modify this behavior by changing the value of the flag, `DeleteOnTermination`.

Spinning up an EC2 instance

Before you spin up any EC2 instance, you need to have some information available. Firstly, you should create an RSA key pair , save, and secure it. In addition, you have to choose an AMI. And then you need to know your network details such as VpcID, subnet, and Security Groups. We have already gone through the process of creating various network components. Refer to the previous chapter for more details. If you do not specify anything, defaults will be used for EC2. Let's get started.

To create a RSA key pair, you can use the following command:

```
PS C:\> (New-EC2KeyPair -KeyName "MyWebPressApp").KeyMaterial | Out-File
C:\AWSKey\MyWebPressApp.pem
```

```
PS C:\> (New-EC2KeyPair -KeyName "MyWebPressApp").KeyMaterial | Out-File C:\AWSKey\MyWebPressApp.pem
PS C:\> Get-Content -Raw C:\AWSKey\MyWebPressApp.pem
-----BEGIN RSA PRIVATE KEY-----
MIIEpAIBAAKCAQEAuW+Vr7gwIq1h/VdbLyQOhg+DOH2Pc0ngbhSrXWVAo+2oVH/wii4we+LoDSL8
J9nr3C95zRlebBDW64WkMSDWNCrjvdctgYpVUdxRgpFItZO9C1ysHwuHEI7Oo9IwVGFGJIdmOeso
5wL7NWPj3f+bO42DszpuA9IlF8ykmbVrRvwDgxIB7AD4kkRyzfq47YBpimPcPRmhN3znBYwjZcD/
rz4A02+w6BYpsGBnPw04gTVmF314aBBLuN+35B/5o+kBLw2/vLlMWEJjVaO026RtLodJrXroFpO2
grINgjuUw5VfNyoolqMuUYqI4+g8nz3NZXfXWls1eUYnEGXb96vXyQIDAQABAoIBAQC5Et5B18Ir
CgLvt70hKop4UIk121NNzGD7XRO/TiwasDq9w0d0klT/gHL7kXw7Ret6QcP96KDtmEz4mdRK2CwR
uvC760PWszr+Tbboapo353DZIzACeB3gb7dbl4921/MKyDxF+CdFkRspqT2mttK2uEHGor1kgNtW
in+JjaC5IWAbeCdi5M/Vwyzr8gM8RYu+bitOvuSYDKciGs3Wq/RMO3mNovU0fg3riHZaM96vlPDh
j0/MQHVjaeU9I9omMHItCrZlJ71QcZ2UMgz3ZKdQdwZN1lfsxUb60UzDnKl8/yH1fquQJpiCGsfr
oJKmCiX3BFtjcrByhqadwVz90k0RAoGBAOKgD0T6FsHjgiFK+FDCEfRHOU+gPnwbJpgDlQaw52V7
R9eIByGCrD4E8GVbuXPMRlRuTfkhsmOLOxtMEb4oSpUH2qjn8kaOGRRQqxnMJTvbFuQ/Gnq/AfiJ
s9Kwod/C5RjqLg/eT1YFzzXSrkqA+U8FznhpUph5mpETy7FtbjF9AoGBANF4xMVZC5xQC1GL5+LU
/8xZZKm0X5x8ndNN1tC9sDGw7WIngTzL/Iv/Y0WvS7vVFGO2Y9rkQPovtFm/2+M3yi1+oJK1XU3f
vRVOh3fFi+Lqa/V194uMcMTdUThofiM5tFEoHi2R2Zj9oEmhIthh4z4fn0eHnTzVv7DRgc61f9E9
AoGAdFYsYIFtq0zKYaL1xDdMFjV14z1ktjsN3d2A5DVuJDdcEvWei4JUP2YzriSfGCXWOMODPZAh
zl4MEqBDP3XZi5XDlw+y3KtXjok2vICC4K5Amx0Vz8s8DMVLza2k+4RGLTsSOE0sNwG2dG/Zzx9U
XE+jxUZ0Axfx0+Xwm/2MItUCgYEAsOVNPt+m6H4biKwewqdf8gGYCdyiVbPDULvOam+WiRBCF/8G
nAIkH1IoUqPr0A7s7hwMDcFuwhlhM93bYvItUeg60EpLJkWJF6I+sr3oGVQgoaTizT1nykigm4Na
6oKFDMf1XERsP1AIecWTeKqJzl/EEhMLjWFxRXBYL+mErH0CgYBi2XuWjDwcdg3aznG9jkMfvEnV
wQFR+r+GZF0MYp75TK+E56MhSYc4e8j6CMJji3wfJxqQNeNFL/fsiE/RTeO2H9opIygdTGafA56u
MxVK/fr9PxIASCxWBbWH+lUl1bBp3UWuyqFjgPcn1ZUNB4eD/00LCk8PUzZJKGLWqgPuOA==
-----END RSA PRIVATE KEY-----
```

`New-EC2KeyPair` lets you create the key pair for your EC2 instance. The key pair is a combination of the public and private keys. AWS stores the public key, and you would be prompted to download or to save a private key. You can only create 5,000 keys in the region. As usual, for lifting the limit, you need to contact AWS.

The sample key created is stored in the file called `MyWebPressApp.pem`. The content of the file is displayed for clarity. So, we now have an RSA key called `MyWebPressApp` ready to use. You can use the same key to spin up a Linux or Windows EC2 instance if needed. To list all the EC2 key pair in the region, you use this:

```
PS C:\> Get-EC2KeyPair
```

```
PS C:\> Get-EC2KeyPair

KeyFingerprint                                               KeyName
--------------                                               -------
f3:fe:95:08:4d:b0:50:0f:ef:0d:ef:cf:a5:8a:b3:48:b3:50:c4:a8  AWSBastion
71:4a:a0:b9:a2:74:dd:b5:de:b4:88:8b:9d:33:ae:5e:1e:73:81:b5  Mysql
bc:44:f7:48:6a:47:ca:e6:af:cf:97:a3:48:a8:d3:98:90:b2:07:06  MyWebPressApp
56:dc:ae:80:2d:c0:31:8f:a8:f9:2c:40:5d:38:95:9e:79:94:2e:2d  PowerShell
d5:4a:b6:7c:a1:a0:8d:3c:8f:f9:c5:36:7f:f4:94:b5:7d:61:82:46  winkey
```

Now, you need to know the AMI ID that you can make use of. `Get-EC2Image` lists the AMI available to you and includes the public images, private images that you own, and private images owned by other AWS accounts but for which you have explicit launch permissions:

```
PS C:\ Get-EC2Image
```

This returns a big list if you are not filtering it properly, hence my advice is that you make use of the AWS console and pick up the AMI ID from there. It is easy to scan through the GUI and pick up the best one suited for your needs:

Be aware of the fact that you could be using the AWS console for viewing your services for your day-to-day work. It is easy to navigate and review your AWS services and components using the AWS console. PowerShell helps you to automate your tasks. Hence, you will be using a combination of both the styles whenever needed.

To get the list of all EC2 instance cmdlets, you can use the following command:

```
PS C:\> Get-Command *EC2Instance*
```

To launch an EC2 instance, run the following command:

```
PS C:\> New-EC2Instance -ImageId ami-c58c1dd3 -AssociatePublicIp $true -
MinCount 1 -MaxCount 1 -SubnetId subnet-c843dd80 -InstanceType t2.micro -
KeyName MyWebPressApp -SecurityGroupId sg-9ec521ef
```

AsscociatePublicIP switch allocates a public IP to the EC2 instance. SubnetID is the subnet in which you want to run the EC2 instance. InstanceType indicates the model that you can use which is a combination of vCPU, RAM, and network bandwidth. KeyName is the RSA key needed for you to login to the servers when there is a need. SecurityGroup is the group for which you defined the ingress appropriately.

To get the list of running EC2 instances, you run the following command:

```
PS C:\> Get-EC2Instance |Format-Table -AutoSize
```

```
PS C:\> Get-EC2Instance |Format-Table -AutoSize

GroupNames Groups Instances        OwnerId      RequesterId ReservationId        RunningInstance
---------- ------ ---------        -------      ----------- -------------        ---------------
{}         {}     {PowerShell}     072316406132             r-03b32f874f10767da  {PowerShell}
{}         {}     {MyWebPressApp}  072316406132             r-084e0e042ac3f4b4a  {MyWebPressApp}
```

There are two EC2 instances running as shown in the output. In this output, you only see the reservation ID for each EC2 instance, which is unique when you deal via PowerShell. In this case, the instance that we launched is the one with the reservation ID `r-084e0e042ac3f4b4a`. To get the details about the instance, you need to expand the collection using the reservation ID. You can do this as:

```
PS C:\> (Get-EC2Instance -Filter @{ Name="reservation-id";
Values="r-084e0e042ac3f4b4a" }).Instances
```

```
PS C:\> (Get-EC2Instance -Filter @{ Name="reservation-id"; Values="r-084e0e042ac3f4b4a" }).Instances

AmiLaunchIndex        : 0
Architecture          : x86_64
BlockDeviceMappings   : {/dev/xvda}
ClientToken           :
EbsOptimized          : False
EnaSupport            : True
Hypervisor            : xen
IamInstanceProfile    :
ImageId               : ami-c58c1dd3
InstanceId            : i-0cab647fc9e824f2c
InstanceLifecycle     :
InstanceType          : t2.micro
KernelId              :
KeyName               : MyWebPressApp
LaunchTime            : 6/15/2017 2:37:38 PM
Monitoring            : Amazon.EC2.Model.Monitoring
NetworkInterfaces     : {ip-10-0-2-122.ec2.internal}
Placement             : Amazon.EC2.Model.Placement
Platform              :
PrivateDnsName        : ip-10-0-2-122.ec2.internal
PrivateIpAddress      : 10.0.2.122
ProductCodes          : {}
PublicDnsName         : ec2-54-209-21-209.compute-1.amazonaws.com
PublicIpAddress       : 54.209.21.209
RamdiskId             :
RootDeviceName        : /dev/xvda
RootDeviceType        : ebs
SecurityGroups        : {bastion_ps}
SourceDestCheck       : True
SpotInstanceRequestId :
SriovNetSupport       :
State                 : Amazon.EC2.Model.InstanceState
StateReason           :
StateTransitionReason :
SubnetId              : subnet-c843dd80
Tags                  : {}
VirtualizationType    : hvm
VpcId                 : vpc-a6bb60df
```

You can see that InstanceID is i-0cab647fc9e824f2c, which you would be mostly using in your scripting for all kinds of operations on AWS and not the reservation ID. Public and private IPs for the instance are also seen as part of the output, which is needed to connect to the instance. Other networking details such as the subnet ID and the associated VPC is also displayed for you to confirm that the instance is running in the subnet assigned by you at the time of launch. There are other variants of the Get-EC2Instance cmdlet, which you can review using the online help posted on the AWS site.

Accessing the EC2 instance

For an EC2 instance that we have created earlier, the public IP is 54.209.21.209. To ease the connectivity demonstration, I spun up the EC2 server in the public subnet. You should follow the appropriate practice in your environment to get connected to your EC2 instance. Whether to use the bastion server, build IPsec VPN, or use direct connect is something you need to think about, considering your network infrastructure requirement. In order to access the EC2 instance, ensure that you have the OpenSSH module installed in your PowerShell environment. Microsoft announced OpenSSH support on PowerShell in 2015. You can download the OpenSSH from https://github.com/PowerShell/Win32-OpenSSH /releases, and follow the instructions posted on https://github.com/PowerShell/Win 32-OpenSSH/wiki/Install-Win32-OpenSSH. This is not the only way that you can get connected to EC2 instances; there are multiple ways in which you can do so. But considering the Windows environment and the PowerShell capability, you can plan to install the OpenSSH Windows module as mentioned on the link and establish the connectivity to the EC2 instance. I installed the OpenSSH module in the C:\Program File\OpenSSH directory and created an alias using the following command:

```
PS C:\> Set-Alias ssh 'c:\Program Files\Openssh\ssh.exe'
```

Then, simply using the `ssh` program and the RSA private key for the instance, you can connect:

```
PS C:\> ssh -i 'C:\Users\ramesh\AWSKey\MyWebPressApp.pem' ec2-
user@54.209.21.209
```

```
PS C:\> Set-Alias ssh 'c:\Program Files\Openssh\ssh.exe'
PS C:\> get-alias ssh

CommandType     Name                                               Version    Source
-----------     ----                                               -------    ------
Alias           ssh -> ssh.exe

PS C:\> ssh -i 'C:\Users\ramesh\AWSKey\MyWebPressApp.pem' ec2-user@54.209.21.209
Last login: Thu Jun 15 23:24:37 2017 from ppp118-210-156-36.bras1.adl6.internode.on.net

       __|  __|_  )
       _|  (     /   Amazon Linux AMI
      ___|\___|___|

https://aws.amazon.com/amazon-linux-ami/2017.03-release-notes/
8 package(s) needed for security, out of 12 available
Run "sudo yum update" to apply all updates.
[ec2-user@ip-10-0-2-122 ~]$ sudo su - root
Last login: Thu Jun 15 23:24:56 UTC 2017 on pts/0
[root@ip-10-0-2-122 ~]#
```

If you are a seasoned Windows professional, then you can also make use of **Cygwin**. It can be downloaded from `https://cygwin.com/install.html`. Pick up the 32-bit or 64-bit version depending on your version of Windows. The installation is straightforward; follow the instructions and proceed. Just make sure that you are choosing the `openssh` package while doing the install, otherwise ssh may not be available. Cygwin is a UNIX-like environment and CLI for the Windows platform. It is easy to install and set up. You then place the RSA private key that you created in the directory created in Cygwin and get connected. You can also use Putty, but for Putty, you need to convert the PEM key to the format that is understood by Putty.

```
$ ls -ltr
total 4
-r-------- 1 ramesh ramesh 1676 Jun 15 19:21 MyWebPressApp.pem

ramesh@apps1 ~/AWSKey
$ ssh -i "MyWebPressApp.pem" ec2-user@54.209.21.209
The authenticity of host '54.209.21.209 (54.209.21.209)' can't be established.
ECDSA key fingerprint is SHA256:w1VQo5RLAwajWD5Fxaq4HYc3L1RuKev1T/j8Z027ZUk.
Are you sure you want to continue connecting (yes/no)? yes
Warning: Permanently added '54.209.21.209' (ECDSA) to the list of known hosts.

       __|  __|_  )
       _|  (     /   Amazon Linux AMI
      ___|\___|___|

https://aws.amazon.com/amazon-linux-ami/2017.03-release-notes/
8 package(s) needed for security, out of 12 available
Run "sudo yum update" to apply all updates.
[ec2-user@ip-10-0-2-122 ~]$ sudo su - root
[root@ip-10-0-2-122 ~]# df -h
Filesystem      Size  Used Avail Use% Mounted on
devtmpfs        488M   56K  488M   1% /dev
tmpfs           497M     0  497M   0% /dev/shm
/dev/xvda1      7.8G  975M  6.8G  13% /
```

In both the cases mentioned earlier, you must ensure that you have restricted permission on the RSA key file; otherwise, you won't be able to establish connectivity. On Windows, do not keep the file permissions too open; and on Linux, you must ensure that it is set to 400.

For a Windows-based EC2 login, you have to get the EC2 password using the `Get-EC2PasswordData` cmdlet, then you can use the `Enter-PSSession` cmdlet to log into the server. I have a Windows-based server spun up the same way as I did the Linux EC2 instance by changing the AMI ID. Get the instance ID for the reservation ID and pull out the EC2 password. You can use the following method to hop on to the Windows EC2 server:

```
PS C:\> $ip = "54.157.244.96"
PS C:\> Set-Item WSMan:\localhost\Client\TrustedHosts $ip
PS C:\> Get-EC2PasswordData -InstanceId i-00dd7a63ca4db18f1 -PemFile
C:\Users\ramesh\AWSKey\MyWebPressApp.pem
PS C:\> Enter-PSSession -ComputerName $ip -Credential ~\Administrator
```

Alternatively, you can type `mstsc` at the PowerShell prompt to get the RDP connection window, which will allow you to supply the administrator user and password to an EC2 instance.

The EC2 instance metadata service

The EC2 instance metadata is the data about your running instance, which can be accessed within the instance itself. This instance data is very useful when you need some details programmatically, such as an instance ID, public IP or private IP, and so on. You can also access user data using the instance metadata that you supply at the time of the EC2 instance launch. You can use the following URL to view all the categories of the instance metadata from within a running instance:

```
http://169.254.169.254/latest/meta-data/
```

You can use a tool such as `curl` to access the instance metadata:

```
curl http://169.254.169.254/latest/meta-data/
```

```
[root@ip-10-0-2-122 ~]# curl http://169.254.169.254/latest/meta-data/
ami-id
ami-launch-index
ami-manifest-path
block-device-mapping/
hostname
instance-action
instance-id
instance-type
local-hostname
local-ipv4
mac
metrics/
network/
placement/
profile
public-hostname
public-ipv4
public-keys/
reservation-id
security-groups
services/[root@ip-10-0-2-122 ~]#
```

These are some of the examples of the instance metadata that you can use:

```
[root@ip-10-0-2-122 ~]# curl http://169.254.169.254/latest/meta-data/instance-id;echo
i-0cab647fc9e824f2c
[root@ip-10-0-2-122 ~]# curl http://169.254.169.254/latest/meta-data/public-ipv4;echo
54.209.21.209
[root@ip-10-0-2-122 ~]# curl http://169.254.169.254/latest/meta-data/hostname;echo
ip-10-0-2-122.ec2.internal
[root@ip-10-0-2-122 ~]# curl http://169.254.169.254/latest/meta-data/ami-id;echo
ami-c58c1dd3
[root@ip-10-0-2-122 ~]# curl http://169.254.169.254/latest/meta-data/local-ipv4;echo
10.0.2.122
```

The user metadata can be accessed using the following command:

```
curl http://169.254.169.254/latest/user-data
```

Stopping the EC2 instance

For stopping an EC2 instance via PowerShell, you can use the `Stop-EC2Instance` cmdlet. You need to use an instance ID with the cmdlet. You can get an instance ID using the `Get-EC2Instance` cmdlet by passing the instance reservation ID. EC2 instances that use Amazon EBS volumes as their root devices can be quickly stopped and started via PowerShell. When an EC2 instance is stopped, the compute resources are released; and you are not billed for an hourly instance usage for the instance. Even though you stop the instance, you will still have your root partition holding data on the EBS volume, and you are charged for EBS volume usage. You can restart your instance at any time.

To stop an EC2 instance, you can use this:

```
PS C:\> Stop-EC2Instance -InstanceId i-0cab647fc9e824f2c
```

```
PS C:\> (Get-EC2Instance -Filter @{ Name="reservation-id"; Values="r-084e0e042ac3f4b4a" }).instances.instanceid
i-0cab647fc9e824f2c
PS C:\> (Get-EC2Instance -Filter @{ Name="reservation-id"; Values="r-084e0e042ac3f4b4a" }).instances.state

Code Name
---- ----
16   running


PS C:\> Stop-EC2Instance -InstanceId i-0cab647fc9e824f2c

CurrentState                  InstanceId          PreviousState
------------                  ----------          -------------
Amazon.EC2.Model.InstanceState i-0cab647fc9e824f2c Amazon.EC2.Model.InstanceState


PS C:\> (Get-EC2Instance -Filter @{ Name="reservation-id"; Values="r-084e0e042ac3f4b4a" }).instances.instanceid
i-0cab647fc9e824f2c
PS C:\> (Get-EC2Instance -Filter @{ Name="reservation-id"; Values="r-084e0e042ac3f4b4a" }).instances.state

Code Name
---- ----
80   stopped
```

Starting the EC2 instance

`Start-EC2Instance` lets you start the EC2 instance. Even though you are not billed for the compute power when an instance is stopped, you would still be charged for the EBS volume attached to those instances. Additionally, AWS charges you for an extra hour when instances are transitioning from one state to another. To start an EC2 instance, you can run this:

```
PS C:\> Start-EC2Instance -InstanceId i-0cab647fc9e824f2c
```

```
PS C:\> (Get-EC2Instance -Filter @{ Name="reservation-id"; Values="r-084e0e042ac3f4b4a" }).instances.instanceid
i-0cab647fc9e824f2c
PS C:\> (Get-EC2Instance -Filter @{ Name="reservation-id"; Values="r-084e0e042ac3f4b4a" }).instances.state

Code Name
---- ----
80   stopped


PS C:\> Start-EC2Instance -InstanceId i-0cab647fc9e824f2c

CurrentState                  InstanceId          PreviousState
------------                  ----------          -------------
Amazon.EC2.Model.InstanceState i-0cab647fc9e824f2c Amazon.EC2.Model.InstanceState


PS C:\> (Get-EC2Instance -Filter @{ Name="reservation-id"; Values="r-084e0e042ac3f4b4a" }).instances.instanceid
i-0cab647fc9e824f2c
PS C:\> (Get-EC2Instance -Filter @{ Name="reservation-id"; Values="r-084e0e042ac3f4b4a" }).instances.state

Code Name
---- ----
16   running
```

The Elastic IP address

As discussed in the earlier section, public IP addresses assigned to the EC2 instance can change when an EC2 instance is stopped and started. An Elastic IP address is a static IP address specifically designed for the dynamic nature of cloud computing. Public IPs and Elastic IP addresses are both public, and they both allow an EC2 instance to communicate over the internet. The Elastic IP address and public IP addresses differ in how long they are associated with the specific EC2 instance. When you stop an EC2 instance, the public IP address is released back to the Amazon public pool, and when you restart an instance, you get a new public IP address for your EC2 instance from the Amazon pool. The Elastic IP address is allocated in the AWS account and associated with an EC2 instance until it's disassociated from it. AWS will charge you for an Elastic IP address if it is associated with an instance that is not running.

A common reason to use an Elastic IP address is the ability to associate it with the active EC2 instance; and if there is a failure, it offers an ability to quickly disassociate it from a failed instance and re-associate it to the new instance. Elastic IP addresses are region specific, and you can use them across multiple availability zones.

`New-EC2Address` acquires an Elastic IP address in the region. An Elastic IP address can still be used in the **EC2-Classic** platform. You can also use it in a VPC for EC2 instances. To create a new Elastic IP, you can run this:

```
PS C:\> New-EC2Address -Domain Vpc
```

`Register-EC2Address` lets you associate an Elastic IP address with an EC2 instance. In case the specified Elastic IP is associated with any existing instance, then AWS disassociates that one from that instance and associates it with the one that you specified to attach it with. Likewise, if your instance has an Elastic IP address associated already, then the Elastic IP is disassociated from the instance and a new one is attached:

```
PS C:\> Register-EC2Address -InstanceId i-0cab647fc9e824f2c -PublicIp
52.22.141.99
```

In the preceding example, I have assigned an EIP created to the instance having a public IP. Now, the EC2 instance public IP will survive the stop and start. It will remain the same until you disassociate it.

```
PS C:\> (Get-EC2Instance -Filter @{ Name="reservation-id"; Values="r-084e0e042ac3f4b4a" }).instances.instanceid
i-0cab647fc9e824f2c
PS C:\> (Get-EC2Instance -Filter @{ Name="reservation-id"; Values="r-084e0e042ac3f4b4a" }).instances.PublicIpAddress
52.54.150.159
PS C:\> New-EC2Address -Domain Vpc

AllocationId    Domain PublicIp
------------    ------ --------
eipalloc-2f34941f vpc    52.22.141.99


PS C:\> Register-EC2Address -InstanceId i-0cab647fc9e824f2c -PublicIp 52.22.141.99
eipassoc-2851b91a
PS C:\> (Get-EC2Instance -Filter @{ Name="reservation-id"; Values="r-084e0e042ac3f4b4a" }).instances.instanceid
i-0cab647fc9e824f2c
PS C:\> (Get-EC2Instance -Filter @{ Name="reservation-id"; Values="r-084e0e042ac3f4b4a" }).instances.PublicIpAddress
52.22.141.99
```

Terminating the EC2 instance

PowerShell has a cmdlet that allows you to remove an EC2 Instance from the account if needed. `Remove-EC2Instance` terminates a stopped or running EC2 instance. The operation will be prompting for confirmation before proceeding. Note that the terminated instances will remain visible after termination for approximately 1 hour but will not accessible:

```
PS C:\> Remove-EC2Instance —InstanceId i-0cab647fc9e824f2c
```

```
PS C:\> (Get-EC2Instance -Filter @{ Name="reservation-id"; Values="r-084e0e042ac3f4b4a" }).instances.instanceid
i-0cab647fc9e824f2c
PS C:\> Remove-EC2Instance -InstanceId i-0cab647fc9e824f2c

Confirm
Are you sure you want to perform this action?
Performing the operation "Remove-EC2Instance (TerminateInstances)" on target "i-0cab647fc9e824f2c".
[Y] Yes [A] Yes to All [N] No [L] No to All [S] Suspend [?] Help (default is "Y"): Y

CurrentState                 InstanceId        PreviousState
------------                 ----------        -------------
Amazon.EC2.Model.InstanceState i-0cab647fc9e824f2c Amazon.EC2.Model.InstanceState


PS C:\> (Get-EC2Instance -Filter @{ Name="reservation-id"; Values="r-084e0e042ac3f4b4a" }).instances.State

Code Name
---- ----
32   shutting-down


PS C:\> (Get-EC2Instance -Filter @{ Name="reservation-id"; Values="r-084e0e042ac3f4b4a" }).instances.State

Code Name
---- ----
48   terminated
```

Placement Groups

A Placement Group is a logical group for your EC2 instance in the single availability zone. Note that Placement Groups cannot span across multiple availability zones. So, the scope of the Placement Group is the availability zone and not the region. It allows for massive network Throughput as compared to other EC2 instances. It allows you to minimize the network latency, as it provides 10 Gbps Throughput . Placement Groups are highly recommended for applications and database set ups that benefits from low network latency and high network Throughput, or both.

In addition to the scope of the Placement Group limitation, there are several more additional limitations that you must be aware of. The name that you specify for the Placement Group must be unique in your AWS account. Only certain types of EC2 instances can be launched in the Placement Group and not all. Compute optimized, GPU, memory optimized, and storage optimized are those instance types that can be launched in the Placement Groups. Though you can launch different types of instances in the same Placement Group, AWS recommendation is to use the same instance type for all the instances in the Placement Group. If you have multiple Placement Groups, you cannot merge them. You cannot move an existing EC2 instance in the Placement Group. If there is a need to move the existing instance in the Placement Group, then you create an AMI from the existing EC2 instance and launch a new instance using that newly created AMI in the Placement Group.

To get the list of existing Placement Groups, you can use this:

```
PS C:\> Get-EC2PlacementGroup
```

To create a new Placement Group, you issue this:

```
PS C:\> New-EC2PlacementGroup -GroupName my-app-group -Strategy cluster
```

```
PS C:\> New-EC2PlacementGroup -GroupName my-app-group -Strategy cluster
PS C:\> New-EC2Instance -ImageId ami-c58c1dd3 -AssociatePublicIp $true -MinCount 3 -MaxCount 6 -SubnetId subnet-c843dd80 -InstanceType c4.large -KeyName MyWe
bPressApp -SecurityGroupId sg-9ec521ef -PlacementGroup my-app-group

GroupNames   : {}
Groups       : {}
Instances    : {MyWebPressApp, MyWebPressApp, MyWebPressApp, MyWebPressApp...}
OwnerId      : 072316406132
RequesterId  :
ReservationId : r-00e3f34d511c7be3d
```

PlacementGroup with the New-EC2Instance cmdlet would let you launch EC2 instances in PlacementGroup. You cannot remove the Placement Group if EC2 instances are running in it. You must ensure that all the running EC2 instances are terminated before you plan to remove an EC2 Placement Group. You can use the Remove-EC2PlacementGroup cmdlet for the removal of a Placement Group.

Assigning an IAM role to the EC2 instance

When applications running on EC2 instances need to access other AWS resources, an application needs credentials, such as access key and secret access key. You can distribute access keys and secret access keys with applications to the EC2 instance, but that is not the best practice. IAM roles are designed in such a way that your applications can make API requests from your EC2 instances without requiring you to manage any security credentials that application needs. Instead, you can assign an IAM role to the EC2 instance that has permissions but does not have any long-term credentials. For example, you can use IAM roles to grant permissions to applications running on your EC2 instances that needs to use a bucket in Amazon S3. You can specify permissions for IAM roles by creating a policy in the JSON format. These are similar to the policies that you create for IAM users. If you make a change to a role, the change is propagated to all the instances. We have seen example of creating role in `Chapter 4`, *AWS Identity and Access Management*.

In order to assign a role to the EC2 instance, first create an instance profile using the `New-IAMInstanceProfile` cmdlet. You can do this as:

PS C:\> New-IAMInstanceProfile –InstanceProfileName S3AccessProfile

```
PS C:\> New-IAMInstanceProfile -InstanceProfileName S3AccessProfile


Arn               : arn:aws:iam::072316406132:instance-profile/S3AccessProfile
CreateDate        : 6/16/2017 4:40:49 PM
InstanceProfileId : AIPAIGXFFJU3ODWHG2PRQ
InstanceProfileName : S3AccessProfile
Path              : /
Roles             : {}
```

Then, add an IAM role to the created instance profile using `Add-IAMRoleToInstanceProfile`:

PS C:\> Add-IAMRoleToInstanceProfile –InstanceProfileName S3AccessProfile –RoleName WorldPressAppRole

You can now use the instance profile to launch an instance. You use a switch called `InstanceProfile_Name` with the `New-EC2Instance` cmdlet.

```
PS C:\> Add-IAMRoleToInstanceProfile -InstanceProfileName S3AccessProfile -RoleName WorldPressAppRole
PS C:\> New-EC2Instance -ImageId ami-c58c1dd3 -AssociatePublicIp $true -MinCount 1 -MaxCount 1 -SubnetId subnet-c843dd80 -InstanceType t2.micro -KeyName MyWebPressApp -SecurityGroupId sg-9ec521ef -InstanceProfile_Name S3AccessProfile


GroupNames    : {}
Groups        : {}
Instances     : {MyWebPressApp}
OwnerId       : 072316406132
RequesterId   :
ReservationId : r-00f0f90d2e69829d0
```

It is possible to detach and reattach a new role now with EC2 instance service. Review some of the online materials associated for this task. If you do not attach a role at the launch time, no worries; you can create a new role and attach it to the running or stopped instance. This is something AWS introduced last year. This was not the possibility prior to 2016.

The types of EBS

There are primarily two types of EBS volumes available for you to choose from. One is based on **Solid State Drive (SSD)** and the other is based on **Hard Disk Drive (HDD)**. EBS is designed for 99.999% service availability and 0.1% to 0.2% **Annual Failure Rate (AFR)**. This means that you may hardly lose 1 to 2 EBS volumes if you are running 1,000 volumes. The industry standard failure rate for the hard drive is around 4%. AWS EBS Volume AFR is far below the industry average, which makes it more suitable to run the production workload. You can choose EBS SSD for your IOPS needs or you can choose EBS HDD for your Throughput needs.

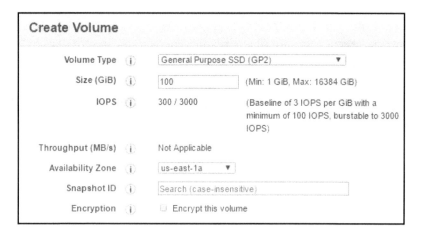

As seen in the preceding screenshot, for creating a volume on the AWS console, EBS SSD permits you to select IOPS and not Throughput. When you select EBS HDD, then you can specify the Throughput that you need. IOPS is a measurement of the number of input/output operations that can be performed in 1 second while Throughput is a measurement of the data that can be transferred in 1 second. You can use a mix of storage types to achieve the best performance. For example, you may want to utilize Provisional IOPS for hosting your database, but you may think of using Throughput which is optimized for backing up the database.

EBS SSD backed volumes

EBS SSD backed volumes are again subdivided into three more categories based on their characteristics:

- General purpose (gp2):
    - Commonly used as the root volume on an EC2 instance
    - Used for development/testing environments and smaller DB instances
    - 3 IOPS/GiB (burstable with baseline performance)
    - Volume size of 1 GiB to 16 TiB
    - Considerations when using T2 instances with SSD root volumes burstable versus baseline performance
- Provisioned IOPS (io1):
    - Mission critical applications that require sustained IOPS performance
    - Large database workloads
    - The volume size of 4 GiB to 16 TiB
    - Performs at provisioned level and can provision up to 20,000 IOPS
- Magnetic:
    - Low storage cost
    - Workloads where performance is not important or data is not frequently accessed
    - Volume size of min 1 GiB and max 1,024 GiB

EBS HDD backed volumes

These types of EBS volumes are the recent addition to the EBS service. EBS HDD are known as low cost and high Throughput volumes:

- Cold (sc1)
    - Lower cost HDD volume as compared to others
    - Designed for large, less frequently accessed, and high Throughput demand workloads
- Throughput optimized (st1):
    - Is again a low cost HDD, but slightly higher than sc1
    - Designed for higher Throughput application workload demanding around 500 MB/s

EBS volumes are available in the availability zone in which they are created. The scope of the EBS volume is the availability zone and not the region. In case you want to move the volume that you created from one availability zone to another, then you have to take the snapshot and copy that snapshot to the other availability zone. You can then use the snapshot to create the new volume. Data on the EBS volumes is replicated in the same availability zone with no additional cost.

EBS also has built-in encryption characteristics. You use it when you need it. Enabling encryption is just like checking one more box. It has out-of-the-box service characteristics provided by AWS. You can encrypt both boot and data volumes if needed. The EC2 instance can have both encrypted and unencrypted volumes attached. By enabling the encryption on the EBS volume, there is no performance impact as such. Encryption is supported on all the EBS volume types. If you take the snapshot on the encrypted EBS volumes, snapshots are encrypted as well.

EBS provides a persistent block storage for the EC2 instance. You can either create or assign EBS volumes at the time of launching an EC2 instance or later. You can get a list of EC2 volume-related cmdlets as follows:

```
PS C:\> Get-Command *EC2Volume*
```

New-EC2Volume creates an EBS volume that can be attached to an instance in the same availability zone.

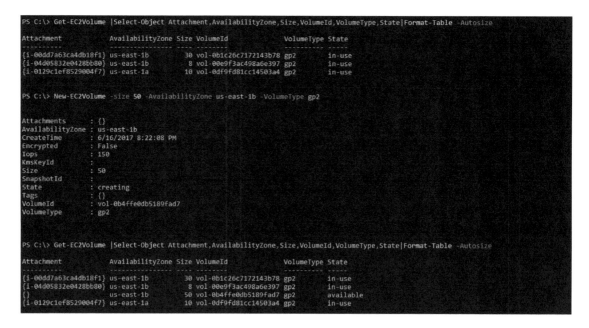

`State` indicates whether the EBS volume is attached to the EC2 instance or not. `in-use` indicates that the EBS volume is attached to an EC2 instance, and `available` means it is not attached to any EC2 instance. You can only attach volumes to an EC2 instance which has a state as `available`. We discussed earlier that there are several types of `Volume` available. Depending on your workload needs, you can choose the volume type. Here are some of the variants of the `New-EC2Volume` cmdlet that you can use:

```
PS C:\> New-EC2Volume -size 50 -AvailabilityZone us-east-1b -VolumeType io1
-Iops 200
PS C:\> New-EC2Volume -size 500 -AvailabilityZone us-east-1b -VolumeType
st1
PS C:\> New-EC2Volume -size 500 -AvailabilityZone us-east-1b -VolumeType
sc1
```

`Add-EC2Volume` attaches an EBS volume to a running or stopped instance and exposes it to the instance with the specified device name:

```
PS C:\> Add-EC2Volume -InstanceId i-0e90b6d5d439175a3 -VolumeId
vol-0b4ffe0db5189fad7 -Device /dev/sdc
```

```
PS C:\> ssh -i 'C:\Users\ramesh\AWSKey\MyWebPressApp.pem' ec2-user@54.175.247.46
Last login: Fri Jun 16 11:00:43 2017 from ppp118-210-156-36.bras1.adl6.internode.on.net

       _|  _|_  )
      _|  (    /   Amazon Linux AMI
      _|\_|_|_|

https://aws.amazon.com/amazon-linux-ami/2017.03-release-notes/
8 package(s) needed for security, out of 12 available
Run "sudo yum update" to apply all updates.
[ec2-user@ip-10-0-2-27 ~]$ ls -ltr /dev/xv*
brw-rw---- 1 root disk 202, 0 Jun 16 10:56 /dev/xvda
brw-rw---- 1 root disk 202, 1 Jun 16 10:56 /dev/xvda1
[ec2-user@ip-10-0-2-27 ~]$ exit
logout
Connection to 54.175.247.46 closed.
PS C:\> Add-EC2Volume -InstanceId i-0e90b6d5d439175a3 -VolumeId vol-0b4ffe0db5189fad7 -Device /dev/sdc


AttachTime          : 6/16/2017 9:02:57 PM
DeleteOnTermination : False
Device              : /dev/sdc
InstanceId          : i-0e90b6d5d439175a3
State               : attaching
VolumeId            : vol-0b4ffe0db5189fad7


PS C:\> ssh -i 'C:\Users\ramesh\AWSKey\MyWebPressApp.pem' ec2-user@54.175.247.46
Last login: Fri Jun 16 11:02:31 2017 from ppp118-210-156-36.bras1.adl6.internode.on.net

       _|  _|_  )
      _|  (    /   Amazon Linux AMI
      _|\_|_|_|

https://aws.amazon.com/amazon-linux-ami/2017.03-release-notes/
8 package(s) needed for security, out of 12 available
Run "sudo yum update" to apply all updates.
[ec2-user@ip-10-0-2-27 ~]$ ls -ltr /dev/xv*
brw-rw---- 1 root disk 202,  0 Jun 16 10:56 /dev/xvda
brw-rw---- 1 root disk 202,  1 Jun 16 10:56 /dev/xvda1
brw-rw---- 1 root disk 202, 32 Jun 16 11:03 /dev/xvdc
[ec2-user@ip-10-0-2-27 ~]$
```

`/dev/xvdc` is attached to the EC2 instance. Note that though we specified a device as `/dev/sdc`, AWS renames those names as `/dev/xvdc`. Usually `s` is replaced by `xv`. I noticed this in all the EC2 instances. Attaching and detaching volumes is easy. You just need to ensure that you are attaching and detaching the right volume; otherwise, you may break your database or application functionality. `Remove-EC2Volume` deletes the specified EBS volume. The volume must be in the available state and not attached to an instance:

```
PS C:\> Remove-EC2Volume -VolumeId vol-0b4ffe0db5189fad7
```

Amazon Machine Images

An **Amazon Machine Image** (**AMI** or **ah-mi**) is a packaged environment containing a software stack along with the required parts to boot and set up an EC2 Instance. AMI is part of the EC2 service and is a basis to build the fault tolerant application. It is a unit of your deployment. You can launch a single EC2 instance or multiple EC2 instances using the same AMI. You can create your own AMIs that correspond to different components, such as those related to web servers, app servers, or database servers. AWS provides a number of ways to create an AMI. You can create an AMI using the AWS console, CLI, or API calls. Here are three type of AMIs that you will find on AWS:

- **Amazon maintained**: These are a set of Linux and Windows images created and maintained by AWS in each region.
- **Community maintained**: These are images published by other AWS users. There are also Linux and Windows-based images. These images are managed and maintained by the AWS marketplace.
- **Own machine images**: These images are created by you in your own account from EC2 instances. You can keep these images as private or shared with other accounts.

An AMI is a vital component used in the deployment methodology of the EC2 instance. There are two different types of deployment considerations you can utilize on the AWS cloud. Whether to choose **Bake an AMI** fully or **Configure Dynamically** depends on your need of bootstrapping of EC2 instances. How soon you want the EC2 instance to join the production service once launched plays a critical role in deciding on the options mentioned here:

- **Bake an AMI**: The baking of an AMI means you configure the EC2 instance first using the Amazon Maintained or Community Maintained AMI, and you then create an AMI from that configured instance, or it means installing/adding all the required software to run your application on the EC2 instance and creating an AMI from that EC2 instance. Because the required software is already installed on the AMI, the EC2 instance does not take a lot of time to be ready for the service. In short, bootstrapping is not a time-consuming task in this case.

- **Configure Dynamically**: In this type of deployment strategy, you have a base AMI, which could be Amazon Maintained, Community Maintained, or your own baked AMI, which is then again updated at the time of launch using the user metadata EC2 service or cloud-init. The downfall of this method is that launching an EC2 instance takes long time. Because of the dynamic nature of the software installation and configuration, bootstrapping is a time-consuming task and may not be ready quickly to join the production instances.

The `New-EC2Image` cmdlet lets you create an AMI from an EC2 instance that can be either running or stopped. In case your customized instance has EBS volumes attached, then the AMI contains some block device mapping information for those volumes. When you use your custom AMI, then AWS will launch an instance with those additional EBS volumes. To get the list of all the AMI-related cmdlets, you can use the following command:

```
PS C:\> Get-Command *EC2Image*
```

To create a new image, you can use `New-EC2Image`:

```
PS C:\> New-EC2Image -InstanceId i-0e90b6d5d439175a3 -Name "my-app-server"
-Description "my app server ami" -NoReboot $true
```

This example creates an AMI with the specified name and description from the specified instance. Amazon EC2 creates the image without shutting down and restarting the instance; therefore, filesystem integrity on the created image can't be guaranteed.

```
PS C:\> New-EC2Image -InstanceId i-0e90b6d5d439175a3 -Name "my-app-server"
-Description "my app server ami"
```

This example creates an AMI with the specified name and description from the specified instance. Amazon EC2 attempts to cleanly shut down the instance before creating the image, and restarts the instance on completion. Filesystem integrity on the created image is guaranteed. This is the recommended way to create images from the EC2 instance. You can get a list of all the AMIs that you created in your own account using this:

```
PS C:\> Get-EC2Image -Owner self |Select-Object
ImageID,Name,State,VirtualizationType|Format-Table -AutoSize
```

EBS snapshots

EBS snapshots are point-in-time copy of your EBS volumes and provide you with disaster recovery solutions for your EBS volumes. You can think of snapshots as full and incremental backups of your EBS volumes. When you create a snapshot of the EBS volume, only the data that is changed since the last snapshot is stored in the new S3 snapshot. In this way, it is an incremental backup. When you use a snapshot to restore the data, all the data from the snapshot is restored as well as all the data from the previous snapshot. This way, it is a full backup. Internally, EBS snapshots are chained together. Snapshots are stored in Amazon S3. However, you do not find your snapshot in any one of the S3 buckets. AWS just makes use of the Amazon S3 infrastructure to store your snapshot, but you cannot access them while they reside in S3.

You can do a number of things with the EBS snapshot. You can copy the EBS snapshot to other regions, within your own AWS account, and to another AWS account. If you create a snapshot on an encrypted EBS volume, all the snapshots are automatically encrypted. Most importantly, you can create EBS volumes using snapshots. Volumes created using the encrypted snapshots are also encrypted. You can encrypt the snapshot for an unencrypted snapshot during the copy process. You can also re-encrypt the snapshot for an encrypted snapshot during the copy process using different encryption keys as well.

There is nothing like an automated process available on AWS to take the snapshot of all your EBS volumes. This is something that you need to script for your account. This can be done using CLI, such as PowerShell or AWS CLI. There are some key best practices that you must utilize before you take a snapshot of the EBS volume. If you have a database running on top of your EBS volumes, then ensure that the cache is flushed and the tables are locked. This way, you will have a consistent copy of the snapshot. There are some `sync` and `fsfreeze` utilities on Linux which can be used to quiesce IO. You can think of snapshotting all the available EBS volumes. As soon as you issue the `CreateSnapshot` API and it returns success, it is safe to resume. You do not need to wait until the snapshot is created. The time taken by the snapshot creation totally depends on the volume size and the amount of change since the last snapshot.

To create a snapshot, you can use the `New-EC2Snapshot` cmdlet:

```
PS C:\> New-EC2Snapshot -VolumeId vol-0b4ffe0db5189fad7 -Description "This
is a snapshot test"
```

Summary

Amazon EC2 is a well-known IaaS platform and is widely used by many organizations to satisfy their on-demand computing needs. The EC2 design allows you to Scale-Up and Scale-Down when needed based on the application node and provides the ability to build fault-tolerant and highly available applications. We have seen some of the basic and important tasks that you can do in regard to the EC2 service via PowerShell. In the next chapter, we will deal with the massive object store S3 and learn some of the cmdlets and functionality provided by S3.

7

AWS Simple Storage Service

AWS **Simple Storage Service** (**S3**) is an unlimited object store service. Almost every customer that I work with uses S3 for data storage because S3 is really cheap, easy to use, and integrated with various other AWS services. This is a core storage service considering the storage options on AWS. S3 offers various storage classes to optimize the cost. It is a highly available and durable object store that has 99.99% of availability and 99.999999999% of durability. Objects within a bucket in the region are synchronized across all the availability zones for extremely high availability and durability. You can think of a bucket as a local drive on your computer and directories as folders inside the bucket. As buckets are region specific, you should always create an S3 bucket in the region that makes sense to its purpose, such as sharing content to customers or sharing data with EC2 instances in the given region. Objects in S3 could be any blob of data, such as backup and archives, log files, videos, images, and audio files. In objects store, objects are stored in a non-hierarchical flat address space, which allows for almost endless scalability and a very fast object retrieval. This is why S3 does not offer an ability to search across all objects natively. S3 is also known as a key value data store. You cannot install any software in S3 as it is just an object store.

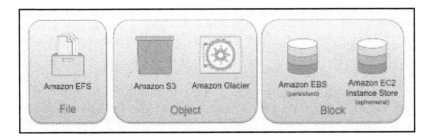

AWS offers several types of storage, as shown above. In theory, S3 provides unlimited storage capacity. It will scale and grow as demanded by your storage needs. There is no defined limit to the amount of content that you can store in S3. At the minimum, objects can be 0 byte in size, and it can be up to five terabytes at the maximum. You can access objects via the AWS console or via CLI and API calls. All the regions now support read after write consistency for putting new objects into S3. This means objects are immediately available after putting objects in S3. In addition, all the regions use eventual consistency for PUTS overwriting existing objects and **deletes** of objects in the S3 bucket. This means there could be a slight delay for those people viewing the objects to get the current content.

In this chapter, we will discuss storage classes in S3, working around the S3 service via PowerShell cmdlet, and managing S3 bucket and object permissions. In addition, we will build S3 endpoint for VPC and learn about S3 Transfer Acceleration, S3 versioning, S3 lifecycle policies, and cross-region replication.

AWS Glacier

Amazon Glacier is a deep archival and extremely low-cost storage service starting at $0.004 per GB per month. It is also a highly durable object store and offers the same durability as S3. That is, 99.999999999% (11 nines) durability, which means that if you store 10,000 objects in the Glacier for 10 million years, you can hardly loose anyone of them. This also indicates a 5-6 order of magnitude higher than the two copies of the tape. AWS introduced three retrieval options ranging from minutes to hours, and are planning to add some more options in the future. This is extremely beneficial for the customer, and retrieval out of the Glacier is not seen as a concern anymore. Because of the new retrieval offering, Glacier can now address full spectrum of archival used cases. All the data stored on the Glacier is encrypted at rest, regardless of how you pass it. Even if you encrypt the data before transferring it to Glacier, AWS will encrypt it again.

Particularly for archival cases in traditional world, there is a long-term investment needed to satisfy regulatory compliance. This demands very huge capital requirements. With Glacier, you do not have any upfront capital investment for your long-term strategy of archival storage. Because you can provision on-demand capacity for your archival storage, you do not need any capacity planning. You only pay as you go. There is no commitment to utilize the service. You also do not have any risk of tape corruption or physical media handling. You can transition S3 objects directly to Glacier based on the lifecycle policy and retain them there for as long as you need them. Though this is a different AWS service, it is highly integrated with S3 using the lifecycle policy to transition objects from one storage class to another. That's why I wanted to refer to this one as an informative section for you at this place before you learn more about S3.

Storage classes on S3

S3 storage class represents the classification for each object in S3. There are several types of storage classes with varying attributes in terms of cost, object availability, object durability, and object accessibility. Object durability represents the percentage that the object is going to be there, meaning it will not be deleted or corrupted on AWS S3. This means the higher the durability percentage of the file, the better the object. Object availability represents the percentage that the object is available when you access it or download it. Having both of these attribute percentages at the higher side means that your chances of losing a particular object are very slim. These attributes differ for different storage classes:

- **Standard**:
  - Most expensive storage class as compared to the rest of the storage classes
  - 99.999999999% (11 nines) durability
  - 99.99% availability
  - Designed for all purpose storage and default option on S3

- **Infrequent Access (IA)**:
  - Less expensive than standard and RRS storage classes
  - 99.999999999% (11 nines) durability
  - 99.90% availability
  - Designed for objects that you do not access frequently, but must be available immediately when accessed

- **Reduced Redundancy Storage (RRS)**:
  - Less expensive than standard storage class
  - 99.99% durability
  - 99.99% availability
  - Designed for non-critical and reproducible objects

- **Glacier**:
  - Cheapest of all the storage classes
  - 99.999999999% (11 nines) durability
  - Object availability depends on the retrieval options that you choose ranging from minutes to hours
  - Designed for long-term deep archival storage

The S3 bucket

The S3 bucket is a container for objects. When creating a bucket, you name the bucket and select the region. The bucket names must be unique across all the S3 namespaces on AWS. Selecting the appropriate region allows you to reduce latency for your end users, minimize cost, and address data residency requirements for compliance. Bucket names range from three to 63 characters in length. They can only contain lowercase letters, numbers, and hyphens. Bucket names should not be formatted as an IP address.

To get the list of all S3-related cmdlets, you can use this:

```
PS C:\> Get-Command *S3*
```

To create a new bucket, you can use the New-S3Bucket cmdlet as follows:

```
PS C:\> New-S3Bucket -BucketName myfirstpowershellbucket
```

```
PS C:\> New-S3Bucket -BucketName myfirstpowershellbucket

CreationDate          BucketName
------------          ----------
6/18/2017 7:10:21 AM  myfirstpowershellbucket
```

If you do not specify the region with the New-S3Bucket cmdlet, it will create the bucket in the region that you specify in the PowerShell profile. For creating the bucket in the particular region, you can use the region parameter with the cmdlet:

```
PS C:\> New-S3Bucket -BucketName mysecondpowershellbucket -region us-west-2
```

```
PS C:\> New-S3Bucket -BucketName mysecondpowershellbucket -region us-west-2

CreationDate          BucketName
------------          ----------
6/18/2017 7:14:01 AM  mysecondpowershellbucket

PS C:\> Get-S3BucketLocation -BucketName mysecondpowershellbucket

Value
-----
us-west-2
```

Get-S3BucketLocation is used to find out the bucket location:

```
PS C:\> Get-S3BucketLocation -BucketName mysecondpowershellbucket
```

I noticed that if you created the bucket in the region for which you created your PowerShell profile, it does return null values for that region only. So be aware on this fact.

```
PS C:\> Get-S3BucketLocation -BucketName myfirstpowershellbucket

Value
-----


PS C:\> Get-S3BucketLocation -BucketName 5b86fe880aaa4764850dcfc52a8a5b0b-logs

Value
-----
us-west-2
```

`myfirstpowershellbucket` is the bucket that I have in the region for which I created my PowerShell profile. So, the value returned is null. To get the list of all buckets in the account, you can use the following command:

```
PS C:\> Get-S3Bucket
```

Folders and objects

Buckets are root level folders, or you can think of it as a local drive in your own computer. You can dump everything in the bucket. But there is a limit on the number of buckets that you can create in the region. So, it is always a best practice to create subfolders inside the bucket, and place the object in those subfolders. This way, you can never hit the limit of max buckets and your storage is infinitely scalable. Objects are any files placed in the bucket or folder.

To get the list of all the folders and objects in the bucket, you can use the following command:

```
PS C:\> Get-S3Object -BucketName myfirstpowershellbucket
```

Let's assume you want to create an `Images` folder in your bucket called `myfirstpowershellbucket` and upload the `D:\sampleimages` folder from your local computer to the S3 bucket; you run the following command:

```
PS C:\> Write-S3Object -BucketName myfirstpowershellbucket -Folder
'D:\sampleimages\' -KeyPrefix Images
```

If the `Images` folder is present, then objects will be simply copied, otherwise this operation would create a folder and place all the objects from `D:\sampleimages` to S3. You can issue `Get-S3Object` to see whether the objects were copied or not:

> PS C:\> Get-S3object -BucketName myfirstpowershellbucket

```
PS C:\> Get-S3Object -BucketName myfirstpowershellbucket
PS C:\> Write-S3Object -BucketName myfirstpowershellbucket -Folder 'D:\sampleimages\' -KeyPrefix Images
PS C:\> Get-S3Object -BucketName myfirstpowershellbucket


ETag         : "d48dd1daf5b6a89018777b4bda33c4d6"
BucketName   : myfirstpowershellbucket
Key          : Images/IMG_0309.JPG
LastModified : 6/18/2017 6:29:16 PM
Owner        : Amazon.S3.Model.Owner
Size         : 1363330
StorageClass : STANDARD
```

To copy a single file called `D:\data\Tax-number-application.txt` from your desktop to your S3 bucket and to save it as `Tax`, you can use the following command:

> PS C:\> Write-S3Object -BucketName myfirstpowershellbucket -Key "Tax" -File
> D:\data\Tax-number-application.txt

To copy all the PDF files in the `D:\data` folder on your local computer to the folder called `Books` inside the bucket, you can use the following command:

> PS C:\> Write-S3Object -BucketName myfirstpowershellbucket -Folder D:\data
> -KeyPrefix Books\ -SearchPattern *.pdf

To create an S3 object with specified content, you can use the following command:

> PS C:\> Write-S3Object -BucketName myfirstpowershellbucket -Key
> "TestSample.txt" -Content "These are my object contents"

Downloading folders and objects from the S3 bucket

With the increasing popularity of S3 and its simplicity, almost every organization started using S3 for their object store. So, you need to know how you can upload and download S3 objects from the S3 bucket. We have already seen this in the previous section on uploading or writing objects/folders to S3. Let's review the download-related cmdlet. The `Read-S3Object` cmdlet lets you download an S3 object optionally, including sub-objects, to a local file or folder location on your local computer.

To download the `Tax` file from the bucket `myfirstpowershellbucket` and to save it as `local-Tax.txt` locally, use the following command. If `local-Tax.txt` is already present, the operation will overwrite the file:

```
PS C:\>Read-S3Object –BucketName myfirstpowershellbucket –Key Tax –File
local-Tax.txt
```

To download the complete folder `Books` under the bucket `myfirstpowershellbucket` and save the folder as `local-books`, use the following command. The operation would overwrite if the folder is already present:

```
PS C:\>Read-S3Object –BucketName myfirstpowershellbucket –KeyPrefix Books –
Folder local-books
```

To search all the buckets that have the name `powershell` in them, and to download all the JPG images, use this next command. The new folder called `Images` will be created locally if not present:

```
PS C:\>Get-S3Bucket | ? { $_.BucketName –like '*powershell*' } | Get-
S3Object | ? { $_.Key –like '*.JPG' } | Read-S3Object –Folder Images
```

```
PS D:\Data\S3Download> dir
PS D:\Data\S3Download> Read-S3Object -BucketName myfirstpowershellbucket -Key Tax -File local-Tax.txt

Mode                LastWriteTime         Length Name
----                -------------         ------ ----
-a----        6/19/2017   9:53 AM           1704 local-Tax.txt


PS D:\Data\S3Download> Read-S3Object -BucketName myfirstpowershellbucket -KeyPrefix Books -Folder local-books

Mode                LastWriteTime         Length Name
----                -------------         ------ ----
d-----        6/19/2017   9:54 AM                local-books


PS D:\Data\S3Download> Get-S3Bucket | ? { $_.BucketName -like '*powershell*' } | Get-S3Object | ? { $_.Key -like '*.JPG' } | Read-S3Object -Folder Images

Mode                LastWriteTime         Length Name
----                -------------         ------ ----
-a----        6/19/2017   9:56 AM        1363330 IMG_0309.JPG
-a----        6/19/2017   9:57 AM        1504457 IMG_0310.JPG
-a----        6/19/2017   9:57 AM        1369265 IMG_0311.JPG
-a----        6/19/2017   9:57 AM        1406505 IMG_0312.JPG
-a----        6/19/2017   9:57 AM        1484573 IMG_0313.JPG
-a----        6/19/2017   9:57 AM        1544019 IMG_0314.JPG
-a----        6/19/2017   9:57 AM        1368887 IMG_0315.JPG
```

Managing S3 permissions

S3 is one of the oldest service offerings in the AWS services portfolio. It is safe to say that S3 is a widely used service on AWS and stores literally trillions of files as objects. Users can interact with S3 directly via the AWS web console or via a variety of third-party tools or CLI/APIs. By default, all the buckets and objects are private. Only the resource owner has access to it and can grant access to the buckets/objects. There are broadly two ways that you can manage access to S3. One is by defining the S3 resource based policies and the other one is through IAM. S3 resource based policies are further divided into two categories:

- Bucket policy
- Access Control List (ACL)

IAM policies

As discussed in `Chapter 4`, *AWS Identity and Access Management*, IAM policies are constructs within an AWS account that defines what a user can and cannot do. In the context of S3, IAM policies are useful because they can be applied to users, roles, and groups.

To demonstrate an IAM policy, I created Neil and Shara as IAM users. By this time, you know how to create IAM users. Refer to the earlier chapter that covers IAM user creation if needed. I also created a PowerShell profile for both the users. We have covered both the concepts in the earlier chapters.

```
PS D:\Data> Get-AWSCredential -ListProfileDetail

ProfileName       StoreTypeName          ProfileLocation
-----------       -------------          ---------------
PowerShellProfile NetSDKCredentialsFile
default           NetSDKCredentialsFile
NeilProfile       NetSDKCredentialsFile
SharaProfile      NetSDKCredentialsFile
```

Consider you have a business case that for each IAM user you need to create a home directory same as their IAM username, and allow them to access only their home folders inside the bucket. They should not be able to view each other's folders. In order to implement the solution for this business case, you can write an inline policy document and attach the policy to every new user that you create in IAM. You can also attach the policy to group and keep adding users in the group. This way, controlling access would be easy rather than defining complex bucket policies and ACL.

Here is the policy document that I used and attach to both the IAM users, Neil and Shara:

```
PS D:\Data> Get-Content -Raw D:\Data\IAMPolicies\S3UserHomeDirectoryAccess.txt
{
  "Version": "2012-10-17",
  "Statement": [
    {
      "Effect": "Allow",
      "Action": [
        "s3:ListAllMyBuckets",
        "s3:GetBucketLocation"
      ],
      "Resource": "arn:aws:s3:::*"
    },
    {
      "Effect": "Allow",
      "Action": "s3:ListBucket",
      "Resource": "arn:aws:s3:::myfirstpowershellbucket",
      "Condition": {"StringLike": {"s3:prefix": [
        "",
        "home/",
        "home/${aws:username}/*"
      ]}}
    },
    {
      "Effect": "Allow",
      "Action": "s3:*",
      "Resource": [
        "arn:aws:s3:::myfirstpowershellbucket/home/${aws:username}",
        "arn:aws:s3:::myfirstpowershellbucket/home/${aws:username}/*"
      ]
    }
  ]
}
```

This policy document allows an IAM user to access a personal home directory that matches the username inside his or her own home directory; each IAM user can perform all the S3 actions such as `ListBucket`, `DeleteObject`, `PutObject`, and `GetObject`. I have also assigned the `IAMReadOnlyAccess` AWS managed policy to both the users in this example so that I can pull out the user metadata.

Let's connect as Neil via PowerShell, and try to create a file in his own directory and Shara's home directory.

```
PS D:\Data> Set-AWSCredentials -ProfileName NeilProfile
PS D:\Data> Get-IAMUser


Arn             : arn:aws:iam::072316406132:user/neil
CreateDate      : 6/19/2017 1:36:31 PM
PasswordLastUsed : 1/1/0001 12:00:00 AM
Path            : /
UserId          : AIDAIEQORPJZR4GX43Y4C
UserName        : neil
```

You use the `Set-AWSCredentials` cmdlet in the PowerShell AWS profile in the current PowerShell session, and `Get-IAMUser` will return the IAM user currently active in the PowerShell session. Let's try to create a file in both Neil and Shara's directory as Neil IAM user.

```
PS D:\Data> Write-S3Object -BucketName myfirstpowershellbucket -Key "home/neil/Myfile.txt" -Content "This is neil file"
PS D:\Data> Write-S3Object -BucketName myfirstpowershellbucket -Key "home/shara/Myfile.txt" -Content "This is neil trying to write in Shara home directory"
Write-S3Object : One or more errors occurred. (Access Denied)
At line:1 char:1
+ Write-S3Object -BucketName myfirstpowershellbucket -Key "home/shara/M ...

    + CategoryInfo          : InvalidOperation: (Amazon.PowerShe...eS3ObjectCmdlet:WriteS3ObjectCmdlet) [Write-S3Object], InvalidOperationException
    + FullyQualifiedErrorId : System.AggregateException,Amazon.PowerShell.Cmdlets.S3.WriteS3ObjectCmdlet
```

You can see that when Neil is trying to create a file in Shara's IAM user home directory, which is `<bucket>/home/shara`, he gets an access denied error and the same goes for Shara as well.

```
PS D:\Data> Set-AWSCredentials -ProfileName SharaProfile
PS D:\Data> Get-IAMUser


Arn             : arn:aws:iam::072316406132:user/shara
CreateDate      : 6/19/2017 1:36:31 PM
PasswordLastUsed : 1/1/0001 12:00:00 AM
Path            : /
UserId          : AIDAJJL2QR42IBOQRNLIG
UserName        : shara

PS D:\Data> Write-S3Object -BucketName myfirstpowershellbucket -Key "home/shara/Myfile.txt" -Content "This is neil file"
PS D:\Data> Write-S3Object -BucketName myfirstpowershellbucket -Key "home/neil/Myfile.txt" -Content "This is shara trying to write in Neil home directory"
Write-S3Object : One or more errors occurred. (Access Denied)
At line:1 char:1
+ Write-S3Object -BucketName myfirstpowershellbucket -Key "home/neil/My ...

    + CategoryInfo          : InvalidOperation: (Amazon.PowerShe...eS3ObjectCmdlet:WriteS3ObjectCmdlet) [Write-S3Object], InvalidOperationException
    + FullyQualifiedErrorId : System.AggregateException,Amazon.PowerShell.Cmdlets.S3.WriteS3ObjectCmdlet
```

So, managing S3 access via IAM policies is a great idea. This fits nicely with the best practice of using IAM to control access to AWS resources. IAM policies is a great tool and is a preferred method of managing S3 permissions as they allow for almost any level of granularity. This is a powerful concept as policies can be assigned to roles, and the EC2 instance can be launched using that role. The ability to attach a role to the server is a big plus, as it removes the need for an IAM access key placed on the server. Another big benefit is how specific they can be. In terms of S3, you can create a policy that allows full access to one bucket, read only access to the second bucket, and no access at all to the third bucket.

Read more about IAM policies on `http://docs.aws.amazon.com/IAM/latest/UserGuide /access_policies.html`

Bucket policies

Bucket policies are the policies that are attached to the S3 bucket directly. These are the security controls placed at the individual bucket level. The permissions in the policy are applied to all the objects in the bucket. The policy specifies what actions are allowed and denied for a particular user. Bucket policies are very useful if you have many S3 buckets, and each of them has its own security requirement. Mostly, it is an ideal mechanism to grant access to a specific bucket across AWS accounts. The most defining features of this control mechanism is that bucket policies allow you to delegate access without sacrificing control. The permission specified in the bucket policy takes precedence.

In order to understand the bucket policy better, let's go back to the example that we discussed in the IAM policy section of S3 permissions. Consider that IAM user Shara, should be able to put the objects in the home directory created for her in the bucket, and she should not have any privilege to delete objects from her own home directory in S3. To tighten the security control, you can now define the bucket policy. The IAM policy that we defined earlier for her is allowing her to put and delete objects from the home directory in the bucket. So, it was more open.

I created the S3 bucket policy document as shown here and attached it to the bucket. Note that you can use an online policy generator for writing such a JSON document, which is very easy to use.

I have used the policy generator at `http://awspolicygen.s3.amazonaws.com/policygen.html`.

```
PS D:\Data> Get-Content -Raw D:\data\Policies\S3BucketPolicyExample.json
{
  "Id": "Policy1497862132609",
  "Version": "2012-10-17",
  "Statement": [
    {
      "Sid": "Stmt1497862055498",
      "Action": [
        "s3:GetObject",
        "s3:PutObject"
      ],
      "Effect": "Allow",
      "Resource": "arn:aws:s3:::myfirstpowershellbucket/*",
      "Principal": {
        "AWS": [
          "arn:aws:iam::072316406132:user/shara"
        ]
      }
    },
    {
      "Sid": "Stmt1497862126133",
      "Action": [
        "s3:DeleteObject",
        "s3:DeleteObjectVersion"
      ],
      "Effect": "Deny",
      "Resource": "arn:aws:s3:::myfirstpowershellbucket/*",
      "Principal": {
        "AWS": [
          "arn:aws:iam::072316406132:user/shara"
        ]
      }
    }
  ]
}
```

The policy document allows the IAM user Shara to add objects, but does not allow her to delete any objects from the bucket. You can now assign this S3 bucket policy to the bucket using `Write-S3BucketPolicy`. To get the existing attached policy on the bucket, you can use `Get-S3BucketPolicy`:

```
PS D:\> Get-S3BucketPolicy -BucketName myfirstpowershellbucket
PS D:\> Write-S3BucketPolicy -BucketName myfirstpowershellbucket -Policy
(Get-Content -Raw D:\data\Policies\S3BucketPolicyExample.json)
```

```
PS C:\> Get-S3BucketPolicy -BucketName myfirstpowershellbucket
PS C:\> Write-S3BucketPolicy -BucketName myfirstpowershellbucket -Policy (Get-Content -Raw D:\data\Policies\S3BucketPolicyExample.json)
PS C:\> Get-S3BucketPolicy -BucketName myfirstpowershellbucket
{"Version":"2012-10-17","Id":"Policy1497862132609","Statement":[{"Sid":"Stmt1497862055498","Effect":"Allow","Principal":{"AWS":"arn:aws:iam::072316406132:user/shara"},"Action":["s3:GetObject","s3:PutObject"],"Resource":"arn:aws:s3:::myfirstpowershellbucket/*"},{"Sid":"Stmt1497862126133","Effect":"Deny","Principal":{"AWS":"arn:aws:iam::072316406132:user/shara"},"Action":["s3:DeleteObject","s3:DeleteObjectVersion"],"Resource":"arn:aws:s3:::myfirstpowershellbucket/*"}]}
```

Now, since this policy is attached to the bucket, IAM user Shara can now only put objects in the home directory created for her in the S3 bucket and cannot delete her own objects from the bucket. Let's try that.

```
PS C:\> Set-AWSCredentials -ProfileName SharaProfile
PS C:\> Get-IAMUser


Arn             : arn:aws:iam::072316406132:user/shara
CreateDate      : 6/19/2017 1:36:31 PM
PasswordLastUsed : 1/1/0001 12:00:00 AM
Path            : /
UserId          : AIDAJJL2QR42IBOQRNLIG
UserName        : shara


PS C:\> Write-S3Object -BucketName myfirstpowershellbucket -Key "home/shara/Myfile.txt" -Content "This is Shara file"
PS C:\> Remove-S3Object -BucketName myfirstpowershellbucket -Key home/shara/Myfile.txt

Confirm
Are you sure you want to perform this action?
Performing the operation "Remove-S3Object (DeleteObjects)" on target "".
[Y] Yes  [A] Yes to All  [N] No  [L] No to All  [S] Suspend  [?] Help (default is "Y"): Y
Remove-S3Object : One or more errors occurred. (Access Denied)
At line:1 char:1
+ Remove-S3Object -BucketName myfirstpowershellbucket -Key home/shara/M ...
+ ~~~~~~~~~~~~~~~~~~~~~~~~~~~~~~~~~~~~~~~~~~~~~~~~~~~~~~~~~~~~~~~~~~~~~~~~
    + CategoryInfo          : InvalidOperation: (Amazon.PowerShe...eS3ObjectCmdlet:RemoveS3ObjectCmdlet) [Remove-S3Object], InvalidOperationException
    + FullyQualifiedErrorId : System.AggregateException,Amazon.PowerShell.Cmdlets.S3.RemoveS3ObjectCmdlet
```

In this example, Shara got an access denied error when she tried to delete the file from her own home directory in S3. It is critical to understand that a bucket policy trumps all other accesses. At the end of the day, a bucket policy takes precedence, even though she had an open IAM policy which allows her to put and delete objects from the home directory in S3 bucket.

Access Control Lists

The first thing to understand about the S3 ACL is that you can apply it to every object that you put in the bucket. Considering trillions of objects stored in S3, that's potentially a lot of ACLs. The next thing to understand is that S3 being one of the oldest services in AWS, S3 ACLs came into being long before IAM existed as a service. Because there are IAM policies and bucket policies available to control the access, you should use an ACL as the last resort. If you cannot solve your access problems using IAM policies and bucket policies, only then plan to use ACL. It is really tricky to keep track of all the security controls if your access policies are spread across IAM Policies, bucket policies, and S3 ACLs. Unless you have a compelling need for diverse permission settings for an individual object in an S3 bucket, you are better off staying away from S3 ACL.

Do not get confused with network ACL and S3 ACL. S3 ACL is meant to control the access to the objects in S3 and has nothing to do with network ACL. There is no corelation as such in anyway. This helps you to grant access to other AWS accounts or to the public if needed. You can define ACL for buckets as well as objects. ACL also allows to share the S3 object with the public via a URL.

Let's create an object in the S3 bucket and assign a public read ACL to the object. You can use the `Set-S3ACL` cmdlet to set the ACL on the specified objects:

```
PS C:\> Write-S3Object -BucketName myfirstpowershellbucket -Key
"home/shara/MyPublicFile.txt" -Content "This is public file"
PS C:\> Set-S3ACL -BucketName myfirstpowershellbucket -Key
home/shara/MyPublicFile.txt -PublicReadOnly
```

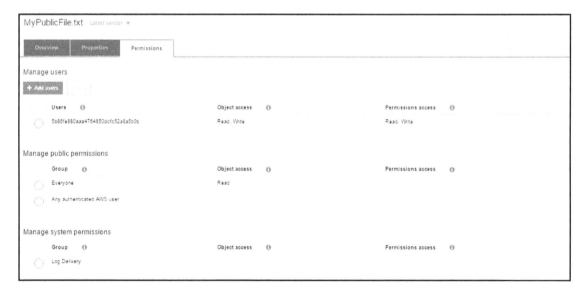

To get better clarity, let's review the AWS console for S3:

You can see the file `MyPublicFile.txt` now has public permission for everyone to read. Everyone means literally everyone on the web. You can also access the S3 objects by a unique URL assigned by AWS. You can click on the **Overview** tab and get the link for the URL. I did not find a way to get that in the PowerShell cmdlet. I feel that functionality will be added sometime in the future.

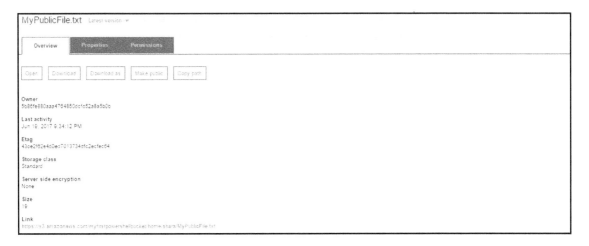

If you now click on the link shown, you can access your file over the public internet. This is a real beauty when you need to share the files over the internet for quick access and download.

Building S3 VPC endpoints

By design, communication between the server you operate locally and S3 is routed via the public internet. The same channel of communication is used for the servers in AWS as well. Even though S3 is an AWS service, and when you access S3 from your EC2, by default, it will get routed via public endpoints and through the open internet.

Suppose, you store a software installation on S3, and you want to install the software on your on-premise server locally. From your on-premise server, you can use an AWS CLI, such as PowerShell, to download the software from S3. You specify the name of the bucket and object in your AWS account with a cmdlet. This communication is done via HTTP over the public internet. Now, suppose you want to do the same thing on your AWS servers. In this case as well, even though you are getting the software from S3, it will still route the request via the public internet. If you want to communicate with S3 privately for your AWS servers, you need to create a VPC endpoint for S3.

The VPC endpoint is a virtual device that lets you interact between AWS servers and S3 to communicate privately without the need to access the internet at all. Your local on-premise server still uses the internet in order to interact with S3. VPC endpoints for S3 let you provide secure access to S3 for running servers in AWS.

As discussed earlier, all cmdlets in regards to VPC are covered under the EC2 service. Hence, to get the list of VPC S3 endpoint-related cmdlets, you can use the following command:

```
PS C:\> Get-Command *EC2VPCEndPoint*
```

To list all the existing endpoints, you can run the following command:

```
PS C:\> Get-EC2VPCEndPoint
```

In order to create a new VPC S3 endpoint, you can use `New-EC2VpcEndpoint`. You need to know the Route Table ID and VPC ID for which you are creating a VPC S3 endpoint and a policy document. Here is the policy document I saved for S3 endpoint:

```
PS C:\> Get-Content -Raw D:\Data\Policies\S3EndPointPolicy.json
{
    "Statement": [
        {
            "Action": "*",
            "Effect": "Allow",
            "Resource": "*",
            "Principal": "*"
        }
    ]
}
```

Before creating the VPC endpoint, first let's check how you can validate if the VPC endpoint is really private and no S3 traffic is going through the open internet. For checking this, issue `traceroute` on the AWS EC2.

```
[root@ip-10-0-1-74 ~]# traceroute us-east-1.s3.amazonaws.com
traceroute to us-east-1.s3.amazonaws.com (52.216.18.232), 30 hops max, 60 byte packets
 1  ip-10-0-2-7.ec2.internal (10.0.2.7)  0.424 ms  0.419 ms  0.415 ms
 2  216.182.224.110 (216.182.224.110)  18.914 ms 216.182.224.104 (216.182.224.104)  19.253 ms 216.182.224.102 (216.182.224.102)  18.496 ms
 3  100.66.8.214 (100.66.8.214)  23.020 ms 100.66.12.36 (100.66.12.36)  12.707 ms 100.66.8.98 (100.66.8.98)  22.139 ms
 4  100.66.14.32 (100.66.14.32)  13.410 ms 100.66.14.128 (100.66.14.128)  18.530 ms 100.66.14.136 (100.66.14.136)  20.875 ms
 5  100.66.22.163 (100.66.22.163)  17.379 ms 100.66.22.119 (100.66.22.119)  23.510 ms 100.66.23.111 (100.66.23.111)  17.597 ms
 6  100.66.21.205 (100.66.21.205)  15.828 ms 100.66.21.193 (100.66.21.193)  14.528 ms 100.66.21.231 (100.66.21.231)  166.901 ms
 7  100.65.47.49 (100.65.47.49)  16.320 ms  15.889 ms  15.185 ms
 8  52.216.18.232 (52.216.18.232)  1.166 ms  1.140 ms  1.042 ms
```

You will notice that when we issue `traceroute` to the S3 infrastructure endpoint in the `us-east-1` region, `traceroute` has several hops to reach the AWS S3 infrastructure. You can now create the S3 endpoint as follows:

```
PS C:\> New-EC2VpcEndpoint -VpcId vpc-a6bb60df -RouteTableId rtb-c24421ba -
ServiceName com.amazonaws.us-east-1.s3 -PolicyDocument (Get-Content -Raw
D:\Data\Policies\S3EndPointPolicy.json)
```

Reading the data is much easier on the AWS console. Here is how you would see an endpoint on the **Route Table**.

As soon as you add a VPC endpoint on the Route Table associated with your EC2 instance, a subsequent request to S3 in that region is now sent over to the private S3 endpoint for the VPC. You can validate this by running `traceroute` once again.

```
[root@ip-10-0-1-74 ~]# traceroute us-east-1.s3.amazonaws.com
traceroute to us-east-1.s3.amazonaws.com (52.216.232.19), 30 hops max, 60 byte packets
 1  * * *
 2  * * *
 3  * * *
 4  * * *
 5  * * *
 6  * * *
 7  * * *
 8  * * *
 9  * * *
10  * * *
11  * * *
12  * * *
13  * * *
14  * * *
15  * * *
16  * * *
17  * * *
18  * * *
19  * * *
20  * * *
21  * * *
22  * * *
23  * * *
24  * * *
25  * * *
26  * * *
27  * * *
28  * * *
29  * * *
30  * * *
```

You will see asterisks (*) in the `traceroute` output. There are no hops seen now. This means that for the given region and VPC, all the communication is sent over the AWS internal network. Ensure that you understand the scope of the VPC and S3 appropriately. VPC cannot span regions, and S3 as well is specific to the region. You would not achieve the desired result if VPC and S3 are for different regions.

S3 Transfer Acceleration

S3 Transfer Acceleration is an optional and added feature supported by S3 that allows clients to transfer the files from remote locations in a fast and secure way. This feature is disabled by default and enabled when needed. When enabled, additional data transfer charges may apply as this feature makes use of the edge location closest to the client.

If you are moving more data between regions, or moving a lot more data across continents, or if your customers are sitting very far away physically from their AWS regions, or if you move large number of objects, S3 Transfer Acceleration is quite a useful feature here. AWS expects that your transfer will be more than 300% faster for most of the use cases and AWS will not charge the customer if the transfer is not faster.

AWS provides you the S3 Transfer Acceleration Speed Comparison tool and it can be accessed using the following:

```
http://s3-accelerate-speedtest.s3-accelerate.amazonaws.com/en/accelerate-spe
ed-comparsion.html?region=region&origBucketName=yourBucketName
```

You replace `region` and `yourBucketName` in the link with the actual values. For example, I have a bucket in the `us-east-1` region called `myfirstpowershellbucket`. So, the actual URL will be as follows:

```
http://s3-accelerate-speedtest.s3-accelerate.amazonaws.com/en/accelerate-spe
ed-comparsion.html?region=us-east-1&origBucketName=myfirstpowershellbucket
```

This tool provides you with an idea about the speed that you can get, and you can guess how much impact S3 Transfer Acceleration can make in the overall data transfer process. In the next sample, you can see that the transfer is 24% faster if enabled. Remember that I am running this one from my laptop, and hence you see that the percent improvement is very low. If you have a good bandwidth, this will be around 300% faster. AWS says that if it is not much faster, then they will not charge you even though you have enabled S3 Transfer Acceleration:

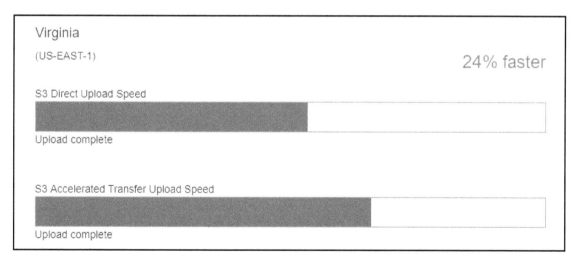

To list all the cmdlets related to S3 Transfer Acceleration, you can use the following command:

```
PS C:\> Get-Command *Accelerate*
```

To enable, S3 Transfer Acceleration on the bucket, you simply run the following command:

```
PS C:\> Write-S3BucketAccelerateConfiguration –BucketName
myfirstpowershellbucket –AccelerateConfiguration_Status enabled
```

```
PS C:\> Write-S3BucketAccelerateConfiguration -BucketName myfirstpowershellbucket -AccelerateConfiguration_Status enabled
PS C:\> Get-S3BucketAccelerateConfiguration -BucketName myfirstpowershellbucket

Value
-----
Enabled
```

Once enabled, you need to use the accelerated endpoint for data transfer, which is usually `<bucketname>.s3-accelerate.amazonaws.com`. In this example case, it would be `myfirstpowershellbucket.s3-accelerate.amazonaws.com`.

You can suspend the S3 acceleration if you do not need it any more using the following command:

```
PS C:\> Write-S3BucketAccelerateConfiguration –BucketName
myfirstpowershellbucket –AccelerateConfiguration_Status suspended
```

```
PS C:\> Write-S3BucketAccelerateConfiguration -BucketName myfirstpowershellbucket -AccelerateConfiguration_Status suspended
PS C:\> Get-S3BucketAccelerateConfiguration -BucketName myfirstpowershellbucket

Value
-----
Suspended
```

S3 versioning

S3 versioning is a feature to manage and store multiple versions of an object. It provides you with a capability to protect accidental deletes or application logic failures. Versioning is disabled by default on the buckets and objects. Versioning can only be set on the bucket level and applied to all objects in the bucket. Once it is enabled, it cannot be fully disabled. Every time a file is uploaded, S3 will create a new version of the file, providing you with a great way for an easy retrieval of deleted objects or roll back to the previous versions. You can only suspend versioning. Suspending versioning prevents new versions from being created. All objects with existing versions will maintain their older versions after being suspended. Lifecycle policies can be applied to specific versions of an object. Both, versioning and lifecycle policies can be enabled on a bucket at the same time. You will learn about lifecycle policies in the next section.

To list all the cmdlets related to the versioning operation, you can use the following command:

```
PS C:\> Get-Command *Versioning*
```

To enable versioning on the bucket, you can run the following command:

```
PS C:\> Write-S3BucketVersioning -BucketName myfirstpowershellbucket -
VersioningConfig_Status Enabled
```

For `VersioningConfig_Status,` the accepted values are `Off`, `Enabled`, and `Suspended`.

```
PS C:\> Write-S3BucketVersioning -BucketName myfirstpowershellbucket -VersioningConfig_Status Enabled
PS C:\> Get-S3BucketVersioning -BucketName myfirstpowershellbucket

Status   EnableMfaDelete
------   ---------------
Enabled  False
```

Once enabled, you can only suspend versioning. You can do this using the following command:

```
PS C:\> Write-S3BucketVersioning -BucketName myfirstpowershellbucket -
VersioningConfig_Status Suspended
```

```
PS C:\> Write-S3BucketVersioning -BucketName myfirstpowershellbucket -VersioningConfig_Status Suspended
PS C:\> Get-S3BucketVersioning -BucketName myfirstpowershellbucket

Status     EnableMfaDelete
------     ---------------
Suspended  False
```

S3 lifecycle policies

S3 lifecycle policies are a great way to automate the data management task for the data in S3 and lower the cost of the data storage based on the access need. These are a set of rules that you can define on the bucket or objects that automate the migration of an object's storage class, or deletion based on the specified time interval. We have seen earlier in this chapter about the different storage classes and their characteristics. By default, lifecycle policies are disabled on buckets and objects.

Consider you have a business case, where your backup files need to be available for quick access for the first 30 days. After 30 days, you may need them only if there is a demand until 60 days; and, after 60 days, you would like to archive them on the long-term archiving storage for overall 1 year from the day of the object creation. For this business case, you can automate the whole lifecycle of the objects without any manual intervention. This is the real beauty of the S3 capability, which allows you automatic tiering and better cost control.

You can combine actions in the lifecycle policies, or you can write different lifecycle policies for each action. In the following example, I have combined three actions. The first one is to transition **Standard-IA**, the second one is to **Glacier**, and the third one is to remove objects from Glacier after 365 days. You can set lifecycle policies by bucket, prefix, or tags, and you can also set them for current and non-current (previous) versions.

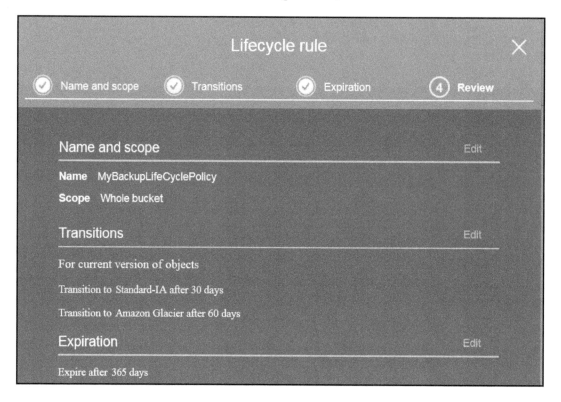

It is best to use the AWS console for setting the lifecycle policies. You can also use the AWS PowerShell cmdlet for defining the lifecycle policies. To list all the cmdlets related to the lifecycle operation, you can use the following command:

```
PS C:\> Get-Command *S3Lifecycle*
```

Though there are cmdlets available for defining lifecycle policies, I prefer to make use of the console, as it is very easy doing this using the AWS S3 console rather through a cmdlet.

Cross-region replication

There are several reasons as to why you may want to replicate the data in S3 across regions. From a compliance perspective, you may want to store data hundreds of miles apart. From a latency perspective, you may want to distribute data to regional customers with very low latency; and from a security perspective, you may just want to create multiple replicas managed by separate AWS accounts.

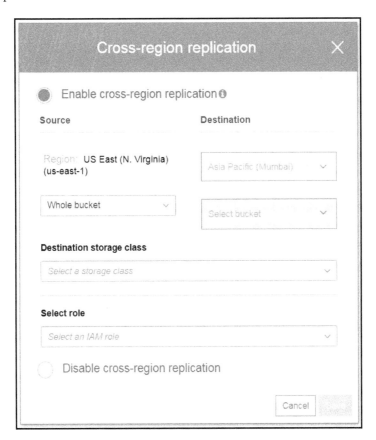

You can either replicate an entire bucket or it can be just prefix based. Once cross-region replication is enabled, it only replicates new PUTs. This means new uploads into the source bucket will be replicated. Cross-region replication is a fast and reliable asynchronous replication and is set between any two regions on a 1:1 basis. Deletes and lifecycle actions are not replicated. You can also change the destination storage class for minimizing the cost.

Removing the S3 bucket

There could be several reasons for which you need to delete the bucket when not needed any more to reduce the cost. This can be done easily using the following cmdlet:

```
PS C:\> Remove-S3Bucket -BucketName myfirstpowershellbucket -
DeleteBucketContent
```

If you do not specify the `DeleteBucketContent` parameter with the cmdlet, the bucket cannot be deleted if it contains data.

```
PS C:\> Remove-S3Bucket -BucketName myfirstpowershellbucket -DeleteBucketContent

Confirm
Are you sure you want to perform this action?
Performing the operation "Remove-S3Bucket (DeleteBucket)" on target "myfirstpowershellbucket".
[Y] Yes  [A] Yes to All  [N] No  [L] No to All  [S] Suspend  [?] Help (default is "Y"): Y
```

Summary

AWS S3 is the most used service because of its simplicity and several powerful capabilities for out-of-the-box data management. The S3 service provides you various choices of storage classes and the ability to simplify your S3 data management using lifecycle policies. It is an unlimited web object store, which is highly durable and available. You have the capability to use S3 with other AWS services with very simple permission setup or configuration. There are a variety of options to store encrypted data. S3 also provides you with high performance for uploads and downloads. There are a number of use cases for which you can use this service. I suggest that you review several use cases published on the AWS website. In the next chapter, you will learn about building a highly available, fault-tolerant environment.

8
Elastic Load Balancer

When you think *Design for Failure*, **Elastic Load Balancing** (**ELB**) is one of the AWS services you need to start using. It is a component used to balance network traffic across multiple EC2 and ECS instances within multiple availability zones. With the introduction of ELB, we can automatically distribute incoming application traffic across multiple applications, microservices, and containers hosted on AWS EC2 instances. You can also think of ELB as a traffic manager. ECS is an AWS EC2 container service, which is not covered in this book, but I would like to encourage you to read more on this service if you are a big fan of Docker containers and Kubernetes. I will limit the scope to EC2 instances load balancing in this chapter. ELB allows you to achieve a greater level of fault tolerance and higher availability. The beauty of this service is, it scales its request handling capacity to meet traffic demands, and it does this without any manual intervention or any additional configuration. The elastic nature of this service is built right into it.

ELB has several in-built characteristics:

- First, ELB can automatically grow and shrink with the demand patterns of the application workload.
- Second, it handles the routing and load balancing of your TCP, HTTP, and HTTPS traffic to EC2 instances.
- Third, it allows a health check to be configured, so it can determine whether or not the instances to which it is routing traffic are healthy and should be used.
- Fourth, it is highly secure and tightly integrated with other AWS services.
- Fifth, the cost of running ELB on AWS is significantly lower than running it on our own. You get charged based on hourly usage or each portion of the hour, and for each gigabyte of data transferred through the load balancer.

When you create a new ELB, AWS creates a single **CNAME** to use for the DNS configuration. The best part of this service is that CNAME does not change, even though ELB scaling happens based on-demand. The CNAME ELB component actually resolves around a round-robin DNS to ELB IP addresses in each availability zone. The representation of this behavior can be seen in the following diagram. As the traffic increases, AWS adds IP addresses to the ELB DNS entry and continues around the round-robin requests across multiple ELBs. Of course, as traffic decreases, it removes the IP addresses from the ELB DNS entry, thereby reducing the number of load balancing components in the system. ELBs are themselves load balanced and AWS takes care of this at the backend with no interruption to the service.

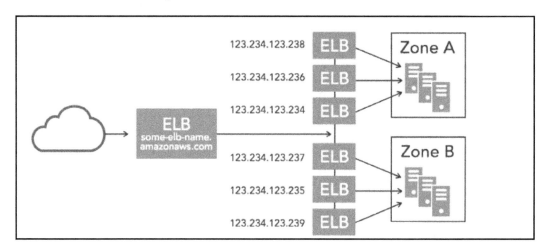

It is possible for ELBs to fail. To address an ELB failure, you can design around it using the Route 53 health checks on ELB. Once you configure the ELB health check on Route 53, and it detects ELB failure, Route 53 can shift traffic to a different ELB. You can configure ELB to be external or internal facing. External facing ELBs are exposed to the internet while the internal facing ELB can be used only for internal applications that cannot reach the internet. Another important feature of the ELB is the easy integration with **AWS Certificate Manager**. AWS Certificate Manager allows you to automate the deployment and renewal process for SSL/TLS certificates with no hassle. ELB also supports sticky sessions. Sticky sessions are great if your application needs to maintain session state between an EC2 instance and the client.

In this chapter, we will discuss different types of load balancers and various components of Application Load Balancer. In addition, we will learn practical implementation of Classic Load Balancer and Application Load Balancer.

Why load balancer?

Traditionally, we install a web application on EC2 and access it directly via HTTP or HTTPS. The following figure depicts this. In such cases, the risk of failure is high. You could have a high capacity EC2 machine at your disposal, and applications could run on top of it with no worries; but in reality, this is not considered fault tolerant or highly available. If you wanted to build a highly available and fault-tolerant environment, you would end up putting various other infrastructure components in place, with much less pain, to manage the ongoing operation.

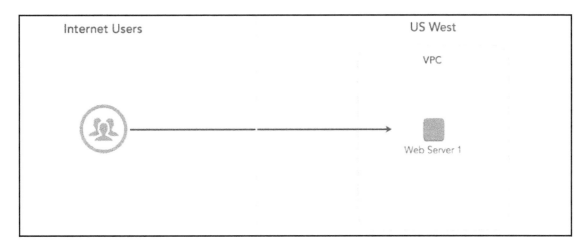

If your application demands more memory or CPU, then there is nothing you can do to handle the on-demand nature of the request. So, having only one powerful EC2 instance to host your application may result in issues to handle the spiky load. In order to handle and overcome this, ELB can help you rescue the situation. You can have a number of EC2 instances running behind ELB, and it is ELB's job to distribute the load across multiple EC2 instances. The following figure depicts this. Adding ELB between your EC2 instances and users will help to mitigate the failure risk and allows your application to scale without any downtime. If anyone of the EC2 instances fail, ELB will stop sending traffic to it, and your application will not experience any issues.

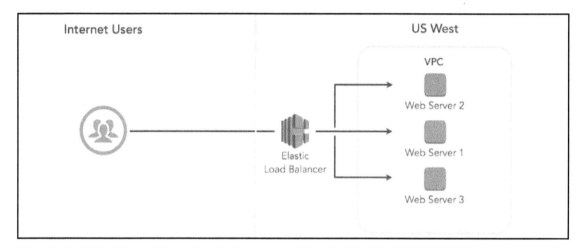

Every other ELB that you create utilizes multiple availability zones by design, even though your application runs out of one availability zone. There are a number of reasons for which you need to use ELB in your environments. They are as follows:

- ELB minimizes the risk of overloading one single EC2 instance
- ELB provides continuous monitoring of the health of the EC2 instances
- It also monitors traffic and redirects it appropriately to healthy and less overloaded EC2 instances
- ELB has its own Security Groups, which helps to open the traffic for specific IP ranges and ports
- You can redirect traffic in one availability zone or multiple availability zones
- You can offload the SSL/TLS processing from EC2 instances to terminate on ELB

Types of Elastic Load Balancers

Elastic Load Balancing is part of the EC2 service. As discussed earlier, ELB lets you design fault-tolerant and highly available applications by distributing incoming traffic to more than one EC2 instance. There are two types of load balancers. One is called **Classic Load Balancer** and other one is known as **Application Load Balancer**.

Classic Load Balancer

Until last year, this was the only available and most widely used load balancer on AWS. Classic Load Balancer is the load balancer that supports either EC2 Classic or VPC EC2. If you have EC2 Classic, this is still applicable to you. If you are still using the TCP/SSL protocol, then this is still a choice to consider, as TCP/SSL protocol is not supported on Application Load Balancer. CLB makes routing decisions at either the transport layer (TCP/SSL) or the application layer (HTTP/HTTPS). You can only host one application with this type of load balancer. CLB also supports cross-zone load balancing, stickiness, and connection draining.

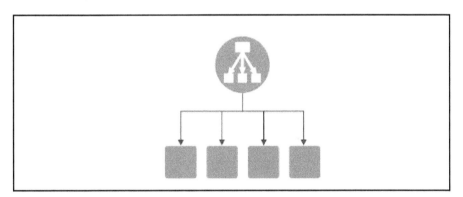

Application Load Balancer

Application Load Balancer (**ALB**) is an entirely new load balancing platform launched in mid 2016. This is not something AWS added on top of Classic Load Balancer; it is a completely new redesign of the load balancing platform they had. This load balancer platform is also fully managed, highly available, and scalable, just like the Classic Load Balancer.

ALB makes routing decisions at the application layer (HTTP/HTTPS). It supports path-based routing and can route requests to one or more ports on each EC2 instance or ECS container instance and microservices supported in your VPC. ALB has some improved health checks and improved CloudWatch metrics. ALB also provides native WebSockets and HTTP/2 support to catch up with all the modern internet applications. WebSockets allows real-time, two-way messaging over the long-running TCP connection. The content-based routing capability of ALB allows requests to be routed to different applications behind a single load balancer, which is a completely new aspect implemented in ALB. This is not seen in Classic Load Balancer at all. With a single ALB, you can now redirect requests to multiple applications. You do not need to have a separate load balancer for each application anymore. This means that ALB allows for multiple applications to be hosted behind a single load balancer. At the time of writing this book, AWS was supporting 100 applications behind a single ALB, which may be enhanced further. This approach of multiple application hosting behind a single load balancer results in some big cost savings.

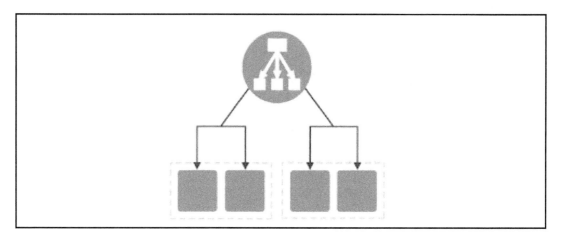

Here are the high-level features of the ELBs for easy reference.

Feature	Classic Load Balancer	Application Load Balancer
Protocols	HTTP, HTTPS, TCP, SSL	HTTP, HTTPS
Platforms	EC2-Classic, EC2-VPC	EC2-VPC
Sticky sessions (cookies)	✓	load balancer generated
Idle connection timeout	✓	✓
Connection draining	✓	✓
Cross-zone load balancing †	✓	Always enabled
Health checks † †	✓	Improved
CloudWatch metrics	✓	Improved
Access logs	✓	Improved
Host-based routing		✓
Path-based routing		✓
Route to multiple ports on a single instance		✓
HTTP/2 support		✓
Websockets support		✓
Load balancer deletion protection		✓

Application Load Balancer components

Before you proceed towards creating an ALB, there are some terminologies that you must be aware of. These are very important to know, to relate them to the various ALB components. The following figure depicts the relationship between various ALB components:

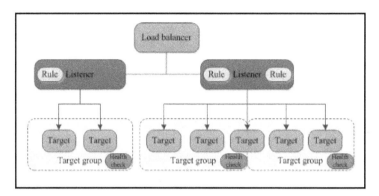

- **Listener**: This defines the protocol and port on which the load balancer listens for incoming connections. Each load balancer needs at least one listener to accept incoming traffic. Routing rules are defined on listeners.
- **Target group**: These are logical groupings of **Target** behind a load balancer. Target groups can exist independently from the load balancer and can be associated with the load balancer when needed.
- **Target**: These are nothing but individual EC2 or ECS instances in the target groups. EC2 instances can be registered in the same target group using multiple ports. A single target can be registered with multiple target groups.
- **Rule**: This provides a link between a **Listener** and a **Target group**. It consists of conditions and actions. When the request meets the condition of the rule, the associated action is taken. Rules can forward a request to a specified **Target group**. Conditions can be specified in path pattern format. A path pattern is case sensitive and can be up to 128 characters in length.

Creating Classic Load Balancer

To find all the related cmdlets for working with Classic Load Balancer, you can use the following command:

```
PS C:\> Get-Command *ELB* |Where-Object {$_.Name -NotLike "*ELB2*"}
```

This will list all the cmdlets for Classic Load Balancer.

 Note that if you run the previous cmdlet without a filter, you will notice that there are cmdlets with `ELB2` in them. Any cmdlet with ELB2 in it is meant for Application Load Balancer.

To get a list of existing CLBs, you run the following command:

```
PS C:\> Get-ELBLoadBalancer
```

To see the Classic Load Balancer limits on the account, you can use the following cmdlet. If a limit needs to be lifted, you have to contact AWS:

```
PS C:\> Get-ELBAccountLimit
```

Let's plan to create a Classic Load Balancer. But before we create it, we need to know the subnet details and its availability zones. We also need to create a Security Group for CLB.

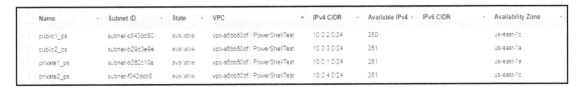

As shown, we discussed the process of creating these subnets in Chapter 5, *AWS Virtual Private Cloud*. The subnet called `subnet-b29d3e9e` has been created in an availability zone called `us-east-1a` and `subnet-c843dd80` is in `us-east-1b`. As we want to create CLB for an internet-facing application, I chose public subnets. Both of these subnets have a route to the internet. The other two subnets are in a private network and do not have a route to the internet.

SecurityGroup `sg-639f1612` has an ingress on port `80` for the HTTP protocol. This is the one I created to attach to the ELB. We also saw a process for creating Security Groups earlier. So, we know Security Groups and subnets that can be used to create CLB. The `New-ELBLoadBalancer` cmdlet can be used to create the CLB as follows:

```
PS C:\> New-ELBLoadBalancer -LoadBalancerName myfirstclassiclb -
SecurityGroup sg-639f1612 -Subnet subnet-b29d3e9e,subnet-c843dd80 -Listener
$httpListener
```

```
PS C:\> $httpListener = New-Object Amazon.ElasticLoadBalancing.Model.Listener
PS C:\> $httpListener.Protocol = "http"
PS C:\> $httpListener.LoadBalancerPort = 80
PS C:\> $httpListener.InstanceProtocol = "http"
PS C:\> $httpListener.InstancePort = 80
PS C:\> New-ELBLoadBalancer -LoadBalancerName myfirstclassiclb -SecurityGroup sg-639f1612 -Subnet subnet-b29d3e9e,subnet-c843dd80 -Listener $httpListener
myfirstclassiclb-1809645133.us-east-1.elb.amazonaws.com
```

The successful cmdlet execution returns CNAME for the ELB. As per the documentation, you can either use the `-Subnet` or `-AvailabilityZone` parameter with `New-ELBLoadBalancer`, but not both. However, I noticed that if you use `-AvailabilityZone` with `New-ELBLoadBalancer`, it will try to create the Classic Load Balancer in the default VPC. Hence, be aware of this fact. Passing the `-Subnet` parameter and subnet ID would create the CLB in the appropriate VPC. In addition, to define the listener, you have to inherit the object from `Amazon.ElasticLoadBalancing.Model.Listener` and define `Protocol` and `Port` on the load balancer and the EC2 instance. There is also another parameter called `-Scheme`, which can be used with `New-ELBLoadBalancer`. It indicates whether the load balancer is internet facing or internal facing. If you do not specify the scheme, then by default, the internet-facing load balancer is created. The valid values for scheme are internet facing and internal. The preceding cmdlet can be rewritten as follows:

```
PS C:\> New-ELBLoadBalancer -LoadBalancerName myfirstclassiclb2 -
SecurityGroup sg-639f1612 -Scheme internet-facing -Subnet subnet-
b29d3e9e,subnet-c843dd80 -Listener $httpListener
```

If you want to create CLB for internal purposes, then you can use the scheme as internal:

```
PS C:\> New-ELBLoadBalancer -LoadBalancerName myfirstclassiclb3 -
SecurityGroup sg-639f1612 -Scheme internal -Subnet subnet-b29d3e9e,subnet-
c843dd80 -Listener $httpListener
```

We have port `80` open on the Security Group and the CLB ready. But, wait, it has no target EC2 instances. Let's go ahead and add EC2 Instances to the CLB. In order to understand the ELB implementation better, let's review the foundational architecture that we discussed in an earlier chapter.

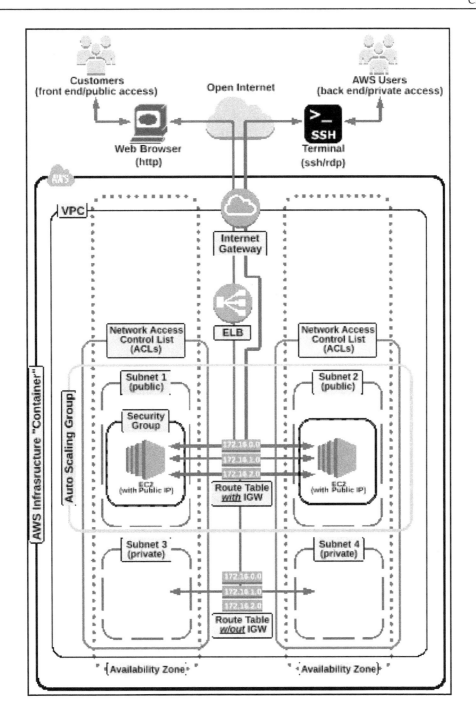

As we created a public facing (internet-facing) CLB, our backend EC2 instances can now go into the private subnet. We created two private subnets. Those are `subnet-b262c19e` and `subnet-f042dcb8`. They reside in `us-east-1a` and `us-east-1b` respectively.

First, we will create the two EC2 instance with a web server installed on it. While spinning the EC2 instances, this time, I will pass on user data to bootstrap the EC2 instance. To explain, user data is the script that can be supplied to the EC2 instance to install your application or update OS, and so on. In this case, I am planning to spin up the Linux EC2 instance and install Apache on it. You can spin up the first EC2 instance using this:

```
PS C:\>New-EC2Instance -ImageId ami-a4c7edb2 -MinCount 1 -MaxCount 1 -
SubnetId subnet-b262c19e -InstanceType t2.micro -KeyName MyWebPressApp -
EncodeUserData -UserDataFile "D:\data\UserData\MyWebServerUserData1.txt" -
SecurityGroupId sg-9ec521ef
```

You might have noticed that, this time, we added a couple of new switches with the `New-EC2Instance` cmdlet, and those are `-EncodeUserData` and `-UserDataFile`. The `-EncodeUserData` parameter instructs that user data is base64 encoded prior to submitting to the EC2 instance. The `-UserDataFile` parameter is the destination of the plain text file in which you have a bootstrapping code. The `-EncodeUserData` switch has to be used when you use `-UserDataFile`.

```
PS C:\> Get-Content -Raw "D:\data\UserData\MyWebServerUserData1.txt"
#!/bin/bash
sudo yum update -y
sudo yum install -y httpd
sudo service httpd start
sudo chkconfig httpd on
sudo groupadd www
sudo usermod -a -G www ec2-user
sudo chown -R root:www /var/www
sudo chmod 2775 /var/www
sudo find /var/www -type d -exec chmod 2775 {} +
sudo find /var/www -type f -exec chmod 0664 {} +
sudo echo "This is my first web server" > /var/www/html/index.html
PS C:\>
PS C:\> New-EC2Instance -ImageId ami-a4c7edb2 -MinCount 1 -MaxCount 1 -SubnetId subnet-b262c19e -InstanceType t2.micro -KeyName MyWebPressApp -EncodeUserData
  -UserDataFile "D:\data\UserData\MyWebServerUserData1.txt" -SecurityGroupId sg-9ec521ef


GroupNames   : {}
Groups       : {}
Instances    : {MyWebPressApp}
OwnerId      : 072316406132
RequesterId  :
ReservationId : r-0549a8195bbc08561
```

For the second EC2 instance, I just changed the last line seen in `UserData` in the preceding script. This is just to ensure that we hit both web servers. Have a look at the following script for the second web server:

```
PS C:\> Get-Content -Raw "D:\data\UserData\MyWebServerUserData2.txt"
#!/bin/bash
sudo yum update -y
sudo yum install -y httpd
sudo service httpd start
sudo chkconfig httpd on
sudo groupadd www
sudo usermod -a -G www ec2-user
sudo chown -R root:www /var/www
sudo chmod 2775 /var/www
sudo find /var/www -type d -exec chmod 2775 {} +
sudo find /var/www -type f -exec chmod 0664 {} +
sudo echo "This is my second web server" > /var/www/html/index.html
PS C:\>
PS C:\> New-EC2Instance -ImageId ami-a4c7edb2 -MinCount 1 -MaxCount 1 -SubnetId subnet-f042dcb8 -InstanceType t2.micro -KeyName MyWebPressApp -EncodeUserData
 -UserDataFile "D:\data\UserData\MyWebServerUserData2.txt" -SecurityGroupId sg-9ec521ef


GroupNames   : {}
Groups       : {}
Instances    : {MyWebPressApp}
OwnerId      : 072316406132
RequesterId  :
ReservationId : r-0186ecc2ed6173293
```

To add these EC2 instances to the Classic Load Balancer, you first need to get the instance IDs for both the instances that we just spun up. You can extract this based on reservation IDs:

```
PS C:\> (Get-EC2Instance -Filter @{ Name="reservation-
id";Values="r-0549a8195bbc08561" }).Instances.InstanceId
PS C:\> (Get-EC2Instance -Filter @{ Name="reservation-
id";Values="r-0186ecc2ed6173293" }).Instances.InstanceId
```

```
PS C:\> (Get-EC2Instance -Filter @{ Name="reservation-id";Values="r-0549a8195bbc08561" }).Instances.InstanceId
i-06ce23d76d459ee3f
PS C:\> (Get-EC2Instance -Filter @{ Name="reservation-id";Values="r-0186ecc2ed6173293" }).Instances.InstanceId
i-03f0f169a698a3a2d
```

`Register-ELBInstanceWithLoadBalancer` lets you add EC2 instances to the load balancer that you created. Again, just ensure that the EC2 instance and ELB belong to the same VPC:

```
PS C:\> Register-ELBInstanceWithLoadBalancer -LoadBalancerName
myfirstclassiclb -Instance i-03f0f169a698a3a2d,i-06ce23d76d459ee3f
```

```
PS C:\> Register-ELBInstanceWithLoadBalancer -LoadBalancerName myfirstclassiclb -Instance i-03f0f169a698a3a2d,i-06ce23d76d459ee3f

InstanceId
----------
i-03f0f169a698a3a2d
i-06ce23d76d459ee3f
```

To ensure that these EC2 instances are in service and ready to accept traffic, you can run the following command:

```
PS C:\> Get-ELBInstanceHealth -LoadBalancerName myfirstclassiclb
```

Both of the instances that we registered with CLB are `InService` state. This means that they are ready to accept traffic and pass the health check. When you create the Classic Load Balancer, the cross-zone load balancing is disabled by default. If the cross-zone load balancing is enabled on the load balancer, it will send the traffic to multiple availability zones and balance the connection. You can enable cross-zone load balancing using this:

```
PS C:\> Edit-ELBLoadBalancerAttribute -LoadBalancerName myfirstclassiclb -
CrossZoneLoadBalancing_Enabled $true
```

Now, we are ready to hit the web browser: just copy and paste the CNAME that we got after creating the load balancer and see the magic. Keep refreshing the page, and you will notice that your browser will display a message like this:

After the browser is refreshed, you will see another message coming from the second server.

The message displayed is the message that you used while bootstrapping the server. This is the message that you added in the userdata script. The created ELB is working as planned. The userdata switch is a great feature of the EC2; by using it, you can pass the bootstrapping script. This way, you can automate the whole process of deployment, and this is one of the ways to handle the deployment.

Now, let's try to understand the various other components of Classic Load Balancer, which are important to know. You can list the details of the load balancer using the following command:

```
PS C:\> Get-ELBLoadBalancer -LoadBalancerName myfirstclassiclb
```

```
PS C:\> Get-ELBLoadBalancer -LoadBalancerName myfirstclassiclb


AvailabilityZones            : {us-east-1a, us-east-1b}
BackendServerDescriptions    : {}
CanonicalHostedZoneName      : myfirstclassiclb-1809645133.us-east-1.elb.amazonaws.com
CanonicalHostedZoneNameID    : Z35SXDOTRQ7X7K
CreatedTime                  : 7/4/2017 11:44:21 AM
DNSName                      : myfirstclassiclb-1809645133.us-east-1.elb.amazonaws.com
HealthCheck                  : Amazon.ElasticLoadBalancing.Model.HealthCheck
Instances                    : {i-03f0f169a698a3a2d, i-06ce23d76d459ee3f}
ListenerDescriptions         : {Amazon.ElasticLoadBalancing.Model.ListenerDescription}
LoadBalancerName             : myfirstclassiclb
Policies                     : Amazon.ElasticLoadBalancing.Model.Policies
Scheme                       : internet-facing
SecurityGroups               : {sg-639f1612}
SourceSecurityGroup          : Amazon.ElasticLoadBalancing.Model.SourceSecurityGroup
Subnets                      : {subnet-b29d3e9e, subnet-c843dd80}
VPCId                        : vpc-a6bb60df
```

You see that DNS Name, VPC ID, Subnets, and associated EC2 instances are displayed for the specified VPC. In addition, the important aspect that you might need to understand here, is the health check. If you do not understand health check properly, then you will have issues troubleshooting the *out of service* status of the EC2 instances on the load balancer. To extract the health check defined for the specified load balancer, you can use the following command:

```
PS C:\> (Get-ELBLoadBalancer -LoadBalancerName
myfirstclassiclb).HealthCheck
```

```
PS C:\> (Get-ELBLoadBalancer -LoadBalancerName myfirstclassiclb).HealthCheck

HealthyThreshold   : 2
Interval           : 5
Target             : TCP:80
Timeout            : 2
UnhealthyThreshold : 2
```

- `HealthyThreshold`: This indicates the number of consecutive health check successes required before marking the instance health check as healthy.
- `Interval`: This indicates the interval in seconds between the health checks of an individual EC2 instance.
- `Target`: This indicates the instance being checked. The protocol is HTTP, HTTPS, TCP, or SSL. The range of valid ports are from `1` to `65535`. The default is TCP.

- `Timeout`: This indicates the amount of time in seconds during which no response means a failed health check. The value must be less than an internal value.
- `UnhealthyThreshold`: This indicates the number of consecutive health check failures required before marking the instance state as unhealthy.

You can use the `Set-ELBHealthCheck` cmdlet to change the threshold value on the load balancer:

```
PS C:\> Set-ELBHealthCheck -LoadBalancerName myfirstclassiclb -
HealthCheck_HealthyThreshold 3 -HealthCheck_Interval 6 -HealthCheck_Target
TCP:80 -HealthCheck_Timeout 3 -HealthCheck_UnhealthyThreshold 5
```

```
PS C:\> Set-ELBHealthCheck -LoadBalancerName myfirstclassiclb -HealthCheck_HealthyThreshold 3 -HealthCheck_Interval 6 -HealthCheck_Target TCP:80 -HealthCheck
_Timeout 3 -HealthCheck_UnhealthyThreshold 5

HealthyThreshold    : 3
Interval            : 6
Target              : TCP:80
Timeout             : 3
UnhealthyThreshold  : 5


PS C:\> (Get-ELBLoadBalancer -LoadBalancerName myfirstclassiclb).HealthCheck

HealthyThreshold    : 3
Interval            : 6
Target              : TCP:80
Timeout             : 3
UnhealthyThreshold  : 5
```

Another aspect that you need to understand is the listeners on the load balancer. We supplied listener information when we created Classic Load Balancer, but that was only for port 80. If you want to check the listeners added on a specific load balancer, then you can extract this as follows:

```
PS C:\> (Get-ELBLoadBalancer -LoadBalancerName
myfirstclassiclb).ListenerDescriptions.Listener
```

```
PS C:\> (Get-ELBLoadBalancer -LoadBalancerName myfirstclassiclb).ListenerDescriptions.Listener

InstancePort      : 80
InstanceProtocol  : HTTP
LoadBalancerPort  : 80
Protocol          : HTTP
SSLCertificateId  :
```

If you want to add an additional listener for port 443, you can use the `New-ELBLoadBalancerListener` cmdlet. When you plan to add a secure listener, you need to get the certificate first, and you can do this using the AWS Certificate Manager for your domain. You can get a new certificate for your domain using the following command:

```
PS C:\> New-ACMCertificate -DomainName "www.example.com"
```

And then, you can pass on the SSL certificate ID to `New-ELBLoadBalancerListener` for the specified load balancer as follows:

```
PS C:\> $httpsListener = New-Object
Amazon.ElasticLoadBalancing.Model.Listener
PS C:\> $httpsListener.Protocol = "https"
PS C:\> $httpsListener.LoadBalancerPort = 443
PS C:\> $httpsListener.InstanceProtocol = "https"
PS C:\> $httpsListener.InstancePort = 443
PS C:\> $httpsListener.SSLCertificateId="arn:aws:acm:us-
east-1:<account_no>:certificate/8e477193-f779-4024-b788-d51ee01bf52b"
PS C:\> New-ELBLoadBalancerListener -LoadBalancerName myfirstclassiclb -
Listener $httpsListener
```

By default, stickiness is disabled. There are two types of stickiness that can be enabled on the load balancer. The first one is load balancer generated cookies stickiness and the second one is application generated cookies stickiness.

To enable the load balancer generated stickiness for the specified time duration, you can use the following command:

```
PS C:\> New-ELBLBCookieStickinessPolicy -LoadBalancerName myfirstclassiclb
-PolicyName MyELBDuration -CookieExpirationPeriod 60
```

To enable application generated cookies stickiness, you can use the following command:

```
PS C:\> New-ELBAppCookieStickinessPolicy -LoadBalancerName myfirstclassiclb
-PolicyName my-app-cookie -CookieName my-app-cookie
```

Creating Application Load Balancer

To find all the related cmdlets for working with Application Load Balancer, you can use the following command:

```
PS C:\> Get-Command *ELB* |Where-Object {$_.Name -Like "*ELB2*"}
```

This will list all the cmdlets for Application Load Balancer. Note that if you run the preceding cmdlet without a filter, you will notice that there are cmdlets without ELB2 in them. Any cmdlet without ELB2 in it is meant for Classic Load Balancer.

To get a list of existing Application Load Balancers, run the following command:

```
PS C:\> Get-ELB2LoadBalancer
```

To obtain the Application Load Balancer limits on the account, you can use the following cmdlet. If the limit needs to be lifted, you have to contact AWS:

```
PS C:\> Get-ELB2AccountLimit
```

```
PS C:\> Get-ELB2AccountLimit

Max  Name
---  ----
20   application-load-balancers
200  target-groups
1000 targets-per-application-load-balancer
10   listeners-per-application-load-balancer
100  rules-per-application-load-balancer
```

When you work with Application Load Balancer, you do not add target EC2 instances directly on the ALB, as we did for Classic Load Balancer. Before you create the Application Load Balancer, you first create `Target Group` and add `Target` (EC2 instances) to `Target Group`. Then, you add `Target Group` to the Application Load balancer. The rest of the process and things are pretty much similar. So, let's head on and create `Target Group`. You can use the `New-ELB2TargetGroup` cmdlet to create `Target Group`:

```
PS C:\> New-ELB2TargetGroup -HealthCheckIntervalSecond 5 -HealthCheckPath
"/" -HealthCheckPort 80 -HealthCheckProtocol http -HealthCheckTimeoutSecond
2 -HealthyThresholdCount 2 -Matcher_HttpCode 200 -Name myfirsttargetgroup -
Port 80 -Protocol http -UnhealthyThresholdCount 2 -VpcId vpc-a6bb60df
```

```
PS C:\> New-ELB2TargetGroup -HealthCheckIntervalSecond 5 -HealthCheckPath "/" -HealthCheckPort 80 -HealthCheckProtocol http -HealthCheckTimeoutSecond 2 -Heal
thyThresholdCount 2 -Matcher_HttpCode 200 -Name myfirsttargetgroup -Port 80 -Protocol http -UnhealthyThresholdCount 2 -VpcId vpc-a6bb60df

HealthCheckIntervalSeconds : 5
HealthCheckPath            : /
HealthCheckPort            : 80
HealthCheckProtocol        : HTTP
HealthCheckTimeoutSeconds  : 2
HealthyThresholdCount      : 2
LoadBalancerArns           : {}
Matcher                    : Amazon.ElasticLoadBalancingV2.Model.Matcher
Port                       : 80
Protocol                   : HTTP
TargetGroupArn             : arn:aws:elasticloadbalancing:us-east-1:072316406132:targetgroup/myfirsttargetgroup/325817ee7a290b52
TargetGroupName            : myfirsttargetgroup
UnhealthyThresholdCount    : 2
VpcId                      : vpc-a6bb60df
```

Once `Target Group` has been created, it's time to add `Target` to it. We created two EC2 instances while creating Classic Load Balancer;, I will use those EC2 instances as part of the `Target Group`. This is just for demonstration. In a real-life scenario, you should have a purpose for using the same instances across multiple load balancers and target groups. AWS allows you to register EC2 instances with multiple target groups. You can create ALB using the `New-ELB2LoadBalancer` cmdlet:

```
PS C:\> New-ELB2LoadBalancer -IpAddressType ipv4 -Name myfirstALB -Scheme
internet-facing -SecurityGroup sg-639f1612 -Subnet subnet-b29d3e9e,subnet-
c843dd80
```

Creating an ALB is similar to CLB; additionally, you will see a switch called `-IpAddressType`, for which the possible values are IPv4 and **Dualstack**. Dualstack means it can support IPv4 and IPv6.

```
PS C:\> New-ELB2LoadBalancer -IpAddressType ipv4 -Name myfirstALB -Scheme internet-facing -SecurityGroup sg-639f1612 -Subnet subnet-b29d3e9e,subnet-c843dd80

AvailabilityZones       : {us-east-1a, us-east-1b}
CanonicalHostedZoneId   : Z35SXDOTRQ7X7K
CreatedTime             : 7/4/2017 6:51:07 PM
DNSName                 : myfirstALB-2030720075.us-east-1.elb.amazonaws.com
IpAddressType           : ipv4
LoadBalancerArn         : arn:aws:elasticloadbalancing:us-east-1:072316406132:loadbalancer/app/myfirstALB/08170653024b5608
LoadBalancerName        : myfirstALB
Scheme                  : internet-facing
SecurityGroups          : {sg-639f1612}
State                   : Amazon.ElasticLoadBalancingV2.Model.LoadBalancerState
Type                    : application
VpcId                   : vpc-a6bb60df
```

To check the state of the ALB, you can use the following command:

```
PS C:\> (Get-ELB2LoadBalancer -Name myfirstALB).state
```

```
PS C:\> (Get-ELB2LoadBalancer -Name myfirstALB).state

Code    Reason
----    ------
active
```

Initially, it shows as *provisioning*. Active means ALB is ready. We created `Target Group` and ALB, but there is no linkage as yet. Before we link both of them, let's add `Target` to `Target Group`. You can use the `Register-ELB2Target` cmdlet to register the targets with `Target Group`. Note that you need to know the `Target Group` ARN and not the name when working with `Target Group`. I picked up the ARN for `Target Group` as shown in the output of the `New-ELB2TargetGroup` cmdlet:

```
PS C:\> Register-ELB2Target -TargetGroupArn
arn:aws:elasticloadbalancing:us-
east-1:<account_no>:targetgroup/myfirsttargetgroup/325817ee7a290b52 -Target
$target1
```

```
PS C:\> $target1 = New-Object Amazon.ElasticLoadBalancingV2.Model.TargetDescription
PS C:\> $target1.id="i-03f0f169a698a3a2d"
PS C:\> $target2 = New-Object Amazon.ElasticLoadBalancingV2.Model.TargetDescription
PS C:\> $target2.id="i-0bce23d76d4598e3f"
PS C:\> Register-ELB2Target -TargetGroupArn arn:aws:elasticloadbalancing:us-east-1:072316406132:targetgroup/myfirsttargetgroup/325817ee7a290b52 -Target $target1
PS C:\> Register-ELB2Target -TargetGroupArn arn:aws:elasticloadbalancing:us-east-1:072316406132:targetgroup/myfirsttargetgroup/325817ee7a290b52 -Target $target2
```

To check the state of the `Target` added to the `Target Group`, you can use the following command:

```
PS C:\> (Get-ELB2TargetHealth -TargetGroupArn
arn:aws:elasticloadbalancing:us-
east-1:<account_no>:targetgroup/myfirsttargetgroup/325817ee7a290b52).Target
Health
```

You can see that both targets have been added to the `Target Group` and the state is unused. It is shown as unused because we still have not linked `Target Group` with ALB. Let's link ALB and `Target Group`. You can link `Target Group` and ALB by creating a rule on the listener using the `New-ELB2Listener` cmdlet:

```
PS C:\> New-ELB2Listener -LoadBalancerArn arn:aws:elasticloadbalancing:us-
east-1:<account_no>:loadbalancer/app/myfirstALB/08170653024b5608 -Port 80 -
Protocol http -DefaultAction $Action1
```

Now, if you run the `Target` health check, both of them should show as healthy.

You are all set. Your first ALB is running now. Go ahead, pull out the DNS CNAME that is allocated to the ALB, and hit the browser.

```
PS C:\> Get-ELB2LoadBalancer -Name myfirstALB

AvailabilityZones      : {us-east-1a, us-east-1b}
CanonicalHostedZoneId  : Z35SXDOTRQ7X7K
CreatedTime            : 7/4/2017 6:51:07 PM
DNSName                : myfirstALB-2030720075.us-east-1.elb.amazonaws.com
IpAddressType          : ipv4
LoadBalancerArn        : arn:aws:elasticloadbalancing:us-east-1:072316406132:loadbalancer/app/myfirstALB/08170653024b5608
LoadBalancerName       : myfirstALB
Scheme                 : internet-facing
SecurityGroups         : {sg-639f1612}
State                  : Amazon.ElasticLoadBalancingV2.Model.LoadBalancerState
Type                   : application
VpcId                  : vpc-a6bb60df
```

Note that, by default, cross-zone load balancing is enabled on Application Load Balancer. So, you do not need to enable cross-zone load balancing, as we did with Classic Load Balancer.

This is my first web server

After a browser refresh, you will see this message coming from the second web server:

This is my second web server

As we used the same web servers created for Classic Load Balancer, we see the same message in the browser. You can secure your environment as much as you can by opening only the required port and protocol on the Security Groups assigned to the `Target` EC2 instances and load balancers. If you would like to add the secure listener on port `443`, ensure that you have a certificate first. The process is the same as we discussed earlier for CLB. Review the online documentation for the cmdlet related to Application Load Balancer. You can pretty much do all the stuff that you can do on the AWS Console via PowerShell.

If you want to enable stickiness, you have to do it on `Target Group` and not on ALB. You can only set load balancer generated cookies stickiness in this case. To enable stickiness, you can use `Edit-ELB2TargetGroupAttribute`:

```
PS C:\> Edit-ELB2TargetGroupAttribute -TargetGroupArn
arn:aws:elasticloadbalancing:us-
east-1:<account_no>:targetgroup/myfirsttargetgroup/325817ee7a290b52 -
Attribute $Action1
```

```
PS C:\> $Action1 = New-Object Amazon.ElasticLoadBalancingV2.Model.TargetGroupAttribute
PS C:\> $Action1.key="stickiness.enabled"
PS C:\> $Action1.value="true"
PS C:\> Edit-ELB2TargetGroupAttribute -TargetGroupArn arn:aws:elasticloadbalancing:us-east-1:072316406132:targetgroup/myfirsttargetgroup/325817ee7a290b52 -At
tribute $Action1

Key                                  Value
---                                  -----
stickiness.enabled                   true
deregistration_delay.timeout_seconds 300
stickiness.type                      lb_cookie
stickiness.lb_cookie.duration_seconds 86400
```

Deleting Elastic Load Balancer

To delete a Classic Load Balancer, you can use `Remove-ELBLoadBalancer`; and to delete an Application Load Balancer, you can use `Remove-ELB2LoadBalance`. These cmdlets delete the specified load balancer from your account. The CNAME associated with the load balancer will no longer be available, and the traffic will not be sent to the target EC2 instances.

In the case of Application Load Balancer, it also deletes the attached listeners to ALB. You won't be able to delete ALB if deletion protection is enabled on the ALB. Both cmdlets will prompt for confirmation before the operation proceeds, unless you specify force switch. You also have to use load balancer ARN to delete Application Load Balancer. For Classic, you would be using the name of the load balancer:

```
PS C:\> Remove-ELBLoadBalancer -LoadBalancerName myfirstclassiclb
PS C:\> Remove-ELB2LoadBalancer -LoadBalancerArn
arn:aws:elasticloadbalancing:us-
east-1:<account_no>:loadbalancer/app/myfirstALB/08170653024b5608
```

```
PS C:\> Remove-ELBLoadBalancer -LoadBalancerName myfirstclassiclb

Confirm
Are you sure you want to perform this action?
Performing the operation "Remove-ELBLoadBalancer (DeleteLoadBalancer)" on target "myfirstclassiclb".
[Y] Yes  [A] Yes to All  [N] No  [L] No to All  [S] Suspend  [?] Help (default is "Y"): Y
```

To delete Application Load Balancer, do this:

```
PS C:\> Remove-ELB2LoadBalancer -LoadBalancerArn arn:aws:elasticloadbalancing:us-east-1:072316406132:loadbalancer/app/myfirstALB/08170653024b5608

Confirm
Are you sure you want to perform this action?
Performing the operation "Remove-ELB2LoadBalancer (DeleteLoadBalancer)" on target
"arn:aws:elasticloadbalancing:us-east-1:072316406132:loadbalancer/app/myfirstALB/08170653024b5608".
[Y] Yes  [A] Yes to All  [N] No  [L] No to All  [S] Suspend  [?] Help (default is "Y"): Y
```

Note that the delete operation only deletes load balancers. There is no impact on `Target Group` and `Target`. In order to delete `Target Group` and the associated `Target`, you need to run Remove-ELB2TargetGroup:

```
PS C:\> Remove-ELB2TargetGroup –TargetGroupArn
arn:aws:elasticloadbalancing:us-
east-1:<account_no>:targetgroup/myfirsttargetgroup/325817ee7a290b52
```

```
PS C:\> Remove-ELB2TargetGroup -TargetGroupArn arn:aws:elasticloadbalancing:us-east-1:072316406132:targetgroup/myfirsttargetgroup/325817ee7a290b52

Confirm
Are you sure you want to perform this action?
Performing the operation "Remove-ELB2TargetGroup (DeleteTargetGroup)" on target
"arn:aws:elasticloadbalancing:us-east-1:072316406132:targetgroup/myfirsttargetgroup/325817ee7a290b52".
[Y] Yes  [A] Yes to All  [N] No  [L] No to All  [S] Suspend  [?] Help (default is "Y"): Y
```

For individual targets, you can use the following command:

```
PS C:\> Remove-EC2Instance –InstanceId i-03f0f169a698a3a2d
PS C:\> Remove-EC2Instance –InstanceId i-06ce23d76d459ee3f
```

```
PS C:\> Remove-EC2Instance -InstanceId i-03f0f169a698a3a2d

Confirm
Are you sure you want to perform this action?
Performing the operation "Remove-EC2Instance (TerminateInstances)" on target "i-03f0f169a698a3a2d".
[Y] Yes  [A] Yes to All  [N] No  [L] No to All  [S] Suspend  [?] Help (default is "Y"): Y

CurrentState                InstanceId          PreviousState
------------                ----------          -------------
Amazon.EC2.Model.InstanceState i-03f0f169a698a3a2d Amazon.EC2.Model.InstanceState

PS C:\> Remove-EC2Instance -InstanceId i-06ce23d76d459ee3f

Confirm
Are you sure you want to perform this action?
Performing the operation "Remove-EC2Instance (TerminateInstances)" on target "i-06ce23d76d459ee3f".
[Y] Yes  [A] Yes to All  [N] No  [L] No to All  [S] Suspend  [?] Help (default is "Y"): Y

CurrentState                InstanceId          PreviousState
------------                ----------          -------------
Amazon.EC2.Model.InstanceState i-06ce23d76d459ee3f Amazon.EC2.Model.InstanceState
```

Almost all the removal and delete operations will prompt you before proceeding, unless you specify a force switch with the cmdlet.

Summary

Elastic Load Balancer is an amazing component of the EC2 service, which allows us to build a highly available and fault-tolerant environment. With the addition of Application Load Balancer to the fleet, the capabilities of the load balancer service have reached a very high level. There is no need to create multiple load balancers for multiple applications, and this actually helps to reduce cost and maintenance. Classic Load Balancer is still a choice if you have TCP and SSL traffic. In the near future, AWS will enhance the limit of the number of applications and listeners that can be supported on the Application Load Balancer. In the next chapter, you will learn about another solution provided by AWS to implement elasticity using Auto Scaling. Elastic Load Balancer and Auto Scaling always go hand in hand and help to achieve a highly available, fault tolerate, and scalable solution.

9
Auto Scaling

When we talk about elasticity in AWS, Auto Scaling is one of the services that will be used the most. Auto Scaling is such a beautiful service that every application has a reason to use it, even if there is no need to scale. This is one of the best-in-class features in the cloud, making the cloud even more popular, and is one of the most considered features in cloud migration. In the on-premise world, when there is a need to satisfy the demands of a spiky load, there is nothing you can do to satisfy it unless you have already provisioned the required capacity, irrespective of the demand load. This means we have to always overprovision the capacity to ensure that spiky load is addressed. This results in a big cost problem if your application is gaining popularity exponentially. In a traditional on-premise environment, there is no secret formula for matching demand and capacity when needed. Either you end up provisioning too much compute capacity, or underprovisioning resources. The following diagram indicates the nature of demand capacity provisioning in the traditional world.

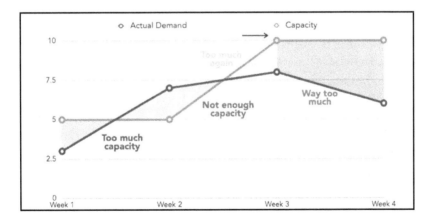

This is where the elastic nature of the cloud has an advantage. Because of this elastic nature, we can increase the capacity exactly when the load demands, and decrease it when the load lightens. To address the issue of the overprovisioning of compute resources, AWS provides Auto Scaling as a solution to handle the demand for the application, thus allowing you to match the need of the spiky load. The following diagram shows the on-demand provisioning of the capacity in the cloud when actually required.

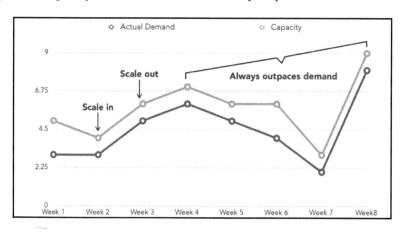

Auto Scaling is a component of the AWS EC2 service. Hence, you can find Auto Scaling under the EC2 Compute service. Note that Scale-Out or Scale-Up, and Scale-In or Scale-Down are used interchangeably. Scale-Out means you are adding capacity to the fleet based on-demand, and Scale-In means you are taking out capacity or shrinking your fleet. Auto Scaling is free to use, however you are charged for the resources that Auto Scaling provisions. There are several benefits of using Auto Scaling for your application architecture.

- **Better availability:** Auto Scaling ensures that the right amount of capacity is available to handle the load at all times to meet traffic demands.
- **Better cost management:** Auto Scaling adds capacity only when you need it, and shrinks it when not needed, thus allowing you to pay only for the time you used the capacity.
- **Better fault tolerance:** Auto Scaling can detect when an EC2 instance is unhealthy, terminate it, and replace it with the new EC2 instance. You can configure Auto Scaling to use multiple availability zones. If a particular availability zone becomes unavailable, it launches instances in another availability zone to compensate.

In this chapter, we will discuss Auto Scaling components, Auto Scaling lifecycle, fleet management, and dynamic scaling. In addition, we will learn how to create launch configuration, Auto Scaling Group, maintaining fleets manually and dynamically, lifecycle hooks and cooldown, termination policies, termination protection, suspending the Auto Scaling process, and standby mode.

Auto Scaling components

There are three major components that you need to be aware of while working with Auto Scaling. They are:

- **Launch configuration**: This defines what to scale. This is a collection of attribute values to be used for launching an EC2 instance in the Auto Scaling Group. This is a kind of template to be used while launching EC2 instances. Attributes are AMI, instance type, Security Groups, block device mapping, and key pairs. Launch configuration is pretty much the same as all the configuration settings that need to be defined when launching a new EC2 instance. This configuration instructs Auto Scaling Group what kind of EC2 instances need to be added to the fleet. You can also add userdata to bootstrap the instances to keep the configuration of your application as dynamic as you can.

- **Auto Scaling Groups**: This is a logical collection of EC2 instances and defines where to launch instances. It also defines the limits on the number of EC2 instances to launch, should a certain event occurs. It also allows you to set the desired capacity to start with. As soon as you create the Auto Scaling Group, it starts by launching EC2 instances to meet the desired capacity. Maintaining the number of EC2 instances in the Auto Scaling Group and automatic scaling is the core functionality of the Auto Scaling service. For effective Auto Scaling architecture ensure that you understand your application well enough.

- **Scaling policies**: This is an optional component, but helps you to implement real-time elasticity in the cloud. You can define when and under what conditions Scaling-Out and Scaling-In should happen. There are several ways for you to scale Auto Scaling Groups. You can either scale based on-demand, or based on a schedule. You can also do manual scaling by just simply changing the minimum, maximum, and desired capacity in the Auto Scaling Group. It is always best practice to have at least two scaling policies being used simultaneously. You should define a minimum of at least one Scale-Out and one Scale-In policy. Your Auto Scaling Group can have more than one scaling policy attached to it at any given time.

Auto Scaling lifecycle

Under the hood, EC2 instances are in the Auto Scaling Group. It's essential for you to understand the lifecycle of those EC2 instances when they are in the Auto Scaling Group. The lifecycle of the EC2 instances in the Auto Scaling Group is different from those that are not part of the Auto Scaling Group. Understanding lifecycle events will help you to properly architect a deployment strategy for your application. The following diagram helps you to understand lifecycle events.

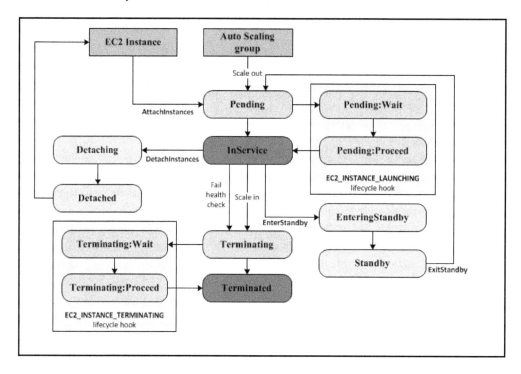

When a Scale-Out event occurs, the Auto Scaling Group launches new EC2 instances using the associated launch configuration. All newly launched EC2 instances start in the **Pending** state. This is the state in which you can add a lifecycle hook and perform a custom action. Lifecycle hooks give you the ability to perform actions before an EC2 instance is **InService** state, or before an instance is in **Terminated** state. This is very useful when deployment of an application takes time due to the bootstrapping process, or you want to perform a specific action before your instance is terminated. Once you add the lifecycle hook, the EC2 instance will not move to the **InService** state unless you complete the lifecycle hook. This capability of the Auto Scaling Group provides you with the ability to fully install and configure an application before the load balancer starts serving traffic to it.

An instance will stay in **InService** state unless a Scale-In event occurs or you put the instance in **Standby** state manually. **Standby** state enables you to take the instance out of service and then troubleshoot the issues associated with the instance, if any. Auto Scaling automatically removes the instance from the Auto Scaling Group if an EC2 instance fails the health check. You can also manually detach an instance from the Auto Scaling Group if needed. A Scale-In event is automatic and removes one or more EC2 instances from the Auto Scaling Group depending on the CloudWatch alarm. We will learn more about the CloudWatch alarm later in the book. You can also attach an existing instance to an Auto Scaling Group, provided it meets some criteria. You can attach an existing EC2 running instance if the AMI used to launch the instance still exists, the EC2 instance is not part of any other Auto Scaling Group, and it is available in the same availability zone as the Auto Scaling Group.

Fleet management

Fleet management is one of the main reasons for managing the EC2 instances for your application in an Auto Scaling Group. You can usually put all the healthy instance behind the load balancer and let it serve the traffic to the healthy instances. As discussed in an earlier chapter, if an EC2 instance becomes unhealthy, the load balancer will stop sending traffic to it, and you have to take appropriate action manually to ensure that instances are healthy and ready to serve traffic again. This is where Auto Scaling plays a vital role, even though you do not have any intention of scaling. Instead of running those EC2 instance independently behind the load balancer, if you add them as part of the Auto Scaling Group, Auto Scaling automatically manages the fleet behind your load balancer and you do not need to take any manual action if any one of the EC2 instances becomes unhealthy.

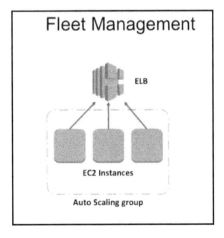

An Auto Scaling health check will detect an impaired instance and replace it with a healthy one, without any manual intervention, as the same instance while running in the Auto Scaling Group. This is a very simple use case in the industry, and is mostly used for self-healing. You just have to define the fleet size that you need to run to serve the traffic.

Dynamic scaling

As you start adapting more and more to your cloud journey and understanding the capability of Auto Scaling, dynamic scaling is what enables you to respond to the dynamic changes in the load that is being placed on your application. In the diagram below, we have four EC2 instances running and there is a metric threshold defined for CPU utilization to Scale-Out the fleet based on the average load on the four EC2 instances. For example, you might want to add another EC2 instance to the fleet if average CPU utilization goes beyond 80%, or remove an instance when average CPU utilization is below 50%. The fleet size will vary depending on the load on your application and you will be charged only for the duration when you add additional instances.

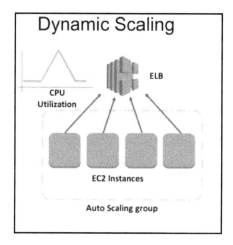

Creating launch configuration

In order to understand the Auto Scaling concept better, let's make use of the same foundational architecture that we used in an earlier chapter. But, instead of load balancer sending traffic to the EC2 instance directly, we will make use of the Auto Scaling Group. To find out all the cmdlets related to Auto Scaling, you can use the following command:

```
PS C:\> Get-Command *-AS*
```

To see the limits of Auto Scaling components in the given account, you can use the following command:

```
PS C:\> Get-ASAccountLimit
```

```
PS C:\> Get-ASAccountLimit

MaxNumberOfAutoScalingGroups MaxNumberOfLaunchConfigurations NumberOfAutoScalingGroups NumberOfLaunchConfigurations
---------------------------- ------------------------------- ------------------------- ---------------------------
20                           100                             0                         0
```

The output indicates that the maximum number of Auto Scaling Groups that can be created in the region is 20, and you can create 100 launch configurations at the most. If you want to change the limit, you have to ask AWS to increase it. To create an Auto Scaling Group, first, we need to create the template called **launch configuration**. To create the launch configuration template, you need to know the AMI ID, Security Group, key name, and userdata, if any, that needs to be passed on. I have a Linux AMI `ami-a4c7edb2` which is just a vanilla OS provided by AWS. You can use your AMI if you've created any. These AMI IDs keep changing. We earlier covered how we can get the AMI ID using console and PowerShell cmdlets. The Security Group that we will use is `sg-7b1f700a`, which has ingress on port `22` for SSH, port `80` for HTTP, and port `443` for HTTPS. I am planning to pass the following userdata scripts to each EC2 instance while bootstrapping.

```
PS C:\> Get-Content -Raw D:\data\UserData\WebAppLCUserData.txt
#!/bin/bash
yum update -y
yum install -y httpd curl
service httpd start
chkconfig httpd on
groupadd www
usermod -a -G www ec2-user
chown -R root:www /var/www
chmod 2775 /var/www
find /var/www -type d -exec chmod 2775 {} +
find /var/www -type f -exec chmod 0664 {} +
echo "I am coming from " > /var/www/html/index.html
export myhost=`curl http://instance-data/latest/meta-data/instance-id`
echo $myhost >> /var/www/html/index.html
```

This script simply sets the Apache web server and creates the `index.html` in the web server's default root directory in which the EC2 instance ID is captured. I have created a key pair called `MyWebPressApp`, and you can confirm that by running `Get-EC2KeyPair`. I am using the same key pair that we used in an earlier chapter. Feel free to create one if you have not retained the private key.

```
PS C:\> Get-EC2KeyPair -KeyName MyWebPressApp

KeyFingerprint                                   KeyName
--------------                                   -------
bc:44:f7:48:6a:47:ca:e6:af:cf:97:a3:48:a8:d3:98:90:b2:07:06 MyWebPressApp
```

Another thing that you can do is to associate the IAM role with the launch configuration, so that EC2 instances are started with that role. This way, you do not need to store any AWS credentials on those servers if needed. Attaching a role to an EC2 is considered a best practice. If you miss out attaching the role at the time of launch, no worries; you can attach the role to the running EC2 instances. This simply administration and maintenance aspects. This was not a possibility prior to 2017. I have a role called `WorldPressAppRole`, to which I have already assigned the `AdministratorAccess` profile. While working through PowerShell, you have to create the instance profile and assign a role to that instance profile. You can do so with the following command:

```
PS C:\> New-IAMInstanceProfile -InstanceProfileName WebAppRoleProfile
PS C:\> Add-IAMRoleToInstanceProfile -InstanceProfileName WebAppRoleProfile
-RoleName WorldPressAppRole
```

```
PS C:\> New-IAMInstanceProfile -InstanceProfileName WebAppRoleProfile


Arn                  : arn:aws:iam::072316406132:instance-profile/WebAppRoleProfile
CreateDate           : 7/10/2017 2:24:39 PM
InstanceProfileId    : AIPAIZQMVKVXB23AWQXYU
InstanceProfileName  : WebAppRoleProfile
Path                 : /
Roles                : {}


PS C:\> Add-IAMRoleToInstanceProfile -InstanceProfileName WebAppRoleProfile -RoleName WorldPressAppRole
```

I have not seen a `Userdatafile` switch with the `New-ASLaunchConfiguration` cmdlet. There is only a `Userdata`. `Userdata` switch, which expects userdata to be in base64 format. Before you pass on the userdata to the `New-ASLaunchConfiguration` cmdlet, you must convert that to base64. To create launch configuration, you can use the following command:

```
PS C:\> New-ASLaunchConfiguration -LaunchConfigurationName WebAppLC -
InstanceType "t2.micro" -ImageId "ami-a4c7edb2" -SecurityGroup
"sg-7b1f700a" -IamInstanceProfile "WebAppRoleProfile" -KeyName
"MyWebPressApp" -AssociatePublicIpAddress $false -Userdata $EncuserData
```

```
PS C:\> $userdata = (Get-Content -Raw D:\data\UserData\WebAppLCUserData.txt)
PS C:\> $EncodeUserData = [System.Text.Encoding]::UTF8.GetBytes($userdata)
PS C:\> $EncuserData = [System.Convert]::ToBase64String($EncodeUserData)
PS C:\> New-ASLaunchConfiguration -LaunchConfigurationName WebAppLC -InstanceType "t2.micro" -ImageId "ami-a4c7edb2" -SecurityGroup "sg-7b1f700a" -IamInstanc
eProfile "WebAppRoleProfile" -KeyName "MyWebPressApp" -AssociatePublicIpAddress $false -Userdata $EncuserData
```

The `AssociatePublicIpAddress` switch indicates whether you want to associate a public IP to the EC2 instance or not. Review the above screenshot for converting the user data to base64 format in PowerShell. Successful execution of the preceding cmdlet will not return anything. You can validate the creation of the launch configuration using the cmdlet `Get-ASLaunchConfiguration`.

```
PS C:\> Get-ASLaunchConfiguration

AssociatePublicIpAddress     : False
BlockDeviceMappings          : {}
ClassicLinkVPCId             :
ClassicLinkVPCSecurityGroups : {}
CreatedTime                  : 7/10/2017 5:15:39 PM
EbsOptimized                 : False
IamInstanceProfile           : WebAppRoleProfile
ImageId                      : ami-a4c7edb2
InstanceMonitoring           : Amazon.AutoScaling.Model.InstanceMonitoring
InstanceType                 : t2.micro
KernelId                     :
KeyName                      : MyWebPressApp
LaunchConfigurationARN       : arn:aws:autoscaling:us-east-1:072316406132:launchConfiguration:2f700b60-94b0-4c16-8731-63902cecbdc8:launchConfigurationName/W
                               ebAppLC
LaunchConfigurationName      : WebAppLC
PlacementTenancy             :
RamdiskId                    :
SecurityGroups               : {sg-7b1f700a}
SpotPrice                    :
UserData                     : IyEvYmluL2Jhc2gNCnl1bSB1cGRhdGUgLXkNCnl1bSB5pbnN0YWxsIC15IGh0dHBkIGN1cmwNCnNlcnZpY2UgaHR0cGQgc3RhcnQNCmNoa2NvbmZpZyBodHRwZCBvb
                               g0KZ3JvdXBhZGQgd3d3DQp1c2Vybw9kIC1hIC1HIHd3dyBlYzItdXNlcg0KY2hvd24gLVIgcm9vdDp3d3cgL3Zhci93d3cNCmNob3d0k1DI3NzUgL3Zhci93d3cNCm
                               ZpbmQgL3Zhci93d3cgLXR5cGUgZCAtZXhlYyBjaG1vZCAyNzc1IHt9ICsNCmZpbmQgL3Zhci93d3cgLXR5cGUgZiAtZXhlYyBjaG1vZCA4NjY0IHt9ICsNCmVjaG8
                               gIkkgYW0gY29taW5nIGZyb20gIiA+IC92YXIvd3d3L2h0bWwvaW5kZXguaHRtbA0KZXhwb3J0IG15aG9zdD1gY3VybCBodHRwOi8vaW5zdGFuY2UtZGF0YS9sYXRlc3
                               c3QvbWV0YS1kYXRhL2luc3RhbmNlLWlkYA0KZWNobyAkbXlob3N0ID4+IC92YXIvd3d3L2h0bWwvaW5kZXguaHRtbA0K
```

You can see that all the details that we passed on to the `New-ASLaunchConfiguration` are seen in the output of `Get-ASLaunchConfiguration`. `Userdata` has encrypted values, but you can ensure that it is what you passed to it using the AWS Console. You can get a nice, clear picture here.

User data

```
#!/bin/bash
yum update -y
yum install -y httpd curl
service httpd start
chkconfig httpd on
groupadd www
usermod -a -G www ec2-user
chown -R root:www /var/www
chmod 2775 /var/www
find /var/www -type d -exec chmod 2775 {} +
find /var/www -type f -exec chmod 0664 {} +
echo "I am coming from " > /var/www/html/index.html
export myhost=`curl http://instance-data/latest/meta-data/instance-id`
echo $myhost >> /var/www/html/index.html
```

With this launch configuration ready, we can create the Auto Scaling Group now. But, before creating the Auto Scaling Group, let's ensure that we have at least one load balancer. You can create a Classic Load Balancer as follows:

```
PS C:\> $httpListener = New-Object
Amazon.ElasticLoadBalancing.Model.Listener
PS C:\> $httpListener.Protocol = "http"
PS C:\> $httpListener.LoadBalancerPort = 80
PS C:\> $httpListener.InstanceProtocol = "http"
PS C:\> $httpListener.InstancePort = 80
PS C:\> New-ELBLoadBalancer -LoadBalancerName MyCLB -SecurityGroup
sg-639f1612 -Subnet subnet-b29d3e9e,subnet-c843dd80 -Listener $httpListener
```

`sg-639f1612` is the security that has ingress on port 80 for HTTP and port 443 for HTTPS traffic. We are just using port 80 to demonstrate the concept. Port 443 requires a certificate and a domain associate with that certificate. Conceptually, we have touched base on the HTTPS and port 443 in the earlier chapter. The subnets that are specified in the cmdlet are public subnets in this case.

```
PS C:\> $httpListener = New-Object Amazon.ElasticLoadBalancing.Model.Listener
PS C:\> $httpListener.Protocol = "http"
PS C:\> $httpListener.LoadBalancerPort = 80
PS C:\> $httpListener.InstanceProtocol = "http"
PS C:\> $httpListener.InstancePort = 80
PS C:\> New-ELBLoadBalancer -LoadBalancerName MyCLB -SecurityGroup sg-639f1612 -Subnet subnet-b29d3e9e,subnet-c843dd80 -Listener $httpListener
MyCLB-553220444.us-east-1.elb.amazonaws.com
PS C:\> Edit-ELBLoadBalancerAttribute -LoadBalancerName MyCLB -CrossZoneLoadBalancing_Enabled $true

LoadBalancerAttributes                                    LoadBalancerName
----------------------                                    ----------------
Amazon.ElasticLoadBalancing.Model.LoadBalancerAttributes  MyCLB
```

Because we created a Classic Load Balancer, we have to ensure that cross-zone balancing is enabled. This is done using `Edit-ELBLoadBalancerAttribute`.

```
PS C:\> Edit-ELBLoadBalancerAttribute -LoadBalancerName MyCLB -
CrossZoneLoadBalancing_Enabled $true
```

Classic Load Balancer is ready as well, and you can access it now using the DNS name `MyCLB-553220444.us-east-1.elb.amazonaws.com`.

Creating an Auto Scaling Group

Once your load balancer and launch configuration are ready, creating an Auto Scaling Group is just a click away. You can use the `New-ASAutoScalingGroup` cmdlet to create the Auto Scaling Group. Note that you must know the subnet ID that Auto Scaling can use. The subnet IDs that are specified following are the private subnet we created earlier. ELB is created in a public subnet and EC2 instances are launched in a private subnet.

```
PS C:\> New-ASAutoScalingGroup -AutoScalingGroupName WebAppASG -
LaunchConfigurationName WebAppLC -MinSize 2 -MaxSize 2 -AvailabilityZone
@("us-east-1a", "us-east-1b") -VPCZoneIdentifier "subnet-b262c19e,subnet-
f042dcb8" -HealthCheckType ELB -HealthCheckGracePeriod 10 -LoadBalancerName
MyCLB
```

```
PS C:\> New-ASAutoScalingGroup -AutoScalingGroupName WebAppASG -LaunchConfigurationName WebAppLC -MinSize 2 -MaxSize 2 -AvailabilityZone @("us-east-1a", "us-east-1b") -VPCZoneIdentifier "subnet-b262c19e,subnet-f042dcb8" -HealthCheckType ELB -HealthCheckGracePeriod 10 -LoadBalancerName MyCLB
```

Successful execution returns nothing. You can review the Auto Scaling Group configuration and status using the following:

```
PS C:\> Get-ASAutoScalingGroup -AutoScalingGroupName WebAppASG

AutoScalingGroupARN             : arn:aws:autoscaling:us-east-1:072316406132:autoScalingGroup:8936441b-7586-42d5-9726-04de681ba047:autoScalingGroupName/Web
                                  AppASG
AutoScalingGroupName            : WebAppASG
AvailabilityZones               : {us-east-1a, us-east-1b}
CreatedTime                     : 7/10/2017 5:41:58 PM
DefaultCooldown                 : 300
DesiredCapacity                 : 2
EnabledMetrics                  : {}
HealthCheckGracePeriod          : 10
HealthCheckType                 : ELB
Instances                       : {WebAppLC, WebAppLC}
LaunchConfigurationName         : WebAppLC
LoadBalancerNames               : {MyCLB}
MaxSize                         : 2
MinSize                         : 2
NewInstancesProtectedFromScaleIn : False
PlacementGroup                  :
Status                          :
SuspendedProcesses              : {}
Tags                            : {}
TargetGroupARNs                 : {}
TerminationPolicies             : {Default}
VPCZoneIdentifier               : subnet-b262c19e,subnet-f042dcb8
```

As soon as you run the `New-ASAutoScalingGroup`, you will have two EC2 instances running in your fleet and will be automatically registered with Classic Load balancer. You can now access ELB CNAME in a web browser and see the magic. We get the CLB URL `myclb-553220444.us-east-1.elb.amazonaws.com`.

```
←  →  C  ⓘ myclb-553220444.us-east-1.elb.amazonaws.com

I am coming from i-07ed4ac4d39667284
```

I am coming from i-0f0f351fb14aaebe3

If you've done your networking part correctly, including the Security Groups ingress, you should be in a position to get something similar to the preceding. Because we have two EC2 instances in the fleet, we get two different instance ID's. Remember, this is what we passed on to the EC2 instance while bootstrapping.

The AWS dashboard shows you that there are two instances running which have no public IP. Because there is no public IP, you cannot access these instances directly. All the application traffic is served via a load balancer. In order to access these servers, you should have a bastion host in the same VPC, and then you can hop on to these servers for any troubleshooting, if needed. You can check the health of the instances in the specified Auto Scaling Group using the following command:

```
PS C:\> (Get-ASAutoScalingGroup -AutoScalingGroupName WebAppASG).Instances
| Get-ASAutoScalingInstance
```

```
PS C:\> (Get-ASAutoScalingGroup -AutoScalingGroupName WebAppASG).Instances | Get-ASAutoScalingInstance


AutoScalingGroupName      : WebAppASG
AvailabilityZone          : us-east-1a
HealthStatus              : HEALTHY
InstanceId                : i-07ed4ac4d39667284
LaunchConfigurationName   : WebAppLC
LifecycleState            : InService
ProtectedFromScaleIn      : False

AutoScalingGroupName      : WebAppASG
AvailabilityZone          : us-east-1b
HealthStatus              : HEALTHY
InstanceId                : i-0f0f351fb14aaebe3
LaunchConfigurationName   : WebAppLC
LifecycleState            : InService
ProtectedFromScaleIn      : False
```

We can see that `LifecycleState` is `InService` and `HealthStatus` is `HEALTHY`.

Increasing a fleet manually

In the previous example, we specified `MinSize` and `MaxSize` as 2 for the Auto Scaling Group. There is another switch that we can pass on to the `New-ASAutoScalingGroup` to instruct Auto Scaling to start the fleet with the desired capacity. As we did not specify `DesiredCapacity`, Auto Scaling assumes the size as the specified `MinSize` . Hence, the fleet we started had the minimum two instances running. `DesiredCapacity` values can be in between the `MinSize` and `MaxSize` of the Auto Scaling Group, and both those numbers are inclusive. Let's try to update the `MaxSize` to 6 and the `DesiredCapacity` of the fleet to 3. You can do this using `Update-ASAutoScalingGroup`.

```
PS C:\> Update-ASAutoScalingGroup -AutoScalingGroupName WebAppASG  -
DesiredCapacity 3 -MinSize 2 -MaxSize 6
```

```
PS C:\> Update-ASAutoScalingGroup -AutoScalingGroupName WebAppASG  -DesiredCapacity 3 -MinSize 2 -MaxSize 6
PS C:\> (Get-ASAutoScalingGroup -AutoScalingGroupName WebAppASG).Instances | Get-ASAutoScalingInstance| format-table -property InstanceId,HealthStatus

InstanceId         HealthStatus
----------         ------------
i-07ed4ac4d39667284 HEALTHY
i-0bc6d110b967ba74f HEALTHY
i-0f0f351fb14aaebe3 HEALTHY
```

As soon as you update the Auto Scaling Group, another EC2 instance fires up automatically. Now, you have three instances in the fleet. This way, you can manually increase the fleet size, if needed. You can also make use of the `Set-ASDesiredCapacity` cmdlet to increase the desired capacity, provided you have `MinSize` and `MaxSize` set correctly.

```
PS C:\> Set-ASDesiredCapacity -AutoScalingGroupName WebAppASG -
DesiredCapacity 4
```

```
PS C:\> Set-ASDesiredCapacity -AutoScalingGroupName WebAppASG -DesiredCapacity 4
PS C:\> (Get-ASAutoScalingGroup -AutoScalingGroupName WebAppASG).Instances | Get-ASAutoScalingInstance| format-table -property InstanceId,HealthStatus

InstanceId         HealthStatus
----------         ------------
i-07ed4ac4d39667284 HEALTHY
i-0bc6d110b967ba74f HEALTHY
i-0c57398c25453eda8 HEALTHY
i-0f0f351fb14aaebe3 HEALTHY
```

Now there are four instances in the Auto Scaling Group and they are healthy. Similarly, if you want to reduce the fleet size from four instances to two, you can use the following cmdlet to do so:

```
PS C:\> Set-ASDesiredCapacity -AutoScalingGroupName WebAppASG -
DesiredCapacity 2
```

```
PS C:\> Set-ASDesiredCapacity -AutoScalingGroupName WebAppASG -DesiredCapacity 2
PS C:\> (Get-ASAutoScalingGroup -AutoScalingGroupName WebAppASG).Instances | Get-ASAutoScalingInstance| format-table -property InstanceId,HealthStatus

InstanceId           HealthStatus
----------           ------------
i-07ed4ac4d39667284  HEALTHY
i-0c57398c25453eda8  HEALTHY
i-0f0f351fb14aaebe3  HEALTHY


PS C:\> (Get-ASAutoScalingGroup -AutoScalingGroupName WebAppASG).Instances | Get-ASAutoScalingInstance| format-table -property InstanceId,HealthStatus

InstanceId           HealthStatus
----------           ------------
i-07ed4ac4d39667284  HEALTHY
i-0f0f351fb14aaebe3  HEALTHY
```

Note that, increasing or decreasing the fleet size will demand some time depending on the configuration that you do during the bootstrapping process.

Scaling-Out and Scaling-In dynamically

To achieve elasticity in the cloud automatically, you can define the scaling policies. It is always a best practice to define at least one Scale-Out and one Scale-In policy for the Auto Scaling Group. You can define the Scale-Out and Scale-In policies using the cmdlet `Write-ASScalingPolicy`. To add one EC2 instance to the fleet, you can use the following command:

```
PS C:\> Write-ASScalingPolicy -AutoScalingGroupName WebAppASG -
AdjustmentType "ChangeInCapacity" -PolicyName "WebAppscaleUp" -
ScalingAdjustment +1
```

Switching `ScalingAdjustment` to a positive value indicates the addition of the EC2 instance, and a negative value indicates removal of the EC2 instance from the Auto Scaling fleet.

```
PS C:\> Write-ASScalingPolicy -AutoScalingGroupName WebAppASG -
AdjustmentType "ChangeInCapacity" -PolicyName "WebAppscaleDown" -
ScalingAdjustment -1
```

```
PS C:\> Write-ASScalingPolicy -AutoScalingGroupName WebAppASG -AdjustmentType "ChangeInCapacity" -PolicyName "WebAppScaleUp" -ScalingAdjustment +1
arn:aws:autoscaling:us-east-1:072316406132:scalingPolicy:81642e7c-9a08-49a1-95ac-132a0cd2af57:autoScalingGroupName/WebAppASG:policyName/WebAppScaleUp
PS C:\> Write-ASScalingPolicy -AutoScalingGroupName WebAppASG -AdjustmentType "ChangeInCapacity" -PolicyName "WebAppScaleDown" -ScalingAdjustment -1
arn:aws:autoscaling:us-east-1:072316406132:scalingPolicy:91b5ec1a-fea4-48ca-8aaa-6e71fb939aeb:autoScalingGroupName/WebAppASG:policyName/WebAppScaleDown
```

For the switch `AdjustmentType`, valid values are `ChangeInCapacity`, `ExactCapacity`, and `PercentChangeInCapacity`. Just adding scaling policies is not sufficient; you need to add a trigger action, and usually, this can be a CloudWatch alarm. I have not found the right switches to relate the CloudWatch alarm to the Auto Scaling Group via PowerShell at the time of writing this book. Hence, I used the AWS Console to define those alarms as following. In the following example, the Auto Scaling Group will add one EC2 instance to the fleet when the aggregate CPU utilization is greater than or equal to 80%, and will remove the EC2 instance from the fleet if the aggregate CPU utilization is less than or equal to 40%.

Scaling on schedule

Instead of scaling manually, you might want to Scale-Up your fleet proactively for the given duration. This is a possibility if you have an Auto Scaling Group. You can schedule an action for the given date and time to increase or decrease the fleet size. This can be done using `Write-ASScheduledUpdateGroupAction`.

```
PS C:\> Write-ASScheduledUpdateGroupAction -AutoScalingGroupName WebAppASG
-ScheduledActionName "MyWebAppScheduleActionUp" -StartTime
"2017-07-10T12:06:00Z" -DesiredCapacity 4
```

In this example, the Auto Scaling Group fleet size is scheduled to increase to the desired capacity of 4 on 10-Jul-2017 at 12:06 PM GMT/UTC. Note that, you have to always specify the time in GMT/UTC. If you feel that you require this fleet size just for an hour, you can schedule the Scale-In an action as per the following:

```
PS C:\> Write-ASScheduledUpdateGroupAction -AutoScalingGroupName WebAppASG
-ScheduledActionName "MyWebAppScheduleActionDown" -StartTime
"2017-07-10T13:06:00Z" -DesiredCapacity 2
```

So, as per our example, on 10-Jul-2017 at 13:06 P.M., a Scale-In event will be triggered and the desired capacity of the fleet will be set back to 2 once again. There is a recurrence switch with this cmdlet which you can use to schedule a cron-like expression if needed. By default, it will run the schedule action once. Review the online documentation for this cmdlet and tweak the parameter values as per your need.

Lifecycle hooks and cooldown

We have seen that health check attributes specified on the load balancer decide whether the EC2 instance is healthy or not. As soon as a health check has been passed, the load balancer starts sending traffic to the EC2 instances, irrespective of whether the application hosted on the EC2 instances is fully configured and installed or not. Often, deploying code and applications take time, and you do not want the load balancer sending traffic until it is fully ready. There is no way for a load balancer to understand whether the EC2 instances are fully configured during bootstrapping. This is where lifecycle hooks play a major role. Lifecycle hooks give us a way to perform actions before an EC2 instance is in **InService** state, or before an EC2 instance is in **Terminated** state.

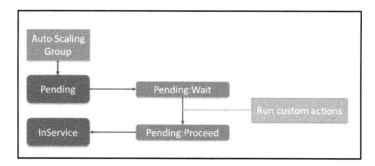

During an EC2 instance launch time, when you add a lifecycle hook to the Auto Scaling Group, the EC2 instance status will move to **Pending:Wait** state. All EC2 instances start in **Pending** state. Because of this, the load balancer will not start sending traffic to an EC2 instance in this state. This allows us to install and configure the application fully on the EC2 instances. By default, an EC2 instance stays for 60 minutes in the **Pending:Wait** state, or you can complete the lifecycle action, which will move the EC2 instance to the **Pending:Proceed**, and then later to the **InService** state.

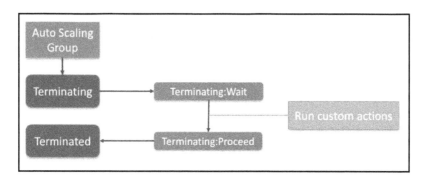

Similarly, you can add a lifecycle hook for the **Terminating** state. There are several reasons as to why you may want to add lifecycle hooks at termination time. You might want to download the log files or perform another action, such as completing batch job or long-running job that is currently running before you terminate the instance.

Let's make use of the load balancer `MyCLB` and the Auto Scaling Group `WebAppASG`, created earlier to understand the lifecycle hook concept better. Check the status of the existing instances registered with the load balancer and Auto Scaling Group. You can do this using the following command:

```
PS C:\> Get-ELBInstanceHealth -LoadBalancerName MyCLB
PS C:\> (Get-ASAutoScalingGroup -AutoScalingGroupName WebAppASG).Instances
| Get-ASAutoScalingInstance| format-table -property InstanceId,HealthStatus
```

You can see that `MyCLB` reports both EC2 instances are in `InService` and Auto Scaling Group shows them as `HEALTHY` and `InService` as well. You can check the desired capacity, minimum, and maximum specified for `WebAppASG` by using the following command:

```
PS C:\> Get-ASAutoScalingGroup -AutoScalingGroupName WebAppASG |Format-
Table DesiredCapacity,MinSize,MaxSize
```

```
PS C:\> Get-ASAutoScalingGroup -AutoScalingGroupName WebAppASG |Format-Table DesiredCapacity,MinSize,MaxSize

DesiredCapacity MinSize MaxSize
--------------- ------- -------
              2       2       6
```

In this example, we will update the desired capacity to 3 and will check the status of the instances after adding the lifecycle hook. You can check the existing lifecycle hooks using the following command:

```
PS C:\> Get-ASLifecycleHook -AutoScalingGroupName WebAppASG
```

There is no hook as of now. First, let's add a lifecycle hook to launch an instance. You can do this as shown below:

```
PS C:\> Write-ASLifecycleHook -AutoScalingGroupName WebAppASG -
LifecycleHookName "MyLCHookAtLaunch" -LifecycleTransition
"autoscaling:EC2_INSTANCE_LAUNCHING"
```

```
PS C:\> Get-ASLifecycleHook -AutoScalingGroupName WebAppASG
PS C:\> Write-ASLifecycleHook -AutoScalingGroupName WebAppASG -LifecycleHookName "MyLCHookAtLaunch" -LifecycleTransition "autoscaling:EC2_INSTANCE_LAUNCHING"

PS C:\> Get-ASLifecycleHook -AutoScalingGroupName WebAppASG


AutoScalingGroupName   : WebAppASG
DefaultResult          : ABANDON
GlobalTimeout          : 172800
HeartbeatTimeout       : 3600
LifecycleHookName      : MyLCHookAtLaunch
LifecycleTransition    : autoscaling:EC2_INSTANCE_LAUNCHING
NotificationMetadata   :
NotificationTargetARN  :
RoleARN                :
```

As we have added a lifecycle hook on the `WebAppASG`, any instance that gets added to this Auto Scaling Group based on the scaling action will be moved to the **Pending:Wait** state and will not be registered with the load balancer. To demonstrate this, let's change the desired capacity to 3 using the following command:

```
PS C:\> Set-ASDesiredCapacity -AutoScalingGroupName WebAppASG -
DesiredCapacity 3
```

As soon as we increase the desired capacity to 3, Auto Scaling will launch a new EC2 instance, transition to **Pending:Wait** state, and stay there until we complete the lifecycle hook, or for 60 minutes.

You can see that EC2 instance i-05ba9441e9d65e0ff has transitioned to the **Pending:Wait** state and is not registered with the ELB. Because of this capability of the Auto Scaling Group, you can install the application and configure it properly and then complete the lifecycle hook action using the following command:

```
PS C:\> Complete-ASLifecycleAction -LifecycleHookName "MyLCHookAtLaunch" -
AutoScalingGroupName WebAppASG -LifecycleActionResult CONTINUE -InstanceId
i-05ba9441e9d65e0ff
```

As soon as the lifecycle hook is completed, the EC2 instance will transition to **Pending:Proceed**, and then later, to **InService**. Transition happens so quickly that I did not get a chance to capture the **Pending:Proceed** state in this case. Once it is seen as HEALTHY and InService by the Auto Scaling Group, the load balancer will automatically register that instance and will start sending traffic.

The default heartbeat timeout for each lifecycle hook that you add is 3600 seconds, but in case you feel that this is not a sufficient time period for you to fully configure the EC2 instance, then you can extend this timeout period to a greater value. If you want to set it to 7200 seconds, you can do this as shown following:

```
PS C:\> Write-ASLifecycleHook –AutoScalingGroupName WebAppASG –
LifecycleHookName "MyLCHookAtLaunch" –HeartbeatTimeout 7200
```

```
PS C:\> Get-ASLifecycleHook -AutoScalingGroupName WebAppASG


AutoScalingGroupName   : WebAppASG
DefaultResult          : ABANDON
GlobalTimeout          : 172800
HeartbeatTimeout       : 3600
LifecycleHookName      : MyLCHookAtLaunch
LifecycleTransition    : autoscaling:EC2_INSTANCE_LAUNCHING
NotificationMetadata   :
NotificationTargetARN  :
RoleARN                :


PS C:\> Write-ASLifecycleHook -AutoScalingGroupName WebAppASG -LifecycleHookName "MyLCHookAtLaunch" -HeartbeatTimeout 7200
PS C:\> Get-ASLifecycleHook -AutoScalingGroupName WebAppASG


AutoScalingGroupName   : WebAppASG
DefaultResult          : ABANDON
GlobalTimeout          : 172800
HeartbeatTimeout       : 7200
LifecycleHookName      : MyLCHookAtLaunch
LifecycleTransition    : autoscaling:EC2_INSTANCE_LAUNCHING
NotificationMetadata   :
NotificationTargetARN  :
RoleARN                :
```

Another important attribute that you should understand is the cooldown period. The default cooldown value is 300 seconds. This value tells the Auto Scaling Group that there is no need to launch or terminate an EC2 instance before the previous scaling activity takes effect. In short, the Auto Scaling Group waits for the duration of the cooldown period before resuming dynamic scaling activities. If you manually Scale-Up your Auto Scaling Group, the default behavior is to not wait for the cooldown period, but that can be overridden and the cooldown period specified on the Auto Scaling Group can be honored. When you use the lifecycle hook, you must ensure that you are using the correct setting for your cooldown, otherwise your dynamic scaling policies will trigger another scaling operation, which you may not want to take place before you finish the configuration on the previously launched EC2 instance. As we changed the heartbeat timeout on the lifecycle hook to 7200 seconds, let's add a similar setting for the Auto Scaling Group cooldown. You can do this using the following command:

```
PS C:\> Update-ASAutoScalingGroup –AutoScalingGroupName WebAppASG –
DefaultCooldown 7200
```

```
PS C:\> Get-ASAutoScalingGroup -AutoScalingGroupName WebAppASG |Format-Table AutoScalingGroupName,DefaultCooldown

AutoScalingGroupName DefaultCooldown
-------------------- ---------------
WebAppASG                        300

PS C:\> Update-ASAutoScalingGroup -AutoScalingGroupName WebAppASG -DefaultCooldown 7200
PS C:\> Get-ASAutoScalingGroup -AutoScalingGroupName WebAppASG |Format-Table AutoScalingGroupName,DefaultCooldown

AutoScalingGroupName DefaultCooldown
-------------------- ---------------
WebAppASG                       7200
```

Now, you might be wondering how to automate the whole process of adding a lifecycle hook. Well, you can make use of the `userdata` attribute of the launch configuration. Initiate an action to add a lifecycle hook operation runtime in the `userdata` script before you start installing and configuring your application from the source code repository. Alternatively, you can be notified via the notification service as and when the EC2 instance launches, and then you hop on to the server and complete the configuration and lifecycle hook. It's up to you how much control you want and to what extent you want to fully automate.

Termination policies

Auto Scaling Group terminate instances when a Scale-In event occurs. It is very important for you to understand how this termination works in order to architect your environment. Auto Scaling Group, use termination policies to determine which EC2 instances should be terminated when a Scale-In event is triggered. Understanding this behavior of Auto Scaling Groups is useful for you to deploy and update the environment. Termination policies are defined in the Auto Scaling Group configurations, and you can view the existing policies using the following command:

```
PS C:\> Get-ASAutoScalingGroup –AutoScalingGroupName WebAppASG |Format-
Table AutoScalingGroupName,TerminationPolicies
```

You can have the following termination policies defined in the ASG. If you have more than one policy defined in the ASG, then these are executed in order. If the evaluated policy does not find a suitable instance to terminate, the next policy in line gets evaluated until the match is found.

Termination policies are **OldestInstance**, **NewestInstance**, **ClosestToNextInstanceHour**, and **OldestLauchConfiguration**.

The names of these policies themselves indicate which actions should be taken by the Auto Scaling Group. Irrespective of the order, the Auto Scaling Group always first checks for an imbalance of EC instances across availability zones before evaluating the first policy. If any one of the availability zones has more instances than the others, the first policy will be applied to that availability zones first, even though **OldestInstance** might be running in the other availability zones. In most of the use cases, the default termination policy would work.

Usually, the following are the reasons behind choosing these policies:

- **OldestInstance**: This is useful when you want to change the instance type
- **NewestInstances**: This is useful when testing a new launch configuration and an instance
- **OldestLaunchConfiguration**: This is useful to phase out the oldest launch configuration
- **ClosetToNextInstanceHour**: This will help you to reduce costs

Termination protection

Termination protection is another feature of the Auto Scaling Group which allows you to protect EC2 instances from Scale-In if you feel that Scaling-In instances is not the right thing for your application. In some cases, you may want to control the scaling of instances manually, rather than trusting the Scale-In dynamically. You can enable instance protection either at the Auto Scaling Group level or on individual EC2 instances.

You can enable the instance protection at the Auto Scaling Group level using the following command:

```
PS C:\> Update-ASAutoScalingGroup –AutoScalingGroupName WebAppASG –
NewInstancesProtectedFromscaleIn $true
```

```
PS C:\> Get-ASAutoScalingGroup -AutoScalingGroupName WebAppASG |Format-Table NewInstancesProtectedFromScaleIn

NewInstancesProtectedFromScaleIn
--------------------------------
                           False


PS C:\> Update-ASAutoScalingGroup -AutoScalingGroupName WebAppASG -NewInstancesProtectedFromScaleIn $true
PS C:\> Get-ASAutoScalingGroup -AutoScalingGroupName WebAppASG |Format-Table NewInstancesProtectedFromScaleIn

NewInstancesProtectedFromScaleIn
--------------------------------
                            True
```

To set the termination protection on an individual EC2 level, you can use the following command:

```
PS C:\> Edit-EC2InstanceAttribute -InstanceId i-05ba9441e9d65e0ff -
DisableApiTermination $true
```

Suspending the Auto Scaling process

When we work with Auto Scaling, there are a number of different processes that Auto Scaling performs in the background. Auto Scaling provides us with an option to suspend the processes that Auto Scaling performs in the background. The reason we might want to suspend these processes is to investigate configuration problems or to troubleshoot any other issue in regard to your application and environment. The processes are as follows:

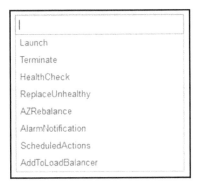

Let's say you want to suspend the terminate process while you troubleshoot the issue, as you want to review the log files on the server and you want to ensure that Scale-In does not trigger the termination of the EC2 instances; you can suspend it as follows:

```
PS C:\> Suspend-ASProcess -AutoScalingGroupName WebAppASG -ScalingProcess
"Terminate"
```

```
PS C:\> Get-ASAutoScalingGroup -AutoScalingGroupName WebAppASG |Format-Table SuspendedProcesses

SuspendedProcesses
------------------
{}

PS C:\> Suspend-ASProcess -AutoScalingGroupName WebAppASG -ScalingProcess "Terminate"
PS C:\> Get-ASAutoScalingGroup -AutoScalingGroupName WebAppASG |Format-Table SuspendedProcesses

SuspendedProcesses
------------------
{Terminate}
```

Once you suspend termination on the Auto Scaling Group, none of the EC2 instances will be terminated. If you want to suspend all the processes on the Auto Scaling Group, you can do so as shown below:

```
PS C:\> Suspend-ASProcess -AutoScalingGroupName WebAppASG
```

```
PS C:\> Suspend-ASProcess -AutoScalingGroupName WebAppASG
PS C:\> Get-ASAutoScalingGroup -AutoScalingGroupName WebAppASG |Format-Table SuspendedProcesses

SuspendedProcesses
------------------
{HealthCheck, ReplaceUnhealthy, AZRebalance, AlarmNotification...}
```

To resume the termination process, you can run the following command:

```
PS C:\> Resume-ASProcess -AutoScalingGroupName WebAppASG -ScalingProcess
"Terminate"
```

And to resume all the suspended processes on the Auto Scaling Group, you can issue the following command:

```
PS C:\> Resume-ASProcess -AutoScalingGroupName WebAppASG
```

```
PS C:\> Resume-ASProcess -AutoScalingGroupName WebAppASG -ScalingProcess "Terminate"
PS C:\> Get-ASAutoScalingGroup -AutoScalingGroupName WebAppASG |Format-Table SuspendedProcesses

SuspendedProcesses
------------------
{AZRebalance, AddToLoadBalancer, AlarmNotification, HealthCheck...}

PS C:\> Resume-ASProcess -AutoScalingGroupName WebAppASG
PS C:\> Get-ASAutoScalingGroup -AutoScalingGroupName WebAppASG |Format-Table SuspendedProcesses

SuspendedProcesses
------------------
{}
```

Standby mode

Auto Scaling provides you with an option for transition from an **InService** EC2 instance to **Standby mode**, so that you can perform the required maintenance, update the EC2, and join the instance back to the Auto Scaling Group. When an instance is transitioned to the Standby mode, it does not receive any traffic from the load balancer, but it is still part of the Auto Scaling Group.

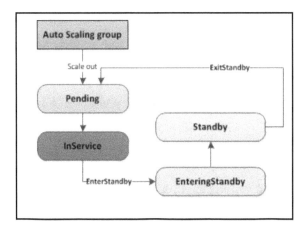

As soon as an EC2 instance is transitioned to the **Standby** state, Auto Scaling will decrement the desired capacity. This is to avoid launching the new instance while you have this instance on standby. If you tell Auto Scaling not to decrement the desired capacity, then a new EC2 instance will be launched as a replacement. Once the instance is in standby mode, Auto Scaling does not perform any health checks on the instance. You can use the `Enter-ASStandby` cmdlet to transition the EC2 instance into standby mode.

```
PS C:\> Enter-ASStandby -InstanceId i-05ba9441e9d65e0ff -
AutoScalingGroupName WebAppASG -ShouldDecrementDesiredCapacity $false
```

```
PS C:\> Enter-ASStandby -InstanceId i-05ba9441e9d65e0ff -AutoScalingGroupName WebAppASG -ShouldDecrementDesiredCapacity $false

ActivityId           : c67a8079-23a0-4e7a-88dc-675216394f52
AutoScalingGroupName : WebAppASG
Cause                : At 2017-07-11T04:33:56Z instance i-05ba9441e9d65e0ff was moved to standby in response to a user request.
Description          : Moving EC2 instance to Standby: i-05ba9441e9d65e0ff
Details              : {"Subnet ID":"subnet-b262c19e","Availability Zone":"us-east-1a"}
EndTime              : 1/1/0001 12:00:00 AM
Progress             : 50
StartTime            : 7/11/2017 2:33:56 PM
StatusCode           : InProgress
StatusMessage        :


PS C:\> (Get-ASAutoScalingGroup -AutoScalingGroupName WebAppASG).Instances | Get-ASAutoScalingInstance| format-table -property InstanceId,HealthStatus,Lifecy
cleState

InstanceId           HealthStatus LifecycleState
----------           ------------ --------------
i-053f08daac48361c7  HEALTHY      InService
i-05ba9441e9d65e0ff  HEALTHY      Standby
i-0c32a482ebe32b44b  HEALTHY      Pending:Wait


PS C:\> Get-ELBInstanceHealth -LoadBalancerName MyCLB

Description InstanceId          ReasonCode State
----------- ----------          ---------- -----
N/A         i-053f08daac48361c7 N/A        InService
```

As we used the `ShouldDecrementDesiredCapacity` switch to not decrement the desired capacity, a new EC2 instance was launched, which is seen as **Pending:Wait** state. This is because we have a lifecycle hook created for the new instance launch. There is one instance in standby mode and only one instance is seen as **InService** on the load balancer.

You can exit standby mode using the following command:

```
PS C:\> Exit-ASStandby -InstanceId i-05ba9441e9d65e0ff -
AutoScalingGroupName WebAppASG
```

```
PS C:\> Exit-ASStandby -InstanceId i-05ba9441e9d65e0ff -AutoScalingGroupName WebAppASG

ActivityId           : beb450ff-2b7e-4ab4-be41-b9f8546bb910
AutoScalingGroupName : WebAppASG
Cause                : At 2017-07-11T04:56:09Z instance i-05ba9441e9d65e0ff was moved out of standby in response to a user request, increasing the capacity
                       from 2 to 3.
Description          : Moving EC2 instance out of Standby: i-05ba9441e9d65e0ff
Details              : {"Subnet ID":"subnet-b262c19e","Availability Zone":"us-east-1a"}
EndTime              : 1/1/0001 12:00:00 AM
Progress             : 30
StartTime            : 7/11/2017 2:56:09 PM
StatusCode           : PreInService
StatusMessage        :


PS C:\> (Get-ASAutoScalingGroup -AutoScalingGroupName WebAppASG).Instances | Get-ASAutoScalingInstance| format-table -property InstanceId,HealthStatus,Lifecy
cleState

InstanceId          HealthStatus LifecycleState
----------          ------------ --------------
i-053f08daac48361c7 HEALTHY       InService
i-05ba9441e9d65e0ff HEALTHY       InService
i-0c32a482ebe32b44b HEALTHY       InService


PS C:\> Get-ELBInstanceHealth -LoadBalancerName MyCLB

Description InstanceId          ReasonCode State
----------- ----------          ---------- -----
N/A         i-053f08daac48361c7 N/A        InService
N/A         i-05ba9441e9d65e0ff N/A        InService
N/A         i-0c32a482ebe32b44b N/A        InService
```

Though you put the original instance back into the **InService** state, the replacement instance that was spun up has not been removed and there is no switch that you can pass on to the `Exit-ASStandby` to reduce the capacity. So, in this case, you may need to manually remove the instance from the Auto Scaling Group and the load balancer.

Deleting an Auto Scaling Group

To delete an Auto Scaling Group, you can use the cmdlet `Remove-ASAutoScalingGroup`. If the Auto Scaling Group has EC2 instances or scaling activities in progress, you must specify the `Force` switch in order for deletion to succeed. If the Auto Scaling Group has policies, deleting the Auto Scaling Group deletes these policies, the underlying alarm actions, and any alarm that no longer has an associated action.

```
PS C:\> Remove-ASAutoScalingGroup -AutoScalingGroupName WebAppASG
PS C:\> Remove-ASAutoScalingGroup -AutoScalingGroupName WebAppASG -
ForceDelete $true -Force
```

```
PS C:\> Remove-ASAutoScalingGroup -AutoScalingGroupName WebAppASG

Confirm
Are you sure you want to perform this action?
Performing the operation "Remove-ASAutoScalingGroup (DeleteAutoScalingGroup)" on target "WebAppASG".
[Y] Yes  [A] Yes to All  [N] No  [L] No to All  [S] Suspend  [?] Help (default is "Y"): Y
Remove-ASAutoScalingGroup : One or more errors occurred. (You cannot delete an AutoScalingGroup while there are instances or pending Spot instance
request(s) still in the group.)
At line:1 char:1
+ Remove-ASAutoScalingGroup -AutoScalingGroupName WebAppASG
+ ~~~~~~~~~~~~~~~~~~~~~~~~~~~~~~~~~~~~~~~~~~~~~~~~~~~~~~~~~~~
    + CategoryInfo          : InvalidOperation: (Amazon.PowerShe...lingGroupCmdlet:RemoveASAutoScalingGroupCmdlet) [Remove-ASAutoScalingGroup], InvalidOper
   ationException
    + FullyQualifiedErrorId : System.AggregateException,Amazon.PowerShell.Cmdlets.AS.RemoveASAutoScalingGroupCmdlet

PS C:\> Remove-ASAutoScalingGroup -AutoScalingGroupName WebAppASG -ForceDelete $true -Force
PS C:\>
```

The first cmdlet did not run to success, as the Auto Scaling Group has EC2 instances running. The second cmdlet had a `ForceDelete` switch, which terminated all the underlying EC2 instances and then removed the ASG.

Summary

Auto Scaling has a bright future. It is the one that allows us to achieve elasticity in the cloud. Architecting your application deployment considering Auto Scaling capability is the key to cloud success. This is one of the most well-known and frequently mentioned reasons for migrating to the cloud. The features and capabilities provided by Auto Scaling help you to architect any type of application in the cloud. We have learnt in this chapter how we can increase the availability of an EC2 instance just by adding it to Auto Scaling, even though there is no intention to scale. Dynamic scaling is what allows us to Scale-Up and Scale-Down when an application demands more capacity. In addition, we learnt a number of management options, such as lifecycle hooks, cooldown, suspending processes, and putting EC2 instances in standby. In the next chapter, we will learn about the Relational Database Service.

10
Laying Foundation for RDS Databases

Data is one of the biggest assets for any organization. Availability, accessibility, and quick recovery of that data after application failure are the most important concerns in order to get back in business. Almost everywhere, and for every application; persistent data is stored in a database. So, a database becomes a critical point in your infrastructure. This is where AWS Relational Database Service, or simply RDS, provides you with a way to provision, operate, and scale a database in the cloud. RDS helps speed up the development process by allowing quick access to the fully-featured database engine without the need to install or configure database software on the server. It also reduces the burden of ongoing database administration by taking on common tasks such as patching, backups, and security management. You can also configure RDS in such a way that you can achieve a highly available and fault-tolerant database. Building a highly available and fault-tolerant database environment requires a lot of work in the traditional world, whereas RDS provides this facility out-of-the-box as part of the RDS service. RDS fits in the **Platform as a Service** (**PaaS**) category of the cloud computing model. PaaS models help you to be more efficient, as you do not need to worry about capacity planning, resource procurement, software maintenance, patching or any other undifferentiated heavy lifting involved in running your application.

In this chapter, we will discuss different database engines available on RDS, RDS deployment consideration, various DB Instance classes, Multi-AZ set up, Read replicas, Compliance, Data Encryption, Database Access and IAM. In addition, we will learn about DB Security Group, DB Subnet Group, DB Parameter Group, and DB Options Group.

Database engines on RDS

AWS RDS is a fully managed service. This means that the underlying host and operating system is fully managed by the AWS. You will have no access to the database host operating system. This will result in you having limited ability to modify configuration on the host operating system, and some of the functions that rely on configuration from host OS will not work. AWS is making attempts to bridge that gap in the future, and there could be a way to have some control at the operating system level as well. At the moment, AWS supports the following database engines on the RDS platform. Both Oracle and SQL Server are proprietary database software, whereas MySQL, PostgreSQL, and MariaDB are all open source database software. AWS has a cloud native database as well, called Aurora, which is MySQL and PostgreSQL compatible.

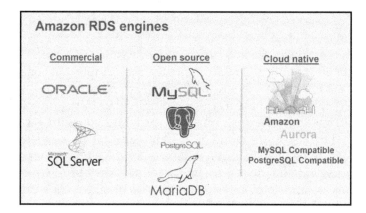

The storage used to host the databases is also fully managed by AWS. You do not need to worry about creating volumes and attaching them to the database host. You just request additional storage by modifying the database instance configuration and you get it! Currently, there is a maximum limit on the database size that you can have on the RDS for each database engine. AWS may raise these limits in the future. The Microsoft SQL Server limit is currently the lowest one, as compared to the other database engines. You can create a database up to a maximum of 4 TB in size. Oracle, MySQL, MariaDB, and PostgreSQL support a database size up to 6 TB, and the last one in the list, Aurora, which is cloud native, can have up to 64 TB. Note that these limits include the space demanded by the operating system and database software as well. That may not be much compared to the size, but always plan considering these aspects. For example, for Oracle, the database software demands around 7 to 8 GB of space. So, if you are expecting your database size to be around 20 GB, then always add up the space demanded by the OS and database software to get the actual database size that you should expect.

Deployment consideration

If you are in a shop where you roll out multiple RDS instances, then my advice would be to consider the following architecture in the overall design for your RDS DB instance deployment. In this architecture, you have a public-facing bastion and RDS Admin Hub in the private subnet. The RDS Admin Hub could be a Linux or Windows machine, ensuring that it has an IAM role assigned which can interact with the RDS using CLI. You then host all your RDS instances in the private subnet. You may also think of integrating the RDS Admin Hub with your bastion. In that case, your bastion and RDS Admin Hub could be the same EC2 instance. It's up to you. I chose to keep RDS Admin Hub in the private subnet, as it is another critical access point to interact with RDS databases and is considered an extra layer of defense. This deployment consideration will allow you to have a standing DBA box all the time to troubleshoot any issues that you may encounter with RDS and also allow you to schedule some jobs, such as Scaling-Out and Scaling-In. In addition, it will help you to do some automation for your database administration work.

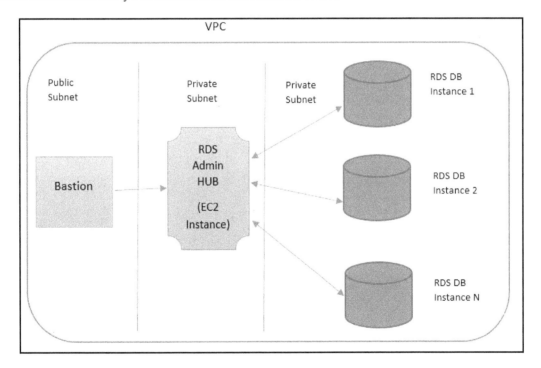

DB instance classes

You have seen that when we work with EC2 instances, we have to choose the appropriate instance type to support the workload. In regard to EC2, the instance type provides you with the required amount of vCPU, memory, and bandwidth. Likewise, when you work with RDS, you have to choose the appropriate DB instance class. DB instance class also provide you with a choice to select the appropriate amount of vCPU, memory, and network speed. The following is a list of the DB instance classes supported on AWS. This list keep changing, so my advice is to review this one on the AWS website, available at `https://aws` `.amazon.com/rds/details/`. Only the Aurora database engine does not support all the DB instance classes. It only supports the **r3** and **t2** DB instance classes.

Instance Type	vCPU	Memory (GiB)	PIOPS-Optimized	Network Performance
Standard				
db.m4.large	2	8	Yes	Moderate
db.m4.xlarge	4	16	Yes	High
db.m4.2xlarge	8	32	Yes	High
db.m4.4xlarge	16	64	Yes	High
db.m4.10xlarge	40	160	Yes	10 Gigabit
db.m3.medium	1	3.75	-	Moderate
db.m3.large	2	7.5	-	Moderate
db.m3.xlarge	4	15	Yes	High
db.m3.2xlarge	8	30	Yes	High
Memory Optimized				
db.r3.large	2	15	-	Moderate
db.r3.xlarge	4	30.5	Yes	Moderate
db.r3.2xlarge	8	61	Yes	High
db.r3.4xlarge	16	122	Yes	High
db.r3.8xlarge	32	244	-	10 Gigabit
Micro instances				
db.t2.micro	1	1	-	Low
db.t2.small	1	2	-	Low

Multi-AZ and standby

On RDS, you have the option of running the RDS DB instance in Multi-AZ mode or standalone mode. The Multi-AZ feature of the RDS service allows you to run the standby database in different availability zones which are synchronously replicated. You must have your standby running only in the same region. You cannot have standby running in a different region. AWS automatically fails over to the standby site if any one of the below situations occur. In this case, AWS will automatically switch the CNAME of the DNS record from the primary DB instance to the standby. The following are the situations when AWS fails over to the standby database.

- Primary database instance failure
- Outage in the primary availability zone
- You change the DB instance class of the primary
- Updating software versions
- Patching of the RDS DB instance
- Manual failover initiated

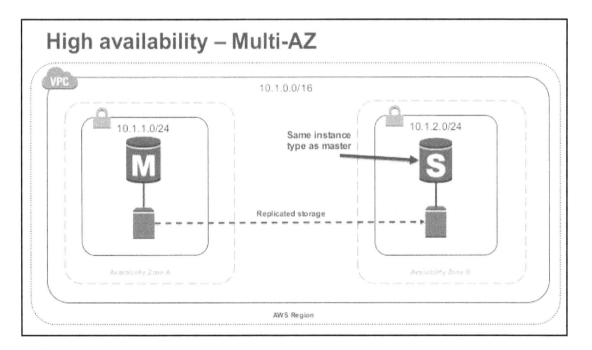

You cannot have more than one standby. When you set up Multi-AZ, only one standby site is created for you and is maintained by AWS. It is highly recommended to utilize the Multi-AZ architecture for your production database. In a Multi-AZ setup, AWS takes the automated backup on the standby database. This adds real value on production, as you do not experience slowness or IO freeze. Otherwise, in a standalone setup, during RDS automated backups, you will experience I/O freeze for a short amount of time.

Read replicas

Read replicas are asynchronous copies of the primary database that are used only for read-only purposes. You can create and have multiple read replicas for your primary database. When new data is written to the primary database, AWS copies that data for you asynchronously to the read replicas. As the data is written asynchronously, AWS provides you with a way to monitor the lag between primary and read replicas using a CloudWatch alarm. Read replicas can be created from other read replicas. This helps you to avoid a performance hit if you have a highly transactional primary database and there is a need for you to have multiple read replicas. Not all the database engines support read replicas. Currently, you can create read replicas for Aurora, MySQL, MariaDB, and PostgreSQL. You cannot create read replicas for SQL Server or the Oracle database engine.

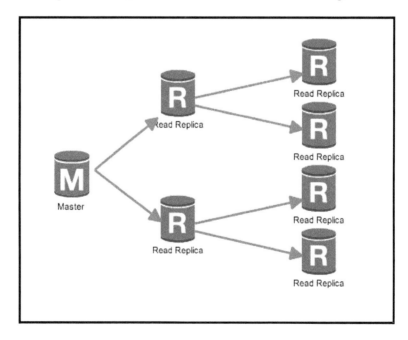

There are a number of benefits to using read replicas. Read replicas allow for all read traffic to be redirected to the read replica from the primary database. This greatly improves the performance of the primary database. If your application is read intensive, you can achieve elasticity using read replicas. You can create another read replica if needed for your read intensive workload. You also have the option to promote your read replica to the primary. You can make use of read replicas to run business functions, such as data warehousing and rebuilding indexes on the primary, if fragmented.

Compliance

AWS understands that many applications and industries have compliance needs. Many enterprises need to be in compliance with certain regulations in the space that enterprise operates in. Understanding this compliance need, AWS has worked with a number of compliance bodies to help them understand how RDS platform functions in order to meet or exceed specific compliance needs. Currently, the following are the regulatory compliance certifications that each database engine supports. If you have an application that needs to be in compliance, then you can run it on top of RDS and achieve compliance certification. Your security team will still have a role to play. They do not need to worry about the underlying infrastructure certification, rather, their focus would be more toward ensuring that application is secure and in compliance with the given regulation. Your security team can download the audit and compliance report for the AWS platform from the AWS Console. AWS Artifact provides on-demand access to AWS Compliance Report.

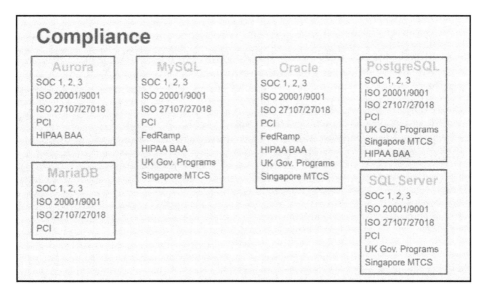

In the case of Aurora, compliance is applicable only for MySQL compatible Aurora for now, and not for PostgreSQL compatible Aurora yet. This compliance list will grow over time. AWS continues to work with other compliance bodies and certifies RDS platforms considering the regulatory requirements for the given industry.

Data encryption

Many compliance bodies have requirements around data protection and the encryption of data in transit and at rest. In order to satisfy these regulatory requirements, RDS provides you with options to encrypt data while in transit and at rest. You can enable SSL for all the database engines, so that your data is encrypted going into and out of the database, to meet your compliance requirements.

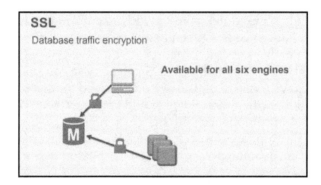

Another common thing for internal and external compliance requirements is the need to have data protected and encrypted at rest. RDS provides you with a way to implement protection at rest using the AWS **Key Management Service** (**KMS**). You can encrypt data at rest using KMS for all the database engines. KMS is a managed service that makes it easy for you to create and control the encryption keys used to encrypt data. KMS is tightly integrated with other AWS services, such as S3, RedShift, and EBS. KMS is part of the AWS Identity and Access Management service. KMS uses industry standard 256 AES encryption, and enabling it on RDS is a straightforward process.

You use a two-tiered key hierarchy using envelope encryption, using which, a unique data key encrypts customer data and the KMS master key encrypts data keys. KMS limits the risk of compromised data keys and provides better performance for encrypting large datasets. It is easier to manage a small number of master keys than millions of data keys. It also provides centralized access and an audit of key activity.

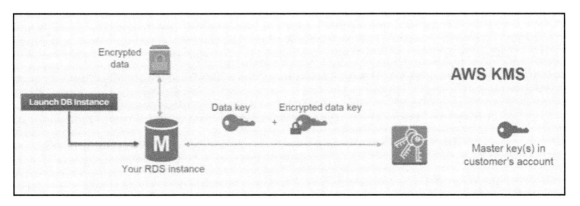

When you launch your RDS instance, it requests an encryption key to use to encrypt the data and passes the reference to the master key in the account. A client request is authenticated based on the permissions set of both the user and the key. A unique data encryption key is created and encrypted under the KMS master key. Plaintext and encrypted data keys are returned to the RDS. The plaintext data key is stored in memory and used to encrypt/decrypt RDS data.

When you use RDS and KMS together, there are some useful tips that you need to know. You can only encrypt database at the time of creation. You cannot encrypt the existing database using KMS. Once encryption is enabled on the database, you cannot remove it. If your master database is encrypted and you create the read replica, then the RDS will automatically encrypt your read replica as well. You can create an encrypted database from an unencrypted database snapshot. The RDS will allow you to choose the key while creating the database from a snapshot. Currently, RDS does not support creation of the Aurora from the encrypted snapshot of the MySQL database and vice versa. You cannot copy an encrypted snapshot to a different AWS region or replicate an encrypted database across regions. AWS is working toward solving these issues in the coming years.

Database access and IAM

Identity and Access Management (**IAM**) provides the way to grant privileges on different AWS resources to IAM Users and, certainly, you can control access to the RDS using IAM. You can provide access to the RDS to only those users who need it. But be aware of the fact that you cannot control the database's internal access using IAM; you still need to use the database engine specific grants to control access to the database and schemas. IAM controls who can access the RDS service, create databases, modify database configuration, and drop those databases; but individual database user creations grant to those users, and applications, specific user access, and restrictions will be controlled at the individual database level.

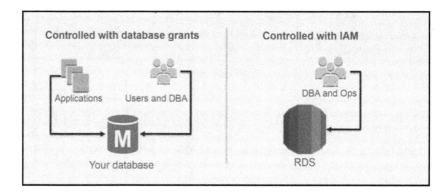

DB Security Groups

This is exactly similar to what we learned in Chapter 6, *AWS Elastic Compute Cloud*. This is also called VPC Security Group. Security Groups are layers of protection and act as a virtual firewall. You create the DB Security Group the same way as we did earlier. Setting up appropriate ingress and egress on the database Security Group will help you control the incoming and outgoing traffic to and from the database. In this case, you also specify the protocol, port, and source of the incoming traffic. The source could be a single IP address, a range of IP addresses, or another Security Group which is an application/web server Security Group.

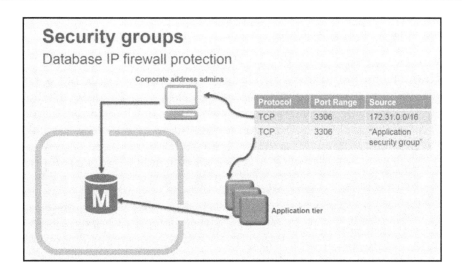

Let's create a Security Group that we can use for spinning up RDS instances. Port 3306 is the default port for MySQL and 1521 is the default port for Oracle. We created a VPC vpc-a6bb60df in Chapter 5, *AWS Virtual Private Cloud*, to demonstrate the AWS Tools for PowerShell. We will create the Security Group in that VPC. I have an RDS Admin Hub running and I have a Security Group sg-6fd1361e assigned to it which allows ingress on port 22 and RDP on port 3389. To create a Security Group, you can use the following command:

```
PS C:\> New-EC2SecurityGroup –GroupName MyRDSSG –Description "Security
Group for RDS" -VpcId vpc-a6bb60df
```

```
PS C:\> New-EC2SecurityGroup -GroupName MyRDSSG -Description "Security Group for RDS" -VpcId vpc-a6bb60df
sg-c97606b8
PS C:\> $ug = New-Object Amazon.EC2.Model.UserIdGroupPair
PS C:\> $ug.GroupId = "sg-6fd1361e"
PS C:\> $ug.UserId = "072316406132"
PS C:\> Grant-EC2SecurityGroupIngress -GroupId sg-c97606b8 -IpPermission @( @{ IpProtocol="tcp"; FromPort="3306"; ToPort="3306"; UserIdGroupPairs=$ug } )
PS C:\> Grant-EC2SecurityGroupIngress -GroupId sg-c97606b8 -IpPermission @( @{ IpProtocol="tcp"; FromPort="1521"; ToPort="1521"; UserIdGroupPairs=$ug } )
PS C:\>
```

Security Group sg-c97606b8 is created, which allows ingress on ports 3306 and 1521. Review the command for allowing a source from another Security Group. In Chapter 5, *AWS Virtual Private Cloud*, we used the IP range as a source. Allowing traffic from other Security Groups has a different format in PowerShell. To ensure a Security Group has appropriate ingress, you can run the following command, as shown in the screenshot:

```
PS C:\> (Get-EC2SecurityGroup -GroupID sg-c97606b8).IPPermissions|Format-Table -AutoSize

FromPort IpProtocol IpRanges Ipv6Ranges PrefixListIds ToPort UserIdGroupPairs UserIdGroupPair IpRange
-------- ---------- -------- ---------- ------------- ------ ---------------- --------------- -------
    1521 tcp        {}       {}         {}              1521 {}               {}              {}
    3306 tcp        {}       {}         {}              3306 {}               {}              {}
```

DB Subnet Groups

When you launch an RDS DB instance inside Amazon VPC, it is always better to create the DB Subnet Group before you spin up the DB Instance. A DB Subnet Group is a collection of subnets (especially private subnets) in the given VPC, and you then associate that DB Subnet Group with your DB instance at the time of launch. Each DB Subnet Group should have subnets in at least two AZs in the given region. If you do not create the DB Subnet Group and leave it to RDS, then at the time of launch, RDS service creates one for you with all the available subnets in the given VPC, which may include all public and private subnets.

It is considered as a best practice to run your databases in your private subnet of the VPC. Creating DB Subnet Group only for the private subnet will allow you to secure your DB instances better. Though you have the option of removing public subnets later from the DB Subnet Group, it may not be a possibility if your RDS picked up the IP range from the one that you want to remove from the DB Subnet Group. Hence, you lose control when letting RDS create it for you.

Earlier, we created two public and two private subnets in the demo VPC `vpc-a6bb60df`. The subnet IDs `subnet-b262c19e` and `subnet-f042dcb8` are two private subnets which we will use to create a DB Subnet Group, and they are in `us-east-1a` and `us-east-1b` availability zone respectively.

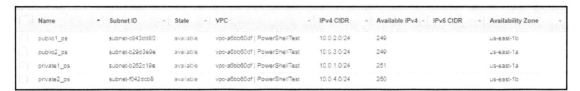

Name	Subnet ID	State	VPC	IPv4 CIDR	Available IPv4	IPv6 CIDR	Availability Zone
public1_ps	subnet-c843dd80	available	vpc-a6bb60df | PowerShellTest	10.0.2.0/24	249		us-east-1b
public2_ps	subnet-b29d3e9e	available	vpc-a6bb60df | PowerShellTest	10.0.3.0/24	249		us-east-1a
private1_ps	subnet-b262c19e	available	vpc-a6bb60df | PowerShellTest	10.0.1.0/24	251		us-east-1a
private2_ps	subnet-f042dcb8	available	vpc-a6bb60df | PowerShellTest	10.0.4.0/24	250		us-east-1b

To list all the cmdlets for creating and maintaining a DB Subnet Group, you can use the following command:

```
PS C:\> Get-Command *DBSub*
```

To get the list of available DB subnets, you can run the following command:

```
PS C:\> Get-RDSDBSubnetGroup
```

`New-RDSDBSubnetGroup` creates a new DB Subnet Group, as shown following:

```
PS C:\> New-RDSDBSubnetGroup -DBSubnetGroupName MySQLDBSub -
DBSubnetGroupDescription "MySQL DB Deployment Subnets" -SubnetId subnet-
b262c19e,subnet-f042dcb8
```

```
PS C:\> New-RDSDBSubnetGroup -DBSubnetGroupName MySQLDBSub -DBSubnetGroupDescription "MySQL DB Deployment Subnets" -SubnetId subnet-b262c19e,subnet-f042dcb8

DBSubnetGroupArn         : arn:aws:rds:us-east-1:072316406132:subgrp:mysqldbsub
DBSubnetGroupDescription : MySQL DB Deployment Subnets
DBSubnetGroupName        : mysqldbsub
SubnetGroupStatus        : Complete
Subnets                  : {Amazon.RDS.Model.Subnet, Amazon.RDS.Model.Subnet}
VpcId                    : vpc-a6bb60df
```

Note that, creating a DB Subnet Group with three subnets is always the safest way to do Multi-AZ deployment. I have used only two, but this is just for demonstration. Always plan to have at least three subnets in your DB Subnet Group. This will help you to run the Multi-AZ setup if any of the availability zones have a problem. It is best practice to always consider more than two in your RDS deployment.

You can use the `Edit-RDSDBSubnetGroup` cmdlet to add and update the existing configuration of the DB Subnet Group and the `Remove-RDSDBSubnetGroup` cmdlet to remove the DB Subnet Group. You cannot remove the DB Subnet Group if there is a DB instance associated with it. Likewise, while updating, just ensure that you are not removing the subnet which is already used by the DB instance.

DB Parameter Groups

DB Parameter Group is a container for database engine configuration values that are applied to one or more DB Instances. If you do not supply your own DB Parameter Group, then RDS instance creates a default one for you. If you create multiple RDS instances for the same database engine and version, this default DB Parameter Group will be used for all the RDS DB instances for that given database engine. The default DB Parameter Group contains database engine specific defaults and AWS system defaults based on the DB instance class and storage size that you specify at the time of launch. You cannot change the configuration values in the default DB Parameter Group. You have to create a new DB Parameter Group and update the values in that newly created group. You can then associate that newly created group with the DB instance. Hence, it is always best practice to create a DB Parameter Group for each RDS DB instance that you spin up for your production use. This way, changing the configuration values in the DB Parameter Group is possible. Your database instance need may be different for different applications, and having a dedicated DB Parameter Group for each RDS instance is the right thing to do.

To list all the cmdlets related to the DB parameter related operation, you can use the following command:

```
PS C:\> Get-Command *DBPara*
```

To get the list of existing DB Parameter Groups, you can issue the following command:

```
PS C:\> Get-RDSDBParameterGroup
```

`New-RDSDBParameterGroup` creates a new DB Parameter Group. This operation creates a new DB Parameter Group with the default configuration values for the database engine used by the DB instance. AWS advises that when you create the DB Parameter Group for the first time, you use it with DB instance, then wait for 5 minutes before you plan to attach it to the existing DB instance or to use it with a new instance. You need to know the parameter group family values that you can pass to this cmdlet. These values are shown in the following screenshot:

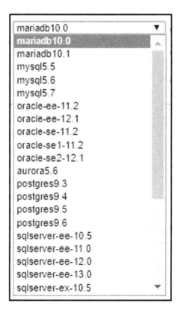

To create a new DB Parameter Group for the `mysql5.7` parameter group family, run the following command:

```
PS C:\> New-RDSDBParameterGroup -DBParameterGroupName "MyWebAppPrd" -
Description "My Web App Production Database" -DBParameterGroupFamily
"mysql5.7"
```

```
PS C:\> New-RDSDBParameterGroup -DBParameterGroupName "MyWebAppPrd" -Description "My Web App Production Database" -DBParameterGroupFamily "mysql5.7"

DBParameterGroupArn                                       DBParameterGroupFamily DBParameterGroupName Description
-------------------                                       ---------------------- -------------------- -----------
arn:aws:rds:us-east-1:072316406132:pg:mywebappprd mysql5.7                       mywebappprd          My Web App Production Database
```

To get the list of default configuration values in the newly created DB Parameter Group, you run the following command:

```
PS C:\> Get-RDSDBParameter -DBParameterGroupName "MyWebAppPrd" |Format-
Table ParameterName,ParameterValue
```

Let's review the current value for the parameter `read_buffer_size` in the DB Parameter Group that we just created. You can use the cmdlet as shown:

```
PS C:\> Get-RDSDBParameter -DBParameterGroupName "MyWebAppPrd" | Where-
Object {$_.ParameterName -eq "read_buffer_size"}
```

```
PS C:\> Get-RDSDBParameter -DBParameterGroupName "MyWebAppPrd" | Where-Object {$_.ParameterName -eq "read_buffer_size"}

AllowedValues        : 8200-2147479552
ApplyMethod          : immediate
ApplyType            : dynamic
DataType             : integer
Description          : Each thread that does a sequential scan allocates this buffer. Increased value may help perf if performing many sequential scans.
IsModifiable         : True
MinimumEngineVersion :
ParameterName        : read_buffer_size
ParameterValue       : 262144
Source               : user
```

The output suggests that `read_buffer_size` is a modifiable parameter because `IsModifiable` is set as True. In this demo, we double the value of this parameter. You can do this as follows:

```
PS C:\> $Parameter1 = New-Object Amazon.RDS.Model.Parameter
PS C:\> $Parameter1.ParameterName="read_buffer_size"
PS C:\> $Parameter1.ParameterValue=524288
PS C:\> $Parameter1.ApplyMethod="Immediate"
PS C:\> Edit-RDSDBParameterGroup -DBParameterGroupName "MyWebAppPrd" -
Parameter $Parameter1
```

```
PS C:\> $Parameter1 = New-Object Amazon.RDS.Model.Parameter
PS C:\> $Parameter1.ParameterName="read_buffer_size"
PS C:\> $Parameter1.ParameterValue=524288
PS C:\> $Parameter1.ApplyMethod="Immediate"
PS C:\> Edit-RDSDBParameterGroup -DBParameterGroupName "MyWebAppPrd" -Parameter $Parameter1
mywebappprd
PS C:\> Get-RDSDBParameter -DBParameterGroupName "MyWebAppPrd" | Where-Object {$_.ParameterName -eq "read_buffer_size"}


AllowedValues       : 8200-2147479552
ApplyMethod         : immediate
ApplyType           : dynamic
DataType            : integer
Description         : Each thread that does a sequential scan allocates this buffer. Increased value may help perf if performing many sequential scans.
IsModifiable        : True
MinimumEngineVersion :
ParameterName       : read_buffer_size
ParameterValue      : 524288
Source              : user
```

The value of the `read_buffer_size` has changed to `524288`. There are some parameters which require the reboot of the DB Instance, in that case you can set the parameter, but use `ApplyMethod` as `PendingReboot`. That way, when you reboot the instance during the maintenance window, the value will take effect.

DB Option Groups

Some of the database engines offer additional features which make it easier for the admin to manage databases to provide additional security or functionality. This is where you have to use option groups to enable and configure database features. You add options in the option groups that are available for the specific database engine, and when you associate that option group with the DB instance, specified features are enabled in the DB instance. Currently, you can have an option group for MariaDB, MySQL, Oracle, and Microsoft SQL Server. At the moment, there are no options that need to be set for PostgreSQL and Aurora.

There are a couple of options that you can set for MySQL DB, as follows.

Option	Option ID	Engine Versions
MariaDB Audit Plugin Support	MARIADB_AUDIT_PLUGIN	MySQL 5.6.29 and later
		MySQL 5.7.11 and later
MySQL MEMCACHED Support	MEMCACHED	MySQL 5.6 and later

The Oracle option list is big compared to the other engines. You can set the following options:

Option	Option ID
Oracle Application Express	APEX
	APEX-DEV
Oracle Enterprise Manager	OEM
	OEM_AGENT
Oracle Label Security	OLS
Oracle Native Network Encryption	NATIVE_NETWORK_ENCRYPTION
Oracle SSL	SSL
Oracle Statspack	STATSPACK
Oracle Time Zone	Timezone
Oracle Transparent Data Encryption	TDE
Oracle UTL_MAIL	UTL_MAIL
Oracle XML DB	XMLDB

SQL Server also allows you to set a couple of options, as follows:

Option	Option ID	Engine Editions
Native Backup and Restore	SQLSERVER_BACKUP_RESTORE	SQL Server Enterprise Edition
		SQL Server Standard Edition
		SQL Server Web Edition
		SQL Server Express Edition
Transparent Data Encryption	TRANSPARENT_DATA_ENCRYPTION	SQL Server Enterprise Edition

MariaDB has just one option that can be enabled:

Option ID	Engine Versions
MARIADB_AUDIT_PLUGIN	MariaDB 10.0.24 and later

To find all the cmdlets related to option group creation and maintenance, you can use the following command:

```
PS C:\> Get-Command *RDSOption*
```

If you do not create the option group prior to launching the DB instance, RDS service will create the default one for you which does not have any options added. As with DB Parameter Group, it is always a best practice to create a separate option group for each RDS instance that you launch. This will ease the administration effort later when there is a need to enable some features in the database or remove them from the database. Using the default option group for all the RDS DB instances will create some challenges for you in terms of managing the individual databases.

To get the list of existing option groups, issue the following command:

```
PS C:\> Get-RDSOptionGroup
```

Another important operational aspect that I would like to highlight is that you can plan to name the database instance, DB Parameter Group, and DB Option Group the same. This will help you to quickly relate to each of them when you have any RDS instances running. There is no hard rule to have the same name, but I notice that this helps with ongoing management of the DB instances. It's up to you. New-RDSOptionGroup creates a new option group for you. You need to specify the engine name and major engine version with this cmdlet. Valid values for engine name are the following:

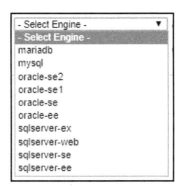

Let's create an option group for `Mysql 5.7`.

```
PS C:\> New-RDSOptionGroup -OptionGroupName "MyWebAppPrd" -EngineName mysql
-MajorEngineVersion 5.7 -OptionGroupDescription "Option Group for Mysql
5.7"
```

```
PS C:\> New-RDSOptionGroup -OptionGroupName "MyWebAppPrd" -EngineName mysql -MajorEngineVersion 5.7 -OptionGroupDescription "Option Group for Mysql 5.7"

AllowsVpcAndNonVpcInstanceMemberships : True
EngineName                            : mysql
MajorEngineVersion                    : 5.7
OptionGroupArn                        : arn:aws:rds:us-east-1:072316406132:og:mywebappprd
OptionGroupDescription                : Option Group for Mysql 5.7
OptionGroupName                       : mywebappprd
Options                               : {}
VpcId                                 :
```

A new option group is created. You can now add options to it using `Edit-RDSOptionGroup`.

```
PS C:\> $Option1 = New-Object Amazon.RDS.Model.OptionConfiguration
PS C:\> $Option1.OptionName = "MARIADB_AUDIT_PLUGIN"
PS C:\> Edit-RDSOptionGroup -OptionGroupName "MyWebAppPrd" -
ApplyImmediately $true -OptionsToInclude $Option1
```

```
PS C:\> $Option1 = New-Object Amazon.RDS.Model.OptionConfiguration
PS C:\> $Option1.OptionName = "MARIADB_AUDIT_PLUGIN"
PS C:\> Edit-RDSOptionGroup -OptionGroupName "MyWebAppPrd" -ApplyImmediately $true -OptionsToInclude $Option1

AllowsVpcAndNonVpcInstanceMemberships : False
EngineName                            : mysql
MajorEngineVersion                    : 5.7
OptionGroupArn                        : arn:aws:rds:us-east-1:072316406132:og:mywebappprd
OptionGroupDescription                : Option Group for Mysql 5.7
OptionGroupName                       : mywebappprd
Options                               : {MARIADB_AUDIT_PLUGIN}
VpcId                                 :
```

To remove an option from the option group, run the following command:

```
PS C:\> Edit-RDSOptionGroup -OptionGroupName "MyWebAppPrd" -
ApplyImmediately $true -OptionsToRemove "MARIADB_AUDIT_PLUGIN"
```

```
PS C:\> Edit-RDSOptionGroup -OptionGroupName "MyWebAppPrd" -ApplyImmediately $true -OptionsToRemove "MARIADB_AUDIT_PLUGIN"

AllowsVpcAndNonVpcInstanceMemberships : True
EngineName                            : mysql
MajorEngineVersion                    : 5.7
OptionGroupArn                        : arn:aws:rds:us-east-1:072316406132:og:mywebappprd
OptionGroupDescription                : Option Group for Mysql 5.7
OptionGroupName                       : mywebappprd
Options                               : {}
VpcId                                 :
```

Note that some of the options are persistent in some database engines. Once added, they cannot be removed. I have particularly seen this behavior with the Oracle database engine. Refer to the documentation for more details in relation to the option groups.

Summary

Amazon RDS is gaining popularity because of its simplicity and out-of-the-box high availability solutions for many mission-critical workloads. Faster provisioning and on-demand capacity makes it a more exciting option, particularly in the development community. Application design considering the strengths of AWS might find RDS as a suitable platform, but as the degree of complexity and datasets increases, RDS gradually gets ruled out. RDS supports broad range of features for some of the commercial databases. We have learnt about some of the operational best practices that should be considered when deploying RDS. In the next chapter, we will learn about spinning up and maintaining RDS instances.

11
DB Instance Administration and Management

As we know, Amazon RDS takes care of time consuming management tasks, such as provisioning and maintenance, freeing you to focus on your application and business. You still need to understand how RDS platform works and how best you can make use of it. In this chapter, we will learn how you can work with RDS platform using PowerShell and perform day-to-day activities. Though there are multiple database engines supported by the RDS platform, I will primarily make use of MySQL database engine to demonstrate the operational aspects of the platform in this chapter. Focusing on all the database engines is beyond the scope of this book, but I would like to advise you to review the RDS User Guide for the database engine that you want to work with. Conceptually, it will be the same for all the other database engines, with the exception of read replicas as they are not something you find in the Oracle or SQL Server database engines.

In this chapter, we will discuss different storage type on RDS, licensing models on RDS, maintenance windows available on RDS, spinning up RDS instances in standalone or multi AZ configuration, enabling encryption on RDS and connecting to RDS with and without SSL. In addition, we will learn general maintenance commands in regard to RDS administration.

RDS storage type

RDS support three storage types. As with EC2, in this case as well, these different storage types differ based on their performance characteristics and cost. You can choose the appropriate storage type depending on the workload that you plan to run on the RDS DB instance. These are the same storage types that we discussed in Chapter 6, *AWS Elastic Compute Cloud*.

- **General Purpose SSD:** These are called **GP2**. These volumes have burstable capability up to 3000 IOPS. GP2 are mostly suitable for preproduction environment. GP2 volume can range from 5 GB to 6 TB for Oracle, PostgreSQL, MySQL, and MariaDB. For SQL Server DB instances, it can range from 20 GB to 4 TB.

- **Provisioned IOPS:** If you are looking for consistent IOPS for your database workload, then this type of storage is more suitable. This storage type is mostly recommended for your production workload. Allocating Provisional IOPS to your database workload comes with a cost. AWS RDS delivers within 10% of the Provisional IOPS performance 99.9% of the time over a given year. For Oracle, PostgreSQL, MariaDB, and MySQL, Provisional IOPS size can range from 100 GB to 6 TB. For SQL Server Enterprise, it can range from 200 GB to 4 TB. For other versions of SQL Server, it can range from 100 GB to 4 TB.

- **Magnetic:** These are meant for workloads where data is not frequently accessed and performance is not a key criteria. This is low-cost storage and is very less frequently used. Even for small workloads, I see many organizations utilizing GP2 instead of this one.

Note that these storage types are not applicable to the Aurora database engine. It uses Amazon proprietary storage. Therefore, you only choose the DB instance Class at the time of launch. It does not prompt you to choose the storage type and storage size at the time of launch. Likewise, for SQL Server DB instances, you cannot change the type of storage and storage capacity after DB instance creation due to the striped storage attached to the Windows instances.

Licensing models on RDS

RDS supports two popular commercial RDBMS database engines, Oracle and SQL Server. When you work with these engines on RDS, it is important for you to know how the licensing works. Both these database engines support two types of licensing models: **License Included** and **Bring-Your-Own-License**, but not all the database editions can be licensed under the License Included model. Under each licensing model, there is a limit to the number of DB instances that you can run in the account. You can always request AWS to lift the limit if needed. By default, you can run 40 DB instances. Out of which, you can have 10 DB instances running on Oracle or SQL Server under the License Included model. You can run 40 DB instances for MySQL, MariaDB, and PostgreSQL, or you can have all 40 running on Bring-Your-Own-License model.

- **License Included**: Under this model, you do not purchase the database engine license separately. AWS holds the license and pricing includes compute resources, AWS Managed Service fee, and software license. If your application does not demand Enterprise Edition-kind of capability, then utilizing the License Included model will save a lot of upfront costs for the business. This is a very attractive option for many AWS customers if they want to run their workload on an Oracle or SQL Server database engine.
- **Bring-Your-Own-License (BYOL)**: Under this model, you purchase the license directly from Microsoft or Oracle. If you select BYOL at the time of launch and purchased the license for Microsoft SQL server, then you must report this on the AWS RDS console using **Microsoft License Mobility Program**. If you do not do this, then AWS will take a snapshot of the database and terminate the DB instance. For Oracle, you are responsible for getting the right license considering the DB instance class that you select. Oracle usually charges based on the vCPU available on the given DB instance class.

Note that, if you configure Multi-AZ for your SQL Server DB instance, you do not need a license for the standby site, but this is not the case for Oracle Multi-AZ set up. You have to license the standby site separately for Oracle DB instance.
MySQL, MariaDB, and PostgreSQL are licensed under General Public License, so there is nothing like the License Included or Bring-Your-Own-License models.

Understanding maintenance windows

RDS is a fully managed service. AWS take cares of regular patching and backups as part of this service. It is critical for you to understand how AWS does the regular patching and backups when you work with RDS. Understanding the maintenance schedule will help you minimize the impact on your database workload. Otherwise, you may have no idea why your RDS has intermittent outage. Broadly, there are two types of maintenance windows:

- **Weekly maintenance window**: Pay very close attention to the RDS maintenance window. This is something you define at the time of DB instance launch or you can modify it later. AWS uses your preferred maintenance window for software patching and upgrades. In addition to the AWS maintenance items, any pending changes to the DB instance configuration will be applied during these maintenance windows. There could be a noticeable impact on the DB instance, as it uses resources on the DB instance host. You may need to adjust the maintenance windows considering your application's peak hours. Ensure that you do not schedule any maintenance during your peak business hours. I would personally advise that your preferred maintenance window should not overlap with the backup schedule maintenance window.

  With a Multi-AZ setup, AWS performs maintenance on the standby, promotes the standby to the primary, and then performs maintenance on the old primary, which becomes the new standby. The following is the current default schedule of the RDS maintenance windows. There is a standard 8-hour block allocated to each region. AWS tries to finish all maintenance in 30 minutes, but it can go beyond the 30-minute time period in some cases. AWS chooses any 30-min block out of the 8-hour maintenance windows. All times are in UTC. If you do not specify the maintenance window at the time of launch, the specific maintenance window is selected for the region in which you are running your DB instance

- **Backup maintenance window**: Database backups, called snapshots, are taken and maintained by AWS. AWS has a defined block of backup maintenance windows in each region. You need to ensure that you know what those default backup windows are in each region. Review the impact of the default backup window on database peak hours and adjust it accordingly. The weekly maintenance window cannot overlap with the backup window. Note that all windows specified are in UTC and you may need to adjust the backup window considering your application's peak and off-peak hours. The good thing is that, when a Multi-AZ setup is used, AWS automatically pushes the backup to the standby site and no impact on production will be noticed. However, when there is no Multi-AZ setup, you need to ensure that backups are scheduled during off-peak hours, as it will freeze the IO for a short amount of time.

If you do not specify the backup window during the DB instance launch, then AWS chooses the one applicable to the region from the following list. In this case, a 30-min block will be selected randomly by AWS out of the 8 hours allocated to each region. If the backup does not finish in the 30-min window, then AWS continues the backup until it finishes. Backup windows can be modified anytime based on your needs.

Region	Time Block
US West (Oregon) Region	06:00–14:00 UTC
US West (N. California) Region	06:00–14:00 UTC
US East (Ohio) Region	03:00–11:00 UTC
US East (N. Virginia) Region	03:00–11:00 UTC
Asia Pacific (Mumbai) Region	16:30–00:30 UTC
Asia Pacific (Seoul) Region	13:00–21:00 UTC
Asia Pacific (Singapore) Region	14:00–22:00 UTC
Asia Pacific (Sydney) Region	12:00–20:00 UTC
Asia Pacific (Tokyo) Region	13:00–21:00 UTC
Canada (Central) Region	06:29–14:29 UTC
EU (Frankfurt) Region	20:00–04:00 UTC
EU (Ireland) Region	22:00–06:00 UTC
EU (London) Region	06:00–14:00 UTC
South America (São Paulo) Region	23:00–07:00 UTC
AWS GovCloud (US)	03:00–11:00 UTC

Spinning up RDS DB instances

By this time, you are aware of the various facts about the RDS platform and ready to rock on. In the previous chapter, you learnt about creating DB Subnet Groups, DB Parameter Groups, and DB Option Groups. We will make use of these groups in this chapter to create the DB instances. As mentioned, we will only learn about the MySQL database creation, administration, and related things to scope out the topics in this chapter.

To find out all the cmdlets related to the RDS platform, you can use the following command:

```
PS C:\> Get-Command *-RDS*
```

To create a new DB instance, you can use the New-RDSDBInstance, as follows:

```
PS C:\> New-RDSDBInstance -DBInstanceIdentifier  "mywebappprd" -DBName
"mywebappprd" -StorageType gp2 -AllocatedStorage 10 -
AutoMinorVersionUpgrade $true -DBInstanceClass db.t2.large -
DBParameterGroupName "mywebappprd" -OptionGroupName "mywebappprd" -
VpcSecurityGroupId sg-c97606b8 -DBSubnetGroupName "mysqldbsub" -Engine
mysql -EngineVersion 5.7 -LicenseModel "general-public-license" -
MasterUsername "rdsdba" -MasterUserPassword "rdsdba123" -
PreferredMaintenanceWindow "SUN:23:00-SUN:23:59" -PreferredBackupWindow
"01:00-02:00" -PubliclyAccessible $false
```

```
PS C:\> New-RDSDBInstance -DBInstanceIdentifier "mywebappprd" -DBName "mywebappprd" -StorageType gp2 -AllocatedStorage 10 -AutoMinorVersionUpgrade $true -DB
InstanceClass db.t2.large -DBParameterGroupName "mywebappprd" -OptionGroupName "mywebappprd" -VpcSecurityGroupId sg-c97606b8 -DBSubnetGroupName "mysqldbsub"
-Engine mysql -EngineVersion 5.7 -LicenseModel "general-public-license" -MasterUsername "rdsdba" -MasterUserPassword "rdsdba123" -PreferredMaintenanceWindow
"SUN:23:00-SUN:23:59" -PreferredBackupWindow "01:00-02:00" -PubliclyAccessible $false


AllocatedStorage                      : 10
AutoMinorVersionUpgrade               : True
AvailabilityZone                      :
BackupRetentionPeriod                 : 1
CACertificateIdentifier               : rds-ca-2015
CharacterSetName                      :
CopyTagsToSnapshot                    : False
DBClusterIdentifier                   :
DBInstanceArn                         : arn:aws:rds:us-east-1:072316406132:db:mywebappprd
DBInstanceClass                       : db.t2.large
DBInstanceIdentifier                  : mywebappprd
DbInstancePort                        : 0
DBInstanceStatus                      : creating
DbiResourceId                         : db-GN33C2COXNNY2A2WQGIHBGH2HY
DBName                                : mywebappprd
DBParameterGroups                     : {mywebappprd}
DBSecurityGroups                      : {}
DBSubnetGroup                         : Amazon.RDS.Model.DBSubnetGroup
DomainMemberships                     : {}
Endpoint                              :
Engine                                : mysql
EngineVersion                         : 5.7.17
EnhancedMonitoringResourceArn         :
IAMDatabaseAuthenticationEnabled      : False
InstanceCreateTime                    : 1/1/0001 12:00:00 AM
Iops                                  : 0
KmsKeyId                              :
LatestRestorableTime                  : 1/1/0001 12:00:00 AM
LicenseModel                          : general-public-license
MasterUsername                        : rdsdba
MonitoringInterval                    : 0
MonitoringRoleArn                     :
MultiAZ                               : False
```

The output has been trimmed in this case, as it did not fit on the screen. The list of switches that you can pass to the cmdlet New-RDSDBInstance are many. Let's review the one that we used in this example. DBInstanceIdentifier is the name used by AWS to identify your DB instance and all the operations that you would do in regard to configuration changes. We will make use of this one. The meaning of the DBName parameter differs from database engine to engine. For Example, in MySQL, RDS will create the specified database, and in Oracle, this is SID. This parameter is not applicable to SQL Server and Aurora.

- StorageType tells the RDS the type of storage to use for creating the DB instance. gp2 indicates that it is a general-purpose SSD. Valid values for StorageType are gp2, io1, and standard. io1 indicates a provisioned IOPS and standard is for magnetic storage. AllocatedStorage is the size of the storage requested for the database instance.
- AutoMinorVersionUpgrade tells RDS that minor database engine upgrades can be applied automatically to the DB instance during the maintenance window. Though we set it to true, that's the default behavior for this switch.
- DBInstanceClass indicates the compute capacity that can be assigned to the DB instance. This is the same as the instance type that we have seen. For valid values, review the online help for this switch.
- DBParameterGroupName holds the configuration values for the database engine. We created a DB Parameter Group in the previous chapter and we used the name mywebappprd. Likewise, OptionGroupName switch indicates whether you want to assign any option group to the DB instance. We created option groups earlier and we used the name mywebappprd.
- VpcSecurityGroupId indicates the Security Group and acts as a virtual firewall at the database level. DBSubnetGroupName indicates the subnet that can be used to launch a DB instance. It is a useful collection of private subnets.
- Engine indicates the type of database engine that you want to launch. Valid values for Engine switch are aurora | mariadb | mysql | oracle-ee | oracle-se2 | oracle-se1 | oracle-se | postgres | sqlserver-ee | sqlserver-se | sqlserver-ex | sqlserver-web. EngineVersion indicates the version to be used for the database engine. There are some valid values as well for this switch. Review the online documentation for the cmdlet New-RDSDBInstance. LicenseModel indicates the type of licensing that you want to use. Valid values for LicenseModel are license-included | bring-your-own-license | general-public-license.

- `MasterUsername` and `MasterUserPassword` are the switches used to define the master username and password, respectively, to log in and administer the RDS instances. Secure these values, as they are key to other administration efforts for your RDS DB instances. Better to come up with a kind of process to secure these usernames and passwords in your environment if there are many RDS DB instances running. Also, always avoid deploying your application schema structure using this username. Always create a separate database of users for application connectivity. Plan to use these credentials only for administration and maintenance purposes. `PubliclyAccessible` indicates whether the instance is open to the internet. If you have spun up a DB instance in a private subnet, even though you specify `PubliclyAccessible` as true, you won't be able to access it via the internet, as the Route Table on the subnet will not permit that. You have to launch a DB instance in a public subnet in order to access it publicly.
- `PreferredMaintenanceWindow` and `PreferredBackupWindow` windows are two maintenance windows that you can define for each RDS DB instance. The values are UTC, hence, always convert it to the appropriate values considering your workload.

To check the status of the DB instance, you can issue the following command:

```
PS C:\> Get-RDSDBInstance -DBInstanceIdentifier   "mywebappprd" |Format-
Table DBInstanceStatus
```

You can expect 10 to 15 minutes before it is flagged as `available`.

```
PS C:\> Get-RDSDBInstance -DBInstanceIdentifier   "mywebappprd" |Format-Table DBInstanceStatus

DBInstanceStatus
----------------
available
```

Once you launch, the DB instance will transition from `creating` to `backing-up` to `available`. The status `available` means that the DB instance is ready for you to use. In this example, the DB instance that we launched is running in standalone mode.

Multi-AZ deployment

If you deploy the DB instance in a Multi-AZ configuration, AWS will set up a standby database in a different availability zone. The standby instance will have synchronous updates from the primary instance. A standby instance is created and maintained by AWS. You do not have any control over the functioning of the standby database. Synchronization and automatic failover is part of the service. It is always recommended to deploy the DB instances in a Multi-AZ configuration to achieve high availability. This is one of the attractive out-of-the-box solutions that AWS provides to the customer.

To deploy a DB instance in a Multi-AZ configuration, you simply add a switch called `MultiAZ` with `New-RDSDBInstance`, as shown following:

```
PS C:\>New-RDSDBInstance -DBInstanceIdentifier  "mywebappprd" -DBName
"mywebappprd" -MultiAZ $true -StorageType gp2 -AllocatedStorage 10 -
AutoMinorVersionUpgrade $true -DBInstanceClass db.t2.large -
DBParameterGroupName "mywebappprd" -OptionGroupName "mywebappprd" -
VpcSecurityGroupId sg-c97606b8 -DBSubnetGroupName "mysqldbsub" -Engine
mysql -EngineVersion 5.7 -LicenseModel "general-public-license" -
MasterUsername "rdsdba" -MasterUserPassword "rdsdba123" -
PreferredMaintenanceWindow "SUN:23:00-SUN:23:59" -PreferredBackupWindow
"01:00-02:00" -PubliclyAccessible $false
```

```
PS C:\> New-RDSDBInstance -DBInstanceIdentifier  "mywebappprd" -DBName "mywebappprd"  -MultiAZ $true -StorageType gp2 -AllocatedStorage 10 -AutoMinorVersionUp
grade $true -DBInstanceClass db.t2.large -DBParameterGroupName "mywebappprd" -OptionGroupName "mywebappprd" -VpcSecurityGroupId sg-c97606b8 -DBSubnetGroupNam
e "mysqldbsub" -Engine mysql -EngineVersion 5.7 -LicenseModel "general-public-license" -MasterUsername "rdsdba" -MasterUserPassword "rdsdba123" -PreferredMai
ntenanceWindow "SUN:23:00-SUN:23:59" -PreferredBackupWindow "01:00-02:00" -PubliclyAccessible $false


AllocatedStorage                     : 10
AutoMinorVersionUpgrade              : True
AvailabilityZone                     :
BackupRetentionPeriod                : 1
CACertificateIdentifier              : rds-ca-2015
CharacterSetName                     :
CopyTagsToSnapshot                   : False
DBClusterIdentifier                  :
DBInstanceArn                        : arn:aws:rds:us-east-1:072316406132:db:mywebappprd
DBInstanceClass                      : db.t2.large
DBInstanceIdentifier                 : mywebappprd
DbInstancePort                       : 0
DBInstanceStatus                     : creating
DbiResourceId                        : db-NHMO4D3KTUZCRS7MHJHGJ4FHCI
DBName                               : mywebappprd
DBParameterGroups                    : {mywebappprd}
DBSecurityGroups                     : {}
DBSubnetGroup                        : Amazon.RDS.Model.DBSubnetGroup
DomainMemberships                    : {}
Endpoint                             :
Engine                               : mysql
EngineVersion                        : 5.7.17
EnhancedMonitoringResourceArn        :
IAMDatabaseAuthenticationEnabled     : False
InstanceCreateTime                   : 1/1/0001 12:00:00 AM
Iops                                 : 0
KmsKeyId                             :
LatestRestorableTime                 : 1/1/0001 12:00:00 AM
LicenseModel                         : general-public-license
MasterUsername                       : rdsdba
MonitoringInterval                   : 0
MonitoringRoleArn                    :
MultiAZ                              : True
```

To check the status of the DB instance in the Multi-AZ configuration, you can run the following command:

```
PS C:\> Get-RDSDBInstance -DBInstanceIdentifier  "mywebappprd" |Format-
Table MultiAZ, DBInstanceStatus
```

I always notice that setting up a DB instance in a Multi-AZ configuration takes a little more time than the standalone.

```
PS C:\> Get-RDSDBInstance -DBInstanceIdentifier "mywebappprd" |Format-Table MultiAZ, DBInstanceStatus

MultiAZ DBInstanceStatus
------- ----------------
   True creating


PS C:\> Get-RDSDBInstance -DBInstanceIdentifier "mywebappprd" |Format-Table MultiAZ, DBInstanceStatus

MultiAZ DBInstanceStatus
------- ----------------
  False modifying


PS C:\> Get-RDSDBInstance -DBInstanceIdentifier "mywebappprd" |Format-Table MultiAZ, DBInstanceStatus

MultiAZ DBInstanceStatus
------- ----------------
   True backing-up


PS C:\> Get-RDSDBInstance -DBInstanceIdentifier "mywebappprd" |Format-Table MultiAZ, DBInstanceStatus

MultiAZ DBInstanceStatus
------- ----------------
   True modifying


PS C:\> Get-RDSDBInstance -DBInstanceIdentifier "mywebappprd" |Format-Table MultiAZ, DBInstanceStatus

MultiAZ DBInstanceStatus
------- ----------------
   True available
```

You can see that the DB instance's status transitions through various statuses before it becomes available.

Enabling encryption on RDS

Enabling encryption on an RDS DB instance is a simple task. There are just a couple of additional switches that need to be passed on to the `New-RDSDBInstance` cmdlet. But, before you enable encryption on the DB instance, you need to have a key created in KMS. For key creation, you need to write a policy document in JSON format first.

I have created a sample policy document, as follows, which indicates that the role
`WorldPressAppRole` can administer the key in my account. I saved the JSON document as
`D:\data\Policies\KMSPolicy.txt` on my desktop.

```json
{
  "Id": "key-consolepolicy-3",
  "Version": "2012-10-17",
  "Statement": [
    {
      "Sid": "Enable IAM User Permissions",
      "Effect": "Allow",
      "Principal": {
        "AWS": [
          "arn:aws:iam::<account_no>:root"
        ]
      },
      "Action": "kms:*",
      "Resource": "*"
    },
    {
      "Sid": "Allow access for Key Administrators",
      "Effect": "Allow",
      "Principal": {
        "AWS": [
          "arn:aws:iam::<account_no>:role/WorldPressAppRole"
        ]
      },
      "Action": [
        "kms:Create*",
        "kms:Describe*",
        "kms:Enable*",
        "kms:List*",
        "kms:Put*",
        "kms:Update*",
        "kms:Revoke*",
        "kms:Disable*",
        "kms:Get*",
        "kms:Delete*",
        "kms:TagResource",
        "kms:UntagResource",
        "kms:ScheduleKeyDeletion",
        "kms:CancelKeyDeletion"
      ],
      "Resource": "*"
    },
    {
      "Sid": "Allow use of the key",
      "Effect": "Allow",
```

```
        "Principal": {
          "AWS": [
            "arn:aws:iam::<account_no>:role/WorldPressAppRole"
          ]
        },
        "Action": [
          "kms:Encrypt",
          "kms:Decrypt",
          "kms:ReEncrypt*",
          "kms:GenerateDataKey*",
          "kms:DescribeKey"
        ],
        "Resource": "*"
      },
      {
        "Sid": "Allow attachment of persistent resources",
        "Effect": "Allow",
        "Principal": {
          "AWS": [
            "arn:aws:iam::<account_no>:role/WorldPressAppRole"
          ]
        },
        "Action": [
          "kms:CreateGrant",
          "kms:ListGrants",
          "kms:RevokeGrant"
        ],
        "Resource": "*",
        "Condition": {
          "Bool": {
            "kms:GrantIsForAWSResource": true
          }
        }
      }
    ]
  }
```

Using this policy document, you can create the KMS key that can be used to encrypt an RDS DB instance. To get the list of all the cmdlets that you can use to work with KMS, you can use the following command:

```
PS C:\> Get-Command "*KMS*"
```

To create a key in KMS, you can issue the following command:

```
PS C:\> New-KMSKey -Description "MySQLDBWebAppKey" -Origin AWS_KMS -Policy
$policydoc
```

```
PS C:\> $policydoc=(Get-Content -Raw D:\data\Policies\KMSPolicy.txt)
PS C:\> New-KMSKey -Description "MySQLDBWebAppKey" -Origin AWS_KMS -Policy $policydoc

Arn                : arn:aws:kms:us-east-1:072316406132:key/8c21ccee-415c-499e-989c-dc9184e07ac1
AWSAccountId       : 072316406132
CreationDate       : 7/14/2017 8:47:54 AM
DeletionDate       : 1/1/0001 12:00:00 AM
Description        : MySQLDBWebAppKey
Enabled            : True
ExpirationModel    :
KeyId              : 8c21ccee-415c-499e-989c-dc9184e07ac1
KeyState           : Enabled
KeyUsage           : ENCRYPT_DECRYPT
Origin             : AWS_KMS
ValidTo            : 1/1/0001 12:00:00 AM
```

`Origin` indicates whether a key is from KMS or from an external source. Once the key has been created, you just need to pick up the `Arn` value shown by this key to use it with an RDS DB instance. Now, with `New-RDSDBInstance`, you supply two additional switches to encrypt the database: `StorageEncrypted` and `KmsKeyId`. The `StorageEncrypted` switch tells the RDS that storage can be encrypted using the key mentioned in `KmsKeyId`.

To create an encrypted database, you can use the following command:

```
PS C:\> New-RDSDBInstance -DBInstanceIdentifier  "mywebappprd1" -DBName
"mywebappprd" -MultiAZ $true -StorageType gp2 -AllocatedStorage 10 -
AutoMinorVersionUpgrade $true -DBInstanceClass db.t2.large -
DBParameterGroupName "mywebappprd" -OptionGroupName "mywebappprd" -
VpcSecurityGroupId sg-c97606b8 -DBSubnetGroupName "mysqldbsub" -Engine
mysql -EngineVersion 5.7 -LicenseModel "general-public-license" -
MasterUsername "rdsdba" -MasterUserPassword "rdsdba123" -
PreferredMaintenanceWindow "SUN:23:00-SUN:23:59" -PreferredBackupWindow
"01:00-02:00" -PubliclyAccessible $false -StorageEncrypted  $true -KmsKeyId
"arn:aws:kms:us-east-1:<account_no>:key/8c21ccee-415c-499e-989c-
dc9184e07ac1"
```

```
PS C:\> New-RDSDBInstance -DBInstanceIdentifier "mywebappprd" -DBName "mywebappprd" -MultiAZ $true -StorageType gp2 -AllocatedStorage 10 -AutoMinorVersionUp
grade $true -DBInstanceClass db.t2.large -DBParameterGroupName "mywebappprd" -OptionGroupName "mywebappprd" -VpcSecurityGroupId sg-c97606b8 -DBSubnetGroupNam
e "mysqldbsub" -Engine mysql -EngineVersion 5.7 -LicenseModel "general-public-license" -MasterUsername "rdsdba" -MasterUserPassword "rdsdba123" -PreferredMai
ntenanceWindow "SUN:23:00-SUN:23:59" -PreferredBackupWindow "01:00-02:00" -PubliclyAccessible $false -StorageEncrypted $true -KmsKeyId "arn:aws:kms:us-east-
1:072316406132:key/8c21ccee-415c-499e-989c-dc9184e07ac1"


AllocatedStorage                    : 10
AutoMinorVersionUpgrade             : True
AvailabilityZone                    :
BackupRetentionPeriod               : 1
CACertificateIdentifier             : rds-ca-2015
CharacterSetName                    :
CopyTagsToSnapshot                  : False
DBClusterIdentifier                 :
DBInstanceArn                       : arn:aws:rds:us-east-1:072316406132:db:mywebappprd
DBInstanceClass                     : db.t2.large
DBInstanceIdentifier                : mywebappprd
DbInstancePort                      : 0
DBInstanceStatus                    : creating
DbiResourceId                       : db-CXTPDFW6R4KKWI6KQOZE7E4TN4
DBName                              : mywebappprd
DBParameterGroups                   : {mywebappprd}
DBSecurityGroups                    : {}
DBSubnetGroup                       : Amazon.RDS.Model.DBSubnetGroup
DomainMemberships                   : {}
Endpoint                            :
Engine                              : mysql
EngineVersion                       : 5.7.17
EnhancedMonitoringResourceArn       :
IAMDatabaseAuthenticationEnabled    : False
InstanceCreateTime                  : 1/1/0001 12:00:00 AM
Iops                                : 0
KmsKeyId                            : arn:aws:kms:us-east-1:072316406132:key/8c21ccee-415c-499e-989c-dc9184e07ac1
LatestRestorableTime                : 1/1/0001 12:00:00 AM
LicenseModel                        : general-public-license
MasterUsername                      : rdsdba
MonitoringInterval                  : 0
MonitoringRoleArn                   :
MultiAZ                             : True
```

 Note that, once you enable encryption on the database, you cannot remove or disable it.

To check the status, you can use the following command:

```
PS C:\> Get-RDSDBInstance -DBInstanceIdentifier "mywebappprd" |Format-
Table MultiAZ, DBInstanceStatus,StorageEncrypted
```

```
PS C:\> Get-RDSDBInstance -DBInstanceIdentifier "mywebappprd" |Format-Table MultiAZ, DBInstanceStatus,StorageEncrypted

MultiAZ DBInstanceStatus StorageEncrypted
------- ---------------- ----------------
   True available                    True
```

You can see that the DB instance is deployed with a Multi-AZ configuration with encryption enabled. To check where your DB instances are running, you can use the following command:

```
PS C:\> Get-RDSDBInstance -DBInstanceIdentifier  "mywebappprd"|Format-Table
AvailabilityZone,SecondaryAvailabilityZone
```

```
PS C:\> Get-RDSDBInstance -DBInstanceIdentifier  "mywebappprd"|Format-Table AvailabilityZone,SecondaryAvailabilityZone

AvailabilityZone SecondaryAvailabilityZone
---------------- -------------------------
us-east-1b       us-east-1a
```

`AvailabilityZone` indicates that the primary DB is running in `us-east-1b` and `SecondaryAvailabilityZone` indicates that the standby is running in `us-east-1a`.

Connecting to an RDS instance with and without SSL

In order to test the connectivity to the DB instance, hop on to the RDS Admin Hub or the bastion server that you have. Ensure that the RDS Admin Hub is part of the same VPC as the DB instance subnets. As mentioned earlier, to demonstrate the concept, I considered my RDS Admin Hub as a bastion server as well. Security Group on my RDS Admin hub allows ingress on port 22 for SSH and RDP on port 3389.

RDS allocates a DNS name to each RDS DB instance that we create. In regard to RDS, these DNS names are called **endpoints**. You need to get the endpoint for the DB instance to establish the connectivity. You can get the endpoint for a specified DB instance by using the following command:

```
PS C:\> (Get-RDSDBInstance -DBInstanceIdentifier  "mywebappprd" ).endpoint
```

```
PS C:\> (Get-RDSDBInstance -DBInstanceIdentifier  "mywebappprd" ).endpoint

Address                                                    HostedZoneId    Port
-------                                                    ------------    ----
mywebappprd.cwrq5w1v98ur.us-east-1.rds.amazonaws.com       Z2R2ITUGPM61AM  3306
```

We got the endpoint address as mywebappprd.cwrq5w1v98ur.us-east-1.rds.amazonaws.com for the DB instance mywebappprd. This is nothing but the hostname. You can now use this hostname to establish the connectivity, either through the application or through bastion. As we have spun up the MySQL DB instance, you just need the MySQL client running on the bastion. You can now connect as shown following:

```
[root@ip-10-0-2-158 ~]# mysql -u rdsdba -prdsdba123 -h
mywebappprd.cwrq5w1v98ur.us-east-1.rds.amazonaws.com
```

```
[root@ip-10-0-2-158 ~]# mysql -u rdsdba -prdsdba123 -h mywebappprd.cwrq5w1v98ur.us-east-1.rds.amazonaws.com
Welcome to the MySQL monitor.  Commands end with ; or \g.
Your MySQL connection id is 37
Server version: 5.7.17-log MySQL Community Server (GPL)

Copyright (c) 2000, 2017, Oracle and/or its affiliates. All rights reserved.

Oracle is a registered trademark of Oracle Corporation and/or its
affiliates. Other names may be trademarks of their respective
owners.

Type 'help;' or '\h' for help. Type '\c' to clear the current input statement.

mysql> show databases;
+--------------------+
| Database           |
+--------------------+
| information_schema |
| innodb             |
| mysql              |
| mywebappprd        |
| performance_schema |
| sys                |
+--------------------+
6 rows in set (0.00 sec)

mysql>
```

The database name that we specified at the time of launch, mywebappprd, can be seen in the list of databases in the DB instance. Provided you have the right ingress rule specified on the Security Group assigned to your DB instance, you should not have any issues connecting to the DB instance. Once connected to it, you can make use of the database mywebappprd and create your own schema structure for the application.

```
mysql> use mywebappprd;
Database changed
mysql> CREATE TABLE pet_master (name VARCHAR(20), owner VARCHAR(20),
    -> species VARCHAR(20), sex CHAR(1), birth DATE, death DATE);
Query OK, 0 rows affected (0.04 sec)

mysql> show tables;
+-----------------------+
| Tables_in_mywebappprd |
+-----------------------+
| pet_master            |
+-----------------------+
1 row in set (0.00 sec)

mysql>
```

The connection method that we tested is without SSL. By default, every time you launch an RDS DB instance, AWS creates and installs an SSL certificate on the DB instance. SSL certificates are signed by the certificate authority. The SSL certificate that is installed on the DB instance host includes an assigned CNAME endpoint to guard against attack. The public key of the certificate is found at `https://s3.amazonaws.com/rds-downloads/rds-combined-ca-bundle.pem`. You can download this certificate to your bastion host and then connect using SSL, as shown following:

```
# wget https://s3.amazonaws.com/rds-downloads/rds-combined-ca-bundle.pem
# mysql -u rdsdba -prdsdba123 -h mywebappprd.cwrq5w1v98ur.us-
east-1.rds.amazonaws.com --ssl-ca=rds-combined-ca-bundle.pem --ssl-verify-
server-cert
```

```
[root@ip-10-0-2-158 ~]# wget https://s3.amazonaws.com/rds-downloads/rds-combined-ca-bundle.pem
--2017-07-14 12:01:28--  https://s3.amazonaws.com/rds-downloads/rds-combined-ca-bundle.pem
Resolving s3.amazonaws.com (s3.amazonaws.com)... 54.231.49.148
Connecting to s3.amazonaws.com (s3.amazonaws.com)|54.231.49.148|:443... connected.
HTTP request sent, awaiting response... 200 OK
Length: 21672 (21K) [binary/octet-stream]
Saving to: 'rds-combined-ca-bundle.pem'

rds-combined-ca-bundle.pem      100%[===================================================================>]  21.16K  --.-KB/s    in 0s

2017-07-14 12:01:29 (108 MB/s) - 'rds-combined-ca-bundle.pem' saved [21672/21672]

[root@ip-10-0-2-158 ~]# ls -ltr
total 24
-rw-r--r-- 1 root root 21672 Oct 18  2016 rds-combined-ca-bundle.pem
[root@ip-10-0-2-158 ~]# pwd
/root
[root@ip-10-0-2-158 ~]# mysql -u rdsdba -prdsdba123 -h mywebappprd.cwrq5w1v98ur.us-east-1.rds.amazonaws.com \
> --ssl-ca=rds-combined-ca-bundle.pem --ssl-verify-server-cert
Welcome to the MySQL monitor.  Commands end with ; or \g.
Your MySQL connection id is 86
Server version: 5.7.17-log MySQL Community Server (GPL)

Copyright (c) 2000, 2017, Oracle and/or its affiliates. All rights reserved.

Oracle is a registered trademark of Oracle Corporation and/or its
affiliates. Other names may be trademarks of their respective
owners.

Type 'help;' or '\h' for help. Type '\c' to clear the current input statement.

mysql> show databases;
+--------------------+
| Database           |
+--------------------+
| information_schema |
| innodb             |
| mysql              |
| mywebappprd        |
| performance_schema |
```

Switch `ssl-ca` indicates the public key for the DB instance that you spun up, and if you have a specific directory to store this certificate, then ensure that you specify the complete path of the certificate file. You can verify whether the connection is encrypted or not just by using `/s` or `status` after connecting to the DB instance, as follows:

```
[root@ip-10-0-2-158 ~]# mysql -u rdsdba -prdsdba123 -h mywebappprd.cwrq5w1v98ur.us-east-1.rds.amazonaws.com \
> --ssl-ca=rds-combined-ca-bundle.pem --ssl-verify-server-cert
Welcome to the MySQL monitor.  Commands end with ; or \g.
Your MySQL connection id is 92
Server version: 5.7.17-log MySQL Community Server (GPL)

Copyright (c) 2000, 2017, Oracle and/or its affiliates. All rights reserved.

Oracle is a registered trademark of Oracle Corporation and/or its
affiliates. Other names may be trademarks of their respective
owners.

Type 'help;' or '\h' for help. Type '\c' to clear the current input statement.

mysql> \s
--------------
mysql  Ver 14.14 Distrib 5.5.56, for Linux (x86_64) using readline 5.1

Connection id:          92
Current database:
Current user:           rdsdba@10.0.2.158
SSL:                    Cipher in use is AES256-SHA
Current pager:          stdout
Using outfile:          ''
Using delimiter:        ;
Server version:         5.7.17-log MySQL Community Server (GPL)
Protocol version:       10
Connection:             mywebappprd.cwrq5w1v98ur.us-east-1.rds.amazonaws.com via TCP/IP
Server characterset:    latin1
Db     characterset:    latin1
Client characterset:    utf8
Conn.  characterset:    utf8
TCP port:               3306
Uptime:                 3 hours 11 min 28 sec

Threads: 2  Questions: 6586  Slow queries: 0  Opens: 174  Flush tables: 1  Open tables: 146  Queries per second avg: 0.573
--------------

mysql>
```

You can see `SSL: Cipher in use is AES256-SHA`. This indicates that the connection from the client to the server is encrypted. You can try to connect once again without the public key and see what you get.

```
[root@ip-10-0-2-158 ~]# mysql -u rdsdba -prdsdba123 -h mywebappprd.cwrq5w1v98ur.us-east-1.rds.amazonaws.com
Welcome to the MySQL monitor.  Commands end with ; or \g.
Your MySQL connection id is 94
Server version: 5.7.17-log MySQL Community Server (GPL)

Copyright (c) 2000, 2017, Oracle and/or its affiliates. All rights reserved.

Oracle is a registered trademark of Oracle Corporation and/or its
affiliates. Other names may be trademarks of their respective
owners.

Type 'help;' or '\h' for help. Type '\c' to clear the current input statement.

mysql> \s
--------------
mysql  Ver 14.14 Distrib 5.5.56, for Linux (x86_64) using readline 5.1

Connection id:          94
Current database:
Current user:           rdsdba@10.0.2.158
SSL:                    Not in use
Current pager:          stdout
Using outfile:          ''
Using delimiter:        ;
Server version:         5.7.17-log MySQL Community Server (GPL)
Protocol version:       10
Connection:             mywebappprd.cwrq5w1v98ur.us-east-1.rds.amazonaws.com via TCP/IP
Server characterset:    latin1
Db     characterset:    latin1
Client characterset:    utf8
Conn.  characterset:    utf8
TCP port:               3306
Uptime:                 3 hours 16 min 24 sec

Threads: 2  Questions: 6745  Slow queries: 0  Opens: 174  Flush tables: 1  Open tables: 146  Queries per second avg: 0.572
--------------
```

This time, you can see SSL: Not in use. This indicates that the connection from the client to the server is not encrypted. If you want to allow only SSL connections from the RDSDBA database user, then you can issue the following command:

```
mysql> GRANT USAGE ON *.* TO 'rdsdba'@'%' REQUIRE SSL;
```

To remove the SSL authentication from the rdsdba user, you can use the following command:

```
mysql> GRANT USAGE ON *.* TO 'rdsdba'@'%' REQUIRE NONE;
```

Stop, start, and restart of a DB instance

The `Stop-RDSDBInstance` cmdlet lets you stop the specified DB instance. After stopping the DB instance, AWS will not release metadata of the DB instance, such as the endpoint. The DB instance will still be associated with the allocated DB Parameter Group and DB Option Group. All the transaction logs will be retained for you to do the point-in-time recovery if required. Even if you stop the DB instance, you will be charged for the underlying resources used by that DB instance. Note that, you cannot stop or start a Multi-AZ or mirrored DB instance. You can only stop and start a single AZ instance. In this example, I have used the single AZ standalone DB instance `WebSingleAZDB`.

To stop the DB instance, you can use the following command:

```
PS C:\> Stop-RDSDBInstance -DBInstanceIdentifier "WebSingleAZDB" -
DBSnapshotIdentifier "Before-stop-Snapshot-20170717"
```

```
PS C:\> Stop-RDSDBInstance -DBInstanceIdentifier "WebSingleAZDB" -DBSnapshotIdentifier "Before-stop-Snapshot-20170717"

AllocatedStorage              : 10
AutoMinorVersionUpgrade       : True
AvailabilityZone              : us-east-1a
BackupRetentionPeriod         : 1
CACertificateIdentifier       : rds-ca-2015
CharacterSetName              :
CopyTagsToSnapshot            : False
DBClusterIdentifier           :
DBInstanceArn                 : arn:aws:rds:us-east-1:072316406132:db:websingleazdb
DBInstanceClass               : db.t2.large
DBInstanceIdentifier          : websingleazdb
DbInstancePort                : 0
DBInstanceStatus              : stopping
DbiResourceId                 : db-3NWSE3Y7T6VBEFSX6Y7U46LXUQ
DBName                        : WebSingleAZDB
```

By specifying the switch `DBSnapshotIdentifier` with the `Stop-RDSDBInstance` cmdlet you can initiate the manual snapshot of the database before the DB instance is stopped. You can confirm the status of the DB instance using the following command:

```
PS C:\> Get-RDSDBInstance -DBInstanceIdentifier  "WebSingleAZDB" |Format-
Table DBInstanceStatus
```

```
PS C:\> Get-RDSDBInstance -DBInstanceIdentifier "WebSingleAZDB" |Format-Table DBInstanceStatus

DBInstanceStatus
----------------
stopping

PS C:\> Get-RDSDBInstance -DBInstanceIdentifier "WebSingleAZDB" |Format-Table DBInstanceStatus

DBInstanceStatus
----------------
stopped
```

After initiating stop, I noticed that the DB instance took around 5 to 7 minutes to transition from `stopping` to the `stopped` state. So, be patient.

The `Start-RDSDBInstance` cmdlet lets you start the DB instance that was stopped previously, either by using CLI or the AWS Console. To start the DB instance, you can run the following command:

```
PS C:\> Start-RDSDBInstance -DBInstanceIdentifier "WebSingleAZDB"
```

```
PS C:\> Start-RDSDBInstance -DBInstanceIdentifier "WebSingleAZDB"

AllocatedStorage                  : 10
AutoMinorVersionUpgrade           : True
AvailabilityZone                  : us-east-1a
BackupRetentionPeriod             : 1
CACertificateIdentifier           : rds-ca-2015
CharacterSetName                  :
CopyTagsToSnapshot                : False
DBClusterIdentifier               :
DBInstanceArn                     : arn:aws:rds:us-east-1:072316406132:db:websingleazdb
DBInstanceClass                   : db.t2.large
DBInstanceIdentifier              : websingleazdb
DbInstancePort                    : 0
DBInstanceStatus                  : starting
DbiResourceId                     : db-3NWSE3Y7T6VBEFSX6Y7U46LXUQ
DBName                            : WebSingleAZDB
```

You can verify the status of the DB instance once again by running the following command:

```
PS C:\> Get-RDSDBInstance -DBInstanceIdentifier  "WebSingleAZDB" |Format-
Table DBInstanceStatus
```

```
PS C:\> Get-RDSDBInstance -DBInstanceIdentifier  "WebSingleAZDB" |Format-Table DBInstanceStatus

DBInstanceStatus
----------------
available
```

The status `available` means the DB instance is ready to serve traffic once again.

The `Restart-RDSDBInstance` cmdlet lets you reboot the DB instance service. If you had any pending database configuration actions, those will be applied during reboot. You will experience outage for a short time during the reboot operation. If you are running a DB instance in Multi-AZ configuration, you can manually failover to the standby database during reboot. This is the only operation that permits you to failover to the standby. In this example, I am using the DB instance `mywebappprd`, which is running in a Multi-AZ.

```
PS C:\> Restart-RDSDBInstance -DBInstanceIdentifier "mywebappprd" -
ForceFailover $true
```

`ForceFailover` is not a mandatory switch.

```
PS C:\> Restart-RDSDBInstance -DBInstanceIdentifier "mywebappprd" -ForceFailover $true

AllocatedStorage                 : 10
AutoMinorVersionUpgrade          : True
AvailabilityZone                 : us-east-1b
BackupRetentionPeriod            : 1
CACertificateIdentifier          : rds-ca-2015
CharacterSetName                 :
CopyTagsToSnapshot               : False
DBClusterIdentifier              :
DBInstanceArn                    : arn:aws:rds:us-east-1:072316406132:db:mywebappprd
DBInstanceClass                  : db.t2.large
DBInstanceIdentifier             : mywebappprd
DbInstancePort                   : 0
DBInstanceStatus                 : rebooting
DbiResourceId                    : db-CXTPDFW6R4KKWI6KQOZE7E4TN4
DBName                           : mywebappprd
```

You can only reboot a DB instance in a Multi-AZ configuration, but for single AZ or standalone DB instances, you can perform stop, start, and reboot or restart. The status of the DB instance can be checked using the following command:

```
PS C:\> Get-RDSDBInstance -DBInstanceIdentifier "mywebappprd" |Format-
Table DBInstanceStatus, AvailabilityZone, SecondaryAvailabilityZone
```

```
PS C:\> Get-RDSDBInstance -DBInstanceIdentifier "mywebappprd" |Format-Table DBInstanceStatus, AvailabilityZone, SecondaryAvailabilityZone

DBInstanceStatus AvailabilityZone SecondaryAvailabilityZone
---------------- ---------------- -------------------------
available        us-east-1a       us-east-1b
```

After initiating reboot, the DB instance transitioned to the `rebooting` status and then back to `available`. We also see that the primary availability zone of the DB instance is now `us-east-1a`. The failover operation made the standby site the primary and the primary site the standby. This is how you can manually failover to the standby site.

Adding space to a DB instance

`Edit-RDSDBInstance` lets you modify one or more configuration items for the DB instance. Almost all the configurational items that you can specify with `New-RDSDBInstance` can be specified with `Edit-RDSDBInstance`, with the exception of enabling encryption. To increase DB instance storage, you can use the `AllocatedStorage` switch with a new value. For all the database engines, the new storage value has to be at least 10% greater than the current allocated storage value. If you do not specify a value at least 10% greater, then RDS will round up to the next 10% value. If you do not specify the `ApplyImmediately` switch with the cmdlet, then changes will occur during the next maintenance window. For immediate allocation, you can set the `ApplyImmediately` switch to true.

To add another 10 GB to the existing DB instance, you can use the following command:

```
PS C:\> Edit-RDSDBInstance -DBInstanceIdentifier "mywebappprd" -
AllocatedStorage 20 -ApplyImmediately $true
```

```
PS C:\> Get-RDSDBInstance -DBInstanceIdentifier  "mywebappprd" |Format-Table DBInstanceIdentifier, StorageType,AllocatedStorage

DBInstanceIdentifier StorageType AllocatedStorage
-------------------- ----------- ----------------
mywebappprd          gp2                       10


PS C:\> Edit-RDSDBInstance -DBInstanceIdentifier "mywebappprd" -AllocatedStorage 20 -ApplyImmediately $true


AllocatedStorage           : 10
AutoMinorVersionUpgrade    : True
AvailabilityZone           : us-east-1a
BackupRetentionPeriod      : 1
CACertificateIdentifier    : rds-ca-2015
CharacterSetName           :
CopyTagsToSnapshot         : False
DBClusterIdentifier        :
DBInstanceArn              : arn:aws:rds:us-east-1:072316406132:db:mywebappprd
DBInstanceClass            : db.t2.large
DBInstanceIdentifier       : mywebappprd
DbInstancePort             : 0
DBInstanceStatus           : available
DbiResourceId              : db-CXTPDFW6R4KKWI6KQOZE7E4TN4
DBName                     : mywebappprd
```

In the above example, you might have noticed that we specified the `AllocatedStorage` value as 20 and not 10. Note that the value that you specify for `AllocatedStorage` is the absolute value and not relative. The initial size of the DB instance was 10 GB and we wanted to extend it by another 10 GB. So, the overall size of the DB instance size will be 20 GB. That's the value that needs to be specified for `AllocatedStorage`. In addition, you can only increase the size of the DB instance, you cannot decrease the DB instance size using `Edit-RDSDBInstance`. To decrease size, you can spin up another DB instance using the snapshot and specify the new size during the launch process. In this case, your DB instance endpoint will change.

To check the status of the operation, you can use the following command:

```
PS C:\> Get-RDSDBInstance -DBInstanceIdentifier  "mywebappprd" |Format-
Table DBInstanceIdentifier, DBInstanceStatus, StorageType, AllocatedStorage
```

```
PS C:\> Get-RDSDBInstance -DBInstanceIdentifier  "mywebappprd" |Format-Table DBInstanceIdentifier, DBInstanceStatus, StorageType, AllocatedStorage

DBInstanceIdentifier DBInstanceStatus StorageType AllocatedStorage
-------------------- ---------------- ----------- ----------------
mywebappprd          available        gp2                       20
```

The status `available` indicates that the DB configuration modification is complete and new additional storage has been provisioned. Review the AWS online documentation for all possible configurational items using the following command:

```
PS C:\> Get-Help Edit-RDSDBInstance  -online
```

RDS backup

AWS RDS is a managed service. Database backups are part of this service. Snapshot and backups are synonymous terms in the case of RDS and are used interchangeably. You do not need to script anything to make backups on an RDS DB instance regularly. You just need to ensure that you have configured the right backup window and backup retention for your DB instance. Both values can be specified at the time of DB instance launch, or you can modify them later, if needed. To check the current backup retention and window, you can use the following command:

```
PS C:\> Get-RDSDBInstance -DBInstanceIdentifier  "mywebappprd" |Format-
Table DBInstanceIdentifier, BackupRetentionPeriod, PreferredBackupWindow
```

```
PS C:\> Get-RDSDBInstance -DBInstanceIdentifier  "mywebappprd" |Format-Table DBInstanceIdentifier, BackupRetentionPeriod, PreferredBackupWindow

DBInstanceIdentifier BackupRetentionPeriod PreferredBackupWindow
-------------------- --------------------- ---------------------
mywebappprd                              1 01:00-02:00
```

If you have `BackupRetentionPeriod` set to 0 (zero), it means that automated backup is disabled for the given instance. In this example, you can see that we have a value of 1. This means only one copy of the automated backup will be retained by AWS. You can specify a `BackupRetentionPeriod` of up to 35 days. To increase the backup retention to 7 days, you can use the following command:

```
PS C:\> Edit-RDSDBInstance -DBInstanceIdentifier "mywebappprd" -
BackupRetentionPeriod 7 -ApplyImmediately $true
```

```
PS C:\> Edit-RDSDBInstance -DBInstanceIdentifier "mywebappprd" -BackupRetentionPeriod 7 -ApplyImmediately $true


AllocatedStorage                     : 20
AutoMinorVersionUpgrade              : True
AvailabilityZone                     : us-east-1a
BackupRetentionPeriod                : 7
CACertificateIdentifier              : rds-ca-2015
CharacterSetName                     :
CopyTagsToSnapshot                   : False
DBClusterIdentifier                  :
DBInstanceArn                        : arn:aws:rds:us-east-1:072316406132:db:mywebappprd
DBInstanceClass                      : db.t2.large
DBInstanceIdentifier                 : mywebappprd
DbInstancePort                       : 0
DBInstanceStatus                     : available
DbiResourceId                        : db-CXTPDFW6R4KKWI6KQOZE7E4TN4
DBName                               : mywebappprd
```

Likewise, you can change the backup window if needed. To ensure that automated backups are running, you can check the status of the snapshots using the following command:

```
PS C:\> Get-RDSDBSnapshot -DBInstanceIdentifier "mywebappprd" |Format-Table
DBSnapshotIdentifier,Encrypted,AvailabilityZone,PercentProgress
```

```
PS C:\> Get-RDSDBSnapshot -DBInstanceIdentifier "mywebappprd" |Format-Table DBSnapshotIdentifier,Encrypted,AvailabilityZone,PercentProgress

DBSnapshotIdentifier              Encrypted AvailabilityZone PercentProgress
--------------------              --------- ---------------- ---------------
rds:mywebappprd-2017-07-14-09-13  True us-east-1b                       100
rds:mywebappprd-2017-07-15-01-10  True us-east-1a                       100
```

In this example, two snapshots are created. As we enabled the DB encryption during the launch time, snapshots created are also encrypted. Different availability zones indicate that there was a failover on standby and, therefore, backups are taken on two different sites. Remember that, in a Multi-AZ configuration, backups are taken on the standby database. PercentProgress indicates that backups have been 100 percent completed.

RDS restore

They are various scenarios in which you may want to restore the DB instance from the previous backup. These include: that you want to test a new DB instance class for your workload, or see how a DB instance performs with Provisional IOPS or you want go back in time and review some of the table data, or your developer wants the latest data from production to test the application. On RDS, restoration is simply a click away. You just need to know the snapshot ID that you want to restore and spin up the new DB instance. Note that you cannot restore a DB instance to the existing DB instance. You have to spin up a new DB instance using the snapshot.

The `Restore-RDSDBInstanceFromDBSnapshot` cmdlet lets you create a new DB instance from the DB snapshot.

```
PS C:\> Restore-RDSDBInstanceFromDBSnapshot -DBInstanceIdentifier
"copymywebappprd" -DBSnapshotIdentifier "rds:mywebappprd-2017-07-15-01-10"
-DBInstanceClass  "db.m3.medium" -DBSubnetGroupName "mysqldbsub" -Engine
mysql -StorageType gp2
```

You can change some of the values when creating the new DB instance from the snapshot. In this example, I have changed the DB instance class to db.m3.medium.

```
PS C:\> Restore-RDSDBInstanceFromDBSnapshot -DBInstanceIdentifier "copymywebappprd" -DBSnapshotIdentifier "rds:mywebappprd-2017-07-15-01-10" -DBInstanceClass
     "db.m3.medium" -DBSubnetGroupName "mysqldbsub" -Engine mysql -StorageType gp2

AllocatedStorage                   : 10
AutoMinorVersionUpgrade            : True
AvailabilityZone                   :
BackupRetentionPeriod              : 1
CACertificateIdentifier            : rds-ca-2015
CharacterSetName                   :
CopyTagsToSnapshot                 : False
DBClusterIdentifier                :
DBInstanceArn                      : arn:aws:rds:us-east-1:072316406132:db:copymywebappprd
DBInstanceClass                    : db.m3.medium
DBInstanceIdentifier               : copymywebappprd
DbInstancePort                     : 0
DBInstanceStatus                   : creating
DbiResourceId                      : db-ENARSHZR74E4DSCBUSJQYRE7NQ
DBName                             : mywebappprd
```

By default, a single AZ DB instance will be created if you do not specify a Multi-AZ switch with `Restore-RDSDBInstanceFromDBSnapshot`. If your original DB instance had encryption enabled, then the new DB instance will also be encrypted. Review the online documentation for this cmdlet and make yourself familiar with its usage.

```
PS C:\> Get-Help Restore-RDSDBInstanceFromDBSnapshot -online
```

Manual snapshot of the RDS instance

In addition to automated backup, you can always initiate a manual snapshot of the DB instance at any time. The manual snapshot that you take does not get deleted when you delete the DB instance, and does not come under the AWS Managed Service umbrella. All automated snapshots are deleted when you delete the DB instance. You can retain the copy of a manual snapshot for as long as you want. Usually, you can always initiate the manual snapshot before making any changes to the DB instance. You can initiate the manual snapshot using the following command:

```
PS C:\> New-RDSDBSnapshot -DBSnapshotIdentifier "before-change-mywebappprd"
-DBInstanceIdentifier "mywebappprd"
```

```
PS C:\> New-RDSDBSnapshot -DBSnapshotIdentifier "before-change-mywebappprd" -DBInstanceIdentifier "mywebappprd"


AllocatedStorage                    : 20
AvailabilityZone                    : us-east-1a
DBInstanceIdentifier                : mywebappprd
DBSnapshotArn                       : arn:aws:rds:us-east-1:072316406132:snapshot:before-change-mywebappprd
DBSnapshotIdentifier                : before-change-mywebappprd
Encrypted                           : True
Engine                              : mysql
EngineVersion                       : 5.7.17
IAMDatabaseAuthenticationEnabled    : False
InstanceCreateTime                  : 7/14/2017 7:03:49 PM
Iops                                : 0
KmsKeyId                            : arn:aws:kms:us-east-1:072316406132:key/8c21ccee-415c-499e-989c-dc9184e07ac1
LicenseModel                        : general-public-license
MasterUsername                      : rdsdba
OptionGroupName                     : mywebappprd
PercentProgress                     : 0
Port                                : 3306
SnapshotCreateTime                  : 1/1/0001 12:00:00 AM
SnapshotType                        : manual
SourceDBSnapshotIdentifier          :
SourceRegion                        :
Status                              : creating
StorageType                         : gp2
TdeCredentialArn                    :
Timezone                            :
VpcId                               : vpc-a6bb60df
```

The DB instance is available during the manual snapshot process. In this case, backups will also be taken on the standby site if you have a Multi-AZ configuration. You can check the status of the snapshot backup using the following command:

```
PS C:\> Get-RDSDBSnapshot -DBInstanceIdentifier "mywebappprd" |Format-Table
DBSnapshotIdentifier,Encrypted,AvailabilityZone,PercentProgress
```

```
PS C:\> Get-RDSDBSnapshot -DBInstanceIdentifier "mywebappprd" |Format-Table DBSnapshotIdentifier,Encrypted,AvailabilityZone,PercentProgress

DBSnapshotIdentifier              Encrypted AvailabilityZone PercentProgress
--------------------              --------- ---------------- ---------------
before-change-mywebappprd              True us-east-1a                    91
rds:mywebappprd-2017-07-14-09-13       True us-east-1b                   100
rds:mywebappprd-2017-07-15-01-10       True us-east-1a                   100
```

In this example, DBSnapshotIdentifier before-change-mywebappprd indicates that the operation is 91% complete.

Deleting an RDS instance

The `Remove-RDSDBInstance` cmdlet lets you remove the existing DB instance. When you remove the DB instance, all the automated snapshot related to the DB instance are also removed and cannot be recovered. All manual snapshots taken by you will be retained. You can initiate the final snapshot of the DB instance as part of the removal operation and the DB instance will have the deleting status until the snapshot is completed. You also have the choice to skip the final snapshot.

To remove a DB instance, you can use the following two variants of the cmdlet.

```
PS C:\> Remove-RDSDBInstance -DBInstanceIdentifier "copymywebappprd" -
FinalDBSnapshotIdentifier "Myfinalsnapshot4webappprd"
```

Or:

```
PS C:\> Remove-RDSDBInstance -DBInstanceIdentifier "copymywebappprd" -
SkipFinalSnapshot $true
```

```
PS C:\> Remove-RDSDBInstance -DBInstanceIdentifier "copymywebappprd" -FinalDBSnapshotIdentifier "Myfinalsnapshot4webappprd"

Confirm
Are you sure you want to perform this action?
Performing the operation "Remove-RDSDBInstance (DeleteDBInstance)" on target "copymywebappprd".
[Y] Yes  [A] Yes to All  [N] No  [L] No to All  [S] Suspend  [?] Help (default is "Y"): Y


AllocatedStorage                 : 10
AutoMinorVersionUpgrade          : True
AvailabilityZone                 : us-east-1a
BackupRetentionPeriod            : 1
CACertificateIdentifier          : rds-ca-2015
CharacterSetName                 :
CopyTagsToSnapshot               : False
DBClusterIdentifier              :
DBInstanceArn                    : arn:aws:rds:us-east-1:072316406132:db:copymywebappprd
DBInstanceClass                  : db.m3.medium
DBInstanceIdentifier             : copymywebappprd
DbInstancePort                   : 0
DBInstanceStatus                 : deleting
DbiResourceId                    : db-ENARSHZR74E4DSCBUSJQYRE7NQ
DBName                           : mywebappprd
```

Checking account limit and attributes

If you are running several hundred DB instances, it is always best practice to schedule an automation around RDS service limits. `Get-RDSAccountAttribute` lets you list all the attributes and limits for your RDS Service in your account. This will list all the current quotas and the maximum usage allowed in your account for the RDS service.

```
PS C:\> Get-RDSAccountAttribute
```

```
PS C:\> Get-RDSAccountAttribute

AccountQuotaName                    Max      Used
----------------                    ---      ----
DBInstances                         40       3
ReservedDBInstances                 40       0
AllocatedStorage                    100000   40
DBSecurityGroups                    25       0
AuthorizationsPerDBSecurityGroup    20       0
DBParameterGroups                   50       1
ManualSnapshots                     100      3
EventSubscriptions                  20       0
DBSubnetGroups                      50       1
OptionGroups                        20       2
SubnetsPerDBSubnetGroup             20       2
ReadReplicasPerMaster               5        0
DBClusters                          40       0
DBClusterParameterGroups            50       0
DBClusterRoles                      5        0
```

`AllocatedStorage Used` limit does not account for the standby site. The utilization displayed is for the primary site. You can still request the AWS raises the limit if needed. But monitoring these limits is essential for your day-to-day operation.

Summary

AWS RDS is a managed service. A lot of time-consuming tasks, such as provisioning, patching, high availability, and backups are part of the service. In this chapter, we have learnt about the various licensing aspects that should be considered. We also learnt about the various storage types available with this service. Multi-AZ configuration provides you out-of-the-box high availability solution for which you might spend a lot of time and money in the traditional world. We learnt how easily encryption can be enabled, and how client-to-server traffic can be encrypted using SSL on RDS. We also touched base on several operational aspects, such as restarting the DB instance, adding more space to the DB instance, and modifying the DB instance configuration. In the next chapter, we will learn about the read replicas that are used to read intensive workloads.

12
Working with RDS Read Replicas

There are a variety of scenarios in which you might want to deploy read replicas for your read-intensive workloads. RDS uses built-in replication functionality in database engine such as PostgreSQL, MySQL, and MariaDB. Note that you cannot deploy read replicas for Oracle and SQL Server database engines. There is a maximum 6 TB size limit on MySQL, MariaDB, and PostgreSQL DB instances. If you want to scale beyond the compute or IO capacity for a single instance, a read-intensive database workload, then using read replicas is a solution. You can also redirect your reporting application to query from read replicas instead of the primary database. Running your reporting queries against read replicas will significantly improve the performance of your primary side. You can also plan to create read replicas in a region closer to your user, so that data locality can be implemented and latency can be reduced.

By default, read replicas are created with the same storage type as a primary DB instance. However, you have the option to create read replicas with a different storage type, as compared to your primary DB instance. Here is a short summary of the things to consider when you create read replicas with a different storage type.

Source DB Instance Storage Type	Source DB Instance Storage Allocation	Read Replica Storage Type Options
PIOPS	100 GB - 3 TB	PIOPS | GP2 | Standard
GP2	100 GB - 3 TB	PIOPS | GP2 | Standard
GP2	Less than 100 GB	GP2 | Standard
Standard	100 GB - 3 TB	PIOPS | GP2 | Standard
Standard	Less than 100 GB	GP2 | Standard

If you have the **GP2** or **Standard** storage type with less than 100 GB, then you cannot change the storage type when creating a read replica. Otherwise, with a minimum of 100 GB of storage, you can change the storage type for read replicas.

In this chapter, we will learn about creating read replicas, rebooting read replicas, connecting to read replicas, and promote read replicas to primary. In addition, we will discuss a real-time use case about balancing traffic between read replicas.

Creating read replicas

The New-RDSDBInstanceReadReplica cmdlet lets you create a read replica for the specified DB instance running PostgreSQL, MySQL, and MariaDB. By default, a read replica will be created as a single AZ deployment and automated backups will be disabled. When you create a read replica on the primary, you must have automated backup enabled. You can create a read replica in different regions as well. In this example, we will be creating the read replica in the same region. Review the online documentation for creating read replicas in different regions. The overall process remains the same.

To create a read replica for a primary DB instance, you can use the following command:

```
PS C:\> New-RDSDBInstanceReadReplica -DBInstanceIdentifier
"mywebapprdrr01" -SourceDBInstanceIdentifier "mywebapprd" -
AutoMinorVersionUpgrade $true -DBInstanceClass "db.t2.large" -StorageType
gp2
```

```
PS C:\> New-RDSDBInstanceReadReplica -DBInstanceIdentifier "mywebapprdrr01" -SourceDBInstanceIdentifier "mywebapprd" -AutoMinorVersionUpgrade $true -DBInst
anceClass "db.t2.large" -StorageType gp2

AllocatedStorage                : 20
AutoMinorVersionUpgrade         : True
AvailabilityZone                :
BackupRetentionPeriod           : 0
CACertificateIdentifier         : rds-ca-2015
CharacterSetName                :
CopyTagsToSnapshot              : False
DBClusterIdentifier             :
DBInstanceArn                   : arn:aws:rds:us-east-1:072316406132:db:mywebapprdrr01
DBInstanceClass                 : db.t2.large
DBInstanceIdentifier            : mywebapprdrr01
DbInstancePort                  : 0
DBInstanceStatus                : creating
DbiResourceId                   : db-GGLMIAJWQBHNGNHNWNPA254J4U
DBName                          : mywebapprd
```

You do not need to specify DBSubnetGroup if you are creating the read replica in the same region as the master. Most of the master DB instance attributes will be inherited as part of this operation. If your primary instance has encrypted storage, the read replica will also be created as encrypted. When you initiate the read replica creation, RDS will modify the database configuration for the primary and initiate the snapshot, which will be used to build the read replicas.

To get the list of read replicas for the master DB instance, you can use the following command:

```
PS C:\> Get-RDSDBInstance -DBInstanceIdentifier  "mywebapprd"|format-table
ReadReplicaDBInstanceIdentifiers
```

```
PS C:\> Get-RDSDBInstance -DBInstanceIdentifier  "mywebapprd"|format-table ReadReplicaDBInstanceIdentifiers

ReadReplicaDBInstanceIdentifiers
--------------------------------
{mywebapprdrr01, mywebapprdrr02}
```

You see, there are two read replicas defined for the DB instance `mywebappprd`. The DB instance status for those two read replicas can be checked using the following command:

```
PS C:\> Get-RDSDBInstance |Format-Table DBInstanceIdentifier,
DBInstanceStatus
```

```
PS C:\> Get-RDSDBInstance |Format-Table DBInstanceIdentifier, DBInstanceStatus

DBInstanceIdentifier DBInstanceStatus
-------------------- ----------------
mywebappprd          available
mywebappprdrr01      available
mywebappprdrr02      creating
websingleazdb        available
```

The read replica `mywebappprdrr02` is still being created.

Rebooting read replicas

You cannot stop or start a read replica. You can only restart a read replica. You can use the same cmdlet, `Restart-RDSDBInstance`, which we used earlier to restart the primary DB instance.

To reboot or restart the read replica, you can run the following command:

```
PS C:\> Restart-RDSDBInstance –DBInstanceIdentifier "mywebappprdrr02"
```

```
PS C:\> Restart-RDSDBInstance -DBInstanceIdentifier "mywebappprdrr02"

AllocatedStorage                : 20
AutoMinorVersionUpgrade         : True
AvailabilityZone                : us-east-1a
BackupRetentionPeriod           : 0
CACertificateIdentifier         : rds-ca-2015
CharacterSetName                :
CopyTagsToSnapshot              : False
DBClusterIdentifier             :
DBInstanceArn                   : arn:aws:rds:us-east-1:072316406132:db:mywebappprdrr02
DBInstanceClass                 : db.t2.large
DBInstanceIdentifier            : mywebappprdrr02
DbInstancePort                  : 0
DBInstanceStatus                : rebooting
DbiResourceId                   : db-2GR5TUTHFA6JI4BWPT5H74BYN4
DBName                          : mywebappprd
```

Connecting to a read replica

The process for connecting to a read replica is the same as connecting to the primary DB instance. You first need to get the endpoint. For every read replica that you create, it also gets a DNS CNAME, which is called an **endpoint**.

To get the endpoint for the read replica `mywebappprdrr01`, you use a cmdlet that we have used previously.

```
PS C:\> (Get-RDSDBInstance -DBInstanceIdentifier
"mywebappprdrr01").endpoint
```

```
PS C:\> (Get-RDSDBInstance -DBInstanceIdentifier  "mywebappprdrr01").endpoint

Address                                                HostedZoneId    Port
-------                                                ------------    ----
mywebappprdrr01.cwrq5w1v98ur.us-east-1.rds.amazonaws.com Z2R2ITUGPM61AM 3306
```

Once you have the endpoint, hop on to the bastion server, then from there, connect using MySQL client, as follows:

```
# mysql -u rdsdba -prdsdba123 -h  mywebappprdrr01.cwrq5w1v98ur.us-
east-1.rds.amazonaws.com --ssl-ca=rds-combined-ca-bundle.pem --ssl-verify-
server-cert
```

```
[root@ip-10-0-2-158 ~]# mysql -u rdsdba -prdsdba123 -h  mywebappprdrr01.cwrq5w1v98ur.us-east-1.rds.amazonaws.com \
> --ssl-ca=rds-combined-ca-bundle.pem --ssl-verify-server-cert
Welcome to the MySQL monitor.  Commands end with ; or \g.
Your MySQL connection id is 27
Server version: 5.7.17 MySQL Community Server (GPL)

Copyright (c) 2000, 2017, Oracle and/or its affiliates. All rights reserved.

Oracle is a registered trademark of Oracle Corporation and/or its
affiliates. Other names may be trademarks of their respective
owners.

Type 'help;' or '\h' for help. Type '\c' to clear the current input statement.

mysql> show databases;
+--------------------+
| Database           |
+--------------------+
| information_schema |
| innodb             |
| mysql              |
| mywebappprd        |
| performance_schema |
| sys                |
+--------------------+
6 rows in set (0.01 sec)
```

In this example, we used the SSL connection method to connect to the read replica. To connect without SSL, just remove `ssl-ca` and `ssl-verify-server-cert` from the command-line option. Note that we are using the same credentials as the primary to connect to the read replica in this case. Only the endpoint has changed. As long as your Security Group ingress is configured properly, you should not have any connectivity issues.

Promoting read replicas to primary

By default, automated backups are disabled on read replicas that we create. AWS recommends that we enable automated backups before promoting the read replica to single AZ standalone mode. You can check the current configuration of the backup using the following command:

```
PS C:\> Get-RDSDBInstance -DBInstanceIdentifier  "mywebappprdrr01" |Format-
Table BackupRetentionPeriod,PreferredBackupWindow
```

```
PS C:\> Get-RDSDBInstance -DBInstanceIdentifier  "mywebappprdrr01" |Format-Table BackupRetentionPeriod,PreferredBackupWindow

BackupRetentionPeriod PreferredBackupWindow
--------------------- ---------------------
                    0 01:00-02:00
```

`BackupRetentionPeriod` to 0 (zero) indicates that automated backups are disabled. Setting this value to any non-zero number (up to a maximum of 35 days) enables the automated backup on the read replica. You can enable the backup as shown following:

```
PS C:\> Edit-RDSDBInstance -DBInstanceIdentifier "mywebappprdrr01" -
BackupRetentionPeriod 7 -ApplyImmediately $true
```

After running `Edit-RDSDBInstance`, you can verify whether the backup retention is modified or not.

```
PS C:\> Get-RDSDBInstance -DBInstanceIdentifier  "mywebappprdrr01" |Format-Table BackupRetentionPeriod,PreferredBackupWindow

BackupRetentionPeriod PreferredBackupWindow
--------------------- ---------------------
                    7 01:00-02:00
```

The `Convert-RDSReadReplicaToStandalone` cmdlet lets you promote the specified read replica to primary. As backups are enabled prior to promoting, RDS will continue to take the backup as per the backup window and retain it for as long as retention is specified.

To promote read replica `mywebappprdrr01`, you can use the following command:

```
PS C:\> Convert-RDSReadReplicaToStandalone -DBInstanceIdentifier
"mywebappprdrr01"
```

```
PS C:\> Convert-RDSReadReplicaToStandalone -DBInstanceIdentifier "mywebappprdrr01"

AllocatedStorage              : 20
AutoMinorVersionUpgrade       : True
AvailabilityZone              : us-east-1b
BackupRetentionPeriod         : 7
CACertificateIdentifier       : rds-ca-2015
CharacterSetName              :
CopyTagsToSnapshot            : False
DBClusterIdentifier           :
DBInstanceArn                 : arn:aws:rds:us-east-1:072316406132:db:mywebappprdrr01
DBInstanceClass               : db.t2.large
DBInstanceIdentifier          : mywebappprdrr01
DbInstancePort                : 0
DBInstanceStatus              : modifying
DbiResourceId                 : db-GGLMIAJWQBHNGNHNWNPA254J4U
DBName                        : mywebappprd
```

Consider that you have a cascaded replication deployment, where MySQL Instance 1 replicates to MySQL Instance 2, and MySQL Instance 2 replicates to MySQL Instance 3. If you promote MySQL Instance 2, then replication from MySQL Instance 1 to MySQL Instance 2 no longer occurs, but MySQL Instance 2 continues to replicate to MySQL Instance 3. If replication is stopped for more than 30 consecutive days, either because of replication error or manual set up, RDS terminates replication between primary and all read replicas to prevent increased storage demand on the primary DB instance, and to avoid a long failover time. In such cases, it is better to create a new read replica from the primary and re-establish the connection.

Deleting read replicas

Removing a read replica is the same process as we did for the standalone DB instance. You can use the `Remove-RDSDBInstance` cmdlet. You have the option to initiate the final snapshot before you delete the read replica.

```
PS C:\> Remove-RDSDBInstance –DBInstanceIdentifier "mywebappprdrr02" –
SkipFinalSnapshot $true
```

```
PS C:\> Remove-RDSDBInstance -DBInstanceIdentifier "mywebappprdrr02" -SkipFinalSnapshot $true

Confirm
Are you sure you want to perform this action?
Performing the operation "Remove-RDSDBInstance (DeleteDBInstance)" on target "mywebappprdrr02".
[Y] Yes  [A] Yes to All  [N] No  [L] No to All  [S] Suspend  [?] Help (default is "Y"): Y

AllocatedStorage                     : 20
AutoMinorVersionUpgrade              : True
AvailabilityZone                     : us-east-1a
BackupRetentionPeriod                : 0
CACertificateIdentifier              : rds-ca-2015
CharacterSetName                     :
CopyTagsToSnapshot                   : False
DBClusterIdentifier                  :
DBInstanceArn                        : arn:aws:rds:us-east-1:072316406132:db:mywebappprdrr02
DBInstanceClass                      : db.t2.large
DBInstanceIdentifier                 : mywebappprdrr02
DbInstancePort                       : 0
DBInstanceStatus                     : deleting
DbiResourceId                        : db-2GR5TUTHFA6JI4BWPT5H74BYN4
DBName                               : mywebappprd
```

If this is the only read replica for the primary, then the primary instance master role will be removed by this operation.

Use case - balancing traffic between read replicas

If your application is read-intensive and you have a single read replica, chances are that if your read replica CPU spikes up to 100 percent, your read replica may not respond at all. To address such a situation, the solution is to add multiple read replicas to your application stack; then you might want to balance the traffic between those read replicas.

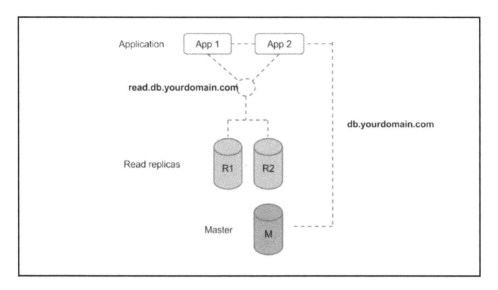

This is where Route 53 can play a role. Route 53 is a scalable DNS service provided by AWS. In this example, we will create a private hosted zone for VPC and then make use of the **Weighted Routing Policy** to direct traffic across two read replicas. Let's create the domain for VPC as `mydb.local`.

To get a list of all the cmdlets related to Route 53, you can use the following command:

```
PS C:\> Get-Command *R53*
```

We created VPC `vpc-a6bb60df` to demonstrate concepts in this book, and it was created in region `us-east-1`. To create a new hosted zone for this VPC, you can issue the following command:

```
PS C:\> New-R53HostedZone -CallerReference mydb.local -Name mydb.local -
HostedZoneConfig_PrivateZone $true -VPC_VPCId vpc-a6bb60df -VPC_VPCRegion
us-east-1
```

In this example, the primary DB instance `mywebappprd` has two read replicas, `mywebappprdrr01` and `mywebappprdrr02`. Let's get the endpoints for those two replicas, as we need their CNAMEs to define two record sets with Route 53 as a hosted zone for our VPC. You can use:

```
PS C:\> Get-RDSDBInstance -DBInstanceIdentifier   "mywebappprd" |Format-
Table ReadReplicaDBInstanceIdentifiers
PS C:\> (Get-RDSDBInstance -DBInstanceIdentifier
"mywebappprdrr01").endpoint
PS C:\> (Get-RDSDBInstance -DBInstanceIdentifier
"mywebappprdrr02").endpoint
```

```
PS C:\> Get-RDSDBInstance -DBInstanceIdentifier "mywebappprd" |Format-Table ReadReplicaDBInstanceIdentifiers

ReadReplicaDBInstanceIdentifiers
--------------------------------
{mywebappprdrr01, mywebappprdrr02}

PS C:\> (Get-RDSDBInstance -DBInstanceIdentifier "mywebappprdrr01").endpoint

Address                                                     HostedZoneId   Port
-------                                                     ------------   ----
mywebappprdrr01.cwrq5w1v98ur.us-east-1.rds.amazonaws.com Z2R2ITUGPM61AM 3306

PS C:\> (Get-RDSDBInstance -DBInstanceIdentifier "mywebappprdrr02").endpoint

Address                                                     HostedZoneId   Port
-------                                                     ------------   ----
mywebappprdrr02.cwrq5w1v98ur.us-east-1.rds.amazonaws.com Z2R2ITUGPM61AM 3306
```

Instead of adding these two endpoints in the Route 53 record set via the cmdlet for the given hosted zone, I made use of the AWS Console dashboard and added it as follows. Adding a record set via the AWS Console is an easy task.

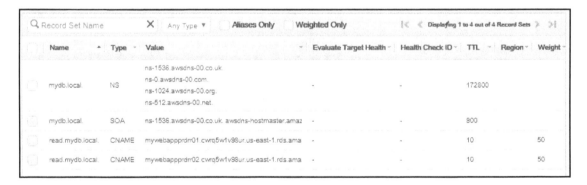

Name	Type	Value	Evaluate Target Health	Health Check ID	TTL	Region	Weight
mydb.local.	NS	ns-1536.awsdns-00.co.uk. ns-0.awsdns-00.com. ns-1024.awsdns-00.org. ns-512.awsdns-00.net.	-	-	172800		
mydb.local.	SOA	ns-1536.awsdns-00.co.uk. awsdns-hostmaster.amaz	-	-	900		
read.mydb.local.	CNAME	mywebapoprdrr01.cwrq5w1v98ur.us-east-1.rds.ama	-	-	10		50
read.mydb.local.	CNAME	mywebappprdrr02.cwrq5w1v98ur.us-east-1.rds.ama	-	-	10		50

You can see at the bottom of the preceding screenshot that both endpoint records have been added with 50 percent weight. The alias that can be used to connect to both endpoints is defined as `read.mydb.local`. Now, hop on to the bastion host and see if that works for you. You can use the `dig` command to test that your weighted routed policy is working.

```
# dig read.mydb.local ANY
```

```
[root@ip-10-0-2-158 ~]# dig read.mydb.local ANY

; <<>> DiG 9.8.2rc1-RedHat-9.8.2-0.62.rc1.55.amzn1 <<>> read.mydb.local ANY
;; global options: +cmd
;; Got answer:
;; ->>HEADER<<- opcode: QUERY, status: NOERROR, id: 26887
;; flags: qr rd ra; QUERY: 1, ANSWER: 1, AUTHORITY: 0, ADDITIONAL: 0

;; QUESTION SECTION:
;read.mydb.local.               IN      ANY

;; ANSWER SECTION:
read.mydb.local.        2       IN      CNAME   mywebappprdrr02.cwrq5w1v98ur.us-east-1.rds.amazonaws.com.

;; Query time: 0 msec
;; SERVER: 10.0.0.2#53(10.0.0.2)
;; WHEN: Sat Jul 15 08:26:50 2017
;; MSG SIZE  rcvd: 103

[root@ip-10-0-2-158 ~]# dig read.mydb.local ANY

; <<>> DiG 9.8.2rc1-RedHat-9.8.2-0.62.rc1.55.amzn1 <<>> read.mydb.local ANY
;; global options: +cmd
;; Got answer:
;; ->>HEADER<<- opcode: QUERY, status: NOERROR, id: 61448
;; flags: qr rd ra; QUERY: 1, ANSWER: 1, AUTHORITY: 0, ADDITIONAL: 0

;; QUESTION SECTION:
;read.mydb.local.               IN      ANY

;; ANSWER SECTION:
read.mydb.local.        10      IN      CNAME   mywebappprdrr01.cwrq5w1v98ur.us-east-1.rds.amazonaws.com.

;; Query time: 3 msec
;; SERVER: 10.0.0.2#53(10.0.0.2)
;; WHEN: Sat Jul 15 08:26:52 2017
;; MSG SIZE  rcvd: 103
```

You can see the internal domain that we created called `read.mydb.local` first contacted `mywebappprdrr02.cwrq5w1v98ur.us-east-1.rds.amazonaws.com` and then `mywebappprdrr01.cwrq5w1v98ur.us-east-1.rds.amazonaws.com`. This means that the weighted record policy that you defined in Route 53 for your read replicas is working fine. Your application can now connect to `read.mydb.local` and Route 53 will ensure that read requests are balanced based on the weight that you define.

You can also make use of `read.mydb.local` to connect to read replicas, as follows:

```
# mysql -u rdsdba -prdsdba123 -h read.mydb.local
```

```
[root@ip-10-0-2-158 ~]# mysql -u rdsdba -prdsdba123 -h read.mydb.local
Welcome to the MySQL monitor.  Commands end with ; or \g.
Your MySQL connection id is 34
Server version: 5.7.17 MySQL Community Server (GPL)

Copyright (c) 2000, 2017, Oracle and/or its affiliates. All rights reserved.

Oracle is a registered trademark of Oracle Corporation and/or its
affiliates. Other names may be trademarks of their respective
owners.

Type 'help;' or '\h' for help. Type '\c' to clear the current input statement.

mysql> show databases;
+--------------------+
| Database           |
+--------------------+
| information_schema |
| innodb             |
| mysql              |
| mywebappprd        |
| performance_schema |
| sys                |
+--------------------+
6 rows in set (0.00 sec)
```

Summary

For read-intensive workloads, RDS read replicas are a very useful component in your infrastructure. In this chapter, we have learnt how to create read replicas and work around them using various cmdlets. Almost all other generic cmdlets for day-to-day functions that you can use with a primary DB instance can be used with read replicas as well. We also know how to enable the backups on read replicas and how to promote them when needed. We also went through a use case that is commonly used in the industry to balance a workload between multiple read replicas using the Route 53 weighted routing policy. In the next chapter, we will learn about the AWS Elastic Beanstalk service for deploying applications, and managing application deployment using Beanstalk's capabilities.

13
AWS Elastic Beanstalk

Traditionally, if you wanted to deploy an application, you needed to have the underlying infrastructure ready. And, you know, infrastructure includes various servers, networking, and storage related components. So, even if you have the application code that needs to be tested ready, you need to work with your infrastructure team and get everything sorted out before you deploy and test your application. Getting the infrastructure ready and testing your code before it goes to production is seen as a long process in every organization. In this cloud era, because of the cloud capability of providing disposable or immutable infrastructures, traditional application deployment and testing has changed significantly. In the last few years, elasticity, on-demand scalability, and time to market have impacted almost every other process in the enterprise to deploy code and manage infrastructure and security.

AWS provides various services to configure and deploy your applications. Though you can deploy your application on EC2, which we discussed earlier, you still need to manage the infrastructure and understand the various other components around it, such as Security Groups, Elastic Load Balancer, and Auto Scaling. AWS Elastic Beanstalk takes heavy-lifting work items off your hands and lets you focus on just your application's code.

This is truly a **Platform as a Service (PaaS)** provided by AWS out-of-the-box. You simply choose the platform that you want and let AWS handle all the heavy-lifting infrastructure work at the backend. The best part, the service is free, you just pay for the resources that are used by your application after launching the stack.

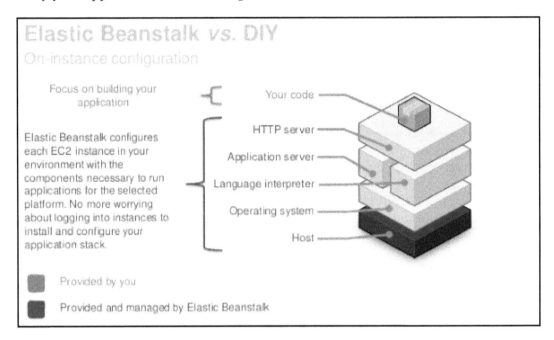

Doing-It-Yourself (DIY) requires a lot of technical expertise to build and maintain underlying platforms for your application. As shown in the diagram, you only focus on your application code and the whole stack is created for you by AWS. Under the hood, Beanstalk does all the work that we have learnt so far, such as launching EC2 instances, load balancer, and Auto Scaling. It also takes care of creating the required Security Group and IAM roles. You just need to ensure that the right VPC and subnets are selected when launching the stack.

In this chapter, we will discuss Elastic Beanstalk components, environment types, and various deployment models. In addition, we will look at creating an application, creating a configuration template, creating an environment, deploying a popular WordPress application on Beanstalk, cloning an environment, and swapping an environment.

What is Elastic Beanstalk?

AWS Elastic Beanstalk is a service that automatically handles all the provisioning of the infrastructure resources to run your application in the cloud. This service takes care of capacity provisioning, load balancing, Auto Scaling, and health monitoring of the application and associated infrastructure components. AWS is regularly adding to the list of platforms supported. At the time of writing this book, the following platforms were supported.

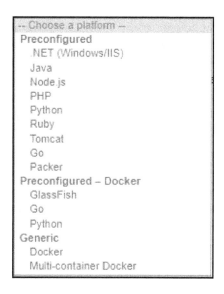

Beanstalk automatically pushes server and application logs to AWS S3. The beauty of Beanstalk is that the full control over the AWS resources been created at the time of launch is retained. With Beanstalk, you can still control the resources supporting your application and the software running on the EC2 instances. There are several ways that you can deploy an application on AWS. Let's review each of them at a high level.

- **AWS EC2**: You can spin up virtual machines with the required capacity and deploy the application. We learnt about deploying applications using EC2 in earlier chapters. We also made use of the load balancer and Auto Scaling Groups to build a highly available and fault-tolerant environment. Doing so, though we had a lot of heavy-lifting work to do, through the whole process, we had control of individual EC2 instances.

- **AWS Elastic Beanstalk**: You have just started learning about this service and, for now, you know that all the heavy-lifting work is done by AWS and you will be focusing on application code only. We will learn more on this in this chapter as we move forward.

- **AWS OpsWorks**: This service provides you with a flexible way to create and manage various resources for your application, as well as the application itself. You create a stack of resources and manage those resources collectively in different layers. Layers can have built-in or chef recipes. Overall, you can also use this service to automate, maintain, and monitor deployments. If you are interested in learning more about this service, then review the service specific AWS documentation, as this is not something covered in this book.

- **AWS CloudFormation**: Using this service, you can create templates that define a set of resources and instructions on how to create those resources. You might have heard many times that AWS provides you with the ability to write infrastructure as code and this is the service which provides you with that capability. You can version control your template and deploy wherever you feel you need to build your stack from scratch. Using CloudFormation, you get a repeatable, reliable, and consistent environment. We will learn more on this service in the next chapter.

Considering all the other services, AWS Elastic Beanstalk is on the convenient side of the spectrum. Using Elastic Beanstalk, you do not need to do anything from an infrastructure perspective. When you want more control of your underlying infrastructure, you can think about utilizing AWS OpsWorks or CloudFormation.

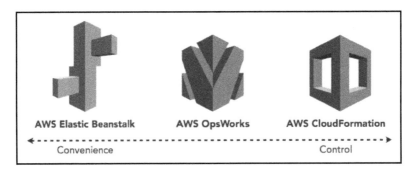

Given the many AWS services for application deployment, you may be wondering when to use Elastic Beanstalk and others. Well, when you do not have any in-house support for the underlying infrastructure for your application and you are looking for quick prototyping, then it is best to use Elastic Beanstalk. In addition, if your application has a shorter lifecycle and if you want to maintain some control over the resources used by your application, then Beanstalk comes to the rescue. If you are looking for complete control over the resource configuration, then Beanstalk is not the answer that you are looking for. But still, I feel, there are many things that you can do with Beanstalk, provided you understand it's configurational aspects very well. There are two types of architecture for deploying Elastic Beanstalk: **Web Server Environment Tiers** and **Worker Environment Tiers**. We will only focus on the Web Server Environment Tiers of the architecture in this chapter.

 I would encourage you to read more on `http://docs.aws.amazon.com/e` `lasticBeanstalk/latest/dg/concepts.concepts.architecture.html`.

Elastic Beanstalk components

Before we jump into deploying an application using Elastic Beanstalk, let's discuss some of the terminology that you need to be aware of. These terminologies will help you to deploy and manage an application in the cloud.

- **Application**: This is a logical collection of components such as environments, application versions, and environment configurations. You can treat an application as a top-level folder, but not actually a folder. It is still your application, holding the code and configurations.
- **Application version**: This is a part of the application. Each application version is unique and applications can have multiple versions. You can run different environments for different application versions or the same application version. These application versions are nothing but deployable code in the form of WAR or ZIP files. You simply upload the application code to the Beanstalk and label the version as you feel for your tracking.
- **Environment**: A version that is deployed with AWS Resources. Each environment runs on a single application version, and you can run the same application version on many environments.

- **Environment configuration**: This is a collection of parameters and settings that define the environment and resources. When you update environment configuration settings, Beanstalk automatically updates the existing underlying resources or redeploys those resources depending on the change.
- **Configuration template**: This is where you start and define the unique environment configuration. It is used to create repeatable environment configurations. When you create a template for the application, those templates are found under *Saved Configuration* on the AWS Console. So, it is nothing but a *Saved Configuration* if you are working via another CLI and AWS Console.

Environment types

Before we discuss the various deployment models that are supported by Elastic Beanstalk, it makes much more sense to understand the various environment types that are provided for you to choose from when deploying your applications on the Beanstalk platform. There are two environment types:

- **Single instance environment**: When you choose this option, you get one EC2 instance with one Auto Scaling Group. Though you will have selected a single instance environment, you get one Auto Scaling Group, which will allow your single instance environment to self-heal if your EC2 instance becomes unresponsive. Beanstalk does not provision a load balancer in this type of environment. One Elastic IP will be allocated and assigned to the instance.

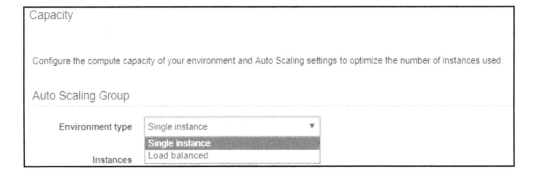

If you are creating an environment via the AWS Console, you choose **Environment type** by clicking on the **Capacity** section of the **Choose more options** section of the **Create New Environment** screen under AWS Elastic Beanstalk service.

- **Load balanced environment**: When you choose this type of environment to run your application, Beanstalk will provision a load balancer and a specified number of EC2 instances in the Auto Scaling Group. Irrespective of whether you use a single instance or load balanced environment type, you get an Auto Scaling Group. The load balancer handles client requests and communicates with backend instances. After launching your Elastic Beanstalk environment, if you want to change the environment type from a single instance to load balanced, this is possible and can be done in the **Scaling** section of the **Environment Configuration.**

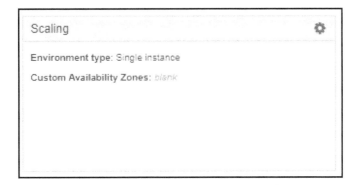

Note that, when you work with Elastic Beanstalk, you should ensure that you choose the right VPC to deploy in, with appropriate subnets for your EC2 instances and for the load balancer. You may want to keep only load balancing subnets as public facing and all other EC2 instances in private subnets. If you do not choose a VPC, then Elastic Beanstalk will launch the environment in your default VPC.

Understanding deployment models on Elastic Beanstalk

Now you know the different environment types, let's discuss the different deployment models available on Elastic Beanstalk. There are five deployments models that you can choose from, depending on your requirement. These models are useful either when you are deploying new versions of the application or reverting back to an old one.

- **All at once deployment**: This is in-place deployment. Beanstalk chooses existing EC2 instances to do this type of deployment. This is one of the fastest methods and requires no DNS change. As the name suggests, all the underlying EC instances will be updated during the deployment at the same time, hence, will cause some downtime. If your deployment fails, you have to redeploy the code from previous versions, causing you some more downtime.

- **Rolling deployment**: This is in-place deployment as well. If your environment cannot afford downtime, then you can make use of the rolling deployment type with Elastic Beanstalk. During this deployment, Beanstalk removes only a batch of instances from the fleet. This means you have complete control over the number of EC2 instances that can be updated with the new version at the same time. You can specify a fixed number of instances that can be updated, or you can specify the percentage of the fleet that you want to update with the new version. After successful deployment, Beanstalk will register those EC2 instances back to the Elastic Balancer and start serving traffic, provided it passes the health check. This method also requires no DNS update. On the downside, because a portion of your fleet is taken out for updating with the new application version, your application may face capacity issues during deployment. If your deployment fails, you redeploy your previous or fixed application version with the rolling deployment strategy once again.

- **Rolling with additional batch deployment**: This is a rolling deployment in response to the capacity concern that was noticed in the earlier rolling deployment strategy. This deployment method updates a batch of EC2 instances at the same time, but with additional capacity. No existing instances have been updated with the new application version. Beanstalk provisions additional capacity in batches as you specify. In this case, you also either provide a fixed number of instances or a percentage of the fleet that can be updated at the same time as part of the batch. After successful deployment, Beanstalk registers a new set of EC2 instances to the load balancer, and once the load balancer passes the health check, traffic will be redirected to the new set of instances. Beanstalk will then terminate the old instances in batches. If the deployment fails, you redeploy the previous or fixed application version again with rolling deployment with additional batch strategy.

- **Immutable deployment**: When you want completely new EC2 instances with new AMI, then this type of deployment method is very helpful. In this type of deployment strategy, Beanstalk replaces existing EC2 instances with new instances by creating a temporary Auto Scaling Group. During this deployment, Beanstalk tests the application version just by spinning one EC2 instance in the temporary Auto Scaling Group. Once that new EC2 instance passes the health check, Beanstalk starts spinning other EC2 instances in the temporary Auto Scaling Group until the size matches the old Auto Scaling Group. Once all the new EC2 instances pass the health check, Beanstalk will then add those new instances in the old Auto Scaling Group. Once they are added in the old Auto Scaling Group, Beanstalk will terminate old EC2 instances and the temporary Auto Scaling Group. This deployment method prevents downtime. On the downside, you will have more EC2 instances than normal, and this may affect the EC2 capacity limit if care is not taken. This will result in costs if you have hundreds of instances behind the scene. If the deployment fails, you clean up the temporary Auto Scaling Group and redeploy your code.

- **Blue/Green deployment**: This strategy of deployment is kind of an immutable deployment. In this type of deployment, you replace all underlying resources including load balancer, Auto Scaling, and EC2 instances. You actually use all new resources instead of the old ones. This method prevents downtime and you get the option to test the application version completely in an isolated environment. On the downside, you double the capacity limit while running the deployment and required DNS change. If your deployment fails, you simply swap the URL.

The following table shows a good summary of the various deployment strategies with Elastic Beanstalk.

Method	Impact of Failed Deployment	Deploy Time	Zero Downtime	No DNS Change	Rollback Process	Code Deployed To
All at once	Downtime	☺	✗	✓	Re-deploy	Existing instances
Rolling	Single batch out of service. Any successful batches prior to failure running new application version.	☺☺†	✓	✓	Re-deploy	Existing instances
Rolling with additional batch	Minimal if first batch fails, otherwise similar to **Rolling**.	☺☺†	✓	✓	Re-deploy	New & existing instances
Immutable	Minimal	☺☺☺☺	✓	✓	Re-deploy	New instances
Blue/green	Minimal	☺☺☺☺	✓	✗	Swap URL	New instances

Creating application

Let's move on to the journey of deploying a popular WordPress application on the Elastic Beanstalk platform. We will name this application `WebWorldPressApp`. Let me tell you first, there is no fun doing this via PowerShell cmdlets. The AWS Console is such a beautiful place that you will love working with Elastic Beanstalk with minimal friction. The intention of this book is to help you to work with AWS via PowerShell. Hence, I will try to demonstrate that working knowledge here can help you to bridge the gap of your learning with Elastic Beanstalk via PowerShell.

To get a list of all the cmdlets related to Elastic Beanstalk, you can run the following command:

```
PS C:\> Get-Command *-EB*
```

Note that, if you want to understand the meaning of each parameter passed to the cmdlet, always review using `Get-Help`.

To create a new application called `WebWorldPressApp`, you can issue the following command:

```
PS C:\> New-EBApplication -ApplicationName "WebWorldPressApp" -Description
"WebWorldPressApp"
```

The `New-EBApplication` cmdlet lets you create an application called `WebWorldPressApp`.

```
PS C:\> New-EBApplication -ApplicationName "WebWorldPressApp" -Description "WebWorldPressApp"

ApplicationName        : WebWorldPressApp
ConfigurationTemplates : {}
DateCreated            : 7/17/2017 2:05:29 PM
DateUpdated            : 7/17/2017 2:05:29 PM
Description            : WebWorldPressApp
ResourceLifecycleConfig : Amazon.ElasticBeanstalk.Model.ApplicationResourceLifecycleConfig
Versions               : {}
```

The application `WebWorldPressApp` is created and there is no configuration template and version assigned. You have not provided any configuration items to the application yet.

Creating a configuration template

For creating a template, you first need to get the solution stack that you can use to create the configuration template. Solution stacks are nothing but the platforms provided by AWS to spin up your AWS resources. You choose the solution stack/platform based on your application dependency. To get the list of solution stacks available, you can use the following command:

```
PS C:\> (Get-EBAvailableSolutionStackList).SolutionStackDetails
```

```
PS C:\> (Get-EBAvailableSolutionStackList).SolutionStackDetails

PermittedFileTypes SolutionStackName
------------------ -----------------
{zip}              64bit Windows Server Core 2016 v1.2.0 running IIS 10.0
{zip}              64bit Windows Server 2016 v1.2.0 running IIS 10.0
{zip}              64bit Windows Server Core 2012 R2 v1.2.0 running IIS 8.5
{zip}              64bit Windows Server 2012 R2 v1.2.0 running IIS 8.5
{zip}              64bit Windows Server 2012 v1.2.0 running IIS 8
{zip}              64bit Windows Server 2008 R2 v1.2.0 running IIS 7.5
{jar, zip}         64bit Amazon Linux 2017.03 v2.5.1 running Java 8
{jar, zip}         64bit Amazon Linux 2017.03 v2.5.1 running Java 7
{zip}              64bit Amazon Linux 2017.03 v4.2.0 running Node.js
```

Note that the list is trimmed in this case. There are many more solution stacks that you can choose from. Pay particular attention to the `PermittedFileTypes` column. You may see values like `zip`, `jar`, `war`, and `json`. It means those are files that you can use to deploy your application on the specific platform/solution stack. The WordPress app runs on the PHP platform, hence, let's choose one from the PHP solution stack.

```
{zip}          64bit Amazon Linux 2017.03 v2.4.1 running PHP 5.4
{zip}          64bit Amazon Linux 2017.03 v2.4.1 running PHP 5.5
{zip}          64bit Amazon Linux 2017.03 v2.4.1 running PHP 5.6
{zip}          64bit Amazon Linux 2017.03 v2.4.1 running PHP 7.0
{zip}          64bit Amazon Linux 2016.03 v2.1.6 running PHP 5.4
{zip}          64bit Amazon Linux 2016.03 v2.1.6 running PHP 5.5
{zip}          64bit Amazon Linux 2016.03 v2.1.6 running PHP 5.6
{zip}          64bit Amazon Linux 2016.03 v2.1.6 running PHP 7.0
{zip}          64bit Amazon Linux 2015.03 v1.4.6 running PHP 5.6
{zip}          64bit Amazon Linux 2015.03 v1.4.6 running PHP 5.5
{zip}          64bit Amazon Linux 2015.03 v1.4.6 running PHP 5.4
{zip}          64bit Amazon Linux 2014.03 v1.1.0 running PHP 5.5
{zip}          64bit Amazon Linux 2014.03 v1.1.0 running PHP 5.4
{zip}          32bit Amazon Linux 2014.03 v1.1.0 running PHP 5.5
{zip}          32bit Amazon Linux 2014.03 v1.1.0 running PHP 5.4
{zip}          64bit Amazon Linux running PHP 5.3
{zip}          32bit Amazon Linux running PHP 5.3
```

These are the solution stacks available for PHP and all of them only support ZIP files as a deployment file type. I am choosing `64bit Amazon Linux 2017.03 v2.4.1 running PHP 7.0` for this demonstration. Using this solution stack, let's create a configuration template `WebWorldPressAppTemplate` for the application `WebWorldPressApp`. You can do this using the following command:

```
PS C:\> New-EBConfigurationTemplate -ApplicationName "WebWorldPressApp" -
TemplateName "WebWorldPressAppTemplate" -SolutionStackName "64bit Amazon
Linux 2017.03 v2.4.1 running PHP 7.0"
```

```
PS C:\> New-EBConfigurationTemplate -ApplicationName "WebWorldPressApp" -TemplateName "WebWorldPressAppTemplate" -SolutionStackName "64bit Amazon Linux 2017.
03 v2.4.1 running PHP 7.0"

ApplicationName    : WebWorldPressApp
DateCreated        : 7/17/2017 2:43:18 PM
DateUpdated        : 7/17/2017 2:43:18 PM
DeploymentStatus   :
Description        :
EnvironmentName    :
OptionSettings     : {}
PlatformArn        : arn:aws:elasticbeanstalk:us-east-1::platform/PHP 7.0 running on 64bit Amazon Linux/2.4.1
SolutionStackName  : 64bit Amazon Linux 2017.03 v2.4.1 running PHP 7.0
TemplateName       : WebWorldPressAppTemplate
```

The configuration template `WebWorldPressAppTemplate` is created with all default values. Let's review those default values and update them for our application. You can review all the default values for the template `WebWorldPressAppTemplate` using the following command:

```
PS C:\> (Get-EBConfigurationSetting –ApplicationName "WebWorldPressApp" –
TemplateName "WebWorldPressAppTemplate").OptionSettings
```

```
PS C:\> (Get-EBConfigurationSetting -ApplicationName "WebWorldPressApp" -TemplateName "WebWorldPressAppTemplate").OptionSettings

Namespace                           OptionName                   ResourceName                                Value
---------                           ----------                   ------------                                -----
aws:autoscaling:asg                 Availability Zones           AWSEBAutoScalingGroup                       Any
aws:autoscaling:asg                 Cooldown                     AWSEBAutoScalingGroup                       360
aws:autoscaling:asg                 Custom Availability Zones    AWSEBAutoScalingGroup
aws:autoscaling:asg                 MaxSize                      AWSEBAutoScalingGroup                       4
aws:autoscaling:asg                 MinSize                      AWSEBAutoScalingGroup                       1
aws:autoscaling:launchconfiguration BlockDeviceMappings          AWSEBAutoScalingLaunchConfiguration
aws:autoscaling:launchconfiguration EC2KeyName                   AWSEBAutoScalingLaunchConfiguration
aws:autoscaling:launchconfiguration IamInstanceProfile           AWSEBAutoScalingLaunchConfiguration
aws:autoscaling:launchconfiguration ImageId                      AWSEBAutoScalingLaunchConfiguration        ami-0f774019
aws:autoscaling:launchconfiguration InstanceType                                                            t1.micro
aws:autoscaling:launchconfiguration MonitoringInterval           AWSEBAutoScalingLaunchConfiguration        5 minute
aws:autoscaling:launchconfiguration RootVolumeIOPS               AWSEBAutoScalingLaunchConfiguration
aws:autoscaling:launchconfiguration RootVolumeSize               AWSEBAutoScalingLaunchConfiguration
aws:autoscaling:launchconfiguration RootVolumeType               AWSEBAutoScalingLaunchConfiguration
aws:autoscaling:launchconfiguration SSHSourceRestriction                                                    tcp,22,22,0.0.0.0/0
aws:autoscaling:launchconfiguration SecurityGroups               AWSEBAutoScalingLaunchConfiguration
```

The list is pretty long. I have trimmed the output in this case for clarity. Let's review it, namespace by namespace, and modify it for our environment. Once you have one configuration template updated properly, you can simply make use of it and spin up the other environment. Note that each configuration template is associated with one application. For namespace `aws:autoscaling:asg`, you can list the existing values using the following command:

```
PS C:\> (Get-EBConfigurationSetting –ApplicationName "WebWorldPressApp" –
TemplateName "WebWorldPressAppTemplate").OptionSettings | Where-Object
{$_.namespace –eq "aws:autoscaling:asg"}
```

```
PS C:\> (Get-EBConfigurationSetting -ApplicationName "WebWorldPressApp" -TemplateName "WebWorldPressAppTemplate").OptionSettings |
>> Where-Object {$_.namespace -eq "aws:autoscaling:asg"}

Namespace           OptionName                ResourceName            Value
---------           ----------                ------------            -----
aws:autoscaling:asg Availability Zones        AWSEBAutoScalingGroup   Any
aws:autoscaling:asg Cooldown                  AWSEBAutoScalingGroup   360
aws:autoscaling:asg Custom Availability Zones AWSEBAutoScalingGroup
aws:autoscaling:asg MaxSize                   AWSEBAutoScalingGroup   4
aws:autoscaling:asg MinSize                   AWSEBAutoScalingGroup   1
```

In this case, you may be interested in changing the default values of `Cooldown` and `MinSize`. I am planning to run at least two instances initially for the WordPress app and then would like to set the default `Cooldown` to `720`. You can do this using the following command:

```
PS C:\> $Option1=New-Object
Amazon.ElasticBeanstalk.Model.ConfigurationOptionSetting
PS C:\> $Option1.Namespace="aws:autoscaling:asg"
PS C:\> $Option1.OptionName="Cooldown"
PS C:\> $Option1.Value=720
PS C:\> $Option2=New-Object
Amazon.ElasticBeanstalk.Model.ConfigurationOptionSetting
PS C:\> $Option2.Namespace="aws:autoscaling:asg"
PS C:\> $Option2.OptionName="MinSize"
PS C:\> $Option2.Value=2
PS C:\> Update-EBConfigurationTemplate -ApplicationName "WebWorldPressApp"
-TemplateName "WebWorldPressAppTemplate" -OptionSetting $Option1,$Option2
```

```
PS C:\> $Option1=New-Object Amazon.ElasticBeanstalk.Model.ConfigurationOptionSetting
PS C:\> $Option1.Namespace="aws:autoscaling:asg"
PS C:\> $Option1.OptionName="Cooldown"
PS C:\> $Option1.Value=720
PS C:\> $Option2=New-Object Amazon.ElasticBeanstalk.Model.ConfigurationOptionSetting
PS C:\> $Option2.Namespace="aws:autoscaling:asg"
PS C:\> $Option2.OptionName="MinSize"
PS C:\> $Option2.Value=2
PS C:\> Update-EBConfigurationTemplate -ApplicationName "WebWorldPressApp" -TemplateName "WebWorldPressAppTemplate" -OptionSetting $Option1,$Option2

ApplicationName    : WebWorldPressApp
DateCreated        : 7/17/2017 2:43:18 PM
DateUpdated        : 7/17/2017 3:04:12 PM
DeploymentStatus   :
Description        :
EnvironmentName    :
OptionSettings     : {}
PlatformArn        : arn:aws:elasticbeanstalk:us-east-1::platform/PHP 7.0 running on 64bit Amazon Linux/2.4.1
SolutionStackName  : 64bit Amazon Linux 2017.03 v2.4.1 running PHP 7.0
TemplateName       : WebWorldPressAppTemplate


PS C:\> (Get-EBConfigurationSetting -ApplicationName "WebWorldPressApp" -TemplateName "WebWorldPressAppTemplate").OptionSettings |
>> Where-Object {$_.namespace -eq "aws:autoscaling:asg"}

Namespace             OptionName                   ResourceName              Value
---------             ----------                   ------------              -----
aws:autoscaling:asg Availability Zones             AWSEBAutoScalingGroup Any
aws:autoscaling:asg Cooldown                       AWSEBAutoScalingGroup 720
aws:autoscaling:asg Custom Availability Zones      AWSEBAutoScalingGroup
aws:autoscaling:asg MaxSize                        AWSEBAutoScalingGroup 4
aws:autoscaling:asg MinSize                        AWSEBAutoScalingGroup 2
```

For namespace `aws:autoscaling:launchconfiguration`, you can list the default setting by using the following command:

```
PS C:\> (Get-EBConfigurationSetting -ApplicationName "WebWorldPressApp" -
TemplateName "WebWorldPressAppTemplate").OptionSettings |Where-Object
{$_.namespace -eq "aws:autoscaling:launchconfiguration"}
```

In this case, you may want to specify `EC2KeyName` and `InstanceType`. Specifying `EC2KeyName` will allow you to log in to the server to troubleshoot your application code if needed. Based on the solution stack that we selected, AWS has assigned AMI ID by default. You can have a custom platform, and I will let you experiment with this one on your own. For now, we will stick to the AMI ID assigned by AWS based on the solution stack that we selected. Pay particular attention to the `SSHSourceRestriction`. By default, anybody can connect to the EC2 instance that will be spun by Beanstalk, and you can restrict this one based on your environment and application. I am leaving that one as it is. `SecurityGroups` will be created by Beanstalk, so we will leave that one as well. To change `EC2Keyname` and `InstanceType`, you can use the following command:

```
PS C:\> $Option3=New-Object
Amazon.ElasticBeanstalk.Model.ConfigurationOptionSetting
PS C:\> $Option3.Namespace="aws:autoscaling:launchconfiguration"
PS C:\> $Option3.OptionName="EC2KeyName"
PS C:\> $Option3.Value="MyWebPressApp"
PS C:\> $Option4=New-Object
Amazon.ElasticBeanstalk.Model.ConfigurationOptionSetting
PS C:\> $Option4.Namespace="aws:autoscaling:launchconfiguration"
PS C:\> $Option4.OptionName="InstanceType"
PS C:\> $Option4.Value="t2.large"
PS C:\> Update-EBConfigurationTemplate -ApplicationName "WebWorldPressApp"
-TemplateName "WebWorldPressAppTemplate" -OptionSetting $Option3,$Option4
```

```
PS C:\> $Option3=New-Object Amazon.ElasticBeanstalk.Model.ConfigurationOptionSetting
PS C:\> $Option3.Namespace="aws:autoscaling:launchconfiguration"
PS C:\> $Option3.OptionName="EC2KeyName"
PS C:\> $Option3.Value="MyWebPressApp"
PS C:\> $Option4=New-Object Amazon.ElasticBeanstalk.Model.ConfigurationOptionSetting
PS C:\> $Option4.Namespace="aws:autoscaling:launchconfiguration"
PS C:\> $Option4.OptionName="InstanceType"
PS C:\> $Option4.Value="t2.large"
PS C:\> Update-EBConfigurationTemplate -ApplicationName "WebWorldPressApp" -TemplateName "WebWorldPressAppTemplate" -OptionSetting $Option3,$Option4


ApplicationName    : WebWorldPressApp
DateCreated        : 7/17/2017 2:43:18 PM
DateUpdated        : 7/17/2017 3:21:29 PM
DeploymentStatus   :
Description        :
EnvironmentName    :
OptionSettings     : {}
PlatformArn        : arn:aws:elasticbeanstalk:us-east-1::platform/PHP 7.0 running on 64bit Amazon Linux/2.4.1
SolutionStackName  : 64bit Amazon Linux 2017.03 v2.4.1 running PHP 7.0
TemplateName       : WebWorldPressAppTemplate


PS C:\> (Get-EBConfigurationSetting -ApplicationName "WebWorldPressApp" -TemplateName "WebWorldPressAppTemplate").OptionSettings |
>> Where-Object {$_.namespace -eq "aws:autoscaling:launchconfiguration"}

Namespace                              OptionName            ResourceName                          Value
---------                              ----------            ------------                          -----
aws:autoscaling:launchconfiguration    BlockDeviceMappings   AWSEBAutoScalingLaunchConfiguration
aws:autoscaling:launchconfiguration    EC2KeyName            AWSEBAutoScalingLaunchConfiguration   MyWebPressApp
aws:autoscaling:launchconfiguration    IamInstanceProfile    AWSEBAutoScalingLaunchConfiguration
aws:autoscaling:launchconfiguration    ImageId               AWSEBAutoScalingLaunchConfiguration   ami-4c74435a
aws:autoscaling:launchconfiguration    InstanceType                                                t2.large
aws:autoscaling:launchconfiguration    MonitoringInterval    AWSEBAutoScalingLaunchConfiguration   5 minute
aws:autoscaling:launchconfiguration    RootVolumeIOPS        AWSEBAutoScalingLaunchConfiguration
aws:autoscaling:launchconfiguration    RootVolumeSize        AWSEBAutoScalingLaunchConfiguration
aws:autoscaling:launchconfiguration    RootVolumeType        AWSEBAutoScalingLaunchConfiguration
aws:autoscaling:launchconfiguration    SSHSourceRestriction                                        tcp,22,22,0.0.0.0/0
aws:autoscaling:launchconfiguration    SecurityGroups        AWSEBAutoScalingLaunchConfiguration
```

Another important change that you may like to make in the configuration template is the subnets. To check the default values for the namespace `aws:ec2:vpc`, you can use the following command:

```
PS C:\> (Get-EBConfigurationSetting -ApplicationName "WebWorldPressApp" -
TemplateName "WebWorldPressAppTemplate").OptionSettings | Where-Object
{$_.namespace -eq "aws:ec2:vpc"}
```

```
PS C:\> (Get-EBConfigurationSetting -ApplicationName "WebWorldPressApp" -TemplateName "WebWorldPressAppTemplate").OptionSettings |
>> Where-Object {$_.namespace -eq "aws:ec2:vpc"}

Namespace       OptionName                ResourceName                          Value
---------       ----------                ------------                          -----
aws:ec2:vpc     AssociatePublicIpAddress  AWSEBAutoScalingLaunchConfiguration
aws:ec2:vpc     ELBScheme                                                       public
aws:ec2:vpc     ELBSubnets
aws:ec2:vpc     Subnets                   AWSEBAutoScalingGroup
aws:ec2:vpc     VPCId                     AWSEBLoadBalancerSecurityGroup
```

If you are planning to run EC2 instances in the private subnet, then there is no point enabling `AssociatePublicIpAddress` to true. I have three private subnets and three public private subnets. `OptionName Subnets` will be spinning the EC2 instance in this subnet and `OptionName ELBSubnets` will be used to spin up the load balancer for your application. `ELBScheme` as `public` suggests that it is an internet-facing ELB. To change `Subnets` and `ELBSubnets`, you can run the following command:

```
PS C:\> $Option5=New-Object
Amazon.ElasticBeanstalk.Model.ConfigurationOptionSetting
PS C:\> $Option5.Namespace="aws:ec2:vpc"
PS C:\> $Option5.OptionName="Subnets"
PS C:\> $Option5.Value="subnet-f042dcb8,subnet-b262c19e,subnet-717bf32b"
PS C:\> $Option6=New-Object
Amazon.ElasticBeanstalk.Model.ConfigurationOptionSetting
PS C:\> $Option6.Namespace="aws:ec2:vpc"
PS C:\> $Option6.OptionName="ELBSubnets"
PS C:\> $Option6.Value="subnet-c843dd80,subnet-b29d3e9e,subnet-2c77fe76"
PS C:\> Update-EBConfigurationTemplate –ApplicationName "WebWorldPressApp"
–TemplateName "WebWorldPressAppTemplate" –OptionSetting $Option5,$Option6
```

```
PS C:\> $Option5=New-Object Amazon.ElasticBeanstalk.Model.ConfigurationOptionSetting
PS C:\> $Option5.Namespace="aws:ec2:vpc"
PS C:\> $Option5.OptionName="Subnets"
PS C:\> $Option5.Value="subnet-f042dcb8,subnet-b262c19e,subnet-717bf32b"
PS C:\> $Option6=New-Object Amazon.ElasticBeanstalk.Model.ConfigurationOptionSetting
PS C:\> $Option6.Namespace="aws:ec2:vpc"
PS C:\> $Option6.OptionName="ELBSubnets"
PS C:\> $Option6.Value="subnet-c843dd80,subnet-b29d3e9e,subnet-2c77fe76"
PS C:\> Update-EBConfigurationTemplate -ApplicationName "WebWorldPressApp" -TemplateName "WebWorldPressAppTemplate" -OptionSetting $Option5,$Option6


ApplicationName    : WebWorldPressApp
DateCreated        : 7/17/2017 2:43:18 PM
DateUpdated        : 7/17/2017 3:45:16 PM
DeploymentStatus   :
Description        :
EnvironmentName    :
OptionSettings     : {}
PlatformArn        : arn:aws:elasticbeanstalk:us-east-1::platform/PHP 7.0 running on 64bit Amazon Linux/2.4.1
SolutionStackName  : 64bit Amazon Linux 2017.03 v2.4.1 running PHP 7.0
TemplateName       : WebWorldPressAppTemplate


PS C:\> (Get-EBConfigurationSetting -ApplicationName "WebWorldPressApp" -TemplateName "WebWorldPressAppTemplate").OptionSettings |
>> Where-Object {$_.namespace -eq "aws:ec2:vpc"}

Namespace    OptionName                    ResourceName                         Value
---------    ----------                    ------------                         -----
aws:ec2:vpc  AssociatePublicIpAddress      AWSEBAutoScalingLaunchConfiguration  false
aws:ec2:vpc  ELBScheme                                                          public
aws:ec2:vpc  ELBSubnets                                                         subnet-c843dd80,subnet-b29d3e9e,subnet-2c77fe76
aws:ec2:vpc  Subnets                       AWSEBAutoScalingGroup                subnet-b262c19e,subnet-717bf32b,subnet-f042dcb8
aws:ec2:vpc  VPCId                         AWSEBLoadBalancerSecurityGroup       vpc-a6bb60df
```

You might have noticed that we did not set `VPCId`. We only set `Subnets`, and `VPCId` is automatically picked up by the configuration template associated with those subnets. If you try to reference subnets from multiple VPCs, the operation will fail. For the load balancer namespace `aws:elb:loadbalancer`, there is only one `OptionName` we need to set.

To get the list of existing values set for `OptionName` under namespace `aws:elb:loadbalancer`, you can use the following command:

```
PS C:\> (Get-EBConfigurationSetting -ApplicationName "WebWorldPressApp" -
TemplateName "WebWorldPressAppTemplate").OptionSettings |Where-Object
{$_.namespace -eq "aws:elb:loadbalancer"}
```

```
PS C:\> (Get-EBConfigurationSetting -ApplicationName "WebWorldPressApp" -TemplateName "WebWorldPressAppTemplate").OptionSettings |
>> Where-Object {$_.namespace -eq "aws:elb:loadbalancer"}

Namespace              OptionName                 ResourceName        Value
---------              ----------                 ------------        -----
aws:elb:loadbalancer   CrossZone                  AWSEBLoadBalancer   false
aws:elb:loadbalancer   LoadBalancerHTTPPort       AWSEBLoadBalancer   80
aws:elb:loadbalancer   LoadBalancerHTTPSPort      AWSEBLoadBalancer   OFF
aws:elb:loadbalancer   LoadBalancerPortProtocol   AWSEBLoadBalancer   HTTP
aws:elb:loadbalancer   LoadBalancerSSLPortProtocol AWSEBLoadBalancer  HTTPS
aws:elb:loadbalancer   SSLCertificateId           AWSEBLoadBalancer
aws:elb:loadbalancer   SecurityGroups             AWSEBLoadBalancer   {"Ref":"AWSEBLoadBalancerSecurityGroup"}
```

By default, Beanstalk launches Classic Load Balancer under the hood, hence you need to enable cross-zone load balancing on the load balancer. You can do this by using the following command:

```
PS C:\> $Option7=New-Object
Amazon.ElasticBeanstalk.Model.ConfigurationOptionSetting
PS C:\> $Option7.Namespace="aws:elb:loadbalancer"
PS C:\> $Option7.OptionName="CrossZone"
PS C:\> $Option7.Value=$true
PS C:\> Update-EBConfigurationTemplate -ApplicationName "WebWorldPressApp"
-TemplateName "WebWorldPressAppTemplate" -OptionSetting $Option7
```

```
PS C:\> $Option7=New-Object Amazon.ElasticBeanstalk.Model.ConfigurationOptionSetting
PS C:\> $Option7.Namespace="aws:elb:loadbalancer"
PS C:\> $Option7.OptionName="CrossZone"
PS C:\> $Option7.Value=$true
PS C:\> Update-EBConfigurationTemplate -ApplicationName "WebWorldPressApp" -TemplateName "WebWorldPressAppTemplate" -OptionSetting $Option7

ApplicationName   : WebWorldPressApp
DateCreated       : 7/17/2017 2:43:18 PM
DateUpdated       : 7/17/2017 3:59:13 PM
DeploymentStatus  :
Description       :
EnvironmentName   :
OptionSettings    : {}
PlatformArn       : arn:aws:elasticbeanstalk:us-east-1::platform/PHP 7.0 running on 64bit Amazon Linux/2.4.1
SolutionStackName : 64bit Amazon Linux 2017.03 v2.4.1 running PHP 7.0
TemplateName      : WebWorldPressAppTemplate

PS C:\> (Get-EBConfigurationSetting -ApplicationName "WebWorldPressApp" -TemplateName "WebWorldPressAppTemplate").OptionSettings |
>> Where-Object {$_.namespace -eq "aws:elb:loadbalancer"}

Namespace              OptionName                 ResourceName        Value
---------              ----------                 ------------        -----
aws:elb:loadbalancer   CrossZone                  AWSEBLoadBalancer   true
aws:elb:loadbalancer   LoadBalancerHTTPPort       AWSEBLoadBalancer   80
aws:elb:loadbalancer   LoadBalancerHTTPSPort      AWSEBLoadBalancer   OFF
aws:elb:loadbalancer   LoadBalancerPortProtocol   AWSEBLoadBalancer   HTTP
aws:elb:loadbalancer   LoadBalancerSSLPortProtocol AWSEBLoadBalancer  HTTPS
aws:elb:loadbalancer   SSLCertificateId           AWSEBLoadBalancer
aws:elb:loadbalancer   SecurityGroups             AWSEBLoadBalancer   {"Ref":"AWSEBLoadBalancerSecurityGroup"}
```

You can review all other default settings seen in the configuration template and update them based on your needs. I will refrain changing other values for our learning. You can now use this template to create the environment. It's always better to script the template and apply the settings for quick creation.

Creating an environment

Creating an environment means you are ready to spin up all the required resources needed for your application. Before you spin up an environment, always ensure that you have the DNS names available for your application. You can quickly check the availability of the DNS names for your application using the `Get-EBDNSAvailability` cmdlet. As I have named the application `Get-EBDNSAvailability`, I want to ensure that CNAME is available in the given region.

To check the DNS names, you can run the following command:

```
PS C:\> Get-EBDNSAvailability -CNAMEPrefix "WebWorldPressApp"
```

```
PS C:\> Get-EBDNSAvailability -CNAMEPrefix "WebWorldPressApp"

Available FullyQualifiedCNAME
--------- -------------------
True      WebWorldPressApp.us-east-1.elasticbeanstalk.com
```

The output indicates that I can use the `CNAMEPrefix` as `WebWorldPressApp`. As we have already taken care of all the configurational aspects in the configuration template, we just need to pass on that template to the `New-EBEnvironment` cmdlet, along with the application and environment name. The rest of the magic will be taken care of the Beanstalk platform.

To create a production environment for your application, you can run the following command:

```
PS C:\> New-EBEnvironment -ApplicationName "WebWorldPressApp" -
EnvironmentName "prd-WebWorldPressApp" -CNAMEPrefix "WebWorldPressApp" -
Description "My Production WebApp site" -TemplateName
"WebWorldPressAppTemplate"
```

```
PS C:\> New-EBEnvironment -ApplicationName "WebWorldPressApp" -EnvironmentName "prd-WebWorldPressApp" -CNAMEPrefix "WebWorldPressApp" -Description "My Produc
tion WebApp site" -TemplateName "WebWorldPressAppTemplate"

AbortableOperationInProgress : False
ApplicationName              : WebWorldPressApp
CNAME                        : WebWorldPressApp.us-east-1.elasticbeanstalk.com
DateCreated                  : 7/17/2017 4:16:15 PM
DateUpdated                  : 7/17/2017 4:16:15 PM
Description                  : My Production WebApp site
EndpointURL                  :
EnvironmentId                : e-vncgsvupfb
EnvironmentLinks             : {}
EnvironmentName              : prd-WebWorldPressApp
Health                       : Grey
HealthStatus                 :
PlatformArn                  : arn:aws:elasticbeanstalk:us-east-1::platform/PHP 7.0 running on 64bit Amazon Linux/2.4.1
Resources                    :
SolutionStackName            : 64bit Amazon Linux 2017.03 v2.4.1 running PHP 7.0
Status                       : Launching
TemplateName                 :
Tier                         : Amazon.ElasticBeanstalk.Model.EnvironmentTier
VersionLabel                 :
```

That's all. Your EC2 instances, with the instance type that you selected along with the load balancer and the Auto Scaling Group will be up and running in a few minutes. You can check the status of the environment by running the following command:

```
PS C:\> Get-EBEvent -ApplicationName "WebWorldPressApp" -EnvironmentName
"prd-WebWorldPressApp"|Format-Table
```

```
PS C:\> Get-EBEvent -ApplicationName "WebWorldPressApp" -EnvironmentName "prd-WebWorldPressApp"|Format-Table

ApplicationName   EnvironmentName       EventDate          Message
---------------   ---------------       ---------          -------
WebWorldPressApp  prd-WebWorldPressApp  7/17/2017 4:18:14 PM  Successfully launched environment: prd-WebWorldPressApp
WebWorldPressApp  prd-WebWorldPressApp  7/17/2017 4:18:13 PM  Application available at WebWorldPressApp.us-east-1.elasticbeanstalk.com.
WebWorldPressApp  prd-WebWorldPressApp  7/17/2017 4:18:10 PM  Adding instance 'i-0b51a6e0daa354f3a' to your environment.
WebWorldPressApp  prd-WebWorldPressApp  7/17/2017 4:18:10 PM  Added EC2 instance 'i-0b51a6e0daa354f3a' to Auto Scaling Group 'awseb-e-vncgsvupfb-stack-AWSEB...
WebWorldPressApp  prd-WebWorldPressApp  7/17/2017 4:18:10 PM  Adding instance 'i-09f237e61a99097bf' to your environment.
WebWorldPressApp  prd-WebWorldPressApp  7/17/2017 4:18:10 PM  Added EC2 instance 'i-09f237e61a99097bf' to Auto Scaling Group 'awseb-e-vncgsvupfb-stack-AWSEB...
WebWorldPressApp  prd-WebWorldPressApp  7/17/2017 4:17:54 PM  Created CloudWatch alarm named: awseb-e-vncgsvupfb-stack-AWSEBCloudwatchAlarmLow-1JVY1OM7HI51O
WebWorldPressApp  prd-WebWorldPressApp  7/17/2017 4:17:54 PM  Created CloudWatch alarm named: awseb-e-vncgsvupfb-stack-AWSEBCloudwatchAlarmHigh-1WRRP7DZVQ2DL
WebWorldPressApp  prd-WebWorldPressApp  7/17/2017 4:17:54 PM  Created Auto Scaling group policy named: arn:aws:autoscaling:us-east-1:072316406132:scalingPol...
WebWorldPressApp  prd-WebWorldPressApp  7/17/2017 4:17:54 PM  Created Auto Scaling group policy named: arn:aws:autoscaling:us-east-1:072316406132:scalingPol...
WebWorldPressApp  prd-WebWorldPressApp  7/17/2017 4:17:54 PM  Waiting for EC2 instances to launch. This may take a few minutes.
WebWorldPressApp  prd-WebWorldPressApp  7/17/2017 4:17:54 PM  Created Auto Scaling group named: awseb-e-vncgsvupfb-stack-AWSEBAutoScalingGroup-1HW16UCON1GOJ
WebWorldPressApp  prd-WebWorldPressApp  7/17/2017 4:16:52 PM  Created Auto Scaling launch configuration named: awseb-e-vncgsvupfb-stack-AWSEBAutoScalingLaun...
WebWorldPressApp  prd-WebWorldPressApp  7/17/2017 4:16:37 PM  Created load balancer named: awseb-e-v-AWSEBLOa-DWSDXYL260H9
WebWorldPressApp  prd-WebWorldPressApp  7/17/2017 4:16:36 PM  Created security group named: sg-830148f2
WebWorldPressApp  prd-WebWorldPressApp  7/17/2017 4:16:36 PM  Created security group named: sg-580a4329
WebWorldPressApp  prd-WebWorldPressApp  7/17/2017 4:16:15 PM  Using elasticbeanstalk-us-east-1-072316406132 as Amazon S3 storage bucket for environment data.
WebWorldPressApp  prd-WebWorldPressApp  7/17/2017 4:16:14 PM  createEnvironment is starting.
```

The top message in the preceding screenshot suggests that it hardly took 2 minutes for the whole environment to be up and running. Review the preceding event log for clarity. You will come to know that Beanstalk created a couple of Security Groups, one Auto Scaling Group, the load balancer, EC2 instances, and a couple of CloudWatch alarms. Now, get the CNAME by running the following command:

```
PS C:\> Get-EBEnvironment -ApplicationName "WebWorldPressApp" -
EnvironmentName "prd-WebWorldPressApp"|Select-Object CNAME
```

And hit the web browser. You should get the demo **Congratulations!** page, something like the following:

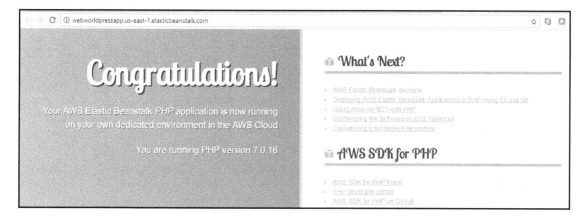

Note that, when creating the configuration template, we selected the solution stack for PHP, hence, we got this PHP default website. If you choose a different solution stack for a different platform, this default website will be different.

Your production environment is ready for application deployment now.

Deploying a popular WordPress application

To deploy to WordPress, first you must download the WordPress files from `https://wordpress.org/download/`. You should extract the downloaded ZIP files into your local directory, called `WordPress`, and ensure that you see following directory and files:

```
PS D:\wordpress> dir


    Directory: D:\wordpress


Mode                LastWriteTime     Length Name
----                -------------     ------ ----
d-----        6/8/2017    2:29 PM            wp-admin
d-----        6/8/2017    2:29 PM            wp-content
d-----        6/8/2017    2:29 PM            wp-includes
------       9/25/2013   12:18 AM        418 index.php
------        1/2/2017    6:58 PM      19935 license.txt
------      12/12/2016    9:01 AM       7413 readme.html
------       9/27/2016    9:36 PM       5447 wp-activate.php
------      12/19/2015   12:20 PM        364 wp-blog-header.php
------       8/29/2016   12:00 PM       1627 wp-comments-post.php
------      12/16/2015   10:58 AM       2853 wp-config-sample.php
------       5/24/2015    5:26 PM       3286 wp-cron.php
------      11/21/2016    3:46 AM       2422 wp-links-opml.php
------      10/25/2016    4:15 AM       3301 wp-load.php
------       5/12/2017    5:12 PM      34327 wp-login.php
------       1/11/2017    6:13 AM       8048 wp-mail.php
------        4/6/2017    6:01 PM      16200 wp-settings.php
------       1/24/2017   12:08 PM      29924 wp-signup.php
------      10/14/2016    8:39 PM       4513 wp-trackback.php
------       8/31/2016    4:31 PM       3065 xmlrpc.php
```

The WordPress application requires a MySQL database as a backend database. I will make use of the database we spun up in the RDS section earlier. You need to copy the file `wp-config-sample.php` as `wp-config.php` and update the database connectivity parameters. The following four parameters need to be updated. I have pasted the updated section from the `wp-config.php` file.

```
// ** MySQL settings - You can get this info from your web host ** //
/** The name of the database for WordPress */
define('DB_NAME', $_SERVER['RDS_DB_NAME']);

/** MySQL database username */
define('DB_USER', $_SERVER['RDS_USERNAME']);

/** MySQL database password */
define('DB_PASSWORD', $_SERVER['RDS_PASSWORD']);

/** MySQL hostname */
define('DB_HOST', $_SERVER['RDS_HOSTNAME']);
```

Because we have not spun up the RDS DB instance used in this case as part of the Beanstalk stack, we have to let the environment know about the DB instance, and you can do this by defining the environment variables for that environment. I have not found the way to do this via PowerShell, hence, you can make use of the AWS Console. Remember, not spinning up RDS as part of Beanstalk is considered best practice for your production application. If you spin up RDS as part of the Beanstalk stack, the DB instance's life will be tied to the life of the environment, and you do not want your database to be deleted when you delete your environment.

You can find the **Environment Properties** in the **Software Configuration** section of the specific environment under the **Configuration** tab, after navigating to the Elastic Beanstalk service on the AWS console. You define those RDS DB variables in the configuration for that specific environment as follows:

Though we did not specify any port number in `wp-config.php`, MySQL assumes that the default port is `3306`. As soon as you hit **Apply**, the environment configuration will be changed and you can confirm once again by checking the event log for the given environment, as follows:

```
PS D:\wordpress> Get-EBEvent -ApplicationName "WebWorldPressApp" -
EnvironmentName "prd-WebWorldPressApp"|Format-Table
```

```
PS D:\wordpress> Get-EBEvent -ApplicationName "WebWorldPressApp" -EnvironmentName "prd-WebWorldPressApp"|Format-Table

ApplicationName   EnvironmentName       EventDate             Message
---------------   ---------------       ---------             -------
WebWorldPressApp  prd-WebWorldPressApp  7/17/2017 5:17:31 PM  Environment update completed successfully.
WebWorldPressApp  prd-WebWorldPressApp  7/17/2017 5:17:31 PM  Successfully deployed new configuration to environment.
WebWorldPressApp  prd-WebWorldPressApp  7/17/2017 5:16:16 PM  Updating environment prd-WebWorldPressApp's configuration settings.
WebWorldPressApp  prd-WebWorldPressApp  7/17/2017 5:16:11 PM  Environment update is starting.
```

As we added `wp-config.php` in the original ZIP, you must now ZIP all the files and upload it to Beanstalk. You can now upload the ZIP file to the application on the AWS Console. I could not find the cmdlet which would let me upload the file. You can upload the file by selecting the specific application on the AWS console. You can review the `New-EBApplicationVersion` cmdlet to create a new version using S3 or Git as a source.

In this example, I uploaded a ZIP file and gave the version label as `V1`. The version label must be unique for each version that you upload to the Beanstalk repository of application versions. You can now deploy your WordPress application by simply running the following command:

```
PS C:\wordpress> Update-EBEnvironment -ApplicationName "WebWorldPressApp" -
EnvironmentName "prd-WebWorldPressApp" -VersionLabel "V1"
```

```
PS D:\wordpress> Update-EBEnvironment -ApplicationName "WebWorldPressApp" -EnvironmentName "prd-WebWorldPressApp" -VersionLabel "V1"


AbortableOperationInProgress : True
ApplicationName              : WebWorldPressApp
CNAME                        : WebWorldPressApp.us-east-1.elasticbeanstalk.com
DateCreated                  : 7/17/2017 4:16:15 PM
DateUpdated                  : 7/17/2017 5:36:31 PM
Description                  : My Production WebApp site
EndpointURL                  : awseb-e-v-AWSEBLoa-DWSDXYL260H9-1146012130.us-east-1.elb.amazonaws.com
EnvironmentId                : e-vncgsvupfb
EnvironmentLinks             : {}
EnvironmentName              : prd-WebWorldPressApp
Health                       : Grey
HealthStatus                 :
PlatformArn                  : arn:aws:elasticbeanstalk:us-east-1::platform/PHP 7.0 running on 64bit Amazon Linux/2.4.1
Resources                    :
SolutionStackName            : 64bit Amazon Linux 2017.03 v2.4.1 running PHP 7.0
Status                       : Updating
TemplateName                 :
Tier                         : Amazon.ElasticBeanstalk.Model.EnvironmentTier
VersionLabel                 : V1
```

You can check the event log once again and see if the deploy has completed.

```
PS D:\wordpress> Get-EBEvent -ApplicationName "WebWorldPressApp" -EnvironmentName "prd-WebWorldPressApp"|Format-Table

ApplicationName  EnvironmentName      EventDate           Message
---------------  ---------------      ---------           -------
WebWorldPressApp prd-WebWorldPressApp 7/17/2017 5:37:56 PM Environment update completed successfully.
WebWorldPressApp prd-WebWorldPressApp 7/17/2017 5:37:56 PM New application version was deployed to running EC2 instances.
WebWorldPressApp prd-WebWorldPressApp 7/17/2017 5:37:12 PM Deploying new version to instance(s).
WebWorldPressApp prd-WebWorldPressApp 7/17/2017 5:36:30 PM Environment update is starting.
```

Once you see that the environment update has completed successfully, that means that your application is ready to serve traffic. You can confirm by hitting the CNAME that we got earlier in the web browser. You should get the **Welcome** page, as follows. The first page will be selecting a language preference for the site.

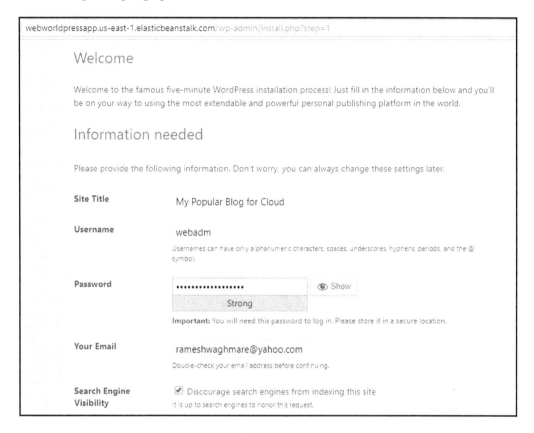

There will be an option to **Install WordPress** on the same screen at the bottom. Just click on that button and all the required tables will be installed in the MySQL database that you configured for this deployment.

You will now get an admin page, as follows, to post your own post.

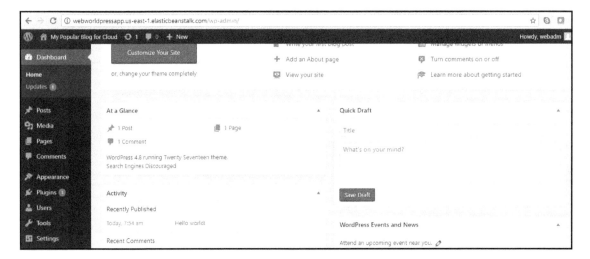

Going back to the CNAME in the browser once again will take you to the home screen of the website. You should now see something like the following:

With this, your popular WordPress blogging website is running on Elastic Beanstalk. During this journey, your focus was only on the application code. You did not do any heavy-lifting work to spin up EC2 instances, the load balancer, and the Auto Scaling Group. All work was done for you by Elastic Beanstalk; you just hosted your application on top of it.

Cloning an environment

Once you have the production application running, you might have several reasons to clone the environment so that you can continue testing it with the production dataset or troubleshoot the actual issue in hand on your production instances. You can make use of PowerShell scripting to automate the clone process, or you can do this on the AWS Console. In this case, I have a PowerShell `clone_env.ps1` which I made using the existing production instance.

```
PS D:\scripts> cat .\clone_env.ps1
#########################################################################
# Declaration of the parameters
#########################################################################
[CmdletBinding()]
Param(
    [Parameter(Mandatory=$True)]
    [string]$vApplicationName,
    [Parameter(Mandatory=$True)]
    [string]$vSourceEnvironmentName,
    [Parameter(Mandatory=$True)]
    [string]$vNewEnvironmentName,
    [Parameter(Mandatory=$True)]
    [string]$vNewEnvironmentCname
)
#########################################################################
# Create Unique Template Name
#########################################################################
$templateName = [Guid]::NewGuid().ToString();
$environment = Get-EBEnvironment -ApplicationName $vApplicationName -EnvironmentName $vSourceEnvironmentName;
#########################################################################
# Get current environment ID and Application Name
#########################################################################
$environmentId = $environment.EnvironmentId;
$ApplicationName = $environment.ApplicationName;
#########################################################################
#Create new template using existing environment set up
#########################################################################
$template = New-EBConfigurationTemplate -ApplicationName $ApplicationName -TemplateName $templateName -EnvironmentId $environmentId;
while (-not (Get-EBApplication -ApplicationNames $ApplicationName)[0].ConfigurationTemplates.Contains($templateName)) {
    echo ([string]::Format("can't find template '{0}'", $templateName));
    Start-Sleep -s 5;
}
(Get-EBApplication -ApplicationNames $ApplicationName)[0].ConfigurationTemplates.Contains($templateName);
Get-EBEnvironment -ApplicationName $ApplicationName -EnvironmentNames $SourceEnvironmentName
#########################################################################
# Create new environment  and remove template
#########################################################################
New-EBEnvironment -ApplicationName $ApplicationName -EnvironmentName $vNewEnvironmentName -CNAMEPrefix $vNewEnvironmentCname -TemplateName $template.Template
Name;
Remove-EBConfigurationTemplate -ApplicationName $ApplicationName -TemplateName $templateName -Force;
```

This script requires four parameters as an input to clone the existing environment. You can run the script as the following command:

```
PS D:\scripts> .\clone_env.ps1

cmdlet clone_env.ps1 at command pipeline position 1
Supply values for the following parameters:
ApplicationName: WebWorldPressApp
SourceEnvironmentName: prd-WebWorldPressApp
NewEnvironmentName: dev-WebWorldPressApp
NewEnvironmentCname: dev-WebWorldPressApp
True
```

Successful execution will stand up another environment for you, the same as the existing one. I know there are not a whole lot of checks that I have added to this script, such as ensuring the CNAME is available, but at a high level you can automate the clone of the environment using this script. When you clone the environment something like this, ensure that the database related environment variables have been updated, otherwise your preproduction applications will end up accessing the same database as production, resulting in data corruption or loss.

Swapping an environment CNAME

Every environment that you stand up with Elastic Beanstalk gets a unique CNAME. These CNAMEs are useful when you manage your deployment using the blue/green deployment strategy, as there is a need for you to swap the URLs, or you may want to route traffic based on the weighted routing policy in Route 53. The Set-EBEnvironmentCNAME cmdlet lets you swap the CNAME of two environments. Let's plan to switch the CNAME of the two environment that we created in this chapter. You can do this as follows:

```
PS D:\scripts> Set-EBEnvironmentCNAME -SourceEnvironmentId "e-vncgsvupfb" -
SourceEnvironmentName "prd-WebWorldPressApp" -DestinationEnvironmentId "e-
s3b62feki2" -DestinationEnvironmentName "dev-WebWorldPressApp"
```

```
PS D:\scripts> Get-EBEnvironment -ApplicationName "WebWorldPressApp" -EnvironmentName "prd-WebWorldPressApp"|Select-Object CNAME

CNAME
-----
WebWorldPressApp.us-east-1.elasticbeanstalk.com


PS D:\scripts> Get-EBEnvironment -ApplicationName "WebWorldPressApp" -EnvironmentName "dev-WebWorldPressApp"|Select-Object CNAME

CNAME
-----
dev-WebWorldPressApp.us-east-1.elasticbeanstalk.com

PS D:\scripts> Set-EBEnvironmentCNAME -SourceEnvironmentId "e-vncgsvupfb" -SourceEnvironmentName "prd-WebWorldPressApp" -DestinationEnvironmentId "e-s3b62fek
i2" -DestinationEnvironmentName "dev-WebWorldPressApp"
PS D:\scripts> Get-EBEnvironment -ApplicationName "WebWorldPressApp" -EnvironmentName "prd-WebWorldPressApp"|Select-Object CNAME

CNAME
-----
dev-WebWorldPressApp.us-east-1.elasticbeanstalk.com


PS D:\scripts> Get-EBEnvironment -ApplicationName "WebWorldPressApp" -EnvironmentName "dev-WebWorldPressApp"|Select-Object CNAME

CNAME
-----
WebWorldPressApp.us-east-1.elasticbeanstalk.com
```

Note that, when you have a production environment and there is a need for you to swap URLs, you should ensure that the DNS cache does not create issues for your user. Some browsers do not respect TTL defined in the DNS configuration, resulting in weird and unexpected behavior in the application.

Deleting an environment and application

The `Stop-EBEnvironment` cmdlet lets you terminate the specified environment and free up the resources, depending on switches that you pass on. If you specify `TerminateResource` as false, then Beanstalk will retain underlying resources, otherwise, whatever is started with the stack will be terminated by this operation in regard to the environment. If you want to terminate the `dev` environment, then just get the environment ID and name, then pass it to the cmdlet, as follows:

```
PS C:\> Stop-EBEnvironment -EnvironmentId "e-s3b62feki2" -EnvironmentName
"dev-WebWorldPressApp" -TerminateResource $true
```

```
PS D:\scripts> Stop-EBEnvironment -EnvironmentId "e-s3b62feki2" -EnvironmentName "dev-WebWorldPressApp" -TerminateResource $true

AbortableOperationInProgress : False
ApplicationName              : WebWorldPressApp
CNAME                        : WebWorldPressApp.us-east-1.elasticbeanstalk.com
DateCreated                  : 7/17/2017 6:26:04 PM
DateUpdated                  : 7/17/2017 7:19:50 PM
Description                  :
EndpointURL                  : awseb-e-s-AWSEBLoa-J6X202CXXBF6-1611547768.us-east-1.elb.amazonaws.com
EnvironmentId                : e-s3b62feki2
EnvironmentLinks             : {}
EnvironmentName              : dev-WebWorldPressApp
Health                       : Grey
HealthStatus                 :
PlatformArn                  : arn:aws:elasticbeanstalk:us-east-1::platform/PHP 7.0 running on 64bit Amazon Linux/2.4.1
Resources                    :
SolutionStackName            : 64bit Amazon Linux 2017.03 v2.4.1 running PHP 7.0
Status                       : Terminating
TemplateName                 :
Tier                         : Amazon.ElasticBeanstalk.Model.EnvironmentTier
VersionLabel                 :
```

`Remove-EBApplication` lets you delete the specified application. When you delete an application, all related versions and configurations will be deleted. Note that Beanstalk keeps a copy of your code in the S3 bucket, and it will not be deleted by this operation. If you have an environment running for the specified application, then you cannot delete the application. But if you specify the switch `TerminateEnvByForce` with this cmdlet as true, then all the running environments will be terminated and the application will be removed.

```
PS C:\> Remove-EBApplication -ApplicationName "WebWorldPressApp"

Confirm
Are you sure you want to perform this action?
Performing the operation "Remove-EBApplication (DeleteApplication)" on target "WebWorldPressApp".
[Y] Yes  [A] Yes to All  [N] No  [L] No to All  [S] Suspend  [?] Help (default is "Y"): Y
```

Summary

AWS Elastic Beanstalk is true PaaS. Amazing capabilities are provided by this platform, thus making it one of the most in the development community. Developers love Elastic Beanstalk for deploying and testing their code, as they do not need to wait for the given infrastructure anymore. This platform really brought speed to the overall development, testing, and deployment of the application. This is also a true example of DevOps capability. We have learnt various deployment strategies that can be adopted with Elastic Beanstalk. We also learnt how we can modify the configuration template to satisfy our requirement. We learnt how applications can be deployed on the Elastic Beanstalk environment that we spun up. In the next chapter, we will learn another way to deploy the AWS infrastructure using CloudFormation.

14
AWS CloudFormation

AWS provides various ways to deploy resources on the AWS Cloud. In the previous chapter, we learnt about AWS Elastic Beanstalk as a service to deploy your resources and applications. **CloudFormation** is another service provided by AWS to deploy your resources. In this chapter, we will learn about the various components of CloudFormation and how to make use of it to define and launch your AWS resources.

In this chapter, we will discuss CloudFormation, template anatomy, intrinsic functions, cross stack references, nested stack, validating a template, submitting a template to AWS CloudFormation, and creating EC2 instance using CloudFormation. In addition, we will touch upon helper script and stack policies.

What is CloudFormation?

AWS CloudFormation is a service which lets you create a template that defines a set of resources and instructions on how to create those resources. CloudFormation aims to provide you with a way to deploy your infrastructure and resources consistently so that the process of deploying your application is frictionless. Consider that you are creating a VPC, subnets, EC2 instances, RDS DB instances, a load balancer, and Auto Scaling Group to host your application either through AWS Console or through CLI. When you need to duplicate the same environment in a different region or different VPC, you have to make all those decisions once again and create those individual resources. This is where CloudFormation plays a vital role. You can define a template with a required action and replay that template as many times as you want to replicate the environments.

The fundamental principle of DevOps is to treat infrastructure as code. CloudFormation provides you with that ability to define the whole infrastructure on AWS as code. When you write application code in any language, you have to respect the syntax and semantics of that specific language in order to write an application. Likewise, AWS allows you to script your code in JSON and YAML format. Every AWS resource that you create, either through AWS Console or CLI, has a corresponding JSON and YAML format. You can version control the code just as you do for your application code, allowing you to encourage collaboration. CloudFormation not only allows you to create resources, but also equips you with the ability to update and delete those resources. You can create a single template to define your entire environment, or you can break up the template into multiple templates for different parts of your environment.

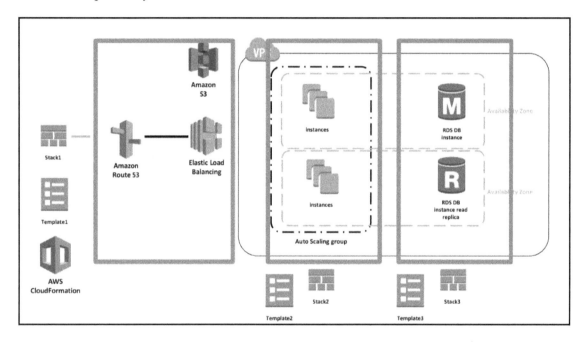

In this example, **Template1** is dedicated to defining **Stack1** for **Amazon Route 53**, **Amazon S3**, and **Elastic Load Balancing**; **Template2** is for the EC2 **Instances** and the **Auto Scaling group** which is part of **Stack2**; **Template3** defines **Stack3**, which includes the **RDS DB Instance** and the **RDS DB Instance read replica**. VPC is a common resource seen in **Template2** and **Template3**. Defining different stacks for different parts of your environment brings modularity to the overall approach to defining your cloud resources. You might have different departments looking after different parts of your infrastructure; having different templates would allow each of them to experience independence to define the practices around their own area.

There are some terminologies that you need to be familiar with while working with CloudFormation.

- **Templates**: There are JSON or YAML formatted test files. This is kind of a blueprint for building your AWS resources. In this chapter, we will be making use of the YAML format. Review the AWS online documentation if you want to work with the JSON format.
- **Stacks**: Sets of resources defined in the template are called stacks. You define those resources, respecting the JSON or YAML format for the specific resources.

Authoring and template anatomy

There are multiple ways to create a template. We will learn YAML based authoring of templates in this chapter. You can author template in JSON format as well. I, personally, like the YAML based format because it is easier to work with. The JSON based format has a lot more braces to deal with; but if you have an editor that can format JSON syntax for you, this format may be easy as well. Another way to create a template is using the **designer**. On the AWS Console, you can make use of the designer to create a template by just dragging the available resources from the resource pane and dropping them on the canvas. The good thing about the designer is that it now supports both formats of text based authoring.

You see that there are different sections in the template, out of which `Resources` is the only mandatory section. Though you can have those sections in any order in the template, it is recommended that you follow the sections as seen in the above template for clarity. Let's touch base on different sections seen in the YAML template. Note that the JSON format also has the same sections. There is nothing different in this; just the way of writing the code is different. The following snippet is a YAML formatted template.

```
---
AWSTemplateFormatVersion: "version date"
Description:
 String
Metadata:
 template metadata
Parameters:
 set of parameters
Mappings:
 set of mappings
Conditions:
 set of conditions
Transform:
 set of transforms
```

```
Resources:
  set of resources
Outputs:
  set of outputs
```

- `AWSTemplateFormatVersion`: The current format version is `2010-09-09` and is the only valid value. If you do not mention this value, AWS CloudFormation assumes the latest format version. This is just a template version which runs independently of other API versions.

```
AWSTemplateFormatVersion: "2010-09-09"
```

- `Description`: This allows you to write any arbitrary comments and it must follow the section `AWSTemplateFormatVersion`. Usually, you can write the purpose of the template in this section:

```
Description: >
  Here are some
  details about
  the template.
```

- `Metadata`: CloudFormation retrieves setting and configuration information from this section for the resources that you define. `AWS::CloudFormation::Init`, `AWS::CloudFormation::Interface`, and `AWS::CloudFormation::Designer` are the three metadata keys that you can use in this section.

```
Resources:
MyInstance:
Type: "AWS::EC2::Instance"
Metadata:
AWS::CloudFormation::Init:
config:
packages:
:
groups:
:
users:
:
sources:
:
files:
:
commands:
:
services:
:
```

```
Properties:
:
```

- `Parameters`: This section allows you to pass on some input values to the template so that the template is customizable for various scenarios. You can also default the parameter values if you are not passing.

```
Parameters:
 InstanceTypeParameter:
 Type: String
 Default: t2.micro
 AllowedValues:
 - t2.micro
 - m1.small
 - m1.large
 Description: Enter t2.micro, m1.small, or m1.large. Default is
 t2.micro.
```

- `Mappings`: You can define mapping keys and associate values to those mapping keys, which can form a condition. By using `Fn::FindInMap` intrinsic function in the `Resources` and `Output` sections, you can extract the value for the given mapping key.

```
Mappings:
 RegionMap:
 us-east-1:
 "32": "ami-6411e20d"
 us-west-1:
 "32": "ami-c9c7978c"
 eu-west-1:
 "32": "ami-37c2f643"
 ap-southeast-1:
 "32": "ami-66f28c34"
 ap-northeast-1:
 "32": "ami-9c03a89d"
```

- `Conditions`: This section defines the condition which controls resources and whether they are created or are assigned value during the stack creation or updation process. For example, you can create a resource that depends on whether the stack is for a development or a production environment.

```
Conditions:
 Logical ID:
 Intrinsic function
```

- `Transform`: This defines the transform that CloudFormation uses to process your template. An `AWS::Serverless` transform is a specific version of the Serverless Application Model on AWS and `AWS::Include` transform is used to work with the templates that are stored separately from the main CloudFormation templates.

```
Transform:
 Name: 'AWS::Include'
 Parameters:
 Location: 's3://MyAmazonS3BucketName/MyFileName.yaml'
```

- `Resources`: You define stack resources and their properties in this section. This is the only mandatory section that you need to specify in the whole template.

```
Resources:
 Logical ID:
 Type: Resource type
 Properties:
 Set of properties
```

- `Outputs`: As the name implies, you can define your output variables in this section. The output values seen in this section can be imported into other templates.

```
Outputs:
 Logical ID:
 Description: Information about the value
 Value: Value to return
 Export:
 Name: Value to export
```

Intrinsic functions

CloudFormation provides various built-in functions that assist you to manage stacks. These intrinsic functions are very useful for you to capture the values of the resource properties that are not available until runtime. This helps to create customizable templates.

Intrinsic functions are as follows:

- `Fn::Base64`: This function returns the `Base64` representation of the input string. It is used to pass encoded data to an EC2 instance via the userdata property of the EC2 instance.

  ```
  Fn::Base64: valueToEncode
  ```

- `Fn::FindInMap`: It returns the mapping value corresponding to the mapping keys declared in the `Mappings` section of the CloudFormation template.

  ```
  Fn::FindInMap: [ MapName, TopLevelKey, SecondLevelKey ]
  ```

- `Fn::GetAtt`: It returns the value of an attribute from the specified resource in the CloudFormation template.

  ```
  Fn::GetAtt: [ logicalNameOfResource, attributeName ]
  ```

- `Fn::GetAZs`: It returns an array that lists availability zones for the specified region.

  ```
  Fn::GetAZs: region
  ```

- `Fn::ImportValue`: It returns the value of an output exported by other stacks. You use this function to create cross stack references.

  ```
  Fn::ImportValue: sharedValueToImport
  ```

- `Fn::Join`: It appends a set of values into a single value, separated by the specified delimiter. If the delimiter is an empty string, values are concatenated with no delimiter.

  ```
  Fn::Join: [ delimiter, [ comma-delimited list of values ] ]
  ```

- `Fn::Select`: It returns the single object from the list of objects by index number. Importantly, this function does not check for null values or whether the index number that you specified is out of bounds. In both cases, stack creation will fail. You must ensure that the index value that you've selected is a valid value and it does not contain any null values.

  ```
  Fn::Select: [ index, listOfObjects ]
  ```

- `Fn::Split`: This allows you to split a string into a list of string values. Usually, you make use of `Fn::Select` to pick up a specific element from a list of string values that you split using `Fn::Split`.

  ```
  Fn::Split: [ delimiter, source string ]
  ```

- `Fn::Sub`: This function substitutes variables in an input string with values that you specify. This function is useful for constructing commands for which values are not available until stack creation or update.

  ```
  Fn::Sub:
    - String
    - { Var1Name: Var1Value, Var2Name: Var2Value }
  ```

- `Ref`: This returns the value of the specified parameter or resource. When you specify the logical parameter name, it returns the value of the parameter. When you specify the resource logical name, it returns the physical ID of the resource.

  ```
  Ref: logicalName
  ```

- **Condition functions**: There are a number of conditional intrinsic functions available for you, such as `Fn::And`, `Fn::Or`, `Fn::If`, `Fn::Equals`, and `Fn::Not` to conditionally create stack resources. You can only reference other conditions and values from the `Parameters` and `Mappings` sections of the CloudFormation template. You cannot reference the logical ID of the resource in the template.

Cross stack references

You can have multiple templates that create multiple stacks in your AWS accounts, and you may have a need to reference resources created in one stack with another. CloudFormation provides you with the ability to export the value of a variable from one stack and import it into another stack. You can export the value of a variable in the `Outputs` section of your CloudFormation source template, and import the value in the `Resources` section of the template where you are making the reference.

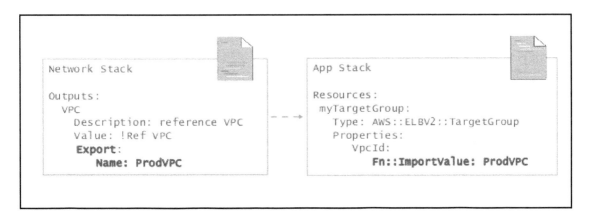

In the preceding example, you can see that Network Stack has the ProdVPC name exported and App Stack has the ProdVPC name imported. The export names that you specify must be unique within the account and the given region. The features of CloudFormation do not allow you to create references across regions. In addition, you cannot delete a stack that is being referenced by another stack, and output in the source template cannot be changed or removed while it is being referenced by the stack.

Creating a base network using CloudFormation

In this section, let's plan to create a similar base network to what we created in Chapter 5, *AWS Virtual Private Cloud*. In that chapter, we learnt how to make use of several individual cmdlets to create the network. In this chapter, we will focus on creating and automating those individual actions using CloudFormation. The business case is, we want to input CIDR Block for VPC and create four individual subnets (two public and two private) inside that VPC, based on the range that you specify as an input to the CloudFormation stack. This means, overall, we will be inputting five parameters to the stack. As an output, we want to get a VPC ID, four subnet IDs, and a Security Group ID. In addition, you want to export those output parameters so that other stacks can reference it.

Creating a template is not that scary, though it sounds like a big task. To understand template creation better, I am going to walk you through the template and help you understand how easy it is. I will be using YAML format here. Ensure that you have a text editor that will help you to catch YAML formatting issues. Since it is YAML, formatting is a key. I used Notepad++ to create the template that I will discuss in this section.

To start with, open any text editor and define the five parameters that you want to input to the template.

```
---
AWSTemplateFormatVersion: '2010-09-09'
Description: Creating Base Network for Application
Parameters:
  VPCCIDRRange:
    Description: My CIDR Block for VPC
    Type: String
  PublicSubnetCIDR1:
    Description: First Public Subnet
    Type: String
  PublicSubnetCIDR2:
    Description: Second Public Subnet
    Type: String
  PrivateSubnetCIDR1:
    Description: First Private Subnet
    Type: String
  PrivateSubnetCIDR2:
    Description: Second Private Subnet
    Type: String
```

The template starts with three dashes (---). You then define the section AWSTemplateFormatVersion and there is only one valid value 2010-09-09. The Description section lets you define the purpose of the template. When you write a template in a plaintext editor, do not indent a line using tab. Use spacebar to create those spaces. The Parameters section has those five variables defined. All of them are defined as type string as that is a valid type for accepting the CIDR block ranges. VPCCIDRRange is a logical name. This can be any name as long as you respect the rule of naming these logical names. Likewise, the same is true for other logical names for subnets such as PublicSubnetCIDR1, PublicSubnetCIDR2, PrivateSubnetCIDR1, and PrivateSubnetCIDR2. Description under the Parameters section is a comment for variables that you input. This helps you to bring in clarity for those variables when others review your template. So, you might have noticed that this is just plain English language, with due respect to the YAML format.

Let's continue to the next section. We would now like to define the resource for the VPC and Internet Gateway. Then we would want to link the Internet Gateway to the VPC.

```
Resources:
  myCFVPC:
    Type: AWS::EC2::VPC
    Properties:
      CidrBlock:
        Ref: VPCCIDRRange
      EnableDnsSupport: 'true'
      EnableDnsHostnames: 'true'
      InstanceTenancy: default
      Tags:
      - Key: Name
        Value: "CFVpc"
  myCFIgw:
    Type: "AWS::EC2::InternetGateway"
    Properties:
      Tags:
      - Key: Name
        Value: "CFIgw"
  AttachGateway:
    Type: AWS::EC2::VPCGatewayAttachment
    Properties:
      VpcId:
        Ref: myCFVPC
      InternetGatewayId:
        Ref: myCFIgw
```

The `Resources` section is the only mandatory section in the template if you just want everything hardcoded underneath it. Once you start planning customization, then other sections start popping up in the template. And you definitely want to make your template repeatable and consistent. So, to me, you always work with different sections in the template. For each resources that you define in the `Resources` section, you have `Type` and `Properties`.

To write this section, always refer to the following link:
`http://docs.aws.amazon.com/AWSCloudFormation/latest/UserGuide/aws-template-resource-type-ref.html`

`myCFVPC` is a logical name given to the VPC and you are instructing CloudFormation that the resource type to be created is `AWS::EC2::VPC`. AWS has a specific name given to each resource type. Each resource that you define in this space will have different `Properties` and you get all those `Properties` details from the link shared here. You will start building the required skills writing this section, as you start working more on the CloudFormation template. Do not try to memorize those properties. Just refer to the link and steal those `Properties` from there. AWS keeps adding additional `Properties` as and when they add new features to the service. Hence, visiting this page is not a choice, you must review this regularly if you work with CloudFormation.

Pay special attention to the `Properties CidrBlock`, which has a value `Ref: VPCCIDRRange`. `Ref` is an *intrinsic function* in CloudFormation, which returns the value specified in the `Parameters` or `Resources` section. You are accepting input in the `Parameters` section for variable `VPCCIDRRange` and passing it to the `CidrBlock` property in the VPC creation section. This is the way you reference the values in the CloudFormation template.

`myCFIgw` is the logical name for the Internet Gateway and it is defined as resource type `AWS::EC2::InternetGateway`. You see that type value is in double quotes in this case. It does not matter in YAML format. You can include the values in double quotes or without quotes. `AttachGateway` is another logical name and we have not referenced it anywhere in the template. This is the only area where you see this name and it can be anything. By defining this resource, you are attaching the Internet Gateway to the VPC. You might have noticed that both the values used in `AttachGateway` were created previously in the same section and do not come from the `Parameters` section. So, `Ref` *intrinsic* function can reference values from the `Parameters` and `Resources` section.

As you are planning to create public and private subnets, you must ensure that there are different Route Tables for those subnets. You do not want to have the Internet Gateway on your private Route Table. You learnt that, once you have Internet Gateway on the Route Table, that route is called a public route. To continue the template creation journey, let's create two Route Tables that you can attach to the public and private subnets respectively.

```
CFPublicRoute:
   Type: AWS::EC2::RouteTable
   Properties:
     VpcId:
       Ref: myCFVPC
     Tags:
     - Key: Name
       Value: CFPublicRT
CFPrivateRoute:
   Type: AWS::EC2::RouteTable
   Properties:
     VpcId:
       Ref: myCFVPC
     Tags:
     - Key: Name
       Value: CFPrivateRT
```

CFPublicRoute and CFPrivateRoute are two logical names for the routes that you are planning to create. Typing AWS::EC2::RouteTable instructs CloudFormation that this is a resource Route Table and it will be created in VPC referenced by Ref: myCFVPC. By default, when you create a Route Table, it will have a local route the same as the CIDR block that you mentioned for the VPC. Moving on, let's create two public subnets and assign the CIDR block that we input.

```
CFPublic1:
  Type: AWS::EC2::Subnet
  Properties:
    VpcId:
      Ref: myCFVPC
    CidrBlock:
      Ref: PublicSubnetCIDR1
    AvailabilityZone: "us-east-1a"
    Tags:
    - Key: Name
      Value: CFPublicSubnet1
CFPublic2:
  Type: AWS::EC2::Subnet
  Properties:
    VpcId:
      Ref: myCFVPC
    CidrBlock:
      Ref: PublicSubnetCIDR2
    AvailabilityZone: "us-east-1b"
    Tags:
    - Key: Name
      Value: CFPublicSubnet2
```

CFPublic1 and CFPublic2 are the two logical IDs for the public subnet. AWS::EC2::Subnet is the resource type that indicates it is a subnet. PublicSubnetCIDR1 and PublicSubnetCIDR2 are the two input parameters, and the subnet is created in the VPC referenced by Ref: myCFVPC. Both subnets are created in different availability zones. Similarly, let's create two private subnets.

```
CFPrivate1:
  Type: AWS::EC2::Subnet
  Properties:
    VpcId:
      Ref: myCFVPC
    CidrBlock:
      Ref: PrivateSubnetCIDR1
    AvailabilityZone: "us-east-1a"
    Tags:
    - Key: Name
      Value: CFPrivateSubnet1
CFPrivate2:
  Type: AWS::EC2::Subnet
  Properties:
    VpcId:
      Ref: myCFVPC
    CidrBlock:
      Ref: PrivateSubnetCIDR2
    AvailabilityZone: "us-east-1b"
    Tags:
    - Key: Name
      Value: CFPrivateSubnet1
```

CFPrivate1 and CFPrivate2 are the two logical IDs for the private subnet. AWS::
EC2::Subnet is the resource type that indicates it is a subnet. PrivateSubnetCIDR1 and
PrivateSubnetCIDR2 are the two input parameters, and the subnet is created in the VPC
referenced by Ref: myCFVPC. Both subnets are created in different availability zones.

As you have now created all the required subnets, it's now time to add the Internet
Gateway to the public route.

```
myCFPublicRoute:
  Type: AWS::EC2::Route
  DependsOn: myCFIgw
  Properties:
    RouteTableId:
      Ref: CFPublicRoute
    DestinationCidrBlock: 0.0.0.0/0
    GatewayId:
      Ref: myCFIgw
```

The AWS::EC2::Route resource lets you add a route on the Route Table that you created.
DestinationCidrBlock is always 0.0.0.0/0 for the Internet Gateway. In this case, you
see that you used the DependsOn attribute for the resource, which instructs
CloudFormation to act on this item only when myCFIgw resource is created. myCFIgw is the
Internet Gateway. This is the way you can build dependencies in the CloudFormation
template. You are adding a route on the public route that you created, referenced as Ref:
CFPublicRoute. You can now associate public subnets with the public route.

```
myCFSubnetRouteTableAssociation1:
  Type: AWS::EC2::SubnetRouteTableAssociation
  Properties:
    SubnetId:
      Ref: CFPublic1
    RouteTableId:
      Ref: CFPublicRoute
myCFSubnetRouteTableAssociation2:
  Type: AWS::EC2::SubnetRouteTableAssociation
  Properties:
    SubnetId:
      Ref: CFPublic2
    RouteTableId:
      Ref: CFPublicRoute
```

`CFPublic1` and `CFPublic2` are the two subnets that will be added on the public route `CFPublicRoute` you created earlier. This process is called subnet association with a Route Table. For a private route, you have to create a **NAT Gateway**, which needs to be spun in a public subnet and then added to the private Route Table.

```
myCFEIP:
  Type: AWS::EC2::EIP
  Properties:
    Domain: vpc
myCFNat:
  Type: AWS::EC2::NatGateway
  Properties:
    AllocationId:
      Fn::GetAtt:
      - myCFEIP
      - AllocationId
    SubnetId:
      Ref: CFPublic1
myCFNatPrivateRoute:
  Type: AWS::EC2::Route
  Properties:
    RouteTableId:
      Ref: CFPrivateRoute
    DestinationCidrBlock: 0.0.0.0/0
    NatGatewayId:
      Ref: myCFNat
myCFSubnetRouteTableAssociation3:
  Type: AWS::EC2::SubnetRouteTableAssociation
  Properties:
    SubnetId:
      Ref: CFPrivate1
    RouteTableId:
      Ref: CFPrivateRoute
myCFSubnetRouteTableAssociation4:
  Type: AWS::EC2::SubnetRouteTableAssociation
  Properties:
    SubnetId:
      Ref: CFPrivate2
    RouteTableId:
      Ref: CFPrivateRoute
```

For a NAT Gateway, you need to have an Elastic IP. So, resource type `AWS::EC2::EIP` lets you create an Elastic IP and resource `AWS::EC2::NatGateway` lets you create a NAT Gateway. After NAT Gateway creation, you can add the NAT Gateway to the private Route Table referenced by `Ref: CFPrivateRoute`. Once the NAT Gateway is added to the private Route Table, you can associate private subnets with the private Route Table. `CFPrivate1` and `CFPrivate2` are the two private subnets and are associated with the private Route Table `CFPrivateRoute`. The final piece of the puzzle is the Security Group for the VPC that will be created as part of this template. You might want that one to be created so that you can use it for the EC2 instance that you are planning to launch.

```
myCFSecurityGroup:
  Type: AWS::EC2::SecurityGroup
  Properties:
    GroupDescription: Allow http and ssh to client host
    VpcId:
      Ref: myCFVPC
    SecurityGroupIngress:
    - IpProtocol: tcp
      FromPort: '22'
      ToPort: '22'
      CidrIp: 0.0.0.0/0
    Tags:
    - Key: Name
      Value: myCFSG
SGBaseIngress:
  Type: AWS::EC2::SecurityGroupIngress
  Properties:
    GroupId:
      Ref: myCFSecurityGroup
    IpProtocol: tcp
    FromPort: '80'
    ToPort: '80'
    CidrIp: 0.0.0.0/0
```

Security Groups are created for the specific VPC. There will be ingress added on the Security Group for port `80` and port `22`. Resource type `AWS::EC2::SecurityGroup` lets you create a Security Group and resource type `AWS::EC2::SecurityGroupIngress` lets you create a ingress rule for that Security Group. I added one with the resource type attribute, and the other one by creating the new resource of type `AWS::EC2::SecurityGroupIngress`. With this, the main resource part for your base network will be created. For outputs, you would want to display the IDs of each resources that you intend for.

```
Outputs:
  myCFVPCId:
    Description: VPC Id
    Value:
      Ref: myCFVPC
    Export:
      Name: 'exmyCFVPC'
  CFPublic1Id:
    Description: Public Subnet 1 Id
    Value:
      Ref: CFPublic1
    Export:
      Name: 'exCFPublic1SubnetId'
  CFPublic2Id:
    Description: Public Subnet 2 Id
    Value:
      Ref: CFPublic2
    Export:
      Name: 'exCFPublic2SubnetId'
  CFPrivate1Id:
    Description: Private Subnet 1 Id
    Value:
      Ref: CFPrivate1
    Export:
      Name: 'exCFPrivate1SubnetId'
  CFPrivate2Id:
    Description: Private Subnet 2 Id
    Value:
      Ref: CFPrivate2
    Export:
      Name: 'exCFPrivate2SubnetId'
  myCFSecurityGroupId:
    Description: Security Group for VPC
    Value:
      Ref: myCFSecurityGroup
    Export:
      Name: 'exCFSecurityGroupId'
```

`myCFVPCId` is the logical name in the output section for the VPC, which will be given a value from `Ref: myCFVPC`. To export this variable from this template to the other template, you can specify the export parameter, as shown, and give a name to the variable that it can be exported as. That's the name the other template will be using. Similarly, review other output variables and export values in the template. You can save the whole template as `basenetwork.txt` on your desktop and proceed to the next section.

Validating a base network template

Once the template has been created, whether it is YAML or JSON, you must ensure that the template is in a valid format. You can do this easily at the PowerShell prompt using `Test-CFNTemplate`. This cmdlet lets you validate the template on your local desktop, or you can specify the `TemplateURL` switch to validate it from the S3. In the example, we are using only the `TemplateBody` switch.

You can get all the cmdlets that you can make use of in regard to CloudFormation using the following command:

```
PS C:\> Get-Command *-CF*
```

To validate the template, you can run the following command:

```
PS C:\> $vpcstack=(Get-Content -Raw D:\scripts\basenetwork.txt)
PS C:\> Test-CFNTemplate -TemplateBody $vpcstack
```

```
PS C:\> $vpcstack=(Get-Content -Raw D:\scripts\basenetwork.txt)
PS C:\> Test-CFNTemplate -TemplateBody $vpcstack


Capabilities       : {}
CapabilitiesReason :
DeclaredTransforms : {}
Description        : Creating Base Network for Application
Parameters         : {VPCCIDRRange, PublicSubnetCIDR1, PrivateSubnetCIDR1, PrivateSubnetCIDR2...}
```

Cmdlet `Test-CFNTemplate` first checks whether the template is valid JSON. If not, then it checks whether it is a valid YAML. Otherwise, it returns an error. Note that, `Test-CFNTemplate` only checks for the valid format of the file; it does not validate the property attribute. You must ensure that properties are written correctly in the template. Now it's time to run the template and spin up your stacks.

Running a base network template

The `New-CFNStack` cmdlet lets you submit the template to create the stack. If there are any property issues at any stage of the operation, it will roll back the whole stack. Otherwise, you should get a CREATE COMPLETE message in the stack events. In this case, you can also make use of the `TemplateURL` switch if your template is available in S3. In the template created, you have five input variables. You can define the values of those input variables by creating the new object using class `Amazon.CloudFormation.Model.Parameter`.

```
$vpcstack=(Get-Content -Raw D:\scripts\basenetwork.txt)
$p1 = New-Object -Type Amazon.CloudFormation.Model.Parameter
$p1.ParameterKey = "VPCCIDRRange"
$p1.ParameterValue = "10.12.0.0/16"
$p2 = New-Object -Type Amazon.CloudFormation.Model.Parameter
$p2.ParameterKey = "PublicSubnetCIDR1"
$p2.ParameterValue = "10.12.1.0/24"
$p3 = New-Object -Type Amazon.CloudFormation.Model.Parameter
$p3.ParameterKey = "PublicSubnetCIDR2"
$p3.ParameterValue = "10.12.2.0/24"
```

```
$p4 = New-Object -Type Amazon.CloudFormation.Model.Parameter
$p4.ParameterKey = "PrivateSubnetCIDR1"
$p4.ParameterValue = "10.12.3.0/24"
$p5 = New-Object -Type Amazon.CloudFormation.Model.Parameter
$p5.ParameterKey = "PrivateSubnetCIDR2"
$p5.ParameterValue = "10.12.4.0/24"
New-CFNStack -StackName "myVpcStack" -TemplateBody $vpcstack -Parameter
@($p1,$p2,$p3,$p4,$p5) -OnFailure "ROLLBACK"
```

```
PS C:\> $vpcstack=(Get-Content -Raw D:\scripts\basenetwork.txt)
PS C:\> $p1 = New-Object -Type Amazon.CloudFormation.Model.Parameter
PS C:\> $p1.ParameterKey = "VPCCIDRRange"
PS C:\> $p1.ParameterValue = "10.12.0.0/16"
PS C:\> $p2 = New-Object -Type Amazon.CloudFormation.Model.Parameter
PS C:\> $p2.ParameterKey = "PublicSubnetCIDR1"
PS C:\> $p2.ParameterValue = "10.12.1.0/24"
PS C:\> $p3 = New-Object -Type Amazon.CloudFormation.Model.Parameter
PS C:\> $p3.ParameterKey = "PublicSubnetCIDR2"
PS C:\> $p3.ParameterValue = "10.12.2.0/24"
PS C:\> $p4 = New-Object -Type Amazon.CloudFormation.Model.Parameter
PS C:\> $p4.ParameterKey = "PrivateSubnetCIDR1"
PS C:\> $p4.ParameterValue = "10.12.3.0/24"
PS C:\> $p5 = New-Object -Type Amazon.CloudFormation.Model.Parameter
PS C:\> $p5.ParameterKey = "PrivateSubnetCIDR2"
PS C:\> $p5.ParameterValue = "10.12.4.0/24"
PS C:\> New-CFNStack -StackName "myVpcStack" -TemplateBody $vpcstack -Parameter @($p1,$p2,$p3,$p4,$p5) -OnFailure "ROLLBACK"
arn:aws:cloudformation:us-east-1:072316406132:stack/myVpcStack/b24bc180-6c42-11e7-bd57-500c2855d8d1
```

It will take some time to create all the required resources as part of the stack. The more complex it is, the more time it takes. You can view the stack events using the following command:

```
PS C:\> Get-CFNStackEvent -StackName myVpcStack|Format-Table
EventId,ResourceType,ResourceStatus
```

```
PS C:\> Get-CFNStackEvent -StackName myVpcStack|Format-Table EventId,ResourceType,ResourceStatus

EventId                                                               ResourceType                             ResourceStatus
-------                                                               ------------                             --------------
1df4ca80-6c43-11e7-8351-503acac5c0fd                                  AWS::CloudFormation::Stack               CREATE_COMPLETE
myCFNatPrivateRoute-CREATE_COMPLETE-2017-07-19T05:28:34.237Z          AWS::EC2::Route                          CREATE_COMPLETE
myCFNatPrivateRoute-CREATE_IN_PROGRESS-2017-07-19T05:28:17.416Z       AWS::EC2::Route                          CREATE_IN_PROGRESS
myCFNatPrivateRoute-CREATE_IN_PROGRESS-2017-07-19T05:28:16.311Z       AWS::EC2::Route                          CREATE_IN_PROGRESS
myCFNat-CREATE_COMPLETE-2017-07-19T05:28:13.161Z                      AWS::EC2::NatGateway                     CREATE_COMPLETE
myCFSubnetRouteTableAssociation2-CREATE_COMPLETE-2017-07-19T05:26:41.855Z  AWS::EC2::SubnetRouteTableAssociation  CREATE_COMPLETE
myCFSubnetRouteTableAssociation1-CREATE_COMPLETE-2017-07-19T05:26:41.556Z  AWS::EC2::SubnetRouteTableAssociation  CREATE_COMPLETE
myCFSubnetRouteTableAssociation4-CREATE_COMPLETE-2017-07-19T05:26:40.142Z  AWS::EC2::SubnetRouteTableAssociation  CREATE_COMPLETE
myCFSubnetRouteTableAssociation3-CREATE_COMPLETE-2017-07-19T05:26:40.064Z  AWS::EC2::SubnetRouteTableAssociation  CREATE_COMPLETE
myCFSubnetRouteTableAssociation2-CREATE_IN_PROGRESS-2017-07-19T05:26:26.134Z AWS::EC2::SubnetRouteTableAssociation  CREATE_IN_PROGRESS
myCFSubnetRouteTableAssociation1-CREATE_IN_PROGRESS-2017-07-19T05:26:25.758Z AWS::EC2::SubnetRouteTableAssociation  CREATE_IN_PROGRESS
myCFPublicRoute-CREATE_COMPLETE-2017-07-19T05:26:25.509Z              AWS::EC2::Route                          CREATE_COMPLETE
myCFSubnetRouteTableAssociation2-CREATE_IN_PROGRESS-2017-07-19T05:26:25.156Z AWS::EC2::SubnetRouteTableAssociation  CREATE_IN_PROGRESS
myCFNat-CREATE_IN_PROGRESS-2017-07-19T05:26:24.745Z                   AWS::EC2::NatGateway                     CREATE_IN_PROGRESS
myCFSubnetRouteTableAssociation1-CREATE_IN_PROGRESS-2017-07-19T05:26:24.717Z AWS::EC2::SubnetRouteTableAssociation  CREATE_IN_PROGRESS
myCFSubnetRouteTableAssociation4-CREATE_IN_PROGRESS-2017-07-19T05:26:24.577Z AWS::EC2::SubnetRouteTableAssociation  CREATE_IN_PROGRESS
myCFSubnetRouteTableAssociation3-CREATE_IN_PROGRESS-2017-07-19T05:26:24.413Z AWS::EC2::SubnetRouteTableAssociation  CREATE_IN_PROGRESS
myCFNat-CREATE_IN_PROGRESS-2017-07-19T05:26:24.086Z                   AWS::EC2::NatGateway                     CREATE_IN_PROGRESS
myCFSubnetRouteTableAssociation3-CREATE_IN_PROGRESS-2017-07-19T05:26:23.464Z AWS::EC2::SubnetRouteTableAssociation  CREATE_IN_PROGRESS
myCFSubnetRouteTableAssociation4-CREATE_IN_PROGRESS-2017-07-19T05:26:23.442Z AWS::EC2::SubnetRouteTableAssociation  CREATE_IN_PROGRESS
```

I have trimmed the output here. You will see a longer listing. It will show you all the events that happened during the stack creation process. Overall, the whole stack for the base network took just less than two minutes for me. You can now check your output variables returned by this stack.

```
PS C:\> (Get-CFNStack -StackName myVpcStack).Outputs
```

```
PS C:\> (Get-CFNStack -StackName myVpcStack).Outputs

Description              OutputKey              OutputValue
-----------              ---------              -----------
VPC Id                   myCFVPCId              vpc-b3d3b6ca
Private Subnet 1 Id      CFPrivate1Id           subnet-ee9f02c2
Private Subnet 2 Id      CFPrivate2Id           subnet-bd2470f5
Public Subnet 2 Id       CFPublic2Id            subnet-ac396de4
Public Subnet 1 Id       CFPublic1Id            subnet-c89e03e4
Security Group for VPC myCFSecurityGroupId sg-15d58564
```

As you mention values to be exported from the base network stack, you can check them using the following command:

```
PS C:\> Get-CFNExport
```

```
PS C:\> Get-CFNExport

ExportingStackId                                                                                                        Name                  Value
----------------                                                                                                        ----                  -----
arn:aws:cloudformation:us-east-1:072316406132:stack/myVpcStack/b24bc180-6c42-11e7-bd57-500c2855d8d1 exCFPrivate1SubnetId subnet-ee9f02c2
arn:aws:cloudformation:us-east-1:072316406132:stack/myVpcStack/b24bc180-6c42-11e7-bd57-500c2855d8d1 exCFPrivate2SubnetId subnet-bd2470f5
arn:aws:cloudformation:us-east-1:072316406132:stack/myVpcStack/b24bc180-6c42-11e7-bd57-500c2855d8d1 exCFPublic1SubnetId  subnet-c89e03e4
arn:aws:cloudformation:us-east-1:072316406132:stack/myVpcStack/b24bc180-6c42-11e7-bd57-500c2855d8d1 exCFPublic2SubnetId  subnet-ac396de4
arn:aws:cloudformation:us-east-1:072316406132:stack/myVpcStack/b24bc180-6c42-11e7-bd57-500c2855d8d1 exCFSecurityGroupId  sg-15d58564
arn:aws:cloudformation:us-east-1:072316406132:stack/myVpcStack/b24bc180-6c42-11e7-bd57-500c2855d8d1 exmyCFVPC             vpc-b3d3b6ca
```

Note that these exported values are region specific and need to be unique.

Creating an EC2 instance using CloudFormation

Your base network stack is now available and you can now run the EC2 instance in the VPC that you created. In this example, let's assume that you want to install nginx web server on the EC2 as part of the bootstrapping process and spin up the EC2 in the first public subnet that you created as part of the above stack. You will want to input only instance type and AMI ID to the stack. Your template should reference the values for the Security Group and first public subnet exported from the base network stack.

In order to achieve this, you can build the stack as follows:

```yaml
---
AWSTemplateFormatVersion: "2010-09-09"
Description: Creating EC2 Instance using CloudFormation
Parameters:
  myAMIId:
    Description: My AMI Id
    Type: String
  InstanceType:
    Type: String
    Default: t2.large
    AllowedValues:
      - t2.nano
      - t2.micro
      - t2.small
      - t2.large
Resources:
  MyEc2Instance:
    Type: AWS::EC2::Instance
    Properties:
      ImageId:
        Ref: myAMIId
      InstanceType:
        Ref: InstanceType
      KeyName: MyWebPressApp
      NetworkInterfaces:
        - AssociatePublicIpAddress: "true"
          DeviceIndex: "0"
          GroupSet:
            - !ImportValue 'exCFSecurityGroupId'
          SubnetId: !ImportValue 'exCFPublic1SubnetId'
      UserData:
        Fn::Base64: |
          #! /bin/bash -xe
          yum install nginx -y
          sudo service nginx start
Outputs:
  MyEC2InstancePublicIP:
    Description: My EC2 Instance Public IP
    Value: !GetAtt MyEc2Instance.PublicIp
  MyEC2InstanceID:
    Description: My EC2 Instance ID
    Value: !Ref MyEc2Instance
```

In the parameters section, you see that you have the AllowedValues attribute, which allows you to define the list of values that parameters can accept. Resource type AWS::EC2::Instance lets you spin up the EC2 instance considering the properties mentioned. !ImportValue is nothing but the short form of Fn::ImportValue in YAML format. You will see that both the exported values exCFSecurityGroupId and exCFPublic1SubnetId are imported in this template using !ImportValue. As a special mention, GroupSet indicates the Security Group IDs list and, because it's a list, you see it in a special way mentioned with a dash (–). Userdata properties need to be encoded using Fn::Base64. The lines added in the userdata section are an installation of the nginx web server and start the nginx service. Save this file as EC2AppServer.txt on your desktop or whenever that you prefer.

To validate the template, you can use the following command:

```
PS C:\> $ec2stack=(Get-Content -Raw D:\scripts\EC2AppServer.txt)
PS C:\> Test-CFNTemplate -TemplateBody $ec2stack
```

```
PS C:\> $ec2stack=(Get-Content -Raw D:\scripts\EC2AppServer.txt)
PS C:\> Test-CFNTemplate -TemplateBody $ec2stack


Capabilities         : {}
CapabilitiesReason   :
DeclaredTransforms   : {}
Description          : Creating EC2 Instance using CloudFormation
Parameters           : {myAMIId, InstanceType}
```

To submit the stack, you can run the following command:

```
PS C:\> $p1 = New-Object -Type Amazon.CloudFormation.Model.Parameter
PS C:\> $p1.ParameterKey = "myAMIId"
PS C:\> $p1.ParameterValue = "ami-a4c7edb2"
PS C:\> $p2 = New-Object -Type Amazon.CloudFormation.Model.Parameter
PS C:\> $p2.ParameterKey = "InstanceType"
PS C:\> $p2.ParameterValue = "t2.large"
PS C:\> New-CFNStack -StackName EC2AppServer -TemplateBody $ec2stack -
Parameter @($p1,$p2) -OnFailure "ROLLBACK"
```

```
PS C:\> $p1 = New-Object -Type Amazon.CloudFormation.Model.Parameter
PS C:\> $p1.ParameterKey = "myAMIId"
PS C:\> $p1.ParameterValue = "ami-a4c7edb2"
PS C:\> $p2 = New-Object -Type Amazon.CloudFormation.Model.Parameter
PS C:\> $p2.ParameterKey = "InstanceType"
PS C:\> $p2.ParameterValue = "t2.large"
PS C:\> New-CFNStack -StackName EC2AppServer -TemplateBody $ec2stack -Parameter @($p1,$p2) -OnFailure "ROLLBACK"
arn:aws:cloudformation:us-east-1:072316406132:stack/EC2AppServer/30507b50-6c4a-11e7-954a-500c28604c82
```

In this case, AMI ID and instance type are supplied as input parameters to the stack. You can track the stack events using the following command:

```
PS C:\> Get-CFNStackEvent -StackName myEC2Instance|Format-Table
EventId,ResourceType,ResourceStatus
```

```
PS C:\> Get-CFNStackEvent -StackName EC2AppServer|Format-Table EventId,ResourceType,ResourceStatus

EventId                                          ResourceType                     ResourceStatus
-------                                          ------------                     --------------
3b145f20-6c4a-11e7-be2a-500c28b4e461             AWS::CloudFormation::Stack CREATE_COMPLETE
MyEc2Instance-CREATE_COMPLETE-2017-07-19T06:19:30.509Z  AWS::EC2::Instance        CREATE_COMPLETE
MyEc2Instance-CREATE_IN_PROGRESS-2017-07-19T06:19:21.058Z AWS::EC2::Instance      CREATE_IN_PROGRESS
MyEc2Instance-CREATE_IN_PROGRESS-2017-07-19T06:19:19.529Z AWS::EC2::Instance      CREATE_IN_PROGRESS
3051b3d0-6c4a-11e7-954a-500c28604c82             AWS::CloudFormation::Stack CREATE_IN_PROGRESS
```

When you see `ResourceType AWS::CloudFormation::Stack` and `ResourceStatus` as `CREATE_COMPLETE`, it means that stack execution has completed successfully. If the stack is rolling back because of some issues, those events will be published in this list. To get the list of output variables that are defined in `EC2AppServer`, you can use the following command:

```
PS C:\> (Get-CFNStack -StackName EC2AppServer).Outputs
```

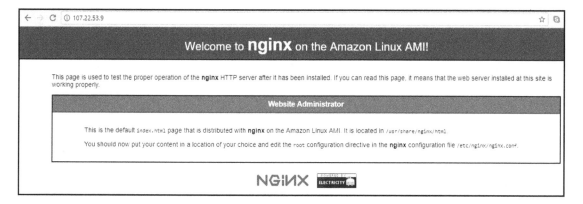

The output suggests that the instance ID is `i-0b01a6ffdd9172756` and the public IP is `107.22.53.9`. You can simply hop on to the browser and type the IP that is seen in this case. You will get a sample **nginx** website page.

If you get this page, it means that your userdata script worked as part of the bootstrapping process. Another way to get the status is to run the `Invoke-Webrequest` cmdlet.

```
PS C:\> Invoke-Webrequest 107.22.53.9
```

`StatusCode 200` is an indication that the web server `nginx` was installed successfully as part of the bootstrapping.

Nested stack

CloudFormation adoption is increasing. So, the complexity of the stack is also increasing. Nested stacks are the stack inside the stack which help you to bring in the modular approach of defining the stack, so that common functionality can be achieved using a single stack across multiple environments. This helps you to reduce the number of stacks that you maintain in your environment. You reference the other stack in the main stack by using the resource type `AWS::CloudFormation::Stack`. Here is the main stack example, which gives you a way to use `myVPC.template` and `mySubnets.template` inside your main code and access the values from the child stack.

```
---
AWSTemplateFormatVersion: "2010-09-09"
Description: Demo of nested stack template
Resources:
  ChildStack01:
    Type: AWS::CloudFormation::Stack
    Properties: "https://s3.amazonaws.com/cloudformation-templates-us-east-1/myVPC.template"
    TimeoutInMinutes: 60
  ChildStack02:
    Type: AWS::CloudFormation::Stack
    Properties: "https://s3.amazonaws.com/cloudformation-templates-us-east-1/mySubnets.template"
    TimeoutInMinutes: 60
    Parameters:
      VpcID: Fn::GetAtt : [ "ChildStack01", "Outputs.VpcID" ]

Outputs:
  StackRef:
    value:
      Ref: ChildStack02
  OutputFromNestedStack:
    value:
      Fn::GetAtt: [ "ChildStack02", "Outputs.SubnetID" ]
```

`TimeoutInMinutes` indicates the wait time for the nested stack to reach `CREATE_COMPLETE` state. In this example, you see `ChildStack01` output `VpcID` was passed as a parameter to `ChildStack02`, and `ChildStack02` output `SubnetID` was passed to `Outputs`.

Stack policies

Stack policies are similar to policies that we learnt in IAM and S3. These are mostly used to control which resources can be updated and by what actions. When setting a stack policy, all resources become protected by default and you must explicitly allow an action on a resource. Stack policies apply to all the users who try to update the stack. By default, if there is no stack policy defined, then all update actions are allowed on all resources. Any IAM user with permissions to perform stack updates can update all the resources.

You could write a JSON document something like the following and attach this policy to the stack.

```
{
"Statement"    :[
    {
        "Effect":"Allow",
        "Action":"Update:*",
        "Principal":"*",
        "Resource":"*"
    },
    {
        "Effect":"Deny",
        "Action":"Update:*",
        "Principal":"*",
        "Resource":"LogicalResourceId/EC2Instance"
    }
]
}
```

The first statement allows all update actions on all resources. The second statement denies all update actions on the EC2Instance resource referenced by logical ID. Overall, this policy allows all update actions on all resources except the EC2Instance logical resource ID in your stack. There are two switches, StackPolicyBody and StackPolicyURL, which you can use with New-CFNStack at the time of stack creation. The Update-CFNStack cmdlet lest you update the stack policy if your resources are already running. Update-CFNStack also has the same two switches.

Helper scripts

CloudFormation provides four helper scripts. These helper scripts can be called directly from your template. These helper scripts are preinstalled on Amazon Linux AMI and are found in /opt/aws/bin. These scripts can be installed on Windows using Python.

- cfn-init: This helper script can fetch and parse template metadata from templates and use that data to install packages, create and write files to disk, enable/disable, and start/stop services.
- cfn-signal: This helper script is used to signal back to a stack a success or failure. Once actions are complete, you can signal back their success to the stack. If an action could not be completed, you can signal back its failure to the stack.
- cfn-hup: This helper script is a daemon that detects changes in resource metadata and then runs actions when a change is detected.
- cfn-get-metadata: This helper script is used to get a metadata block from CloudFormation and print it out to standard output.

Dropping the template

`Remove-CFNStack` lets you delete the stack and associated resources. If you are trying to delete a stack which has been referenced in another stack, CloudFormation does no action on that stack. You must ensure that there are no references for the stack that you are planning to delete. This operation cleans up all the resources that are spun by the stack. You can use the following command:

```
PS C:\> Remove-CFNStack -StackName EC2AppServer
```

```
PS C:\> Remove-CFNStack -StackName EC2AppServer

Confirm
Are you sure you want to perform this action?
Performing the operation "Remove-CFNStack (DeleteStack)" on target "EC2AppServer".
[Y] Yes  [A] Yes to All  [N] No  [L] No to All  [S] Suspend  [?] Help (default is "Y"): Y
PS C:\>
PS C:\> Get-CFNStackEvent -StackName EC2AppServer|Format-Table EventId,ResourceType,ResourceStatus

EventId                                             ResourceType                  ResourceStatus
-------                                             ------------                  --------------
MyEc2Instance-DELETE_IN_PROGRESS-2017-07-19T11:16:09.666Z AWS::EC2::Instance      DELETE_IN_PROGRESS
a91a2030-6c73-11e7-ba18-500c217b26c6                AWS::CloudFormation::Stack  DELETE_IN_PROGRESS
3b145f20-6c4a-11e7-be2a-500c28b4e461                AWS::CloudFormation::Stack  CREATE_COMPLETE
MyEc2Instance-CREATE_COMPLETE-2017-07-19T06:19:30.509Z    AWS::EC2::Instance      CREATE_COMPLETE
MyEc2Instance-CREATE_IN_PROGRESS-2017-07-19T06:19:21.058Z AWS::EC2::Instance      CREATE_IN_PROGRESS
MyEc2Instance-CREATE_IN_PROGRESS-2017-07-19T06:19:19.529Z AWS::EC2::Instance      CREATE_IN_PROGRESS
3051b3d0-6c4a-11e7-954a-500c28604c82                AWS::CloudFormation::Stack  CREATE_IN_PROGRESS
```

Summary

AWS CloudFormation is increasing in popularity, as it provides the way to define a consistent and repeatable environment. You can do all the things that you can do either on the AWS Console or through CLI. You learnt the required details to build the stack and created the base network and one EC2 instance as an example. CloudFormation documentation is vast and not all the aspects of writing the YAML CloudFormation template are covered here. But this chapter will definitely help you to groom your skills in building the CloudFormation template. When building templates, intrinsic functions are key to capture the runtime values and perform an action based on the value. Understand those intrinsic functions. We have touched base on nested stack and cross stack references, which help you bring modularity into the CloudFormation template. In the next chapter, you will learn about the AWS monitoring service CloudWatch.

15
AWS CloudWatch

AWS provides a number of different services for different purposes. Monitoring AWS services that you use for your consumption is key to efficient and cost-effective service delivery. In order to monitor your AWS infrastructure, AWS provides a built-in service called **CloudWatch**. In this chapter, we will learn key elements of CloudWatch and how this service can be used for your day-to-day monitoring.

In this chapter, we will discuss CloudWatch monitoring service, the types of CloudWatch monitoring available, CloudWatch alarm state, simple notification service, monitoring EC2 instances using CloudWatch and creating custom metrics in CloudWatch for EC2. In addition, we will learn how to monitor RDS DB instances and setting up CloudWatch logs for application logs.

CloudWatch

CloudWatch is a built-in native service provided by AWS for monitoring your AWS infrastructure. Almost every other service that is supported by the AWS Cloud can be monitored using CloudWatch. In fact, it is highly integrated with other services, for which you do not need any plugins. CloudWatch has two important aspects that you must understand: metrics and alarm. We could say that CloudWatch is a collection of metrics repository for the services and products that you use on the AWS Cloud.

Alarms are kind of triggers that initiate action depending on the threshold that you define on the metrics data set for the specific dimension. At a high level, here is how CloudWatch works.

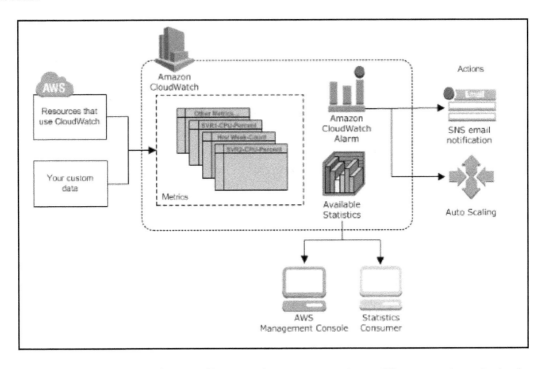

As mentioned, CloudWatch is a collection of metrics repository. These metrics exist in the region in which they are created. Metric data is retained for 15 months by AWS for historical analysis. Metric data older than 15 months is automatically purged and the metrics will no longer be available if no new data comes in. As we learnt in the Auto Scaling chapter, dynamic scaling of the fleet is totally managed via the CloudWatch alarm. In addition, alarms can talk to the notification service to notify the group of subscribers about the breach of the threshold so that the support staff can action the item and take the appropriate proactive precaution. You can review the statistics for the given metric on the dashboard. The AWS CloudWatch dashboard is the best place to review the data points in graphical format.

Types of CloudWatch monitoring

There are basically two types of monitoring available. In both cases, you do not need to install an agent on the guest operating system.

- **Basic monitoring**: It is collected at 5-minute intervals. Basic monitoring gives you visibility into a limited set of metrics, such as CPU utilization, disk activity, and network activity. Status check metrics are included in basic monitoring. Status check metrics indicate the relationship between EC instances and the underlying hypervisor. If the hypervisor deems an EC2 instance to be unhealthy, the status check metrics will show that status.

- **Detailed monitoring**: If the 5-minute interval does not provide the granularity of data you need, it is possible to enable detailed monitoring, which collects additional data points at 1-minute intervals. Detailed monitoring comes with an extra cost. With this type of monitoring, you get all that you get with basic monitoring. As there is a cost associated with detailed monitoring, you can enable it only on the required servers for better cost control.

CloudWatch alarm states

Before using CloudWatch, it's important to understand CloudWatch alarm states in more detail. Understanding these alarm states will allow you use CloudWatch more optimally. It has three possible states: ALARM, INSUFFICIENT_DATA, and OK.

- ALARM: This state indicates that the threshold defined for the specific CloudWatch alarm has breached the threshold value. For example, if you are monitoring the CPU utilization of the server and define an alarm to notify you when the CPU utilization goes beyond 75 percent, then as soon as the server has over 75 percent utilization of the CPU, CloudWatch will trigger an alarm, and the state of the alarm will be ALARM. You may want to be notified when the alarm is in this state.

- INSUFFICIENT_DATA: This state indicates that CloudWatch did not have sufficient data for the number of consecutive periods defined during the alarm creation definition. When such a thing happens, the state of the alarm will be INSUFFICIENT_DATA. For example, you are monitoring the CPU utilization of the server, but the server was accidentally shutdown by some process, then the alarm state would be INSUFFICIENT_DATA. You may want to be notified when the alarm is in this state.

- OK: This indicates that CloudWatch is getting data points continuously and there are no breaches of the thresholds. Relating this to the CPU utilization case mentioned, if it is under 75 percent all the time, the alarm state will be OK.

Simple Notification Service

AWS **Simple Notification Service** (**SNS**) is a messaging service. SNS coordinates and manages the sending and delivery of messages to specific endpoints. Endpoints are the targets where notifications need to be sent out. You can use SNS to receive notifications when an event occurs in your AWS environment. SNS is integrated into many AWS services, so it is easy to set up notifications based on events that occur in those services. With CloudWatch and SNS, full environment monitoring solutions can be created that notify developers, administrators, or IT staff about various issues in the environment. It is not just related to issues, but you can also extend the CloudFormation template capability to notify other resources based on the stack components it creates. The more you use this service, the more you become a fan of it.

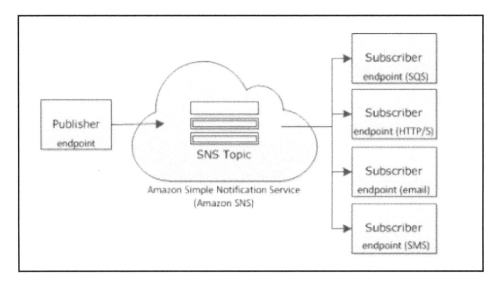

There are three basic elements of the SNS service that you must be aware of. This service makes use of the publish-subscribe model.

- **Publisher**: This is an entity that triggers the sending of a message. This can be an S3 event, human, or CloudWatch alarm.
- **Subscription**: This is an endpoint where the message is sent. Available endpoints are HTTP, HTTPS, email, Email-JSON, SQS, Lambda, application, mobile app, and SMS.
- **Topic**: This represents the group of subscribers that you send a message to.

Creating SNS topics

Before we continue creating alarms, let's create the SNS topic and subscribe an email to it. To get a list of all the cmdlets related to SNS, you can run the following command:

```
PS C:\> Get-Command *-SNS*
```

To list existing SNS topics, you can use the following command:

```
PS C:\> Get-SNSTopic
```

New-SNSTopic lets you create a topic to which notifications can be published. You can create maximum of 100,000 topics. If the topic that you create already exists then no error will be returned. Instead, you will be provided with a topic ARN. Let's create a topic called PowerShellSNS.

```
PS C:\> New-SNSTopic -Name PowerShellSNS
```

```
PS C:\> New-SNSTopic -Name PowerShellSNS
arn:aws:sns:us-east-1:072316406132:PowerShellSNS
PS C:\>
PS C:\> New-SNSTopic -Name PowerShellSNS
arn:aws:sns:us-east-1:072316406132:PowerShellSNS
PS C:\>
```

You might have noticed that, when I ran the same cmdlet with the same topic name, no error was returned.

Subscribing to the topic

In order to register a subscriber with the topic created, let's make use of the AWS Console instead of the PowerShell cmdlet. I have not found an easy way of doing this via PowerShell. First, navigate to the messaging service on the console and get on the SNS dashboard. Then, click on **Subscriptions** and hit the **Create subscription** button. It will prompt you to enter the following details, as shown. Fill in the required details.

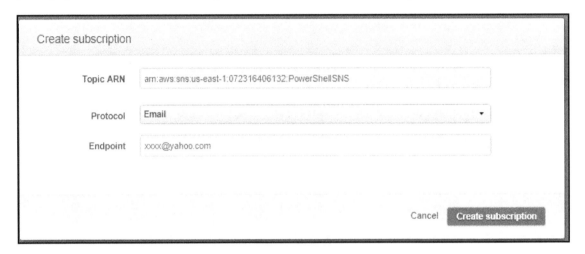

Replace xxxx@yahoo.com with your email ID for testing. You should receive an email asking you to confirm the subscription. Just click on the confirmation link and you should receive the alert as and when it is sent to the topic. Topic ARN is the one that you get when you create the topic.

To test, make use of the Publish-SNSMessage cmdlet to see if you are receiving messages. To do this, you can use the following command:

```
PS C:\> Publish-SNSMessage -TopicArn arn:aws:sns:us-
east-1:<account_no>:PowerShellSNS -Message "This is test from powershell" -
Subject "Welcome to Powershell"
```

You should receive an email from AWS with the content that you passed on in the preceding cmdlet. I received the message as follows. You will always get a link to unsubscribe if you need to do so.

With this, your SNS topic will be ready.

Monitoring EC2 instances

To monitor EC2 instances, it is good to monitor the status checks metrics in addition to default metrics or some custom metrics. AWS does not provide an in-built way to monitor memory utilization, swap utilization, or disk utilization, but they do provide the script so that you can create the required metrics and publish them to CloudWatch. Once you have the metric data available in CloudWatch, you can create an alarm and get notified. There are two types of system checks available for EC2 instances.

- **System status checks**: Things that are outside of your control are indicated by this status check. These include:
  - Loss of system power
  - Hardware issues on the physical host
  - Software issues on the physical host
  - Loss of network connectivity

  In order to solve this status check, you must stop and restart the EC instance. This way, AWS will launch an EC2 instance on different hardware.

- **Instance status checks**: These are indications of software issues that we can control. These include:
  - Corrupted file system
  - Exhausted memory
  - Incompatible kernel
  - Failed system status checks
  - Misconfigured networking
  - Misconfigured startup configuration

  In order to solve this status check, you must reboot the EC2 instance or fix the filesystem related configuration issues.

By default, CloudWatch monitors metrics that can be viewed at the host level and not at the software level. Default metrics on EC2 instances are:

- CPU credit balance
- CPU credit usage
- CPU utilization
- Network in/out

To monitor OS-level metrics, you must install the Perl script provided by AWS. These metrics provide you with the ability to monitor:

- Memory utilization, memory used, and memory available
- Disk swap utilization
- Disk space utilization, disk space used, and disk space available

Creating an alarm for an EC2 instance

As discussed, AWS provides in-built metrics for EC2 instances. Before creating an alarm, first let's find out the metrics that are provided by AWS for a specific EC2 Instance. For demonstration, I have an EC2 instance running in my account, which is running Amazon Linux. To find out all the default metrics related to the EC2 instance, you can use the cmdlet `Get-CWMetricList`. It will list all the default metrics provided for the specific EC2 instance.

```
PS C:\> $p1 = New-Object Amazon.CloudWatch.Model.DimensionFilter
PS C:\> $p1.Name = "InstanceId"
PS C:\> $p1.Value = "i-09ca5e201782643e7"
PS C:\> Get-CWMetricList -Namespace "AWS/EC2" -Dimension $p1
```

```
PS C:\> $p1 = New-Object Amazon.CloudWatch.Model.DimensionFilter
PS C:\> $p1.Name = "InstanceId"
PS C:\> $p1.Value = "i-09ca5e201782643e7"
PS C:\> Get-CWMetricList -Namespace "AWS/EC2" -Dimension $p1

Dimensions    MetricName                     Namespace
----------    ----------                     ---------
{InstanceId}  StatusCheckFailed_System       AWS/EC2
{InstanceId}  DiskWriteBytes                 AWS/EC2
{InstanceId}  DiskWriteOps                   AWS/EC2
{InstanceId}  NetworkPacketsIn               AWS/EC2
{InstanceId}  NetworkIn                      AWS/EC2
{InstanceId}  DiskReadOps                    AWS/EC2
{InstanceId}  StatusCheckFailed              AWS/EC2
{InstanceId}  DiskReadBytes                  AWS/EC2
{InstanceId}  NetworkOut                     AWS/EC2
{InstanceId}  NetworkPacketsOut              AWS/EC2
{InstanceId}  CPUCreditUsage                 AWS/EC2
{InstanceId}  CPUCreditBalance               AWS/EC2
{InstanceId}  CPUUtilization                 AWS/EC2
{InstanceId}  StatusCheckFailed_Instance     AWS/EC2
```

You have to use a filter, as shown preceding, to get the list for the specific instance. You can see that there are 14 different types of metrics provided for the EC2 instance. Because you know the list and the metrics provided, you can further narrow down your search for an instance for a specific `MetricName CPUUtilization`. This can be done as shown:

```
PS C:\> $p1 = New-Object Amazon.CloudWatch.Model.DimensionFilter
PS C:\> $p1.Name = "InstanceId"
PS C:\> $p1.Value = "i-09ca5e201782643e7"
PS C:\> $p2 = New-Object Amazon.CloudWatch.Model.DimensionFilter
PS C:\> $p2.Name = "MetricName"
PS C:\> $p2.Value = "CPUUtilization"
PS C:\> Get-CWMetricList -Namespace "AWS/EC2" -Dimension $p1,$p2
```

```
PS C:\> $p1 = New-Object Amazon.CloudWatch.Model.DimensionFilter
PS C:\> $p1.Name = "InstanceId"
PS C:\> $p1.Value = "i-09ca5e201782643e7"
PS C:\> $p2 = New-Object Amazon.CloudWatch.Model.DimensionFilter
PS C:\> $p2.Name = "MetricName"
PS C:\> $p2.Value = "CPUUtilization"
PS C:\> Get-CWMetricList -Namespace "AWS/EC2" -Dimension $p1,$p2

Dimensions    MetricName      Namespace
----------    ----------      ---------
{InstanceId}  CPUUtilization  AWS/EC2
```

Let's create an alarm on the `MetricName` `CPUUtilization` for an EC2 instance under consideration in this case. You can create an alarm using the `Write-CWMetricAlarm` cmdlet.

```
PS C:\> $powershellsns="arn:aws:sns:us-east-1:<account_no>:PowerShellSNS"
PS C:\> $p1 = New-Object Amazon.CloudWatch.Model.Dimension
PS C:\> $p1.Name = "InstanceId"
PS C:\> $p1.Value = "i-09ca5e201782643e7"
PS C:\> $p2 = New-Object Amazon.CloudWatch.Model.Dimension
PS C:\> $p2.Name = "MetricName"
PS C:\> $p2.Value = "CPUUtilization"
PS C:\> Write-CWMetricAlarm -Namespace "AWS/EC2" -MetricName
"CPUUtilization" -AlarmName "WebAppServerCPU" -AlarmDescription "Alarm for
WebApp CPU" -AlarmAction $powershellsns -Dimension $p1,$p2 -
EvaluationPeriod 1 -Statistic "Average" -Threshold 50 -Period 300 -
ComparisonOperator "GreaterThanOrEqualToThreshold"
```

```
PS C:\> $powershellsns="arn:aws:sns:us-east-1:072316406132:PowerShellSNS"
PS C:\> $p1 = New-Object Amazon.CloudWatch.Model.Dimension
PS C:\> $p1.Name = "InstanceId"
PS C:\> $p1.Value = "i-09ca5e201782643e7"
PS C:\> $p2 = New-Object Amazon.CloudWatch.Model.Dimension
PS C:\> $p2.Name = "MetricName"
PS C:\> $p2.Value = "CPUUtilization"
PS C:\> Write-CWMetricAlarm -Namespace "AWS/EC2" -MetricName "CPUUtilization" -AlarmName "WebAppServerCPU" `
>> -AlarmDescription "Alarm for WebApp CPU" -AlarmAction $powershellsns -Dimension $p1 -EvaluationPeriod 1 `
>> -Statistic "Average" -Threshold 50 -Period 300 -ComparisonOperator "GreaterThanOrEqualToThreshold"
PS C:\>
```

To clarify the switches used in cmdlet, `Namespace` is a kind of indication of a specific AWS service and they use some notation. In this case, you can see that the AWS EC2 compute service notation used for namespace is AWS/EC2. You can find details in regard to this one in the AWS documentation. As we are mostly focusing on EC2, I have made use of AWS/EC2. So, the namespace value for all the EC2 instances for which you will create an alarm is AWS/EC2.

`MetricName` is picked up from the default list, as preceding. `AlarmName` is something you use to identify an alarm. Come up with an operational practice to name an alarm in your environment. `AlarmAction` indicates an action that the alarm should take when breached. In this case, we are sending a notification to the SNS topic that we created earlier. There are some more automatic actions that you can take, such as instance stop, terminate, recover, and reboot. Review the documentation for this and tweak as per your need.

`EvaluationPeriod` indicates the number of periods over which data is compared to the specified threshold. The threshold is the value against which the specific statistics are compared. Valid values for statistics are average, minimum, maximum, samplecount, and sum. Period indicates the duration in seconds over which the specified statistics are applied. The other switches are self-explanatory. You can check the status of the alarm now by using the following command:

```
PS C:\> Get-CWAlarm |Format-Table AlarmName,MetricName,StateValue,
ActionsEnabled
```

```
PS C:\> Get-CWAlarm |Format-Table AlarmName,MetricName,StateValue, ActionsEnabled

AlarmName       MetricName     StateValue         ActionsEnabled
---------       ----------     ----------         --------------
WebAppServerCPU CPUUtilization INSUFFICIENT_DATA          True
```

`StateValue` is in `INSUFFICIENT_DATA` state and, by default, alarm is enabled. Likewise, you can create an alarm for an instance status check and system status check. You can do this as shown here:

```
PS C:\> $powershellsns="arn:aws:sns:us-east-1:<account_no>:PowerShellSNS"
PS C:\> $p1 = New-Object Amazon.CloudWatch.Model.Dimension
PS C:\> $p1.Name = "InstanceId"
PS C:\> $p1.Value = "i-09ca5e201782643e7"
PS C:\> $p2 = New-Object Amazon.CloudWatch.Model.Dimension
PS C:\> $p2.Name = "MetricName"
PS C:\> $p2.Value = "StatusCheckFailed_Instance"
PS C:\> Write-CWMetricAlarm -Namespace "AWS/EC2" -MetricName
"StatusCheckFailed_Instance"  -AlarmName "WebAppServerInstanceSysChk" -
AlarmDescription "Alarm for Instance Status Check" -AlarmAction
$powershellsns -Dimension $p1 -EvaluationPeriod 1 -Statistic "Average" -
Threshold 1 -Period 300 -ComparisonOperator "GreaterThanOrEqualToThreshold"
PS C:\> $powershellsns="arn:aws:sns:us-east-1:<account_no>:PowerShellSNS"
PS C:\> $p1 = New-Object Amazon.CloudWatch.Model.Dimension
PS C:\> $p1.Name = "InstanceId"
PS C:\> $p1.Value = "i-09ca5e201782643e7"
PS C:\> $p2 = New-Object Amazon.CloudWatch.Model.Dimension
PS C:\> $p2.Name = "MetricName"
PS C:\> $p2.Value = "StatusCheckFailed_System"
PS C:\> Write-CWMetricAlarm -Namespace "AWS/EC2" -MetricName
"StatusCheckFailed_System" -AlarmName "WebAppServerSystemSysChk" -
AlarmDescription "Alarm for System Status Check" -AlarmAction
$powershellsns -Dimension $p1 -EvaluationPeriod 1 -Statistic "Average" -
Threshold 1 -Period 300 -ComparisonOperator "GreaterThanOrEqualToThreshold"
```

```
PS C:\> $powershellsns="arn:aws:sns:us-east-1:072316406132:PowerShellSNS"
PS C:\> $p1 = New-Object Amazon.CloudWatch.Model.Dimension
PS C:\> $p1.Name = "InstanceId"
PS C:\> $p1.Value = "i-09ca5e201782643e7"
PS C:\> $p2 = New-Object Amazon.CloudWatch.Model.Dimension
PS C:\> $p2.Name = "MetricName"
PS C:\> $p2.Value = "StatusCheckFailed_Instance"
PS C:\> Write-CWMetricAlarm -Namespace "AWS/EC2" -MetricName "StatusCheckFailed_Instance" `
>> -AlarmName "WebAppServerInstanceSysChk" -AlarmDescription "Alarm for Instance Status Check" `
>> -AlarmAction $powershellsns -Dimension $p1 -EvaluationPeriod 1 -Statistic "Average" `
>> -Threshold 1 -Period 300 -ComparisonOperator "GreaterThanOrEqualToThreshold"
PS C:\>
PS C:\> $powershellsns="arn:aws:sns:us-east-1:072316406132:PowerShellSNS"
PS C:\> $p1 = New-Object Amazon.CloudWatch.Model.Dimension
PS C:\> $p1.Name = "InstanceId"
PS C:\> $p1.Value = "i-09ca5e201782643e7"
PS C:\> $p2 = New-Object Amazon.CloudWatch.Model.Dimension
PS C:\> $p2.Name = "MetricName"
PS C:\> $p2.Value = "StatusCheckFailed_System"
PS C:\> Write-CWMetricAlarm -Namespace "AWS/EC2" -MetricName "StatusCheckFailed_System" `
>> -AlarmName "WebAppServerSystemSysChk" -AlarmDescription "Alarm for System Status Check" `
>> -AlarmAction $powershellsns -Dimension $p1 -EvaluationPeriod 1 -Statistic "Average" `
>> -Threshold 1 -Period 300 -ComparisonOperator "GreaterThanOrEqualToThreshold"
PS C:\>
```

`Threshold` is defined for the system, and the instance status is 1. That should be OK for you to be notified that there are some issues with the instance. We have already discussed the action that you can take when the system and instance checks fail. You can take those actions that are automatically provided to fit your requirements. So, instead of sending it to the SNS topic, you can initiate the reboot/stop/terminate actions based on a threshold breach.

You can disable and enable individual alarms as shown following:

```
PS C:\> Disable-CWAlarmAction -AlarmName "WebAppServerCPU"
PS C:\> Enable-CWAlarmAction -AlarmName "WebAppServerCPU"
```

```
PS C:\> Disable-CWAlarmAction -AlarmName "WebAppServerCPU"
PS C:\>
PS C:\> Get-CWAlarm |Format-Table AlarmName,MetricName,StateValue, ActionsEnabled

AlarmName                  MetricName                  StateValue         ActionsEnabled
---------                  ----------                  ----------         --------------
WebAppServerCPU            CPUUtilization              INSUFFICIENT_DATA           False
WebAppServerInstanceSysChk StatusCheckFailed_Instance  INSUFFICIENT_DATA           True
WebAppServerSystemSysChk   StatusCheckFailed_System    INSUFFICIENT_DATA           True


PS C:\> Enable-CWAlarmAction -AlarmName "WebAppServerCPU"
PS C:\>
PS C:\> Get-CWAlarm |Format-Table AlarmName,MetricName,StateValue, ActionsEnabled

AlarmName                  MetricName                  StateValue         ActionsEnabled
---------                  ----------                  ----------         --------------
WebAppServerCPU            CPUUtilization              INSUFFICIENT_DATA           True
WebAppServerInstanceSysChk StatusCheckFailed_Instance  INSUFFICIENT_DATA           True
WebAppServerSystemSysChk   StatusCheckFailed_System    INSUFFICIENT_DATA           True
```

Custom monitoring for an EC2 instance

For custom metrics for memory, swap, and disk usage, you can make use of the AWS supplied script published on `http://docs.aws.amazon.com/AWSEC2/latest/UserGuide/mon-scripts.html`. This script will let you push the data for custom dimensions to CloudWatch, and then you create the alarm on those custom metrics. For Amazon Linux, you need to perform the following steps. For your platform, refer to the link shared. AWS provides these scripts as a sample and there is no support provided if there are any issues with the script.

```
#sudo yum install perl-Switch perl-DateTime perl-Sys-Syslog perl-LWP-
Protocol-https -y
#curl
http://aws-cloudwatch.s3.amazonaws.com/downloads/CloudWatchMonitoringScript
s-1.2.1.zip -O
#unzip CloudWatchMonitoringScripts-1.2.1.zip
#cd aws-scripts-mon
```

To test the execution, you run the following command:

```
# ./mon-put-instance-data.pl --mem-util --mem-used --mem-avail --swap-util
--swap-used --disk-path=/ --disk-space-util --disk-space-used --disk-space-
avail
```

```
[root@ip-10-0-2-158 aws-scripts-mon]# ./mon-put-instance-data.pl --mem-util --mem-used --mem-avail --swap-util \
> --swap-used --disk-path=/ --disk-space-util --disk-space-used --disk-space-avail

Successfully reported metrics to CloudWatch. Reference Id: a816f47e-6d4f-11e7-b707-119735027c55
```

This will push all the available custom metrics provided by this script to CloudWatch. Note that it takes around 15 minutes for those metrics to be visible in CloudWatch. So, be patient. You can schedule this job in your cron so that data is published to CloudWatch every 5 minutes. You must ensure that your server has a role which allows you to write to CloudWatch, or you may need to make use of the access key and secret access key. Having a role assigned to an EC2 instance is the best practice.

 There are similar scripts available for Windows instances as well. Refer AWS documentation on `http://docs.aws.amazon.com/AWSEC2/latest/WindowsGuide/send_logs_to_cwl.html`

As you installed a script for collecting custom metrics, you can check the number of metrics available now in CloudWatch for the given instance. You can do this by using the following command:

```
PS C:\> $p1 = New-Object Amazon.CloudWatch.Model.DimensionFilter
PS C:\> $p1.Name = "InstanceId"
PS C:\> $p1.Value = "i-09ca5e201782643e7"
PS C:\> Get-CWMetricList -Dimension $p1
```

```
PS C:\> $p1 = New-Object Amazon.CloudWatch.Model.DimensionFilter
PS C:\> $p1.Name = "InstanceId"
PS C:\> $p1.Value = "i-09ca5e201782643e7"
PS C:\> Get-CWMetricList -Dimension $p1

Dimensions                            MetricName                      Namespace
----------                            ----------                      ---------
{InstanceId}                          NetworkPacketsIn                AWS/EC2
{InstanceId}                          NetworkIn                       AWS/EC2
{InstanceId}                          DiskWriteBytes                  AWS/EC2
{InstanceId}                          NetworkPacketsOut               AWS/EC2
{InstanceId}                          NetworkOut                      AWS/EC2
{InstanceId}                          DiskReadBytes                   AWS/EC2
{InstanceId}                          StatusCheckFailed               AWS/EC2
{InstanceId}                          DiskReadOps                     AWS/EC2
{InstanceId}                          CPUCreditBalance                AWS/EC2
{InstanceId}                          CPUUtilization                  AWS/EC2
{InstanceId}                          StatusCheckFailed_Instance      AWS/EC2
{InstanceId}                          DiskWriteOps                    AWS/EC2
{InstanceId}                          StatusCheckFailed_System        AWS/EC2
{InstanceId}                          CPUCreditUsage                  AWS/EC2
{InstanceId}                          SwapUtilization                 System/Linux
{InstanceId}                          SwapUsed                        System/Linux
{InstanceId}                          MemoryUsed                      System/Linux
{InstanceId}                          MemoryUtilization               System/Linux
{InstanceId}                          MemoryAvailable                 System/Linux
{MountPath, InstanceId, Filesystem}   DiskSpaceUtilization            System/Linux
{MountPath, InstanceId, Filesystem}   DiskSpaceAvailable              System/Linux
{MountPath, InstanceId, Filesystem}   DiskSpaceUsed                   System/Linux
```

You can see that custom metrics are collected under the namespace System/Linux and not AWS/EC2. So, you can use the namespace to further drill down the metrics list for the given EC2 instance, as shown:

```
PS C:\> $p1 = New-Object Amazon.CloudWatch.Model.DimensionFilter
PS C:\> $p1.Name = "InstanceId"
PS C:\> $p1.Value = "i-09ca5e201782643e7"
PS C:\> Get-CWMetricList -Namespace "System/Linux" -Dimension $p1
```

```
PS C:\> $p1 = New-Object Amazon.CloudWatch.Model.DimensionFilter
PS C:\> $p1.Name = "InstanceId"
PS C:\> $p1.Value = "i-09ca5e201782643e7"
PS C:\> Get-CWMetricList -Namespace "System/Linux" -Dimension $p1

Dimensions                              MetricName            Namespace
----------                              ----------            ---------
{InstanceId}                            MemoryUsed            System/Linux
{InstanceId}                            MemoryUtilization     System/Linux
{InstanceId}                            MemoryAvailable       System/Linux
{InstanceId}                            SwapUtilization       System/Linux
{InstanceId}                            SwapUsed              System/Linux
{MountPath, InstanceId, Filesystem}     DiskSpaceUtilization  System/Linux
{MountPath, InstanceId, Filesystem}     DiskSpaceAvailable    System/Linux
{MountPath, InstanceId, Filesystem}     DiskSpaceUsed         System/Linux
```

This time, you used the namespace in the cmdlet for the instance. You can now create the alarm as you usually do on the default EC2 metrics. Let's plan to create one for swap utilization going to more than 60 percent.

```
PS C:\> $powershellsns="arn:aws:sns:us-east-1:<account_no>:PowerShellSNS"
PS C:\> $p1 = New-Object Amazon.CloudWatch.Model.Dimension
PS C:\> $p1.Name = "InstanceId"
PS C:\> $p1.Value = "i-09ca5e201782643e7"
PS C:\> Write-CWMetricAlarm -Namespace "System/Linux" -MetricName
"SwapUtilization" -AlarmName "WebAppServerSwapUtil" -AlarmDescription
"Alarm for Swap Check Check" -AlarmAction $powershellsns -Dimension $p1 -
EvaluationPeriod 1 -Statistic "Average" -Threshold 60 -Period 300 -
ComparisonOperator "GreaterThanOrEqualToThreshold"
```

```
PS C:\> $powershellsns="arn:aws:sns:us-east-1:072316406132:PowerShellSNS"
PS C:\> $p1 = New-Object Amazon.CloudWatch.Model.Dimension
PS C:\> $p1.Name = "InstanceId"
PS C:\> $p1.Value = "i-09ca5e201782643e7"
PS C:\> Write-CWMetricAlarm -Namespace "System/Linux" -MetricName "SwapUtilization" `
>> -AlarmName "WebAppServerSwapUtil" -AlarmDescription "Alarm for Swap Check Check" `
>> -AlarmAction $powershellsns -Dimension $p1 -EvaluationPeriod 1 -Statistic "Average" `
>> -Threshold 60 -Period 300 -ComparisonOperator "GreaterThanOrEqualToThreshold"
PS C:\> Get-CWAlarm |Format-Table AlarmName,MetricName,StateValue, ActionsEnabled

AlarmName                   MetricName                   StateValue          ActionsEnabled
---------                   ----------                   ----------          --------------
WebAppServerCPU             CPUUtilization               OK                  True
WebAppServerInstanceSysChk  StatusCheckFailed_Instance   OK                  True
WebAppServerSwapUtil        SwapUtilization              INSUFFICIENT_DATA   True
WebAppServerSystemSysChk    StatusCheckFailed_System     OK                  True
```

Now, there are four alarms created for the instance, which will notify you if there are any threshold breaches and this is the way you can monitor EC2 instances. As long as StateValue is in OK state for the given alarm, you are good, and you do not have any issues. StateValue as ALARM or INSUFFICIENT_DATA indicates that there could be some problems with the EC2 instance.

Monitoring RDS DB instances

By default, RDS provides you with some default metrics that you can use to monitor the RDS instances. RDS provides metrics for the following items:

- The number of connections to a DB instance
- The amount of read and write operations to a DB instance
- The amount of storage that a DB instance is currently utilizing
- The amount of memory and CPU being utilized for a DB instance
- The amount of network traffic to and from a DB instance

To get a list of the default metrics provided for the specific DB instance `mywebappprd`, you can use the following command:

```
PS C:\> $p1 = New-Object Amazon.CloudWatch.Model.DimensionFilter
PS C:\> $p1.Name = "DBInstanceIdentifier"
PS C:\> $p1.Value = "mywebappprd"
PS C:\> Get-CWMetricList -Namespace "AWS/RDS" -Dimension $p1
```

```
PS C:\> $p1 = New-Object Amazon.CloudWatch.Model.DimensionFilter
PS C:\> $p1.Name = "DBInstanceIdentifier"
PS C:\> $p1.Value = "mywebappprd"
PS C:\> Get-CWMetricList -Namespace "AWS/RDS" -Dimension $p1

Dimensions                     MetricName                    Namespace
----------                     ----------                    ---------
{DBInstanceIdentifier} DatabaseConnections          AWS/RDS
{DBInstanceIdentifier} CPUCreditUsage               AWS/RDS
{DBInstanceIdentifier} WriteLatency                 AWS/RDS
{DBInstanceIdentifier} CPUCreditBalance             AWS/RDS
{DBInstanceIdentifier} ReadIOPS                     AWS/RDS
{DBInstanceIdentifier} NetworkTransmitThroughput    AWS/RDS
{DBInstanceIdentifier} WriteThroughput              AWS/RDS
{DBInstanceIdentifier} SwapUsage                    AWS/RDS
{DBInstanceIdentifier} CPUUtilization               AWS/RDS
{DBInstanceIdentifier} FreeStorageSpace             AWS/RDS
{DBInstanceIdentifier} WriteIOPS                    AWS/RDS
{DBInstanceIdentifier} FreeableMemory               AWS/RDS
{DBInstanceIdentifier} ReadThroughput               AWS/RDS
{DBInstanceIdentifier} NetworkReceiveThroughput     AWS/RDS
{DBInstanceIdentifier} ReadLatency                  AWS/RDS
{DBInstanceIdentifier} BurstBalance                 AWS/RDS
{DBInstanceIdentifier} DiskQueueDepth               AWS/RDS
{DBInstanceIdentifier} BinLogDiskUsage              AWS/RDS
```

Note that the namespace name for RDS is `AWS/RDS`, which you use with cmdlet. You can create an alarm the same way as we did for the EC2 instance. To start with, you may be interested in creating an alarm for `FreeStorageSpace` and `CPUUtilization`. You can do this as shown:

```
PS C:\> $powershellsns="arn:aws:sns:us-east-1:<account_no>:PowerShellSNS"
PS C:\> $p1 = New-Object Amazon.CloudWatch.Model.Dimension
PS C:\> $p1.Name = "DBInstanceIdentifier"
PS C:\> $p1.Value = "mywebappprd"
PS C:\> Write-CWMetricAlarm -Namespace "AWS/RDS" -MetricName
"CPUUtilization"  -AlarmName "RDSmywebappprdCPUUtil" -AlarmDescription
"Alarm for RDS CPU Check" -AlarmAction $powershellsns -Dimension $p1 -
EvaluationPeriod 1 -Statistic "Average" -Threshold 80 -Period 300 -
ComparisonOperator "GreaterThanOrEqualToThreshold"
PS C:\> $powershellsns="arn:aws:sns:us-east-1:<account_no>:PowerShellSNS"
PS C:\> $p1 = New-Object Amazon.CloudWatch.Model.Dimension
PS C:\> $p1.Name = "DBInstanceIdentifier"
PS C:\> $p1.Value = "mywebappprd"
PS C:\> Write-CWMetricAlarm -Namespace "AWS/RDS" -MetricName
"FreeStorageSpace" -AlarmName "RDSmywebappprdCPUUtil" -AlarmDescription
"Alarm for free storage for RDS" -AlarmAction $powershellsns -Dimension $p1
-EvaluationPeriod 1 -Statistic "Average" -Threshold 80 -Period 300 -
ComparisonOperator "LessThanOrEqualToThreshold"
```

```
PS C:\> $powershellsns="arn:aws:sns:us-east-1:072316406132:PowerShellSNS"
PS C:\> $p1 = New-Object Amazon.CloudWatch.Model.Dimension
PS C:\> $p1.Name = "DBInstanceIdentifier"
PS C:\> $p1.Value = "mywebappprd"
PS C:\> Write-CWMetricAlarm -Namespace "AWS/RDS" -MetricName "CPUUtilization" `
>> -AlarmName "RDSmywebappprdCPUUtil" -AlarmDescription "Alarm for RDS CPU Check" `
>> -AlarmAction $powershellsns -Dimension $p1 -EvaluationPeriod 1 -Statistic "Average" `
>> -Threshold 80 -Period 300 -ComparisonOperator "GreaterThanOrEqualToThreshold"
PS C:\>
PS C:\> $powershellsns="arn:aws:sns:us-east-1:072316406132:PowerShellSNS"
PS C:\> $p1 = New-Object Amazon.CloudWatch.Model.Dimension
PS C:\> $p1.Name = "DBInstanceIdentifier"
PS C:\> $p1.Value = "mywebappprd"
PS C:\> Write-CWMetricAlarm -Namespace "AWS/RDS" -MetricName "FreeStorageSpace" `
>> -AlarmName "RDSmywebappprdCPUUtil" -AlarmDescription "Alarm for free storage for RDS" `
>> -AlarmAction $powershellsns -Dimension $p1 -EvaluationPeriod 1 -Statistic "Average" `
>> -Threshold 80 -Period 300 -ComparisonOperator "LessThanOrEqualToThreshold"
PS C:\>
```

CloudWatch logs

AWS provides CloudWatch metrics for most of the services that they offer, which you just need to pick up based on your needs and create an alarm to be notified or to send a message to any other endpoint. You run your applications on top of AWS resources, so you need to have a mechanism to monitor your application and server logs. This is where CloudWatch logs help you. Note that CloudWatch and CloudWatch logs are different and not used interchangeably. Monitoring your application logs and server logs in addition to metrics provided by AWS will help you to build a unified monitoring system for your application using CloudWatch. To understand this better, let's review the following diagram:

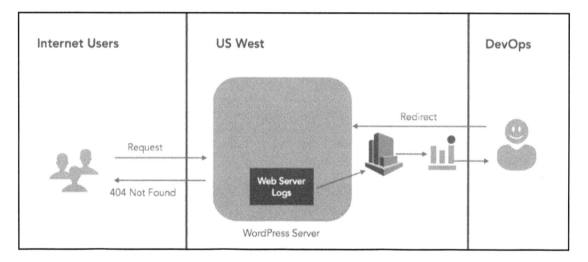

If you have a WordPress application running on the server and you get a user experience page not found message, then your web server log will have this entry. You can ingest your web server log directly into CloudWatch. You can do this by installing an agent on the server. This agent code is provided by AWS and is available for download to everybody. Once data is available in CloudWatch, you can create a filter on the datasets to find 404 and create a CloudWatch alarm to notify you that there are 404 messages in the web server log. This way, your DevOps team can take a look at the server and correct the issue about the page not found error that users are experiencing.

To install and start the agent, you can issue the following command:

```
# yum install -y awslogs
# service awslogs start
# chkconfig awslogs on
```

This code snippet will install, start, and autostart the `awslogs` agent on the server. Usually, many DevOps guys add these steps as part of the bootstrapping steps, so that it is automatically installed when EC2 instances are launched, either via Auto Scaling or through Beanstalk.

For your operating system, specific install notes can be found on `http://docs.aws.amazon.com/AmazonCloudWatch/latest/logs/WhatIs CloudWatchLogs.html`.

Successful installation of the CloudWatch log agent will create the configuration file `/etc/awslogs/awslogs.conf`. This is the file in which you specify the log location. Review the file and understand the format. This configuration file consists of a default entry, as below. You may also want to monitor `/var/log/messages` for any system-level issues.

```
[/var/log/messages]
datetime_format = %b %d %H:%M:%S
file = /var/log/messages
buffer_duration = 5000
log_stream_name = {instance_id}
initial_position = start_of_file
log_group_name = /var/log/messages
```

Usually, you can keep these entries as they are and add new ones for your web server. For HTTP, `access_log` is created in the `/var/log/httpd` directory. Let's plan to add the entries regarding `access_log` in the `/etc/awslogs/awslogs.conf`.

```
[/var/log/messages]
datetime_format = %b %d %H:%M:%S
file = /var/log/messages
buffer_duration = 5000
log_stream_name = {instance_id}
initial_position = start_of_file
log_group_name = /var/log/messages

[/var/log/httpd/access_log]
datetime_format = %b %d %H:%M:%S
file = /var/log/httpd/access_log
buffer_duration = 5000
log_stream_name = {instance_id}
initial_position = start_of_file
log_group_name = MyWebServerApp
```

Most important is naming the `log_stream_name` and having the right file specified in the block, as shown. Once you add entries, you simply need to restart the agent as follows:

```
# service awslogs restart
```

This operation will create a new log group in CloudWatch, where you can see the actual file content. To get the list of log groups created based on the file content that you specified, you can run the following command:

```
PS C:\> Get-CWLLogGroup
```

```
PS C:\> Get-CWLLogGroup

Arn                : arn:aws:logs:us-east-1:072316406132:log-group:/var/log/messages:*
CreationTime       : 5/27/2016 9:13:56 AM
LogGroupName       : /var/log/messages
MetricFilterCount  : 0
RetentionInDays    :
StoredBytes        : 7916696

Arn                : arn:aws:logs:us-east-1:072316406132:log-group:MyWebServerApp:*
CreationTime       : 7/21/2017 8:36:35 AM
LogGroupName       : MyWebServerApp
MetricFilterCount  : 0
RetentionInDays    :
StoredBytes        : 0
```

You see that we have two log groups now, which we specified in the configuration file. If you have a pretty long list, plan to filter them out based on the switches provided by this cmdlet. Refer to online documentation for the same. AWS creates a stream inside your log group. If you refer to the content of /etc/awslogs/awslogs.conf, we specified the stream name as an instance ID, you can name this however you want. To get the list of stream names for your log group, you can use the following command:

```
PS C:\> Get-CWLLogStream -LogGroupName MyWebServerApp
```

```
PS C:\> Get-CWLLogStream -LogGroupName MyWebServerApp

Arn                 : arn:aws:logs:us-east-1:072316406132:log-group:MyWebServerApp:log-stream:i-09ca5e201782643e7
CreationTime        : 7/21/2017 8:36:36 AM
FirstEventTimestamp : 7/21/2017 8:36:34 AM
LastEventTimestamp  : 7/21/2017 9:19:49 AM
LastIngestionTime   : 7/21/2017 9:19:55 AM
LogStreamName       : i-09ca5e201782643e7
StoredBytes         : 0
UploadSequenceToken : 49567849214004609375172139535762070659501364771293283570
```

For the given stream and log group name, you can find the list of event entries using the following command:

```
PS C:\> (Get-CWLLogEvent  -LogGroupName MyWebServerApp -LogStreamName
i-09ca5e201782643e7).Events
```

This indicates your actual server log that is pushed to the CloudWatch by the CloudWatch agent. Because it is available now, you can create the metric and namespace for this data. Let's say you want to create a namespace called `webserver` and a metric `web404` for all the 404 errors, you can do this as follows:

```
PS C:\> $p1 = New-Object Amazon.CloudWatchLogs.Model.MetricTransformation
PS C:\> $p1.MetricName="web404"
PS C:\> $p1.MetricNamespace="webserver"
PS C:\> $p1.MetricValue=1
PS C:\> Write-CWLMetricFilter -LogGroupName MyWebServerApp -FilterName
"404_MyWebServerApp" -FilterPattern 404 -MetricTransformation $p1
```

Note that this may take some time to pop up in the list of available namespaces and metrics. Because the metric is created, you can simply create a CloudWatch alarm to get notified based on this metric filter. You can do this using the following command:

```
PS C:\> $powershellsns="arn:aws:sns:us-east-1:<account_no>:PowerShellSNS"
PS C:\> $p1 = New-Object Amazon.CloudWatch.Model.Dimension
PS C:\> $p1.Name = "WebError404"
PS C:\> $p1.Value = "web404"
PS C:\> Write-CWMetricAlarm -Namespace "webserver" -MetricName "web404" -
AlarmName "WebSever404" -AlarmDescription "Alarm for 404 error for web
server" -AlarmAction $powershellsns -Dimension $p1 -EvaluationPeriod 1 -
Statistic "Average" -Threshold 1 -Period 300 -ComparisonOperator
"GreaterThanOrEqualToThreshold"
```

```
PS C:\> $powershellsns="arn:aws:sns:us-east-1:072316406132:PowerShellSNS"
PS C:\> $p1 = New-Object Amazon.CloudWatch.Model.Dimension
PS C:\> $p1.Name = "WebError404"
PS C:\> $p1.Value = "web404"
PS C:\> Write-CWMetricAlarm -Namespace "webserver" -MetricName "web404" `
>> -AlarmName "WebSever404" -AlarmDescription "Alarm for 404 error for web server" `
>> -AlarmAction $powershellsns -Dimension $p1 -EvaluationPeriod 1 -Statistic "Average" `
>> -Threshold 1 -Period 300 -ComparisonOperator "GreaterThanOrEqualToThreshold"
```

Overall, you pushed the application log file to CloudWatch and then created the metric filter based on the filter pattern which you wanted to track, and then created the alarm on that filter pattern so that you get notified. This is the way application monitoring is achieved on AWS. Everything can be added in the CloudFormation template and you simply duplicate the environment using that template, instead of manually issuing all the cmdlets. With this, I am sure you have a pretty good understanding of how to monitor AWS using AWS provided metrics and your custom metrics.

Summary

AWS CloudWatch is a monitoring service which is native to the AWS Cloud, and all the services that are supported on AWS can be monitored using this service. In this chapter, we learnt how you can monitor EC2 instances using AWS supplied metrics and custom metrics. We also learnt how RDS databases can be monitored. In addition to EC2 and RDS, we used CloudWatch logs to extend the capability of CloudWatch to monitor application and server logs. The Simple Notification Service plays a vital role in delivering the messages from CloudWatch to the endpoint. In the next chapter, we will learn about AWS Config and AWS auditing capabilities using CloudTrail.

16
AWS Resource Auditing

AWS is a digital ocean and is built upon the core concept, *everything as a service*. There are several dozen services that are already up there, which you can simply hook up to your application and extend the capabilities of your application's functionality. Whichever AWS services you use, you should place a focus on three major management services: CloudTrail, AWS Config, and Trusted Advisor. You should use these services irrespective of how big your cloud deployment is. Without making use of these services, you may be fishing in the desert. These services are at the very core when addressing compliance, reviewing the attack surface, and optimizing your AWS environment.

In this chapter, we will learn how CloudTrail and Config can be enabled so that you are in better control of your AWS infrastructure. In addition, there is no reason for you to not use Trusted Advisor. You can optimize your AWS environment using the data that you get from Trusted Advisor.

Introduction to CloudTrail

CloudTrail is a service which provides you with a record of AWS API calls. This is a kind of auditing service provided by AWS. Using the log data provided by CloudTrail, you can audit what your users are doing, or you can troubleshoot operational and security incidents. CloudTrail also helps you to demonstrate compliance with your policies or regulatory standards. As and when API calls are made, CloudTrail records those calls in an S3 log file.

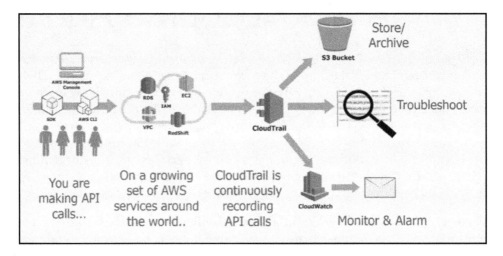

You can look up specific API activity, such as which IAM user made the call to the AWS, which service or which API calls failed because of permission issues, and so on. Most importantly, you can send CloudTrail logs to CloudWatch logs. We learnt in the previous chapter how we can create metrics and then use an alarm on the data in CloudWatch logs. Do not get confused between CloudWatch and CloudTrail. I have seen that there is a lot of confusion around CloudWatch and CloudTrail. CloudWatch is an alerting service and CloudTrail is meant for the recording of API calls. You can create two types of trails:

- A trail that applies to one region
- A trail that applies to all regions

If you create more than one trail, there is a cost associated with the trail. AWS delivers log files in S3 bucket; you can specify the time of trail creation and the logs are delivered within 15 minutes of the API activity.

Why CloudTrail?

There are a number of use cases enabled by CloudTrail.

- IT auditors can use log files generated by CloudTrail as a compliance aid
- DevOps engineers can troubleshoot operational issues
- DevOps engineers and IT administrators can track changes to your AWS infrastructure
- Security administrators can use CloudTrail log data to perform security analysis

CloudTrail events

CloudTrail events are actual log data entries for a specific API call. You can usually find the following entries in CloudTrail events:

- Who made the API call for AWS resources?
- What was the API call all about?
- When was the call made?
- Which AWS resources were acted upon in the API call?
- Where was the API call made from and made to?

A sample trail event looks like this.

AWS access key	AKIAIVQ7QQR7ISZUBY2A	Event source	monitoring.amazonaws.com
AWS region	us-east-1	Event time	2017-07-21, 07:18:35 PM
Error code		Request ID	927314fa-6df5-11e7-898f-3527badd2291
Event ID	4cad45f1-b0a0-4302-9b22-991f0e9698e1	Source IP address	202.161.5.17
Event name	PutMetricAlarm	User name	awsadmin

Create CloudTrail

Before you create a trail, ensure that you have a dedicated S3 bucket created. In addition to this, your S3 bucket should have the following policy attached. This policy will allow CloudTrail to write to your bucket. Replace the `account_number` with your own AWS account number. I will be using a sample bucket called `myenterpriseawslog` and the following policy is attached to it.

```
{
    "Version": "2012-10-17",
    "Statement": [
        {
            "Sid": "AWSCloudTrailAclCheck20150319",
            "Effect": "Allow",
            "Principal": {
                "Service": "cloudtrail.amazonaws.com"
            },
            "Action": "s3:GetBucketAcl",
            "Resource": "arn:aws:s3:::myenterpriseawslog"
        },
        {
            "Sid": "AWSCloudTrailWrite20150319",
            "Effect": "Allow",
            "Principal": {
                "Service": "cloudtrail.amazonaws.com"
            },
            "Action": "s3:PutObject",
            "Resource": "arn:aws:s3:::myenterpriseawslog/powershell/AWSLogs/<account_number>/*",
            "Condition": {
                "StringEquals": {
                    "s3:x-amz-acl": "bucket-owner-full-control"
                }
            }
        }
    ]
}
```

To get a list of all the cmdlets in relation to the CloudTrail service, you can use the following command:

```
PS C:\> Get-Command *-CT*
```

To get a list of all the trails that are have been created in the region, you can run the following command:

```
PS C:\> Get-CTTrail
```

To create a new trail called `MyFirstTrail`, you can issue the following command:

```
PS C:\> New-CTTrail -Name MyFirstTrail -S3BucketName myenterpriseawslog -
S3KeyPrefix powershell -EnableLogFileValidation $true -
IncludeGlobalServiceEvent $true -IsMultiRegionTrail $true
```

```
PS C:\> New-CTTrail -Name MyFirstTrail -S3BucketName myenterpriseawslog -S3KeyPrefix powershell `
>> -EnableLogFileValidation $true -IncludeGlobalServiceEvent $true -IsMultiRegionTrail $true


CloudWatchLogsLogGroupArn  :
CloudWatchLogsRoleArn      :
IncludeGlobalServiceEvents : True
IsMultiRegionTrail         : True
KmsKeyId                   :
LogFileValidationEnabled   : True
Name                       : MyFirstTrail
S3BucketName               : myenterpriseawslog
S3KeyPrefix                : powershell
SnsTopicARN                :
SnsTopicName               :
TrailARN                   : arn:aws:cloudtrail:us-east-1:072316406132:trail/MyFirstTrail
```

You can create a maximum of five trails in any specific region.
`IncludeGlobalServiceEvent` specifies whether the trail publishes events from global
services, such as IAM, to the log files and `IsMultiRegionTrail` specifies whether the trail
is created in the current region or in all regions. The default is false.

To check the status of the trail, you can use the following command:

```
PS C:\> Get-CTTrailStatus -Name  MyFirstTrail
```

```
PS C:\> Get-CTTrailStatus -Name  MyFirstTrail


IsLogging                          : False
LatestCloudWatchLogsDeliveryError  :
LatestCloudWatchLogsDeliveryTime   : 1/1/0001 12:00:00 AM
LatestDeliveryAttemptSucceeded     :
LatestDeliveryAttemptTime          :
LatestDeliveryError                :
LatestDeliveryTime                 : 1/1/0001 12:00:00 AM
LatestDigestDeliveryError          :
LatestDigestDeliveryTime           : 1/1/0001 12:00:00 AM
LatestNotificationAttemptSucceeded :
LatestNotificationAttemptTime      :
LatestNotificationError            :
LatestNotificationTime             : 1/1/0001 12:00:00 AM
StartLoggingTime                   : 1/1/0001 12:00:00 AM
StopLoggingTime                    : 1/1/0001 12:00:00 AM
TimeLoggingStarted                 :
TimeLoggingStopped                 :
```

`IsLogging` indicates that the trail is not logging any events.

Enabling CloudTrail

`Start-CTLogging` lets you start the recording of AWS resources, API calls, and log file delivery for a trail to S3. To start logging, you must enable it from the region in which the trail was created.

You can do this by using the following command:

```
PS C:\> Start-CTLogging -Name MyFirstTrail
```

```
PS C:\> Start-CTLogging -Name MyFirstTrail
PS C:\>
PS C:\> Get-CTTrailStatus -Name MyFirstTrail


IsLogging                            : True
LatestCloudWatchLogsDeliveryError    :
LatestCloudWatchLogsDeliveryTime     : 1/1/0001 12:00:00 AM
LatestDeliveryAttemptSucceeded       :
LatestDeliveryAttemptTime            :
LatestDeliveryError                  :
LatestDeliveryTime                   : 1/1/0001 12:00:00 AM
LatestDigestDeliveryError            :
LatestDigestDeliveryTime             : 1/1/0001 12:00:00 AM
LatestNotificationAttemptSucceeded   :
LatestNotificationAttemptTime        :
LatestNotificationError              :
LatestNotificationTime               : 1/1/0001 12:00:00 AM
StartLoggingTime                     : 7/22/2017 12:42:32 PM
StopLoggingTime                      : 1/1/0001 12:00:00 AM
TimeLoggingStarted                   : 2017-07-22T12:42:32Z
TimeLoggingStopped                   :
```

An `IsLogging` status of `True`, indicates that the trail has started logging the events. You can verify this one in the S3 bucket that you created. You can now use the `Find-CTEvent` cmdlet to find out specific events. The `Find-CTEvent` cmdlet supports the following lookup attributes:

- Event ID
- Event name
- Event source
- Resource name
- Resource type
- User name

To find out the root user activity, you can use the following command:

```
PS C:\> Find-CTEvent -LookupAttribute @{ AttributeKey="Username";
AttributeValue="root" } -MaxResult 5
```

AWS Config

Getting visibility of resource changes and the relationship between different AWS resources is the key to tracking compliance in your AWS infrastructure. AWS offers Config and it helps to ease the burden of implementing and tracking compliance control. Config is a managed service that simplifies compliance reporting. Config help you to get the inventory of AWS resources, discover new resources, track deleted AWS resources, continuous recording of configuration changes, and to be notified when those configuration changes occur.

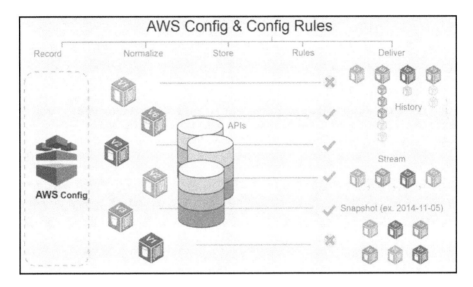

Overall, AWS Config does five things, as shown in the preceding diagram. It records changes to your AWS resources and then normalizes them into the consistent format called **configuration items**. It then stores the data in the data store managed by AWS. Config Rules are another feature within Config, which can help you to focus on compliance issues of particular interest. You then apply those Config Rules. Data is also delivered to S3 for offline analysis. Instead of time travel, you can take the on-demand snapshot of the resource that shows you the current state of your resources, which is also delivered to S3.

Enabling Config

To enable the Config service in your account, you have to first create the recorder and then the delivery group for that recorder. If you do the same thing on the AWS Console, both operations are combined. But if you do this via PowerShell, it sounds like it is a two-step process.

To get a list of all the cmdlets related to Config, you can use the following command:

```
PS C:\> Get-Command *-CFG*
```

You can have only one recorder running in a region, so you can check whether you have a recorder using the following command:

```
PS C:\> Get-CFGConfigurationRecorder
```

Write-CFGConfigurationRecorder lets you create a new configuration recorder to record the selected resource configurations. After recorder creation, you can make use of this same cmdlet to change the role, if needed. There is no separate cmdlet provided for this. As mentioned, only one recorder per region is allowed. If you do not specify the RecordingGroup_ResourceType switch, AWS will start recording for all the supported resource types. To create the recorder named MyFirstConfigRecorder, you can run the following command:

```
PS C:\> Write-CFGConfigurationRecorder -ConfigurationRecorderName
"MyFirstConfigRecorder" -RecordingGroup_AllSupported $true -
RecordingGroup_IncludeGlobalResourceType $true -
ConfigurationRecorder_RoleARN "arn:aws:iam::<account_no>:role/AWSConfig"
```

```
PS C:\> Write-CFGConfigurationRecorder -ConfigurationRecorderName "MyFirstConfigRecorder" `
>> -RecordingGroup_AllSupported $true `
>> -RecordingGroup_IncludeGlobalResourceType $true `
>> -ConfigurationRecorder_RoleARN "arn:aws:iam::072316406132:role/AWSConfig"
PS C:\>
```

RecordingGroup_AllSupported specifies whether AWS Config records configuration changes for every supported resource in the region, and RecordingGroup_IncludeGlobalResourceType specifies whether AWS Config includes all supported types of global resources, such as IAM. You must specify the role ARN. The role that is assigned in this case just has the grant on AWS Config service.

Once you create the recorder, you can create the delivery channel for this recorder. Write-CFGDeliveryChannel lets you create a delivery channel object to deliver configuration information to an Amazon S3 bucket and Amazon SNS topic. Note that you should have created the recorder before running this cmdlet. As with the recorder, you can have only one delivery channel per region. To update the delivery channel, you can use this same cmdlet.

To create the delivery channel in the region, run the following command:

```
PS C:\> Write-CFGDeliveryChannel -DeliveryChannelName "MyConfigDelivery" -
ConfigSnapshotDeliveryProperties_DeliveryFrequency One_Hour -
DeliveryChannel_S3BucketName "myaccountconfiglog" -
DeliveryChannel_S3KeyPrefix powershelltest -DeliveryChannel_SnsTopicARN
"arn:aws:sns:us-east-1:<account_no>:PowerShellSNS"
```

```
PS C:\> Write-CFGDeliveryChannel -DeliveryChannelName "MyConfigDelivery" `
>> -ConfigSnapshotDeliveryProperties_DeliveryFrequency One_Hour `
>> -DeliveryChannel_S3BucketName "myaccountconfiglog" `
>> -DeliveryChannel_S3KeyPrefix powershelltest `
>> -DeliveryChannel_SnsTopicARN "arn:aws:sns:us-east-1:072316406132:PowerShellSNS"
PS C:\>
```

ConfigSnapshotDeliveryProperties_DeliveryFrequency indicates the frequency with which AWS Config delivers configuration snapshots. Valid values are One_Hour, Six_Hours, Three_Hours, Twelve_Hours, and TwentyFour_Hours. DeliveryChannel_S3BucketName indicates the name of the Amazon S3 bucket to which AWS Config delivers configuration snapshots and configuration history files. You can reference the bucket from other accounts. You need to ensure that the bucket has the right set of permissions so that Config can write to it. DeliveryChannel_S3KeyPrefix indicates a prefix for the specified Amazon S3 bucket. DeliveryChannel_SnsTopicARN indicates an SNS topic to which AWS Config sends notifications about configuration changes. You do not specify the recorder with this cmdlet, even though you created it earlier. This is because AWS Config automatically identifies the recorder you created and you can only have one recorder in the region. To check the status of the recorder, you can run the following command:

```
PS C:\> Get-CFGConfigurationRecorderStatus -ConfigurationRecorderName
"MyFirstConfigRecorder"
```

```
PS C:\> Get-CFGConfigurationRecorderStatus -ConfigurationRecorderName "MyFirstConfigRecorder"


LastErrorCode         :
LastErrorMessage      :
LastStartTime         : 1/1/0001 12:00:00 AM
LastStatus            :
LastStatusChangeTime  : 1/1/0001 12:00:00 AM
LastStopTime          : 1/1/0001 12:00:00 AM
Name                  : MyFirstConfigRecorder
Recording             : False
```

Recording is seen as False. This means the recorder is not recording yet. You can start the recorder using the following command:

```
PS C:\> Start-CFGConfigurationRecorder -ConfigurationRecorderName
"MyFirstConfigRecorder"
```

```
PS C:\> Start-CFGConfigurationRecorder -ConfigurationRecorderName "MyFirstConfigRecorder"
PS C:\> Get-CFGConfigurationRecorderStatus -ConfigurationRecorderName "MyFirstConfigRecorder"


LastErrorCode         :
LastErrorMessage      :
LastStartTime         : 7/23/2017 10:22:59 AM
LastStatus            : Pending
LastStatusChangeTime  : 7/23/2017 10:22:59 AM
LastStopTime          : 1/1/0001 12:00:00 AM
Name                  : MyFirstConfigRecorder
Recording             : True
```

Note that, if you do not specify the name of the recorder and delivery channel, AWS creates them as the default. A Recording status of True means your recorder is active and Config is enabled. If you follow the steps as preceding, the subscriber to the SNS topic will be notified as and when there are changes in your AWS environment. Config will also take a snapshot every hour and deliver it to your S3 bucket.

Config provides you with a set of AWS managed Config rules. It's easy to work with managed Config Rule via the AWS Console. You might use the AWS Console more as compared to the command-line option, particularly for management services such as Config and Trusted Advisor. AWS is constantly adding to the new set of Config Rules. Hence, it's always better to refer to the AWS Console for Config frequently. I will let you experiment with the Config rules on the AWS Console. It's really easy, has a user-friendly interface, and you will make out the screen navigation. You can also write your custom Config rules using a **lambda** function. Both of these options are out of the scope of this book. Review online documentation and increase your learning for both items.

Removing the delivery channel and recorder

Remove-CFGDeliveryChannel lets you delete the delivery channel. Before you can delete the delivery channel, you must stop the configuration recorder by using the Stop-CFGConfigurationRecorder action.

```
PS C:\> Stop-CFGConfigurationRecorder -ConfigurationRecorderName
"MyFirstConfigRecorder"
PS C:\> Remove-CFGDeliveryChannel -DeliveryChannelName "MyConfigDelivery"
```

`Remove-CFGConfigurationRecorder` lets you delete the configuration recorder. After deletion of the recorder, AWS stops recording configuration changes, but does not delete the old configuration information. You can still access old recorded information by using the `Get-ResourceConfigHistory` cmdlet, but you cannot access it in the Config console until you create a new recorder.

```
PS C:\> Remove-CFGConfigurationRecorder –ConfigurationRecorderName
"MyFirstConfigRecorder"
```

```
PS C:\> Stop-CFGConfigurationRecorder -ConfigurationRecorderName "MyFirstConfigRecorder"
PS C:\> Remove-CFGDeliveryChannel -DeliveryChannelName "MyConfigDelivery"

Confirm
Are you sure you want to perform this action?
Performing the operation "Remove-CFGDeliveryChannel (DeleteDeliveryChannel)" on target "MyConfigDelivery".
[Y] Yes  [A] Yes to All  [N] No  [L] No to All  [S] Suspend  [?] Help (default is "Y"): Y
PS C:\> Remove-CFGConfigurationRecorder -ConfigurationRecorderName "MyFirstConfigRecorder"

Confirm
Are you sure you want to perform this action?
Performing the operation "Remove-CFGConfigurationRecorder (DeleteConfigurationRecorder)" on target "MyFirstConfigRecorder".
[Y] Yes  [A] Yes to All  [N] No  [L] No to All  [S] Suspend  [?] Help (default is "Y"): Y
PS C:\>
```

Summary

AWS CloudTrail and Config are most important management services for tracking the resources API calls and compliance. Irrespective of any other services, you should always plan to implement CloudTrail and Config in your account. This will provide you with the required logs for your security analysis, and to satisfy auditing compliance needs. In this chapter, we learnt about the CloudTrail implementation and how to work around it. I hope you have enjoyed this book and have received the required knowledge base to work with AWS via PowerShell.

Index

C

D